Digitization in the Real World

Lessons Learned from Small and Medium-Sized Digitization Projects

Edited by
Kwong Bor Ng & Jason Kucsma

Metropolitan New York Library Council

i

Published in the United States of America by
Metropolitan New York Library Council
57 East 11th Street, 4th floor
New York, NY 10003-4605
p: (212) 228-2320 f: (212) 228-2598

Web site: http://www.metro.org

ISBN: 978-0-615-379998-2

Cover Design: Jason Kucsma *(illustration by Smartone Design, licensed via iStockphoto.com)*

Reviewers Committee: Mark F. Anderson, Jill Annitto, Anna Craft, Jody DeRidder, Renate Evers, Wei Fang, Maureen M. Knapp, Sue Kunda, Mandy Mastrovita, Ken Middleton, Emily Pfotenhauer, Mark Phillipson, Alice Platt, Mary Z. Rose, Stacy Schiff, Jennifer Weintraub, Andrew Weiss.

The views expressed in this book are those of the authors, but not necessarily those of the publisher.

About the Editors

Kwong Bor Ng (kbng@qc.cuny.edu) is an associate professor at the Graduate School of Library and Information Studies, Queens College, CUNY. His research interests are in the technical and technological areas of knowledge representation, organization, storage and retrieval. Dr. Ng has published more than 20 academic papers in refereed journals. His most recent publications include *Using XML: A How-to-do-it Manual and CD-ROM for Librarians* (published by Neal Schuman in 2007) and *Collaborative Technologies and Applications for Interactive Information Design: Emerging Trends in User Experiences* (co-edited with S. Rummler, published by Information Science Reference, IGI-Global, Inc. in 2009.)

Jason Kucsma (jkucsma@metro.org) is the Emerging Technologies Manager at the Metropolitan New York Library Council where he manages METRO's Digitization Grant Program and is the point person for member inquiries related to the resources, training and referral services associated with digitization, digital preservation and emerging technologies issues. Jason received his M.A. in American Culture Studies from Bowling Green State University and an M.L.S. from the University of Arizona School of Information Resources and Library Science. He is currently a part-time lecturer in Rutgers's Library and Information Science graduate program, and is a recent graduate of ALA's 2009 Emerging Leaders Program.

Table of Contents

Part III – The Digital Campus: Digitization in Universities and Their Libraries

Part IV – One Plus One is Greater Than Two: Collaborative Projects

Foreword

Dottie Hiebing (METRO Executive Director)

For more than 45 years, METRO has worked to provide opportunities for libraries to share best practice strategies to address many critical needs. In these efforts, we have often seen that the best learning comes through examples of libraries that have addressed important challenges successfully – and sometimes not so successfully. This has been especially true in efforts to support large and small digitization projects.

For more than a decade – and continuing today – digitization has been established as an essential focus for many libraries as well as for research centers, museums, and cultural and arts organizations. METRO has worked to support our members in these efforts with a range of grants, training programs and instructional materials.

Digitization in the Real World represents a significant new milestone in our commitment to providing library professionals with the hands-on experience and guidance they need to plan, execute, and manage digitization projects over the long term. In many ways, the examples presented in this volume show library professionals how to maximize the value and impact of digitization efforts for their libraries and their users.

This book also represents the first self-published text METRO has ever sponsored. As we continually look for new ways to help libraries stay ahead of the curve in digitization, technology and other areas, this strategy has the clear potential to be a major focus of our work in the years ahead. We will welcome your feedback and look forward to seeing how self-published materials such as this can support our mission and your needs moving forward.

On behalf of METRO, I would like to congratulate and thank editors Kwong Bor Ng and Jason Kucsma and all of the members of the library community who supported this project and who contributed of their time and insight in the development of these outstanding digitization case studies. They have created a vital new resource to help libraries continue to advance important digitization projects, and their efforts will have a profound and lasting impact on the future of these efforts in the years ahead.

Preface

Kwong Bor Ng & Jason Kucsma

For more than a decade, digitization has been both a critical need and a formidable challenge for libraries, archives, and museums around the world. To support these important projects, the Metropolitan New York Library Council (METRO) has been awarding annual grants to support digitization projects in New York City and Westchester County since 2005. Thus far, METRO has provided support for approximately 40 digitization projects at 25 different institutions. In those five years, we have learned a great deal about managing digitization projects effectively. In these efforts, METRO members have also shared best practice strategies in digitization through project showcase events and through the work of the METRO-sponsored Digitization Special Interest Group.

All digitization projects begin with some critical questions. How do we start a digitization project? What standards should we use for digital conversion and metadata? What are the best practices for workflow? What equipment or software should we use? Should we digitize in-house or outsource? What organizational or technological obstacles should we anticipate, and how should we negotiate them? Where can we turn for help in the middle of a project?

Naturally, the response to these questions will differ for different institutions. Even discrete projects within an institution will have many unique characteristics and challenges. But shared stories of successes (and failures) can be immensely helpful in supporting future digitization projects. To that end, Professor Ng came to METRO in the summer of 2009 with a great suggestion. Why not collect some of the most compelling examples of recent digitization projects? Many of us are familiar with the large-scale mass digitization projects of recent years. But Ng suggested — and we agreed — that there was a great opportunity to share insights from lesser-known examples from the "real world." That's not to say that large-scale projects don't pose their own unique issues and learning opportunities for librarians, archivists, and technologists. But many libraries are more likely to proceed with smaller-scale digitization projects made possible by a special need or unique opportunity, a first-time grant, or the special dedication of a team of library professionals. Collectively, these efforts can provide many invaluable perspectives and procedural models.

This book was initially conceived as an opportunity to highlight digitization efforts in the New York metropolitan area. Our research quickly showed that there were many other project examples worth sharing. The response to our initial call for proposals was overwhelming; we received hundreds of chapter proposals from all over the world in just the first few months. Contacts from many of the world's leading knowledge-based organizations, cultural institutions and university libraries presented examples of projects representing a wide range of topics, perspectives, approaches, concerns, and lessons-learned.

The effort to choose from among these examples the examples that would be presented in the book was a daunting task. We were unable to include many great case studies. Each of the chapters presented was reviewed in a double-blind peer-review process to assess quality, accuracy and relevance. The 34 papers presented in this book represent our best effort to present a diverse and comprehensive overview of key issues in the management and realization of digitization projects.

We have divided the case studies into four primary groups. The first section focuses on small projects. They are digitization endeavors that moved forward with limited resources and staffing. The second group showcases digitization projects from diverse cultural institutions including public libraries, museums, research institutes, and cultural organizations. The third group consists of digitization projects based on medium-sized collections at universities and their libraries. The last group features projects that brought together multiple institutions to work in collaboration on a project of mutual interest.

This book would not have been possible without the participation and hard work of all of the authors and reviewers involved, including those who submitted chapters that we were not able to accommodate. We're also greatly indebted to Dottie Hiebing, Executive Director of METRO, for recognizing the need for this important resource and for supporting this effort from inception. This is the first of what we hope will become a series of instructional self-publishing projects supported by METRO in the years ahead.

This is, above all, a book written by practitioners for practitioners who together recognize the critical needs and goals in digitization in our industry. Our hope is that it will be useful to students who are preparing for a career in library or research science and to practitioners who will shape the future of digitization for the library community. We know reading these stories has been enlightening for both of us, and we hope it will be for you as well. Thank you for reading.

Part I – Small is Beautiful:
Planning and Implementing Digitization Projects with Limited Resources

DIY Digitization: Creating a Small-scale Digital Zine Exhibit

Melissa L. Jones (College Summit)

Abstract

The Barnard Library Zine Collection is an innovative special collection of dynamic popular culture artifacts. The zines in the collection provide a democratic and vibrant glimpse into the movements and trends in recent feminist thought through the personal work of artists, writers, and activists. The author finds that in order to improve access to and generate interest in such niche collections, institutions have a responsibility to overcome barriers to digitization and begin sharing their collections online. This chapter discusses the development of Barnard's first zine digitization project: *the Elections and Protests: Zines from the Barnard Library Collection Online Exhibit,* launched in the summer of 2008. The successful project demonstrates that it is possible to build effective and engaging small-scale digital collections using simple and inexpensive technologies.

Keywords: Barnard College Library, Copyleft, Copyright, Education, Elections, Lesson plans, Online exhibit, Political zines, Primary sources, Protest, Special collections, Zines.

Introduction

The Barnard College Library began collecting zines in 2003 in an effort to document third wave feminism and riot grrrl culture. Zines are self-published, usually inexpensively produced works by writers who subscribe to a Do It Yourself (DIY) philosophy. Generally, zines are created out of an interest to communicate or express ideas that might not otherwise find acceptance in the mainstream media. Although zines as we know them today were born from the punk movement of the early 1970s (Duncombe, 1997, p. 21), they are part of a long history of small-run and "amateur" publication. Whether calling colonialists to arms in the days of the American Revolution or subverting censorship and challenges to free speech in Soviet Russia (Wright, 1997), alternative publications are a natural and important tool for preserving free speech.

Although zines are low rent ephemera, several public and academic libraries across the country have begun to recognize their value. At the forefront of the field, Barnard's collection has nearly 2,500 holdings providing unmediated access to the voices of young women on such subjects as race, gender, sexuality, childbirth, motherhood and politics. Zine Librarian Jenna Freedman's outreach and advocacy work helps to legitimize zines, not as radical historical footnotes but as valid literary and historic works worthy of collection, preservation and study.

As the Zine Intern in summer 2008, my role was to help Freedman to increase access to and interest in the Zine Collection. The result of my work was Barnard Library's first digital collection, an online exhibit entitled, *Elections and Protests: Zines from the Barnard Library Collection*. This project employed a DIY approach to digitization, making use of materials and resources at hand to solve problems and overcome challenges rather than relying on mainstream or out-of-the-box technologies. This project demonstrates that small-scale digitization projects can be topical, useful and impactful for a variety of stakeholders.

Literature Review and Needs Assessment

The literature surrounding zines reveals that, as unique primary source documents, they can serve as valuable research tools. Alternative press advocates such as librarians Chris Dodge and Jim Danky argue that self-published ephemera like zines, handbills, and military newspapers can provide a glimpse into a part of history that includes the voices of marginalized individuals and groups which would otherwise be lost were they not collected (Dodge, 2008).

Dempsey (2006) notes that to collect the ephemeral and radical "long tail" is not enough; institutions have a responsibility to provide users with access points and contextual materials in order to maximize use. Liu (2007) notes that in order to better serve users, "academic library Web sites should ... switch the focus from presenting information arranged according to library functions and resources to providing targeted and customizable tools and services to library users ... and give users opportunities to express, share, and learn." In addition to their value as historical documents, zines also serve as powerful teaching tools for media literacy (Wan 1999; Congdon, 2003; Daly, 2005), but scholars and teachers need both access to zines and support for teaching with these unique documents in order to capitalize on this potential.

Lesk (2007) acknowledges the legal and philosophical issues that are inherent in digitization work, but advocates strongly for institutions and copyright holders to work together to overcome challenges due to the potential value of digital materials for research. In order to support online research, some public and academic institutions have begun digitizing their special collections. Unfortunately at the time of this project, no public or academic institution had moved to digitize their zine collections.

The lack of high-quality materials for studying and teaching zines online makes interacting with the genre impossible for anyone without physical access to a collection. Most public and academic institutions allow access to their zine collections mainly through catalog search. Some institutions occasionally mount online exhibits that include scans of zine covers only.

This has been due, in part, to the same barriers that hinder other digitization projects such as prohibitive cost, lack of time, and technological limitations. Additionally, zine librarians and scholars identify the intrinsically physical nature of the genre as another reason not to prioritize zine digitization. Migrating zine content to a digital form is seen by many in academia to undermine the very heart of the genre, which is to be rooted in physical interaction between zinester, zine, and reader. Duke University's Zine Librarian argues that, "...zines are created by hand, crafted with paper, scissors, tape, glue, staples. They were meant to be handed from person to person, physically shared. The experience of handling zines in person, turning each page to reveal intimate secrets, funny comics, and poetry, can't be duplicated on-line. You would get the content, but miss out on the physical experience (Wooten, 2009)." Any academic digital Zine Collection would need to be very conscious of its treatment of digital surrogates.

Concerns about copyright, permission and privacy create another barrier to digitization. Copyright is a sticky issue when it comes to zines as a genre, which, by definition are created to be shared. Thus, many zines contain a copyleft statement, or some other notation of whether the owner has given permission for its contents to be reproduced. "Copyleft" is a term coined by open-source software pioneers to describe a "flipping" of traditional copyright laws that allows content owners to grant broader permission for their work to be shared. This "General Public License" can be applied in any situation where copyright might apply, including software, books, images and music (Söderberg, 2002). Generally, copyleft permission or GPL is considered to be conditional; zinesters who select copyleft status for their work, or those who claim no legal protection at all, still expect to be credited, or at least respected, for their work. It is poor zine etiquette to steal, borrow, or sell someone else's zine for personal gain.

Private zine online library and archive groups, run by zinesters and fans, have developed to fill the void of zines on the web. The sites digitize a large number of zines and serve as valuable repositories of content for experts in the field. Because they have grown organically from the zine community, these sites maximize their relationships to avoid and address concerns about copyright.

For Barnard Library, the the benefits of digitization digitization provided an incentive to overcome potential barriers, challenges and costs. An *Access and Use Survey* of known users administered in

2008 revealed that, while the Zine Collection has a strong contingent of feminist and zinester stakeholders, Barnard Library could be doing more to attract users outside the immediate scholarly and cultural community (see Figure ZINE-1.).

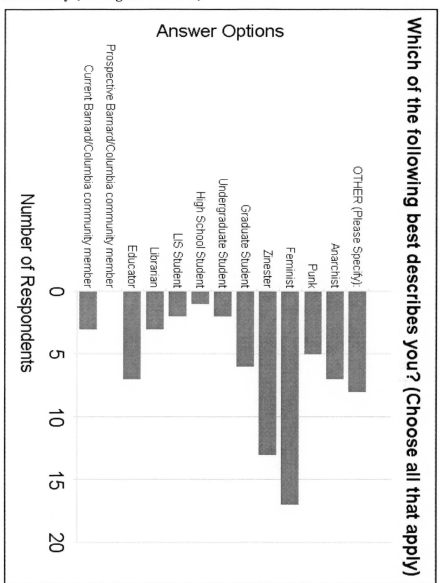

Figure ZINE-1: Results of the Barnard Library Zine Collection Access and Use Survey, administered to 25 known users in July 2008.

The survey confirmed that a small-scale digitization project would be a valuable addition to Barnard Library's existing services. 81% of known users reported that they would use curated, online exhibits about zines and zine history. Additionally, 81% of users said that they would use digital scans of selected zines.

The findings of the survey reflect the expectation by users that a library's website provide more than just access to information. By digitizing the popular and well-respected zine collection, Barnard Library could capitalize on the strength of its special collection to meet the needs of existing users, attract new users, and fill a need in the existing digital zine landscape. Additionally, a digital Zine Collection could help spread the word about the value of zines as historical documents and teaching tools to a new generation of potential stakeholders.

Project Planning

After making the decision to create a small digital zine collection, I created a project plan that included setting clear goals for the project.

Goal Setting

Digitizing even a small portion of Barnard's Zine Collection would have many benefits for the institution, its users, and the historical record. These included:

Improving access: Currently, membership in the Barnard/Columbia learning community is required in order to secure free access to the zine collection. Digitization would allow zines to be downloaded and shared easily, improving the ability of people from across the globe to access and learn from the collection.

Raising awareness about zines as legitimate historical objects: Freedman's work as an advocate for zine and other radical special collections would be complemented by a well-selected digitization project that is supported by descriptive and educational materials.

Highlighting Barnard's women's studies collection and drawing researchers to the institution: Barnard's Zine

Collection sets its women's studies research collection apart from other academic institutions. An online exhibit of materials from the Zine Collection could emphasize its uniqueness and eventually bring more researchers to the collection.

Preservation of the collection: Because most zines are produced cheaply using poor quality paper and inks, long-term conservation can be an issue. Digitizing zines makes their content available to future generations of researchers, students, and other stakeholders while preserving their physical form.

Project Scope

The scale of this project was by necessity very small. No fund was designated for the project. The site would need to be built and function within the existing Library website's structure; no money was available for purchasing a Content Management System or developing a complex metadata or image database. All work would need to be done using hardware and software already in Barnard Library's possession, or available open-source on the Web. As the Zine Intern, I would be the sole staff member available to work on the project. Freedman would supervise and approve my work. The project would need to be completed over the course of my summer internship, lasting only 100 hours over the course of 10 weeks.

Content Selection

Digitizing the collection as a whole proved to be too time consuming and technologically complex given these limitations. Selecting a small group of zines in a given theme or subject area to digitize first seemed a good model to begin with. Prioritizing digitization by demonstrated user need is a model that has been successful for other institutions. The University of Warwick in the UK, for example, developed an innovative research project in which students created digital surrogates of the 18th century French plays they used in their coursework (Astbury, 2006). Following a similar needs-based model would ensure that Barnard's first digital collection would be used by its most immediate stakeholders.

In 2008, the country was gearing up for an historic presidential election. Earlier that year, the previous Zine Intern, Julie Turley had created an exhibit of "Election and protest themed zines" to connect the institution's holdings with current events. The physical exhibit, which lived in the library's lobby, featured copies of selected zines and photocopied extracts of pages. From the Republican National Convention to the presidential election, from deciding to take your child to a political rally to challenging politicians to be responsible to their electorate, the featured zines addressed participation in -- or protest against -- the American political process.

The exhibit was a natural fit for this digitization project. The presidential election was only months away, we knew conversations about the political process would be a hot topic on campus. The selected zines offered a little-seen counterpoint to mainstream political coverage, rejecting voting as the sole means to make change in this nation. Moreover, educators across the nation would be looking for ways to talk about elections and the political process in their classrooms. It would be an excellent opportunity to demonstrate that zines can be relevant political and educational tools. Since zines are political in nature and often overtly political in topic, our digital collection would be reflective of the genre as a whole, even though we could only digitize a small number of zines. Finally, because the zines in this subset were already on display in the lobby, we knew that none were in need of conservation work or otherwise in danger of being damaged by the process of digitization.

Project Implementation

To maximize the benefits of digitization while addressing the barriers faced by the institution, I undertook a multi-step process for digitizing and presenting Barnard zines online. The process, like the zines themselves, was low-rent, low-tech, and outside the mainstream. The DIY approach was limiting in many ways, but also served as an excellent opportunity for learning and innovation.

DIY Digitization Project Timeline – May 5th through July 24th, 2008	
Task	**Timeline**
Needs assessment and literature review	Prior to project start
Goal setting and scope definition	Prior to project start
Content selection	May 5th
Generating metadata	May 12th
Competitive landscape analysis	May 12th through May 20th
Creating site maps and wireframes	May 12th through May 13th
Copyright requests to publish sent to zinesters	May 19th
Scanning and digitization	May 19th through June 17th
Designing an intuitive user interface	May 20th through July 21st
Writing original content	June 1st through July 18th
Usability testing	July 19th through July 21st
Site launch and publicizing	July 23rd through July 24th
Evaluation and reporting	Ongoing

Figure ZINE-2: Project Timeline – May 5th through July 24th, 2008

Copyright Status and Securing Permissions

After selecting the zines to be digitized, securing permission to present their content on the web was the next step. Educational use, such as the creation of an exhibit, would likely fall within any zinester's definition of copyleft. Only one zine of the ten selected, "Radical Cheerbook," contained an explicit copyleft statement. We felt confident that we could use its content in the exhibition.

Because the other nine zines selected for this exhibit contained some kind of copyright statement or did not contain an explicit copyleft statement, an effort was made to contact and secure permissions from the original author. This effort was difficult, however, since many zines were published using pseudonyms or contain contact information that is out of date. To track down the zinesters, I used a combination of Google searches, MySpace, and a pre-catalog Microsoft Access database that Freedman maintains to identify current email addresses. For one zinester, I was only able to identify a mailing address, so I sent a letter and awaited a response.

By the time the site was ready to go live in mid-July, I received written permission to publish from six zinesters, with most expressing excitement about the project. One zinester requested that I send scans of the specific pages I'd hoped to include before giving permission. At the bottom of each zine's page on the site, I made a note that the copyright holder had given permission for Barnard to use scans from the zines.

In three cases, I was not able to secure permission before the launch of the website. In these cases, I added a note to each zine's page that we had made a diligent effort to contact the copyright holder and would remove the images used in the event that there was an objection. I also made the decision to include only minimal excerpts from these zines as compared to the more extensive scans used from the zines for which we had permission.

Site Design & Comparative Landscape Analysis

Once permissions requests were sent, I focused my work on designing the site's architecture and layout. Close analysis of the features of similar sites can be a good way to begin planning. In order to understand how zines and zine-like publications can be presented online, I analyzed five sites with similar collections to Barnard. Because there were at the time no academic institutions with large-scale digital zine projects, I reviewed three sites run by private groups. I also reviewed two academic digital collections that feature radical or obscure publications.

My analysis revealed several qualities that most online exhibits of zine-like material share.

Asset management: (1) All five sites included full-color image scans with legible text and graphics; (2) All but one site included an option to download the asset in PDF form; (3) Four out of five sites included descriptive metadata about subject, author, and publication date to aid in discovery and to give context to the asset

Navigation: (1) Every site evaluated had a descriptive homepage and a consistent look and feel; (2) All five sites utilized global navigation on each page to keep the user oriented.

Search and discovery: (1) Four out of five sites allowed users to browse for a zine by title; (2) Four out of five sites offered a keyword search function; (3) None of the sites offered a search by author or issue number function; (4) Four out of five sites made searching or browsing for a known-item simple and pleasurable.

Tools and customization: Every site evaluated offered a "printer-friendly" version of their assets

Aesthetics and usability: (1) Every site took care to ensure that all links and functions worked as they were expected to; (2) Four out of five sites used some type of backend content-management system to organize assets; (3) For the qualities adopted by all sites evaluated, I attempted to include them.

Site Name and URL	Launch Date	Assets
Zine Library.net http://www.zinelibrary.info/	None given	"hundreds" of zines
The Queer Zine Archive Project http://www.qzap.org	Nov 2003	154 issues
Punk Zine Archive http://www.operationphoenixrecords.com/archivespage.html	2004	120 issues
Ling Long Woman's Magazine @ Columbia University http://www.columbia.edu/cu/lweb/digital/collections/linglong/index.html	2005	241 issues
Anarchism Pamphlets in the Labadie Collection @ The University of Michigan http://www.lib.umich.edu/spec-coll/labadie/	1999	478 pamphlets

Figure ZINE-3: Sites Evaluated for Competitive Landscape Analysis

There were other qualities present in some sites but not in others. These included RSS feeds, customizable user accounts and high-tech page turners. Because these qualities appeared in only some sites, I considered them to be optional for my site.

Interestingly, none of the sites offered any curriculum or supporting finding aids that would add necessary context to the materials. I planned to include lesson plans and a bibliography to accompany my zine scans.

Creating a sitemap and wireframes.

I first sketched wireframes for my site using paper and pencil, then translated those sketches into digital files. The wireframes turned out to be ambitious, and due to time and skill constraints, I was forced to scale down my original vision, but the creation of the sitemap and wireframes helped me synthesize all my ideas for the site into one visual presentation.

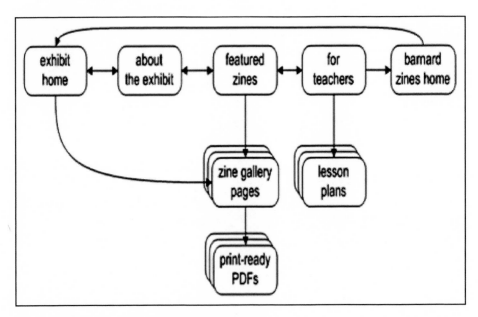

Figure ZINE-4. Final site map for the exhibit.

Generating Content

Scanning and digitization.

Ideally, for this project, preservation-quality scans should be made of each zine, along with its entire contents at the highest possible resolution in addition to any presentation and/or thumbnail versions. However, I was limited in my ability to create high-resolution scans due to several factors. The first issue was the constraints of the hardware and software at my disposal. I worked on scanners and computers that Barnard undergraduates have access to in the library's computer lab. More sophisticated equipment might have resulted in better scans.

The condition of the zines themselves also contributed to poor resolution. Because most zines are produced using cheap materials, many of the oldest were beginning to deteriorate as the paper yellowed and the ink faded. Additionally, poor photocopying resolution in the original zine made some of the digitized page images appear grainy and pixilated.

After much experimentation, I balanced preservation and presentation needs with time and resource scarcity by scanning each zine once at 600 DPI or higher. Next, I saved two JPG versions of each zine: a presentation copy at a maximum height of 600px and a thumbnail copy at a maximum height of 90px. I preserved the aspect ratio of each scan each time I resized the image. When necessary, I used image editing software -- either the open-source GIMP (http://www.gimp.org) or Adobe Photoshop, depending on what was installed on the computer I was working on that day – to tweak the contrast levels of the scan and improve legibility. For each zine's cover, I created a slightly larger thumbnail which is presented on the Home page and the "Featured Zines" page. The last step was to convert all of the JPGs to PDF and create a print version of each zine for users to download.

These digitization decisions allowed me to produce legible copies of each zine while maximizing disk space. Because I didn't have access to an image database or a content management system, I simply organized all of the files in a series of folders on my desktop, giving each file a descriptive name following a clear convention. When the exhibit was complete, these folders were uploaded, along with the HTML and CSS files to the Barnard server.

Generating metadata.

I was able to take the metadata for the exhibit from the existing OPAC records. Each zine is currently assigned cataloged in a MARC record as part of the Barnard/Columbia joint OPAC, CLIO. Current metadata includes: title, an author or creator (when applicable), physical description, a publisher and date, Library of Congress subject headings and a summary or abstract. For each zine's gallery page, I used only the author, title, summary and call number fields. Additionally, I included a link to CLIO so users could locate the zine, check on its availability, and order it through interlibrary loan. I was able to add additional metadata about individual zinesters who responded to my copyright requests, including links to each zinester's current projects or personal websites.

Writing Original Content

A major component of the site was the contextual material that would add value and meaning to the zine scans for users. To meet this need, I wrote an "About" page describing the exhibit, as well as a "For Teachers" page that included:

- a brief explanation of why zines make good teaching tools
- three essential questions related to zines which could be used to frame curriculum planning
- A list of suggested resources for educators

The most time consuming content pieces to develop were the three lesson plans designed to help educators teach with the zines in the exhibit. Drawing on my background as a teacher, I designed these lesson plans around essential questions related to media literacy and social science content areas, then aligned them to three different learning levels: intermediate, secondary, and post-secondary. The lesson plans are student-centered and challenge students to interact with the zines in the exhibit through discussion and evaluation.

Building and Testing the Site

Ideally, the user interface for any site should be intuitive and promote discovery. For this project, I was limited to very basic web design software and programming languages that have a low-barrier to mastery, but I was determined to make the site as usable as possible given the constraints.

To build the site, I again used hardware and software in the Barnard Library computer lab. I first attempted to build the site using Microsoft FrontPage, and then switched to an open-source HTML editor called Mozilla Kompozer (http://www.kompozer.net). Both FrontPage and Kompozer have "WYSIWYG" interfaces – an acronym for "what you see is what you get" – in that they allow users to create web pages using an interface that mirrors how the final product will appear (Myers, 1998). I needed to have a firm grasp on what was happening in the actual code behind my pages as I made changes. Additionally, I wanted to be able to customize my site, and the templates available in FrontPage and Kompozer felt limiting.

After a few days of struggle, I settled on developing the code for my site by hand using the simple text editing software available on most computer operating systems. The flexibility of being able to work on my files from any location made this project much easier to complete in only 10 weeks. I created and edited my files in Microsoft Notepad at Barnard Library, and could easily open them at home on my Apple laptop using either TextEdit or a free trial version of the excellent application, Coda (http://www.panic.com/coda/) which combines a WYSIWYG interface with an easy-to-use text editor. During the initial coding phase, I began by building a framework for each site using a common layout, menu bar, and footer using simple HTML tags such as those for images, links and tables. I also selected a patriotic red-white-and-blue color scheme and created an image banner to run along the top of the page that included the site's title in a typewriter-style font and some randomly-placed stars to mimic a zine-like feel. Later, the color scheme was changed to a more punk-inspired pink and black, to better reflect the lack of overt patriotism expressed in the zines themselves.

Once a basic page template was complete, I created a Cascading Style Sheet (CSS) file which governed the look and feel of each page and made coding the rest of the site easier. Using a CSS file is a simple way to add style (such as fonts, colors and spacing) to every page in a website without having to edit each page individually (Bos, 2010). In order for the CSS file to work, I added a line of code in each page's HTML file that directed a user's web browser to "link" to my style sheet file, called "text.css". This file dictated the background and font colors of each part of each page, the margins for the different dividers and tables, and even the spacing of thumbnail images in my photo gallery. Before beginning this project, I had never worked in CSS. However, I found the language simple to learn and easy to use once I understood the fundamentals. As I worked, I referenced countless tutorials and open-source code available on the web to hack my way through the rest of the coding process.

The biggest coding challenge was creating a workable photo display gallery to present my zine scans. During the site mapping and wire-framing (see Figure 8), I had determined that I wanted users to interact with thumbnail versions of a zine's pages and select which pages they'd like to see in a larger, presentation-quality view. At first, I tried copying an open-source photo gallery HTML file that I found online. This allowed me to build the bare bones of my page layout, and indeed included thumbnail images and presentation-quality views. However, the photo gallery had one weakness: every time I moved my mouse off of the thumbnail I wanted to view, the presentation-quality view disappeared! This would have made my site very difficult to use, as it was impossible to scroll, zoom, or even save the presentation-quality view while still keeping your mouse over the thumbnail view. Finally, a programmer friend-of-the-collection helped out by producing a small piece of JavaScript code that allowed me to keep the presentation-quality view open without having to keep my mouse perfectly still. This code allowed me to create a version of the site that I was excited to test with users.

Usability Testing

Before going live, I tested the site's usability with three different test subjects, each representing a different group of Barnard Library stakeholders. Each test subject was given the same set of tasks to complete. Figure ZINE-5 lists the tasks administered and whether or not the subject was able to complete the task without guidance.

Task	A	B	C
Choose and read through all the pages of a zine you're interested in.	✓	✓	✓
Find the author of the zine, "Don't blame me..."	✓	✓	✓
Find out if Barnard has permission to publish, "Subliminal Criminal"	✓	✓	✗
Find out who first put together the zines in this exhibition and when.	✓	✓	✓
Locate information about how to use these zines in your classroom.	✓	✓	✓
Send an email to the zines collection	✓	✓	✓
Download a copy of page 3 of "Mama Sez no war"	✓	✓	✓
Find out why zines are used for protest	✓	✓	✓
Go to the homepage of Barnard Library	✓	✓	✓
Go to the homepage of the zine collection	✓	✓	✓
Download a lesson plan for use in your classroom	✓	✓	✗
Use CLIO to check the availability of the zine, "Dear Mr. Bush"	✓	✓	✗

Summary of Test Subjects:
Subject A: Female, Age 20, Barnard Undergraduate Student
Subject B: Female, Age 28, Librarian
Subject C: Male, Age 31, Columbia Alumnus

Key:
✓   Task completed
✗   Task not completed

Figure ZINE-5: "Exhibits and Protest" Site Usability Tasks and Results.

In addition to identifying tasks that would be difficult for users to complete, I also made anecdotal records of the test subjects' comments and feedback. Based on the results of the testing, I made the following improvements to the site:

- Increased the size of all fonts used by 1px
- Added a mouse-over function to each zine cover image on the homepage that listed its title to aid in identification
- Added a "download all" link to a PDF containing all image files associated with each zine
- Made the copyright documentation on each zine more prominent

Launching and Publicizing

Upon completion of testing, the final version of the online exhibit (http://www.barnard.edu/library/zines/exhibits/online/elections/index.html) was launched on July 23rd, 2008. A link to the exhibit was posted on the Barnard College Library homepage, and a blog post about it was added to the institution's Livejournal (http://barnardzines.livejournal.com/). Emails were sent to a zine librarians' listserve and to other contacts and friends of the Zine Collection. I also sent a link to the exhibit to colleagues and friends in K-12 schools across the country. Since the initial launch, Freedman has continued to publicize the online exhibit in her talks and outreach activities for the collection.

Results and Next Steps

Informal evaluation of the project demonstrates that it has begun to meet its goals. User feedback on the site has been overwhelmingly positive. By making Barnard's zines accessible on the web to millions of people across the globe, the exhibit has indeed improved access to the collection. In an age when discovery on the web is primarily done through Google or other search (Belden, 2008), it is encouraging that search terms such as "zine lesson plans," "zines and elections," and "teaching with zines" consistently return the site in the first page of search results. This is an indication of how many sites continue to link to the exhibit since its launch.

It is obvious from the *Access and Use Survey* that such an effort is both desired and respected by stakeholders. The exhibit only scanned selections of the zines featured, not entire issues, it may not be seen to contribute to the long-term preservation of the individual artifacts. However, creating a home on the web for zines around a contemporary issue can be seen to be contributing to the long-term preservation of the genre by making zines relevant in the digital age.

It remains to be seen whether this site will indeed drive users to the Zine Collection's other resources. Further evaluation should be done in order to determine whether or not this exhibit is directly contributing to increased access or use of the collection by Barnard/Columbia community members, outside researchers, K-12 educators, and other stakeholders. Repeating the Access and Use Survey annually may be a step in that direction.

Long-term sustainability and continued effectiveness of the exhibit are an issue. Freedman or future interns will need to take on the responsibility for maintaining and updating the exhibit as necessary over time. As Barnard Library further develops its web presence, the exhibit's look, feel, and even its content could become outdated. At this time, however, there is no reason why the exhibit cannot stay live for the foreseeable future without financial cost or significant staff time commitment. In order to maximize the exhibit's effectiveness, Barnard could consider:

- Continuing to promote and publicize the current exhibit, focusing on alternative outlets such as Wikipedia, educator websites, and media literacy blogs
- Developing an evaluation plan to determine the impact of the online exhibit on the stated project goals.
- Securing site analytics data on page usage and download stats to measure usage of the exhibit, as well as effectiveness of marketing techniques

Due to the support for this project from users, Barnard could consider digitizing more of the collection. Next steps could include:

- Creating more online exhibits around themes or subjects of interest to stakeholders if this first exhibit proves valuable
- Creating more subject guides, lesson plans and bibliographies about zines and zine history, and making them available online
- Collaborating with Columbia's New Media Teaching and Learning group in order to ensure that the user interface promotes teaching and learning with zines as primary sources, art objects and media literacy teach tools.

An open question is whether or not Barnard should move forward with digitizing the entire collection. Although this project was able to overcome many barriers to digitization of the genre (Wooten, 2009), a larger-scale project might open the door to more difficulty with copyright, permissions, privacy, and preserving the user experience of interacting with a zine's physical form.

Conclusion

This project showed that it is possible to create innovative web resources for a variety of stakeholders with a minimum level of technological and know-how. It provided a great opportunity for Barnard to continue to lead in the field of zine librarianship. This online exhibit supports teaching, learning, and research with quality and findable digital assets that highlight Barnard Library's strengths. With the current low barrier to web authorship, it is not enough for academic special collections to simply have a web page. Instead, more libraries and institutions can take advantages of the resources available to them – whether it is an eager intern, an exciting collection, or a timely theme –to create a resource that will meet the needs of users and make their holdings accessible to and available for generations to come.

References

Astbury, K. (2006). *French theatre of the first empire: Enhancing research-based learning.* Warwick Interactions Journal 28. Retrieved from http://www2.warwick.ac.uk/services/cap/resources/pubs/interactions/archive/issue28/abastbury/astbury

Belden, D. (2008). Harnessing social networks to connect with audiences: If you build it, will they come 2.0? *Internet Reference Services Quarterly, 13*(1), 99-111.

Bos, B. (2010). *Cascading style sheets.* W3C Consortium. Retrieved from: http://www.w3.org/Style/CSS/

Congdon, K. G., & Blandy, D. (2003). Zinesters in the classroom: Using zines to teach about postmodernism and the communication of ideas. *Art Education. 56*(3), 44-52.

Daly, B. O. (2005). Taking whiteness personally: Learning to teach testimonial reading and writing in the college literature classroom. *Pedagogy, 5*(2), 213-246.

Dempsey, L. (2006). Libraries and the long tail: Some thoughts about libraries in a network age. *D-Lib Magazine, 12*(4). doi:10.1045/april2006-dempsey

Dodge, C. (2008). Collecting the wretched refuse: Lifting a lamp to zines, military newspapers and Wisconsonalia. *Library Trends, 56*(3), 667-677.

Duncombe, S. (1997) *Notes from underground: Zines and the politics of alternative culture.* New York : Verso.

Jones, M. (2008). *Elections and protest: Zines from the Barnard Library collection.* Barnard Library Website. Retrieved from http://www.barnard.edu/library/zines/exhibits/online/elections/index.html

Lesk, M. (2007). *From data to wisdom: Humanities research and online content. Academic Commons.* Retrieved from http://www.academiccommons.org/commons/essay/michael-lesk

Liu, S. (2008). Engaging users: The future of academic library web sites. College & Research Libraries, 69(1), 6-27

Myers, B. (1998). *A brief history of human computer interaction technology.* ACM interactions, 5(2), 44-54. Retrieved from: http://www.cs.cmu.edu/~amulet/papers/uihistory.tr.HTML

Söderberg, J. (2002). *Copyleft vs. copyright: A Marxist critique. First Monday, 7*(3). Retrieved from: http://ojphi.org/htbin/cgiwrap/bin/ojs/index.php/fm/article/viewArticle/938/860

Wan, A. J. (1999). Not just for kids anymore: Using zines in the classroom. *Radical Teacher, 55*, 15-19.

Wooten, K. (2009). *Why we're not digitizing zines.* Duke University Libraries Digital Connections Blog. Retrieved from http://library.duke.edu/blogs/digital-collections/2009/09/21/why-were-not-digitizing-zines/

Wright, F. (1997) *The history and characteristics of zines. The Zine & E-Zine Resource Guide.* Retrieved from http://www.zinebook.com/resource/wright1.HTML

Digitizing Civil Rights: An Omeka-based Pilot Digital Presence for the Queens College Civil Rights Archive

Valery Chen, Jing Si Feng, Kevin Schlottmann
(Queens College, CUNY)

Abstract

The Queens College Civil Rights Archive of the Department of Special Collections partnered with the Queens College Graduate School of Library and Information Studies to create a pilot web presentation using the open-source Omeka platform. Phase I of the project, conducted during the Spring 2010 semester, outlined a method for institutions of limited means to enter into the world of digitization using existing resources while highlighting the difficulties involved with metadata and IT support, and the advantages of involving graduate students.

Keywords: Civil rights, Digitization project, Omeka, Plug-ins.

Introduction

In the spring of 2010, the Queens College Civil Rights Archive of the Department of Special Collections partnered with the Queens College Graduate School of Library and Information Studies to create a pilot web presentation using the open-source Omeka platform. The synergy created between the technological skills found in the library school faculty and student body and the desire of the Civil Rights Archive to begin digitization of key holdings allowed the rapid creation of a powerful web presentation platform. The process also outlined a method for institutions of limited means to enter into the world of digitization.

Queens College Civil Rights Archive

The Civil Rights Archive of the Queens College Department of Special Collections and Archives collects published and unpublished works relating to civil rights activities such as personal papers, community materials, organizational records, non-print materials, and artifacts. It also conducts oral histories to supplement its collections. The archive is particularly strong in materials documenting civil rights work by Queens College students during the early 1960s. The Archive seeks to provide evidences of the under-documented Northern involvement in the civil rights movement.

The Archive was founded in late 2008 around an estimable collection of personal papers donated by alumnus Mark Levy. Since then almost a dozen other personal collections relating to civil rights work in the 1960s have been donated by College alumni, and the Archive continues to actively collect in this area.

Queens College Graduate School of Library and Information Studies

The Queens College Graduate School of Library and Information Studies prepares library/information service professionals to meet the information and literacy needs of the New York metropolitan region and beyond. It is the only American Library Association accredited program for library and information studies within the City University of New York. The school prepares graduates to serve a broad segment of the metropolitan area's multicultural, multiethnic and multi-lingual population in a variety of institutional and informational settings. Through research, publication and other forms of scholarly activity, the school contributes and transmits new knowledge to society and the profession. The faculty provides opportunities for students to attain the competencies needed to participate in the evolving electronic age by providing a technologically rich teaching/learning environment.

Project Origin

The Queens College Department of Special Collections, wherein the Civil Rights Archive is located, was acutely aware of the need for its collections to have a digital presence. It will soon be true that archival materials that are not electronically accessible in some way, whether via an OPAC or on website, will be no better served than in a dark archive. Given the limited resources of an urban public university, the Department had been unable to secure sufficient financial and technological support for an independent digitization project. Head of Special Collections Dr. Ben Alexander is also teaching in the Graduate School of Library and Information Studies, and he approached Dr. Kwong Bor Ng to discuss a mutually beneficial way to begin the process of building a digital presence. Drs. Ng and Alexander decided to expand the Special Collections Fellowship program, which provides archival graduate students at Queens College with a broad range of professional archival experience, to include a technology component. Dr. Ng selected two graduate students with extensive coding skills to do the actual work of creating an Omeka presentation website. The hope was to create a mutually beneficial arrangement: under Dr. Ng's supervision, the two graduate students were able to gain real-world experience in building an Omeka platform, while the Civil Rights Archive was able to lay sufficient groundwork to seek grant funding in support of a larger digitization project.

Staffing/Workflow

Drs. Alexander and Ng served as project coordinators. The semantic team, which was co-extensive with the Department of Special Collections staff, consisted of Dr. Alexander, Archives Adjunct Katie Hughes and Archives Assistant Kevin Schlottmann. The technical team was headed up by Dr. Ng, who supervised two of his technology graduate students, Valery Chen and Jing Si Feng. They were given academic credit as independent study students and Special Collections

Fellows to build the Omeka website. The semantic team was responsible for selection, digitization, and metadata creation. The technological team was responsible for the installation and development of the Omeka presentation. Both teams were involved in the development of the Dublin Core metadata schema, and they also collaborated in creating the user experience of the website.

The project began with a meeting in February 2010. This meeting was initially a brainstorming session, but the teams were able to agree to the basic semester goal of a pilot website, as well as a rough timeline. Once the semantic team completed selection and the metadata schema was ready, a few items from the Civil Rights Archive were digitized per week and forwarded to the technological team. Meanwhile, the technological team was preparing the Omeka website for import of digital items. This continued as an iterative process for the entire Spring 2010 semester. At biweekly meetings, the website and the digital items were discussed, and both were constantly improved.

Implementation – Semantic Team

The semantic team, consisting of the Department of Special Collections staff (Department Head Dr. Benjamin Alexander, Archives Adjunct Katie Hughes and Archives Assistant Kevin Schlottmann) was responsible for selection, digitization, and metadata creation.

Selection

When the semantic team began discussing what to digitize, it considered materials from the Civil Rights Archive, the College Archive, the Performing Arts collection, and the Rare Book, Zine, and Artists Book collections. It quickly became clear that the civil rights materials were best suited for this pilot project, for reasons such as processing status, donor relations, fitting into the Archive's specific mission of engaging with the broader community, copyright status of the materials, and the attraction of having students continue to work with the material.

First and foremost, the Civil Rights Archive had the best-cataloged collections in the Department. The majority of the Archive's holdings are fully processed, have finding aids, and are under archival control. This level of processing also allowed for existing contextual information to be used by the teams.

The civil rights materials are among the most prized and high-profile holdings in Special Collections. The recent founding of the Archive garnered attention from campus and activist communities, and received local press coverage as well. From a donor relations viewpoint, digitizing these collections would generate goodwill within the alumni activist community that contains future donors and supporters. The Archive's living donors are still very interested in their materials and legacies, and have repeatedly expressed strong interest having their materials digitized.

The semantic team also conducted a review of existing civil rights digital archives, which showed many worthy efforts already underway. The University of Southern Mississippi, which holds one of the largest archival collections about civil rights work in Mississippi, created the Civil Rights in Mississippi Digital Archive, an "Internet-accessible, fully searchable database of digitized versions of rare and unique library and archival resources on race relations in Mississippi" (University of Southern Mississippi Special Collections, 2006a). The Civil Rights Digital Library, hosted by the University of Georgia, is "a partnership among librarians, technologists, archivists, educators, scholars, academic publishers, and public broadcasters" that provides federated searching of digital civil rights materials from almost 100 different institutions (Digital Library of Georgia, 2009).

These two excellent examples, among dozens of others, illustrated two major reasons why the semantic team chose to digitize materials from the Civil Rights Archive, rather than from other special collections. First, it was found that there exists a vigorous online community that any institution holding archival civil rights materials must join to remain relevant and accessible. Second, the team found a paucity of material that relates specifically to Northern contributions to the civil rights movement, and thus digitization of the Queens

College Civil Rights Archive would add new perspectives to the online community, in keeping with the Archive's stated mission of engaging the broader archival civil rights community.

The copyright status of the many of the materials in the Civil Rights Archive was clear, because photographs and personal papers of known provenance could be easily cleared by the creators with whom the Department has a relationship. Many of the other areas in special collections have a murkier copyright status, which is a major potential impediment to digitization.

Finally, the civil rights materials were primarily processed by archival students from the Queens College Graduate School of Library and Information Studies as part of the Special Collections Fellowship program. It seemed natural to continue the collaborative effort between the library school and Special Collections by having the student-processed materials brought into the digital realm by Fellows as well.

Digitization

The actual scanning of the items was not the focus of this pilot project. A proper scanning procedure that will create archival images in the TIFF format, such as that developed by the University of Southern Mississippi (University of Southern Mississippi Special Collections, 2006b), will be developed during Phase II in conjunction with implementation of a digital asset management system. The items digitized for this project were scanned with an Epson 10000XL scanner using Adobe Photoshop CS3. After cropping, deskewing, and adjustments to contrast and level, the images were saved as 300-dpi Web-optimized jpegs and provided to the technical team.

Metadata

The development of a robust metadata schema was a primary goal of this project. The semantic team examined a range of available schemas, such as METS, MODS, and PREMIS, but it very quickly became clear that Dublin Core (DC) was ideal for a variety of reasons. Unqualified DC is compatible with basic Omeka; it is a simple and easily-understood schema; it can be extended by using qualified DC; it is well-established; and similar projects are using it. The latter was a particular influence, both because the Civil Rights Archive hopes to digitally collaborate with other institutions as well as because there are a wealth of relevant resources available. The two key sources used by the semantic team were published DC schemas from the University of Southern Mississippi and the North Carolina Exploring Cultural Heritage Online project (Graham & Ross, 2003; NC ECHO, 2007).

The semantic team created a detailed qualified Dublin Core schema, but after much discussion the teams decided to work with an unqualified schema, because that was the Omeka default. The semantic team continued to create qualified DC, so that in the future the project will be able to implement this more detailed schema.

The project utilized many controlled vocabularies. Library of Congress Name and Subject Authorities were used for person and subject terms; DCMI and IAMA for type and digital format, respectively; and ISO 8601 for dates. For the analog Medium field, the Getty's Art and Architecture Thesaurus proved most useful. Geographic data were placed in the Coverage field. LC subjects were used for the general geographic area, such as the town or state, while latitude and longitude data were taken from Google Maps by manually entering a known address and harvesting the geospatial data provided. The technology team was able to use the latitude and longitude data to create a Google Map reflecting the geographic location of the digitized items.

The teams both felt it important to offer maximum searchability, and the semantic team thus also provided the full text of digitized items, using OCR software. This proved to be a time-consuming additional step, in particular the proofreading of the computer-generated text. The print quality of some materials was quite poor, and the many drawings and photographs were also difficult for the software to interpret. Better software and more experience creating OCR text should make this easier as the project moves forward.

Omeka also has the ability for users to add tags. The teams decided to take selected controlled-subject values from the Dublin Core metadata and use them as tags as well, to allow testing of features such as the tag cloud. The teams engaged in an interesting discussion about how tags would be used in this project – some wanted to keep the vocabulary controlled, while others wanted to encourage users to add tags as they saw fit. The teams decided to allow tags to be used as user-generated metadata, in keeping with the Web 2.0 spirit of Omeka.

The metadata was created manually by the semantic team in an MS Word table, and transferred into Omeka by the technology team. A future goal is an automated process for metadata transfer.

Implementation – Technology Team

The technology team for the project consisted of two independent study graduate students, Valery Chen and Jing Si Feng, as part of the Special Collections Fellows program, and their instructor and project coordinator Dr. Ng. These Fellows began working on the project after the first meeting with the semantic team on February 16, 2010. Over the next ten weeks, the Fellows downloaded, installed, and modified Omeka, an open-source web-publishing system, and completed the first phase of the project on May 13, 2010.

Why Omeka?

The purpose of this project was to create a web presentation to showcase the unique and valuable holdings of the Queens College Civil Rights Archive, and at the same time provide the Fellows an opportunity to learn how to build a digital archive using a web-publishing system. In any project, it is important to consider the use of proprietary system versus nonproprietary/open-source. Omeka is relatively a new software package that describes itself as a web-publishing platform on its website:

Omeka is a free, flexible, and open source web-publishing platform for the display of library, museum, archives, and scholarly collections and exhibitions. Its "five-minute setup" makes launching an online exhibition as easy as launching a blog. Omeka is designed with non-IT specialists in mind, allowing users to focus on content and interpretation rather than programming. It brings Web 2.0

technologies and approaches to academic and cultural websites to foster user interaction and participation. It makes top-shelf design easy with a simple and flexible templating system. Its robust open-source developer and user communities underwrite Omeka's stability and sustainability. (Omeka, 2010, Project section.)

Omeka is an open-source web-publishing system developed by the Center for History and New Media at George Mason University. According to the Omeka web site (Center for History and New Media, George Mason University, 2010) Omeka is easy to install, allows great flexibility for customized web interface, and supports multiple plugins. All these features were appealing for this project.

Another compelling reason to choose Omeka was the potential inherent in the exhibit feature. Omeka has the Web 2.0 ability of allowing users to create their own exhibits from the digital collections. A primary goal of the Civil Rights Archive is to engage the educational community and encourage use of its materials. By providing digital surrogates and contextual information, this website would allow a teacher or professor to tailor their use of the materials in an exhibit, and also make them accessible to other educators seeking similar uses. This type of educational contextualization was a key reason to digitize the collection.

Description of Phase I (Feb 16, 2010 – May 13, 2010)

This section discusses the installation of Omeka, the addition of various plugins, the details of the most heavily manipulated pages, and examines particular technical problems and solutions encountered during Phase I of this project.

Installation

Initially, separate Omeka instances were created for each Fellow on the technology team to experiment independently. After both instances were adequately developed, the best features were selected from each and transferred over to a new Omeka installation, running on version 1.2.

Omeka 1.1, the latest version available at the time of the first installation process, was downloaded by the technology team and installed. The Omeka system was in a zip file, and the technology team had to unzip the file to extract all the necessary files for installation. Each Fellow downloaded the zip file and unzipped the files successfully. The next step was to connect to the server remotely and upload the files for installation. Omeka consists of thousands of files, and Adobe Dreamweaver could not handle such a massive upload. Using an FTP client, such as FireFTP, was found to be the best practice. FireFTP supports large uploads and does not terminate in the middle of an upload. If termination does occur, FireFTP automatically reconnects to the server to continue with the upload.

The Omeka installation folder in the directory was removed by bash shell script for security. Administrator and Super accounts were created, and the system was up and running.

Creating Items, Tags, and Collections

A collection can be created in the Omeka Admin page by filling in the name and description of a collection. An item can be created by filling in the Dublin Core fields in the Omeka Admin page and adding the item to a collection. Tags can be added to each item to create more access points.

All image values in the Omeka General Setting should be defined before importing any image files. The values Fullsize Image Size, Thumbnail Size, and Square Thumbnail Size are crucial for Omeka to generate image output. Omeka automatically generates full size image and thumbnails during item creation. The technology team decided to change the full size image output and thumbnail size in the middle of the project, thus resulting in two different image sizes throughout the site. This meant that all the files needed to be uploaded again at the conclusion of the project, to ensure uniform image sizes.

Selecting a Theme

The public interface of Omeka was controlled by the files inside the "themes" folder. The Super can log on to the Omeka Admin page to choose a desired theme. More themes can be downloaded from the Omeka website and uploaded to the server. Both Fellows selected a different theme for their individual pilot Omeka sites. One chose "santa-fe" while the other chose "spring."

Plugins

Many plugins are available for download from the Omeka website. The technology team installed Geolocation, Simple Pages, Dublin Core Extended, Dropbox, ExhibitBuilder, and Lightbox for the pilot site. Several outside interactive effects were also installed, including animated collapsible panels, text truncation, and a slideshow. Most of the plugins were easy to use and install without any hassles; the plugins specifically named above are discussed in more detail below. One plugin issue was that some of the plugins were written in plain JavaScript while others were written using jQuery. This often created clashes in the code as the dollar sign symbol ($) was used for different purposes in both JavaScript and jQuery. In JavaScript, the $ indicates a variable, while in jQuery the $ represents the start of a command. Since jQuery is technically a JavaScript library, the double meaning of the $ was problematic.

Geolocation

Geolocation uses features from Google Maps and allows users to view items in various geographic locations by clicking on the balloon pointers. The technology team decided to install this plugin because it gives users a visual, spatial representation of the materials in the archive. This visual aid can be useful for quickly identifying locations of particular interest, and it allows users an additional non-textual method of accessing digitized items.

In order to use the Google Map functionality, the technology team first had to obtain a Google Maps API (application programming interface) key by creating an account with Google. Once the key was obtained, the team downloaded the packaged Google Map plugin from Omeka and uploaded it to the server. The key was then supplied through the administrator interface to activate the plugin. From the administrator interface, it is possible to customize the Google Map API. For example, the administrator can set the default location, which is controlled by latitude and longitude, and the zoom level ranging from 1 to 20, where 1 displays a view of the Earth and 20 displays a street level map.

The geographic location was added manually through the administrator interface. The latitude and longitude were entered for each digital item's metadata. The technology team hopes to create a plugin in the future that will automatically locate the spatial location information from the Dublin Core metadata and supply it accordingly so that as items are uploaded they will automatically appear on the map.

All items with geographical coordinates are represented by the default red pinWhen users click on the marker, the corresponding item will pop up in a balloon with limited metadata identifying the item. Users can then click on the balloon, which brings them to the particular item's display page. The team plans to enhance the map by creating a color-coding scheme that will correspond to an item's categorization. For example, items relating to a protest could have a red marker, while Freedom School items could have a blue marker. This functionality will add additional visual meaning to the map.

Simple Pages

Simple Pages provides the ability to handle html codes input by the Super at the admin page. The team used the Simple Page plugin to create the "About Us" section of the website.

Dublin Core Extended

Omeka defaults to Unqualified Dublin Core. A Dublin Core Extended Plugin can be installed to create more descriptive fields. A primary consideration when installing Dublin Core Extended is whether all the additional fields are necessary for a given project. Too many fields slow down the data entry process and scrolling time, and since all the Omeka data entries are web-based, a wrong click by the mouse can result in loss of data. The teams hope to take advantage of qualified Dublin Core in Phase II.

Dropbox

Omeka uses a web-based data entry system; each field needs to be typed in separately. A Dropbox plugin can be installed to facilitate bulk file uploads, allowing multiple files to be uploaded at the same time into a Dropbox Folder. When adding a digital item to the collection, the user can then select that item from the Dropbox. Dropbox also supports the creation of multiple items, and allows bulk creation of Tags, Collections, and Titles. Other Dublin Core fields still need to be entered separately.

ExhibitBuilder

ExhibitBuilder was a more complex installation, as the architecture of the exhibit pages had to first be determined. The structure of the exhibit was defined as a Main Title Page with descriptions, a Sub-Section with descriptions, and individual pages with items in the layout of choice. The interface of an exhibit can be changed by accessing the screen.css file under the ExhibitBuilder directory.

Lightbox

In order to enhance the user experience, a Lightbox was installed for viewing full size images. The Lightbox feature creates an overlay around an image and enhances the clarity of the image in the center. The latest version of Lightbox was downloaded from http://www.huddletogether.com/projects/lightbox2/, and installation process was closely followed from the Omeka Documentation page (Ebellempire, 2009).

Heavily Manipulated files

This section describes two particular areas of the Omeka platform that were heavily edited by the technology team.

Item Display Page

The default display page for each item is a non-stylized, exhaustive list of metadata that requires extensive vertical scrolling. Moreover, some of the DC and Omeka metadata are duplicative. In order to create a more user-friendly display of information, multiple files were heavily manipulated and outside plugins were incorporated to make the display page more interactive.

The technology team found it challenging to determine which files control the item display page, because there are many files with the same name in different directories. However, once the structure of how Omeka arranges its files was ascertained, the team was able to manipulate the code and customize the display.

The first step after locating the correct file was to understand the predefined functions created by Omeka. This was achieved with the help from the documentation on the Omeka website. This stage was time consuming, as the team used a trial-and-error approach to learn how to use the different available functions. Once it was determined which function handled the selection of individual metadata, the team was able to control where each piece of metadata would be displayed.

The display page was designed so that the most important information was provided in a clear, easy-to-read format. To minimize the scrolling, certain technical metadata was hidden from the user. The technology and semantic teams jointly examined each DC and Omeka data field, and decided on a short of list of fields to display. These included the collection, subject, tag, and rights fields. Creator, date, location and citation were included under the item's thumbnail image. Hidden fields included type, source, publisher, upload date, and extent. These fields were merely hidden – users may click on the "show" link to reveal the hidden metadata if desired. The show-and-hide functionality was made possible by installing jQuery, a lightweight JavaScript library, and the appropriate toggle-display code. The teams agreed that while an average user would not need to see this information on first viewing a page, more sophisticated users might want the option. The semantic team in particular found in its review of similar web projects that many sites did not include technical metadata, to the disappointment of archivists and librarians seeking to learn from how other institutions handle metadata.

If a particular item had an accompanying full text, it was made available to the user. However, since a typical full text would cover an extensive area of the display page, the technology team used a truncation function to display a snippet of the full text along with a link to show more. This was also accomplished through jQuery.

While most of the display page reorganization was controlled by the php files, CSS files controlled the final style touches, such as spacing, font sizes, and background color.

Homepage

The default homepage also underwent a major redesign. Instead of the default static thumbnails representing the featured item, the team added a dynamic slideshow with captions that rotate through the featured items. The initial plan was to implement the slideshow using Adobe Flash. However, that idea was discarded as inefficient because new .swf files would have to be created for each new imaged added and each image taken down. Therefore, the best solution with the least amount of maintenance was to find a method to automatically pull images for display. The team achieved this by installing a jQuery slideshow. These images are thus easily maintained by a few lines of code.

The technology team also added a right sidebar that allowed users to browse by various categories, including tag, date, location, subject, and type. The sidebar was initially occupied by a list of recently accessed items, but in conversation with the semantic team it was decided that creating multiple access points would be more useful to the user for navigation purposes. Currently, the list of categories is manually created through simple HTML code. The technology team hopes to automate the generation of categories in this sidebar, to simplify site maintenance.

Goals and Discussion

Phase II Goals

The teams have many goals for Phase II. The stabilization and scalability of the project are a top priority, and this includes development of a scanning process and a streamlined metadata creation process, as well as finding stable server space and implementing a digital asset management system behind the Omeka website.

In terms of the Omeka, the technology team hopes to add more sophisticated features to the map, such as item categorization. On the metadata side, it will implement qualified Dublin Core, and may attempt to install the OAI-PMH Harvester. Finally, a long-term goal is the creation of a plugin that would allow use of TEI.

Discussion

This pilot project identified issues that might be similar in other institutions with limited resources. The three key lessons from Phase I of this project relate to technical support, metadata, and the involvement of graduate students.

Technical Support

Proper server space is absolutely vital for any digitization project. The extremely limited IT resources available at Queens College mean that this pilot project is limited in its ability to grow beyond Phase I. This also impacts the Department of Special Collection's ability to implement a digital asset management system. If continued efforts to obtain College server space are unsuccessful, the project will examine other options such as approaching another CUNY school for a partnership, or perhaps even renting commercial server space.

Metadata

The semantic team spent the majority of its time and effort on metadata, both in developing the schema and creating the actual records.

Creating metadata from scratch is extremely time-consuming. For each individual image, the team created titles and descriptions, applied a variety of controlled vocabularies, harvested geographic data, and proofread OCR text. With the current human resources, this process would be impossible to scale up. Thus, in Phase II the teams will attempt to streamline the process by automating some aspects of metadata creation. For example, technical specifications could be automatically imported and drop-down menus created for oft-repeated controlled vocabulary terms. Once a robust and well-described process is in place, Special Collections Fellows working on civil rights materials could be recruited to enter much of the metadata, which would provide the administrative team time to engage in other tasks, such as selection, quality control, and project planning.

Another issue the teams discussed was the extent to which existing archival description is helpful. As archival description by definition is not item-level, existing finding aids were only of limited use this pilot project, primarily providing contextual information. In the future however, incorporation of EAD finding aids would certainly allow additional types of categorization and searching.

Bulk Metadata Creation in Omeka

In order to facilitate the slow process of metadata entry for each item in Omeka, the technology team is experimenting with CSV Import in Phase II of the project. CSV Import, a plugin that handles bulk metadata creation, allows each Dublin Core field to be imported via a comma-separated file. However, more technical support is needed to define the PHP-CLO path setting with the server administrator.

Graduate Students

The collaboration of the Department of Special Collections with the Graduate School of Library and Information Studies was beneficial to both parties. Special Collections was able to lay the groundwork for future digitization and also to create a prototype Omeka website to show potential donors and partners, while the graduate Fellows gained valuable skills in actual implementation of a sophisticated software package. It should be noted that such a collaboration requires continuous interaction between and dedication from both the library school faculty and Department of Special Collections, to maintain standards and momentum as different classes of Fellows participate in the semantic and technology sides of the project.

References

Center for History and New Media, George Mason University. (2010). *Omeka: about*. Retrieved from http://omeka.org/about/

Ebellempire. (2009). *Adding Lightbox to Omeka*. Retrieved from http://omeka.org/codex/Adding_LightBox_to_Omeka

Digital Library of Georgia. (2009). *Welcome to the Civil Rights Digital Library*. Retrieved from http://crdl.usg.edu/?Welcome

Graham, S. R. & Ross, D. D. (2003). Metadata and authority control in the Civil Rights in Mississippi Digital Archive. *Journal of Internet Cataloging 6*(10), 33-42.

NC ECHO. (2007). *North Carolina Dublin Core implementation guidelines.* Retrieved from http://www.ncecho.org/dig/ncdc2007.shtml

University of Southern Mississippi Special Collections. (2006). *About the Civil Rights in Mississippi Digital Archive.* Retrieved from http://www.lib.usm.edu/~spcol/crda/about.htm

University of Southern Mississippi Special Collections. (2006). *Guidelines for digitization.* Retrieved from http://www.lib.usm.edu/~spcol/crda/guidelines/index.html

Digitization on a Dime: How a Small Library and a Big Team of Volunteers Digitized 15,000 Obituaries in Just Over a Year

Elizabeth Goldman (Kingston Frontenac Public Library)

Abstract

In 2006 and 2007, Chelsea District Library, a small public library in Chelsea, Michigan, digitized a collection of 15,000 obituaries on a small budget by using a staff of nearly 50 volunteers and open source software. The author describes the research and planning that led up to the project; unique aspects of the staffing and technology for the project; and the resulting database, which contributed to the library being named "Best Small Library in America" for 2008 by *Library Journal*. The database continues to be updated, expanded, and improved, and the use of volunteers as the primary workforce has had long term rewards for the library. The chapter demonstrates the accessibility of digitization projects to libraries, even those without pre-existing expertise, large staffs, or big budgets.

Keywords: Database, Digitization, Genealogy, Obituaries, Open source, Volunteers.

Introduction and background

Especially in small towns, the public library may serve multiple roles as library, museum, archives, and community center. In many cases, libraries accept donations of rare or unique historical material from families in the area with little thought for long-term maintenance. Technological advances in the last few decades have given libraries new options for preserving local history collections and making them more accessible through digitization. While even the smallest libraries have staff educated in reference and circulation procedures, however, relevant training in archival methods and technology is rare, making the prospect of a digitization project overwhelming. At the same time, small public libraries often have little or no funding for such projects.

Chelsea District Library is a single-branch public library serving 14,000 people in southeast Michigan, about 50 miles west of Detroit. The library was established in 1932 by the local Women's Club and, in 1999, became a district library system serving both the town of Chelsea (population 5,000) and surrounding townships. The earliest settlements in the Chelsea area date back to the 1830s and many local families can trace their roots back to the town's founders, resulting in a rich history. From its earliest days, the library served as a repository for local historical and genealogical material, housing a local history room on the cramped third floor of the McKune House, its location from 1959-2000. In 2006, after extensive renovations and additions to the McKune House, the library moved from temporary quarters back to its historic home on Main Street in Chelsea, leading to renewed interest in the local history collection.

A collection of about 50,000 index cards known as the Family History Index made up a major component of the local history material. A retired lawyer and amateur genealogist named Harold Jones started the collection as a hobby, clipping obituaries from the local Chelsea Standard newspaper and other sources and pasting them onto 4 x 6 index cards, along with cross references that allow women to be located by maiden name. Upon his death in 1987, Jones' family donated the collection to the library, where it received extensive use by local and visiting genealogists. Library staff and volunteers completed a project from 2000-2002 to clean up and update the collection, since then volunteers have continued adding new clippings.

As part of a planning process leading up to an election to fund an expansion of the building and the staff, the library identified local history as a priority for Chelsea area taxpayers and the Family History Index as a prime candidate for digitization work. At the time, the professional librarian staff consisted of the director, three department heads (adult services, youth services, technology services), and a part-time librarian, leaving few resources to focus on a project of this scope. In the spring of 2005, the library replaced the departing part-time librarian with a full-time librarian (the author), adding additional duties of managing the library's website and digitizing the Family History Index.

This paper will describe how a librarian and a team of four dozen volunteers completed the digitization of 15,000 records from the Family History Index in just over a year, resulting in a highly usable database that helped Chelsea District Library earn its distinction of "Best Small Library in America" for 2008 from Library Journal and the Bill and Melinda Gates Foundation. The first section will describe preparation for the project, including research in archival standards and digitization techniques, as well as the recruitment and training of the volunteer workforce. Section two will describe the decision-making process that went into the choice of open source software in order to create a user-friendly, free database of the records on a limited budget, as well as the work of developing and testing the database itself. Section three will offer an overview of the workflow for staff and volunteers as they did data entry, scanning, and proofreading of the records. Finally, the paper will describe the resulting database, current upkeep and expansion, and how the project served as a model for additional digitization work.

Project preparation

Research

Initial research focused on archival and digitization standards. No one on the staff had a specific background in either archives or genealogy that would fit the requirements of the project, so research started from a very basic level. Research was conducted largely online and in books, as well as by speaking with archivists and libraries that had done similar projects. Internal research played a role, too:

understanding how the Family History Index had historically been used and its importance to the community; exploring the scope, size, and fragility of the collection; and agreeing on project goals.

At the time, in mid-2005, quite a few libraries had launched efforts to put obituary indexes online for use by genealogists and historical researchers. The vast majority of these projects resulted in static webpages or simple databases that provided access to citations but not complete text. This early wave of digitization projects represented an important first step on the path toward full electronic access by giving researchers more complete information about the contents of a library's collection. However, those who found an obituary citation online still had to contact the library to obtain more detailed information or the complete text of the obituary.

Chelsea District Library was lucky enough to have a collection that included full-text clippings of obituaries on a significant portion of the cards in the Family History Index. Because of this and advances in technology, one of the library's primary goals was to make complete text available freely online, meaning genealogists and researchers had at least the possibility of meeting their research needs without leaving their computer or contacting the library at all. To further this goal, the library sought to develop a database that was free, simple to use, and contained relatively small image files accessible even by those with dial-up internet connections.

Important sources, although they sadly have not been updated in recent years, were the book and accompanying website, "Moving Theory into Practice," and the Making of Modern Michigan project. Moving Theory into Practice: Digital Imaging for Libraries and Archives by Anne R. Kenney and Oya Y. Rieger (Mountain View, CA: Research Libraries Group, 2000) provided a good grounding in what to consider when planning a digitization project, as well as minimum standards for use and long-term preservation. An online tutorial of housed at Cornell University Library (2010) offered step-by-step instructions for taking a project successfully through to completion. The Making of Modern Michigan was an IMLS-funded joint effort by the Michigan State University Library, the Library of Michigan, the

Michigan Library Consortium, and others (Michigan State University Libraries, 2005). Although its heyday had already passed by the time Chelsea embarked project, the website provided helpful background information on the structure of digitization projects and, especially, scanning equipment that had been vetted. The scanner models in the Making of Modern Michigan are no longer produced and libraries may have moved to higher minimum DPIs for scanning, but the advice offered at both sites remains sound.

Two more recent resources, available freely online, are BCR's CDP Digital Imaging Best Practices, from the Bibliographical Center for Research in Colorado (Collaborative Digitization Program, 2008) and NISO's IMLS-funded A Framework of Guidance for Building Good Digital Collections (National Information Standards Organization, 2007), which within the framework includes links to many other resources on more specific topics.

Project scope

Armed with this information, Chelsea District Library took a look at the Family History Index. While the cards had been stored away from the light in filing drawers, they also had been used heavily by patrons over the years, resulting in some wear and tear. In addition, neither the index cards nor the glue were acid free, and newsprint is one of the most acidic papers. The oldest cards and the oldest clippings dated back to the 1950s, resulting in some that were in very delicate condition. Along with the unique and irreplaceable nature of the collection, this delicate condition led the library director to decide that the cards should be scanned manually in-house rather than sent to a contractor who would likely feed them into a scanner, possibly resulting in damage.

This decision meant significant labor for library staff members and volunteers. In May 2005, the library applied for a grant from the State of Michigan to fund the digitization, which would have allowed for the hiring of contractors, but the application was turned down. Luckily, the library already had a well-established volunteer services program. Lacking any funding beyond $5,000 committed by the library, the project manager developed a volunteer-driven plan and made the choice to seek an open source solution for the database, resulting in savings on the equipment side. An RFP was opened to competitive bidders in the fall of 2005, with selection of a contractor and design and testing of the database completed by early 2006.

During this time, the library also made decisions about the scope of the project. While the collection itself was estimated to consist of more than 50,000 cards, closer to 25,000 obituaries were represented, due to Jones' system of cross-referencing women by maiden name. A database eliminated the need for this. The remaining set of obituaries came from a number of sources:

- gravestone transcriptions from Chelsea's three cemeteries and several others in neighboring areas
- notes culled from early histories of the area, as well as scrapbooks and other material in the local history collection
- notes from death notices published in the local newspaper, The Chelsea Standard, taken from microfilmed versions of the paper, dating from about 1887-1950
- complete obituaries from The Chelsea Standard, clipped and pasted on cards, dating from about 1950 to the present
- complete obituaries from the newspapers in two nearby cities, Ann Arbor and Jackson, clipped and pasted on cards, dating in the 1970s and 80s.

Of this material, the first three could be included in the project without further consideration of copyright, as the donation of the Family History Index to the library included rights to copying the material. The Chelsea Standard, a weekly publication owned by Heritage Newspapers, supported the project from the beginning, granting copyright release for material originally printed in its pages.

Unfortunately, the publisher of both the Ann Arbor News and Jackson Citizen-Patriot declined to grant copyright permission. The library considered this a minor setback, as obituaries from those two newspapers covered a span of only about 20 years. The impetus for collecting from newspapers in the neighboring cities was that some Chelsea area residents chose to publish obituaries only in these publications. The number of citizens who fit this scenario, however, was greatly outweighed by the number of obituaries of people who had no connection to the library's primary service area at all. The library considered entering data from these obituaries but refraining from scanning them, which would not have violated copyright law, but chose instead to leave the cards for a potential future project and focus instead on truly local residents.

Staffing

At this project's initiation, Chelsea District Library had about twenty employees. The project could not be completed by paid staff, and the small budget precluded the hiring of contract labor.

The library had a well-established and strong volunteer program, including a tradition of volunteers working with the Family History Index. Started as a volunteer effort in 1932, the library had always had strong support from volunteers, and genealogy in general is a topic that draws volunteers. Nevertheless, bringing in volunteers double the size of the library's own staff would not have been possible without a coordinator, who had developed procedures, documentation, and processes for intake, training, and evaluation.

Building on this strong foundation, the library advertised through its newsletter, the local newspaper, word-of-mouth, and presentations to organizations such as the county genealogical society. The Family History Index was a well-used collection and one of the best sources for obituaries for the area, so the library was able to to draw in volunteers who did not live in the Chelsea district itself. Volunteers filed standard application forms, which covered basic contact information, times available for work, and special skills. The initial group of about three dozen volunteers received training at one of two sessions set up in early February 2006, after which additional volunteers received training one-on-one or in small groups as they signed on. Later, existing volunteers would train new recruits. Over the course of the project, nearly 50 volunteers contributed to various aspects of the project.

Database development

In considering technology options the library's predominant constraints related to both funding and expertise. In 2005, Chelsea District Library contracted most of its technology services to the library cooperative of which it was part, including website hosting. The library itself at the time had only six public computers and about a dozen non-networked staff computers, with the single on-site server running the public computer time management system. No one on staff had knowledge of server administration, leaving staff nervous about hosting a server for the digitization project but also open to any of a number of configurations.

Open source software has seen increasing adoption by public libraries in recent years. While often referred to as "free," open source software is monetarily free only in the sense that to obtain a copy of the code requires no exchange of funds. In the truer sense, "free" refers to the user's freedom to view and adapt the software, generally with an agreement to then share improvements with the larger community. Chelsea District Library initially considered both proprietary and open source options for this project, as well as both in-house and contract solutions. While the librarian hired as project manager had extensive experience with Microsoft Access, the licensing costs for the accompanying Microsoft SQL server allowing multiple simultaneous users made that option prohibitive. An open source database based on PHP and MySQL appeared to be a more realistic option, with the drawback that no one on staff had the requisite familiarity with these programming languages. The library decided to solicit requests for proposals to get a better sense of its options. Replies to the RFP highlighted the range of options: from a $40,000 proposal that involved proprietary software and taking cards offsite for more efficient scanning to a $1,500 proposal based on open source software and leaving data entry and scanning purely up to the library. The library selected the able services of a programmer who worked at a nearby library and who recommended the purchase of a server and quickly designed and built a PhP/MySQL database meeting specifications. While open source was not the initial goal, that such software ended up forming the basis for the database contributed greatly to the library's ability to produce a high-functioning, easy-to-use database on a limited budget.

Once the library selected the underlying software, the real work of database design began. Priorities were a simple interface on both the administrative and public ends; completely web-based access for both data entry and retrieval; and the ability to attach multiple images to each record. The library pictured a database that would be simple and fast for access by users all over the world and one that could be expanded to meet larger goals for the local history collection. Starting with attached obituary images, the library envisioned eventually allowing researchers to submit their own photos, family trees, marriage licenses, or other material that could supplement the library's own collection to tell the broader story of each person represented in the database. Flexibility for growth of both the size and scope of the collection was important.

These ambitious plans remained in the future. In the near term, the library had to balance providing extensive access to the obituaries with completing the work within a relatively brief time frame. The poor quality of the newsprint and cards meant doing optical character recognition (OCR) was not realistic. Thus, while researchers would be able to view an image of the complete obituary, searching would be limited to data entered by volunteers. This meant maximizing the number of access points was ideal; at the same time, too many access points could slow work to a crawl. In the end, after consultation with genealogical researchers, the library chose the following fields:

- first, middle, last, and maiden names of subject in separate fields
- first and last names in one field for: mother, father, spouse(s), children
- date and place (city, state) of birth and death
- cemetery and funeral home
- metadata covering obituary source and date and source of digital record

The database allowed for multiple spouses and children. It also included a notes field which, at the early stages, was left blank but proved to be invaluable for later expansion.

The database would be accessed via the library's website by users through either a basic or advanced search. Upon visiting the Family History Index Online, users see a basic search screen for the name field, which searches all name-related fields. This is often enough to get users to the obituary they need.

Users also have access to an advanced search screen, which searches first, last, and maiden name as separate fields. It also allows access via date and place of birth or death, cemetery, and funeral home, making it useful to those who may not be searching for a specific person but for more general historical information. Data typed into any of the fields on the basic or advanced search screens will also search the notes field, which may contain additional data from various sources.

The designer brought another feature to the database that would set the *Family History Index Online* apart from similar projects at other libraries, a hyperlinking feature that makes Chelsea's project unique in allowing researchers to jump from record to record, following the obituaries of family members represented in the database. If the parent, child, or spouse of an obituary subject is represented in the database, his or her name will appear as an active link. Clicking on this link takes the user to that person's obituary record. In this way, researchers may discover family connections they did not know existed and be better able to visualize how families relate to each other. Rather than noting the names of relatives, backing out to the initial search screen, and starting a new search, database users can simply hop from one relevant record to the next.

Once the database design was complete, both staff and an initial group of volunteers participated in testing. Volunteers tested for ease of use from the administrative and public perspectives as well as for how the database would meet the needs of genealogy researchers. The library was lucky to have a number of experienced genealogical researchers among its volunteer corps. They provided invaluable feedback throughout the project. The database designer and project manager worked together to tweak the database in late 2005 and early 2006, leading up to training of volunteers and beginning of data entry work.

Timeline

- April 2005 – Chelsea District Library creates a librarian position with duties including digitization of the Family History Index
- October 2005 – Database development begins
- January 2006 – Database development and testing completed
- February 2006 – Volunteer training and data entry work begins
- May 2006 – Scanning of obituary cards begins
- October 2006 – Data entry of 15,000 records completed/ library closes to move to new building
- January 2007 – Scanning resumes; proofreading and database updates continue
- June 2007 – Final image attached to database
- October 2007 – Family History Index Online released to public; timed to coincide with Family History Month in Michigan

Digitization process

The library had two old PCs available for use by volunteers in a back office, a setup that proved beneficial to the project, as volunteers found they could often focus better on the mundane task of data entry while working in pairs. Because the database was entirely web-based, no software installation was required. Volunteers also used each other as resources to answer questions such as the interpretation of unclear wording or how to enter data in a particular field. Each volunteer had committed to working two hours per week for a period of at least three months, in an attempt to minimize the amount of retraining that would need to be done. Most volunteers stayed much longer, seeing the project through to completion, and many also worked multiple shifts each week. Through the volunteer program, these workers were able to sign up for shifts during all hours the library was open, including evenings and weekends, maximizing the number of people who could be involved.

As the project progressed, it became clear both that some volunteers wanted to participate but lacked interest or ability in data entry and also that volunteer tasks existed beyond what the library had originally envisioned. This led to some refocusing of efforts before a final workflow developed. In particular, a pair of volunteers took on the task of taking cards from the filing cabinet and sorting out those that need digitization. They stored the sorted cards in a box and transported them to the office where volunteers were engaged in data entry. Cards not in use remained in the files, which prominently displayed signs explaining the project. Volunteers doing data entry took the sorted cards and entered them into the database. Cards that brought up questions went into a separate pile for review by the librarian. The rest went into a "completed" file and moved on to step 2, proofreading. Two volunteers with especially good eyes for detail, as well as genealogical research experience, were recruited as proofreaders, tasked with checking every fifth card. While it would have been ideal to have a second set of eyes on every single database record, this was not realistic, and conferral with professional archivists confirmed that a 20 percent rate was more than sufficient.

After proofreading, cards moved on to scanning. Scanning represented another challenge, in part because the library had only one scanner which was also used for other purposes. In addition, while the scanning software that accompanied the purchase HP Scanjet 5500c was relatively simple, not all volunteers felt they had the requisite level of computer skills. As a result, scanning did not begin until about three months after data entry and was handled by a subset of about 10 volunteers. Volunteers scanned cards at 300 dpi and saved them in the archival standard TIF format. Because they were on black-and-white newsprint and newsprint already has a very low resolution, a higher resolution would not provide any benefits. These archival copies of the cards have been retained in separate, backed up files so that the original cards should never require rescanning. The entire database, including these archival images, was set to copy to a tape drive, with the tape changed daily. After one week, tapes were reused for new backup copies, leaving the library with multiple recent backups for added security.

At this point, the cards were refiled by a volunteer, returning access to the public who still relied on the paper file for research. The digital images then underwent additional processing. The TIF images were converted, using Adobe Photoshop Elements into compressed JPEG images with small file sizes. In general, the image of each card posted to the database was no more than 100 Kb. It would download quickly even with dial-up internet connections. Volunteers manually attached these images to each database record, completing the cycle.

Data entry work progressed remarkably quickly, with volunteers putting in close to 2,000 hours between February and October 2006. In October 2006, the project went on hiatus while the library packed up its temporary quarters and moved into a new facility. Volunteers completed data entry for the final card just before the move commenced, adding more than 15,000 records into the database in eight months. Between half and two-thirds of the scanning had also been completed at this point. The move to the new facility caused significant delays in the project due to other priorities for the library's technology staff. Scanning resumed in February 2007, however, and the final image was attached to the database in June. The library used the next few months to continue proofreading and to test the robustness of the database, releasing it to the public in conjunction with Michigan's Family History Month in October 2007.

Results

Chelsea District Library's Family History Index digitization project was a major success. Through a combination of creativity, open source software, and volunteer contributions, the library produced a highly usable online database providing full access to more than 15,000 obituaries for less than $5,000, completing work in about 15 months. It demonstrates that even at an institution with little staff and little specific expertise, a project can be developed to meet both the community's needs and the standards set by the library and archives world. The community involvement and grassroots nature of this project made it truly special for those who participated. It drew attention to the library, increased the volunteer corps, and gave community members a sense of ownership for a key piece of the library's collection.

The flexibility with which the database was designed has proven vital to its success. Once done with the initial work of populating the database, the library turned its attention to improvements. One goal was to provide full-text access to all obituaries, even those from newspapers old enough that the only existing copies were on microfilm. In early 2008, the Friends of the Library applied for and received grant funding to help purchase a digital microfilm machine, which volunteers are currently using to scan obituaries from the Chelsea Standard going as far back as copies survive, into the late 1800s. These digital images are then either added to existing database records or used to supplement the database.

There also remained the problem of providing access to obituaries of local residents that were printed in neighboring newspapers. To this end, the library looked to its partnerships with local businesses. Chelsea is represented by two local funeral homes, and directors of both proved willing to provide the library with access to their files. When the funeral homes submit obituaries to any area newspaper, they also send an electronic copy, including photo where available, to the library. These partnerships have allowed the library to enrich the database with full-text access and color photos for more recent obituaries. The text that is sent electronically is pasted into the notes field, and images are higher quality than those ultimately printed in the newspaper. Along with this material, if the final obituary is printed in the *Chelsea Standard*, the scanned newspaper clipping is attached. The funeral homes have also indicated that they have computerized files going back a number of years, and the library is investigating the possibility of further enhancing the database with this material.

As another extension, the library returned to its initial contractor in 2008 to develop a database on the same platform to house the library's local history collection, which had been brought out of storage and organized only in 2007. Much of this material was even more valuable and unique than the obituaries, leaving the library with a strong desire to have it made accessible to the public primarily, if not exclusively, in digital format. Scanning of material and database development have continued in 2009. While working on this and other local history initiatives, including a series of oral history projects, the library has found additional material to enhance the obituary database records of members of Chelsea's founding and prominent families.

Aside from the primary lesson that ambitious digitization projects are not beyond the reach of even very small libraries, the Family History Index digitization project provided additional lessons that apply to similar projects and beyond:

- The existence of a well-setup volunteer program allows a library to think much bigger than would otherwise be practical. People are out there in all communities who have the time, expertise, and interest to contribute.
- Planning is good but flexibility is essential. Projects may stray somewhat from their original vision or carefully thought out procedures, but that isn't necessarily bad. Being open to new opportunities and listening to workers and users can ultimately make a project much richer.
- Open source doesn't have to be terrifying. In fact, open source solutions are generally very stable, as the Family History Index Online has proven to be. Aside from minor software upgrades, the server has provided consistent access to the database for more than two years with virtually no staff intervention required.
- There's nothing wrong with thinking big, but it doesn't hurt to be realistic. Ambition leads to projects being even more successful than initially imagined. That said, a realistic assessment of aspects such as which tasks could be handled in-house (project management) and which should be contracted out (database design) prevented later stumbles.
- Partnerships enhance any library activity. In this case, a good working relationship with the local newspaper eased the process of gaining copyright access, and new partnerships with funeral homes have enhanced both the database and the library's reputation in the larger community. In other situations,

partnerships could be used to gain access to services or material the library cannot pay for or obtain on its own.

Small libraries often represent their communities' best hope for preserving local history. Preserving this history, even with little or no budget, is within reach if libraries combine their expertise in information management with technology decisions geared toward simplicity and a lack of hesitation in taking advantage of the knowledge and goodwill in their communities. Digitization projects not only preserve the past but provide an opportunity for greater community involvement, partnerships, and identification of the library as a key to the community's overall health.

References

Chelsea District Library. (2009). *Chelsea District Library Family History Index Online*. Retrieved on Jun 30, 2010 from http://fh.chelsea.lib.mi.us/

Collaborative Digitization Program. (2008). *Western States digital imaging best practices*, version 2.0. Retrieved on March 31, 2010 from http://www.bcr.org/dps/cdp/best/wsdibp_v1.pdf

Michigan State University Libraries. (2005). *The making of modern Michigan: Digitizing Michigan's hidden past*. Retrieved March 15, 2010, from http://mmm.lib.msu.edu/.

Cornell University Library. (2010). *Moving theory into practice digital imaging tutorial*. Retrieved March 15, 2010, from http://www.library.cornell.edu/preservation/tutorial

National Information Standards Organization. (2007). *A framework of guidance for building good digital collections*. Retrieved March 15, 2010, http://framework.niso.org/

Building the ALBA Digital Library

Jill Annitto (Archivist)

Abstract

This chapter serves as a case study of how a professional digital library can be successfully built with a small staff and budget. It discusses the planning and experiments with beta versions of the Abraham Lincoln Brigade Archives (ALBA) Digital Library, the final version of which is available on ALBA's website, through Metropolitan New York Library Council's (METRO) Digital Metro New York program, and OCLC WorldCat. The sensitive issues of digitizing another institution's collection while maintaining ownership of the final product are also explored.

Keywords: Copyright, CONTENTdm, Database, Digital archive, Electronic classroom, Educational resources, Funding, Indexing, Planning, Ownership issues, Small budgets

Introduction

In 1979, recognizing the vital importance of their radical history, and the need to collect writings, letters, photographs, oral histories and artifacts that would preserve their story, the Veterans of the Abraham Lincoln Brigade, the American volunteers who fought with Republican forces against Generalissimo Francisco Franco during the Spanish Civil War (1936-39), formed the Abraham Lincoln Brigade Archives (ALBA). Today ALBA lends its name to a major archive at New York University's (NYU) Tamiment Library and independently supports cultural and educational activities related to the war. The ALBA collections are the most requested at the Tamiment Library. ALBA's relationship with NYU is non-traditional, which makes the ALBA Digital Library unique. NYU owns and maintains the Archives and hosts many of ALBA's programs, yet the ALBA name gives a different impression.

This chapter explores the challenges of digitizing a collection that is owned by another institution and how to overcome working with a limited budget, dated technology, and minimal staff to produce a professional digital resource. The ALBA Digital Library (Abraham Lincoln Brigade Archives, 2008) evolved from an ineffective form-based website tool to a fully indexed resource using CONTENTdm in a matter of months.

ALBA Goes Digital

Until a full-time Executive Director was hired in 2007, ALBA was initially run by a group of volunteers followed by a string of part-time administrators. The ALBA Board of Governors hired me as the Assistant Director in May 2008 just as they began reconsidering their outdated website, a major step for the small organization.

By June 2008 the Executive Director had resigned, leaving me as ALBA's only employee. It provided me with a great opportunity to help redesign the website alongside a subcommittee of the Board of Governors. The Web Committee, consisting of four history professors living across the United States, set a timeline of four months for the site's overhaul, with an anticipated launch date of early October. The Board wanted to stake a claim as the premier electronic resource for information on the Spanish Civil War.

The Impetus for a Digital Library

In July 2008 ALBA launched its first annual ALBA Teachers Summer Institute at NYU. The Institute hosts teachers from New York City public schools and exposes them to the history, art, and politics of the Spanish Civil War. Part of this immersion includes a trip to NYU's Tamiment Library to view the Brigade's Archives where teachers receive an overview by the collection's archivists as well as professors from various departments at NYU.

After this initial success, ALBA decided to sponsor two more Summer Institutes (as well as year-round professional development seminars) in Tampa and San Francisco in 2009. The new settings precluded a site visit to the Archives so we needed to find a way to bring the Archives to the teachers.

The solution to this dilemma was the creation of a digital library or archive to be launched in conjunction with the new website. The website redesign was going to make ample use of ALBA's collection at NYU's Tamiment Library anyway, slowly integrating digital collections of letters and photos, and eventually including video clips and oral histories. These primary resources would strengthen existing lesson plans and other educational modules once the site was completed and allow for a more dynamic classroom experience. Since the site was already being designed, we thought it would be a great opportunity to have a collections database created for ALBA by our website designers.

Defining the Digital Library

In my experience archives or library staff working in conjunction with a representative from the information technology department does most digital library planning. At ALBA, I was the only staff member and every decision required consensus of the Web Committee, busy professionals with jobs and other responsibilities. Every time an issue arose it could take nearly a week to be resolved. This is a problem that small museums with very active boards will be familiar with, particularly when board members have little time, experience or interest in the digital project at hand.

We quickly ran into a problem of defining the digital library; the Web Committee believed everything created by ALBA was archival. I was in favor of a more traditional, primary source, collections-based digital library with a thesaurus and cataloging guidelines. My idea for ALBA's digital library was to create a system that would recall only primary sources from the war itself. The digital library would be its own entity containing items that are separate from all other files posted to the website.

After several weeks of negotiations via email and conference calls, the Web Committee decided the best option would be to include all online documents in the digital library. The Web Committee charged the website designers with creating a web-based, simple form-based recall system as part of their contract.

The Beta Versions

Albita

Named *Albita* (or 'little ALBA') this resource was first launched in November 2008 along with the debut of the new website. It included the organization's quarterly newsletter, book reviews, and transcribed letters, not primary archival sources. Uploaded items were listed in random order rather than alphabetically or by date. In the end the design did not conform to the standards of information professionals; *Albita* had become a "junk drawer" of every single file uploaded to the website.

Document Library

Even renaming it and reconfiguring the display, the *Document Library* was not robust enough. To recall specific items, the user had to consciously use certain keyword strings, e.g. "George Watt Prize Winner," when retrieving items. It did not include a thesaurus and the plain-text description field did not allow for paragraph breaks. These descriptions were displayed as a solid block of text.

Media Library

Simultaneously added to the site was the *Media Library*. This database appears three pages deep within our Resources tab. It is the only way to access images (from archival photographs to logos of partner organizations) without using the ALBA Digital Library or slogging through the results from a general site search. Unfortunately because it is not linked to any other page, it is not often accessed. The plain-text description field is displayed as a block of text and does not allow indexing.

Once the Web Committee saw *Albita*, the *Document Library*, and the *Media Library* in action the problems became apparent. We considered going back to the drawing board with our website designers, to create a thesaurus or a more sophisticated database system. Unfortunately, our original contract did not cover building a true digital library; the cost would have been prohibitively expensive.

I explained the possibilities of a professional digital library: adding our records to a consortium's collection, making them widely available through WorldCat, including them in an NYU catalog at the item level. It was difficult to convince the Web Committee that we still had affordable, professional options that would blend seamlessly into the new website.

Building a Better Mousetrap

As the only person on staff who could design and implement the digital library, I had to balance time spent on digitization with my other duties, including grant writing, public programming, and administrative issues.

The first problem for ALBA to overcome was the lack of any type of digitization equipment. The nature of ALBA's work and budget did not necessitate having a full flatbed scanner or laptop on hand.

Another major concern for ALBA was the high cost of software. A rough estimate for a full software package ran to the thousands of dollars. We didn't intend to scan the entire collection, just highlights; for our purposes what we needed was something that would allow us to scan part of the collection but offer maximum exposure.

In January 2009 I became aware of the Metropolitan New York Library Council's (METRO) Digital New York program. NYU's status as an institutional member of METRO allowed ALBA to benefit from the digitization program, a partnership between METRO and OCLC and CONTENTdm. As a separate organization, ALBA's much smaller annual budget resulted in a nominal $200 annual fee, paid to METRO for access to the CONTENTdm desktop module and the upload of 500 discrete items. With software issues out of the way, we could focus on permissions and access to the collection.

Since ALBA's intention was to work with a collection that is owned by another large institution, we had to be very thorough and diplomatic about the project. We presented a sample record that would name NYU and Tamiment Library as the copyright holders, as well as instructions on obtaining permission to use the images. We assured NYU that the digital library pages on ALBA's website would include the same information. A distinction is made on both the website and in each record that the ALBA Digital Library is published by ALBA while the copyright is held by NYU. After several weeks of negotiation, we were free to move ahead with the project.

With software and permissions settled we were left with the issue of hardware. ALBA Board Member and NYU Professor of Spanish and Portuguese James Fernandez offered his laptop and Epson flatbed scanner for the duration of the project. After several weeks of further negotiation in order to gain access to the collections, Michael Nash, ALBA Board Member and Director of Tamiment Library, allowed us to scan the items ourselves, free of charge.

Selection, Policies, and Standards

In general there is a lack of digitized archival resources available on the Spanish Civil War. The closest to any kind of digital information on the subject is through Spartacus Educational (Simkin, 1997), an online British encyclopedia dedicated to educating students on history, with a significant amount of information on progressive history. But even this site is lacking in primary source materials.

Besides the Abraham Lincoln Brigade Archives, there are other Spanish Civil War archives in the United States: the Southworth Collection at the University of California at San Diego (see University of California, San Diego, n.d.) and the Spanish Civil War Collection at the University of Illinois – Urbana Champaign (see University of Illinois at Urbana-Champaign, n.d.) Still, the Abraham Lincoln

Brigade Archives at NYU is the largest collection of American volunteers' archives in the US.

Our goal was to put forth a curated collection of the most compelling and historically significant items in the Archives; the original plan was to digitize 500 items, but the realities of time and staff restraints reduced this number to an initial 150 items. These items included postcards, letters, newspaper articles, a multi-lingual newsletter, and a telegram from Ernest Hemingway.

Dr. Fernandez performed the selection of four collections based on the following criteria: size (only one manuscript box each), condition (stable enough for handling and scanning), and variety (each collection included letters from a variety of people). These same collections had been used in the Teachers Summer Institute and they proved to be popular with the teachers.

When it came to setting the scanning standards I turned to the University of Wisconsin-Milwaukee Libraries' Digital Collections (see University of Wisconsin-Milwaukee, 2006) pages, namely the *Transportation Around the World, 1911-1993* collection that I worked on as a graduate student there in 2003. The collection was built using CONTENTdm, then in its infancy. I followed UWM's digitization standards and policies as well as their formula for long-term archival storage as a basis for the ALBA Digital Library.

Digitization Standards

All items were scanned in full-color at a resolution of 600 dpi using an Epson flatbed scanner. The items were saved as the highest quality TIFF files and stored on an external hard drive. We refer to these TIFF files as the Archival Images as they are used only to create access images (PDFs or JPEGs) and are otherwise not accessed.

Access Images were created for web delivery, in the form of thumbnails on the ALBA site and for display within the CONTENTdm records, as well as for everyday use. The letters in the collection do not have OCR capabilities nor are the PDFs searchable. These were saved on both DVDs and the external hard drive. Because the METRO contract only covered 500 discrete items, we used Photoshop to stitch the JPEGs together to create a single PDF file for multiple-page items. Not only did this save room in CONTENTdm, it was also useful to have multiple-page documents combined for reproduction purposes and to better keep track of collections.

All of this information is posted on the Digitization page of the ALBA Digital Library section. Sharing this information shows researchers (and potential donors) that the digital library adheres to archival standards while also helping other librarians and archivists plan their projects.

To access the images it is important to label them properly. Some scanners and scanning programs assign numbers that may or may not be useful. Auto-numbering systems can cause problems if the items are not easily identified by sight (letters, manuscripts). I named the files according to the manuscript collection followed by a number that corresponded to the letter's order in the folder, followed by a decimal that corresponded to the page number. For example, Lardner.1.4 would be the fourth page of the first letter of the Lardner Collection. The stitched PDF file would read Lardner.1.

Indexing

The documents were indexed using Dublin Core metadata (Dublin Core Metadata Initiative, 2010) which are standard in CONTENTdm, including: Creator, Date, Identifier, Type, Source, Description, Format, Coverage, References, Relation, Language, Publisher, Rights, and ALBA Reference Number.

Included in CONTENTdm is a default thesaurus (Thesaurus for Graphic Materials) for the Identifier field. Similarly, a default thesaurus provided the terms for geographic location in the Coverage field. Those fields for which the thesaurus was unique to the Abraham Lincoln Brigade Archives, I built a new thesaurus. These fields were: Type (e.g. text, image), Format (e.g. paper + size in centimeters), Identifier (e.g. envelope, autograph letter signed, typed letter), Publisher, Rights, and Creator. I added new Creators as they came up in each collection; some collections had as many creators as there were letters. In addition, for collections that had an online finding aid at NYU I included a link to that page.

In all, the ALBA Digital Library took four months for 150 items to be scanned, stitched, catalogued, and uploaded. I generally spent about fifteen minutes cataloguing each letter, sometimes longer depending on the length of the document. I worked on the digital library an average of eight hours per week with some weeks going by without any work at all. As collections were completed I added information to the ALBA Digital Library page and continued to redesign the website as necessary.

Final Product and Reception

The final product can be found at http://www.alba-valb.org /resources/digital-library. The Teachers Institute Alumni find the resource easy to use and helpful in the classroom, and ALBA even used the scanned collections to create facsimile copies of the Archives for the Tampa and San Francisco seminars.

As of publication, the digital library is available as a discrete collection on Digital Metro New York (http://cdm128401.cdmhost. com/cdm4/search.php), the digital program of the Metropolitan New York Library Council, the New York Heritage Digital Collections (New York Heritage, 2008) website, as well as at the item level on OCLC WorldCat (http://www.worldcat.org).

Seeing a Digital Project from Beginning to End

Planning is Key

Work backwards and set aside a day or two to really think about what you want to see in the final product. The small team (just myself most of the time) helped keep bureaucracy to a minimum. Remember: it is cheaper to do it right the first time.

Unofficial market research

I asked librarian and archivist friends what they liked to see in digital libraries and to give me advice on moving forward. I also reflected on what struck me in online collections, both the positive and the negative.

Tread Lightly

Occasionally it was necessary to receive approvals and it was important to remember that when dealing with large institutions there will be politics. This exists everywhere and I learned not to take it personally. Many of these issues were deep-seated and existed long before I joined the organization. I also learned that having a board member installed in a specific department or company does not guarantee easy access or donated materials.

Within my own organization, some board members did not understand the potential of planned, professional digital libraries, or that one person could undertake such a project. Price was also an issue; it was only after *Albita* and the *Document Library* failed was CONTENTdm considered and accepted as an amazing deal. In the end, waiting for the Web Committee members to come around in their own time was the best plan of action for this project.

Push the PR

As I completed each collection I sent information about the digital library everywhere: from Facebook and Archivists' Roundtable of Metropolitan New York to ALBA's listserv, e-news, quarterly newsletter, and fundraising appeals. While this publicity was mainly sent to people within the ALBA network, it also garnered the attention of local archivists and library students interested in doing small digital projects on limited resources.

References

Abraham Lincoln Brigade Archives. (2008). ALBA Digital Library. Retrieved March 30, 2010, from http://www.alba-valb.org/ resources/digital-library

Dublin Core metadata initiative. (2010). Retrieved March 30, 2010, from http://dublincore.org

New York Heritage. (2008). Retrieved March 30, 2010, from http://www.newyorkheritage.org

Simkin, J. (1997). *Spartacus educational.* Retrieved March 30, 2010, from http://www.spartacus.schoolnet.co.uk/Spanish-Civil-War.htm

University of California, San Diego. (n.d.). *Southworth Spanish Civil War Collection.* Retrieved March 30, 2010, from UC San Diego Libraries website, http://libraries.ucsd.edu/locations/mscl/collections/southworth-spanish-civil-war-collection.html

University of Illinois at Urbana-Champaign. (n.d.). *Spanish Civil War Collection.* Retrieved March 30, 2010, from University of Illinois at Urbana-Champaign Rare Book and Manuscript Library website, http://www.library.illinois.edu/rbx/SCWPeople.htm

University of Wisconsin-Milwaukee. (2006). *Transportation around the World, 1911-1993.* Retrieved March 30, 2010, from Digital Collections -Transportation around the World, 1911-1993 website, http://www4.uwm.edu/libraries/digilib/transport/index.cfm

Digitization and Access of Louisiana Oral Histories: One Oral History Center's Experience in the Digital Realm

Gina R. Costello (Louisiana State University Libraries)

Abstract

The Louisiana State University (LSU) Libraries Center for Oral History began an effort to digitize at risk and high demand collections in 2007. The Center acquired digitization equipment, server space, and collaborated with the Libraries Special Collections Digital Services librarian to offer digitized oral histories online via the statewide Louisiana Digital Library (LDL). This paper details the history of the ongoing development of a digitization program for oral history materials using two staff members and limited resources. Decisions about what materials to digitize and how, equipment and software, and issues with access and preservation will be discussed.

Keywords: Audio digitization standards, CONTENTdm, Digitizing audio, Digitization equipment, Digital library, Digitization workflow, Oral history, Oral history interviews.

Introduction

The Louisiana State University (LSU) Libraries T. Harry Williams Center for Oral History began to digitize at risk and high demand collections in late 2007. Planning for the systematic digitization of the primarily analog collection began a year prior to any digitization efforts. The Center sought advice from an expert in the field, acquired digitization equipment and server space, hired a full time employee to manage digitization, and collaborated with the Libraries Special Collections Digital Services Librarian to offer digitized oral histories online via the statewide Louisiana Digital Library (LDL).

The Center staff and the Digital Services Librarian have prioritized collections for digitization based on fragility or patron demand, made decisions about organization and access of the audio materials for the public, and addressed copyright issues. Only a small number of oral history collections have been added to the LDL, although over 700 hours of tape have been digitized so far.

This paper details the history of the ongoing development of a digitization program for oral history materials with one full time staff person and partial effort from another staff member. Decisions about what materials to digitize and how, equipment and software, and issues with access and preservation will be discussed. Results of the digitization and online access efforts have been mixed, but may serve as an example for oral history programs wishing to develop a more programmatic approach to digitization.

Center History and Description

The T. Harry Williams Center for Oral History at LSU Libraries Special Collections documents the social, political, and cultural history of LSU and the state of Louisiana by conducting, collecting, preserving, and making available to the public oral history interviews of folk artists, war veterans, governors, congressmen, state and local officials, civil rights activists, and other historically prominent figures in Louisiana. The Center maintains over 4,000 hours of tape-recorded interviews. The three person staff and a number of student workers transcribe, index, and deposit oral history interviews for archival storage at LSU Libraries Special Collections.

The Center, opened in 1991, is named after a man who helped legitimize the field of oral history. Dr. T. Harry Williams, a popular and acclaimed southern history professor at LSU spent more than ten years researching the biography, Huey Long. Published in 1969, this Pulitzer Prize and National Book Award winning book drew upon

Williams' tape-recorded interviews with nearly 300 individuals. Williams used a 30 pound Webster Electric Ekotape reel-to-reel tape recorder to capture the interviews.

The primary mission of the Center is to document the history of LSU. Since the history of the state and university are closely intertwined, many broader Louisiana subjects are documented as well. Public outreach through training workshops, consultations, and collaborations with individual researchers, community groups, classes, and institutions, enhance oral history collections throughout the state. Often, the collections are donated to LSU Libraries for preservation and public access. In many cases copies are provided to libraries, schools, museums, providing access for members of the communities in which the oral histories were collected.

The Center differs from some oral history centers in its commitment to providing fully edited transcriptions of all recorded interviews. Barring any restrictions placed on interviews by the interviewee or interviewer, the audio and a full transcription are made available to scholars and the general public. Because of the large volume of interviews that are collected each year, the Center maintains a backlog of interviews that are not fully processed (i.e., digitized if applicable, transcribed, audited, and cataloged). Interviews are organized into more than 40 different series, including Civil Rights, Military History, and Political History.

The Center Director has taken a more programmatic rather than project-based approach to the digitization of the collected oral histories. To ensure that preservation issues are addressed and collection access is a top priority, the Director employs a full time sound technician/webmaster at the Center. Center staff also works with the Special Collections Digital Services Librarian to mount oral history collections to the Louisiana Digital Library (LDL) (http://www.louisianadigitallibrary.org).

The Center makes available materials that are not restricted by the interviewee or interviewer. Interviews are digitized on demand for patrons, for preservation purposes, and for public access on the LDL. Prior to the acquisition of digitization equipment, patron requested copies were recorded from cassette tape to cassette tape. Now materials are delivered to patrons via CD unless a cassette tape is requested. Copies are provided for a fee to patrons, although a small number of oral histories maintained by the Center are available for listening free online in the LDL. Center staff generally digitize fewer than five interviews per month for patron requests.

The funding for the Center is a mix of Libraries monies and endowment funding. The Libraries pays the salaries of the Director and two full time employees. Student workers' pay, a portion of travel money, and some supplies are also paid for by the university. The Libraries purchases and provides support for computers for the Center staff and student workers. Endowment funds cover most travel expenses, the majority of the equipment (specifically the field recorders, digitization station, software, fax machine, scanner), any Graduate Assistantships, additional student workers, and the majority of the transient workers' (e.g., professional interviewers, transcribers, editors) wages

Early Forays in Digital Access

One of the earliest digital projects the Center was involved with was a pilot project to digitize oral histories that are part of the University History Series sub-series, Integration and the African American Experience at LSU. The sub-series contains interviews with black students, faculty, and administrators at LSU during integration (1950-1970), plus interviews with lawyers and their clients who were involved in key lawsuits, as well as politicians and others who were vocal opponents or supporters of integration. The resulting digital collection, named "Integration and the Black Experience at LSU" (2003) contains audio files and transcriptions of three individuals interviewed between 1985 and 1998.

This legacy digital collection is scheduled to be revamped soon. The ".rm" or ".ram" audio files are available for listening only in RealPlayer and must be downloaded to the listener's computer before playing. The digital files were created more than eight years ago, so the sound quality could be improved and the information about equipment and digitization method has been lost. The analog tapes will be re-digitized and optimized using current technologies.

Between 2001 and 2005, the Center utilized the skills of their part time webmaster and other staff members to create several online exhibitions and presentations (*T. Harry Williams Center for Oral History Exhibits and Presentations*, 2009) using readily available software and tools: simple HTML, PowerPoint, and Windows Movie Maker. Notable among these is the digital exhibition, "Baton Rouge Bus Boycott of 1953. A Recaptured Past" (2009) which includes a background and chronology of the event complete with photographs and audio excerpts. "Leaving Vietnam" is a nine minute presentation of audio clips from the Americans in Vietnam collection, featuring stories of escape from three Vietnamese refugees who immigrated to Louisiana around 1975 while fleeing Communist takeover. The presentation debuted at the 2005 Oral History Association annual conference and is currently available on YouTube, where it has been viewed over 6,000 times. Two other presentations were also mounted on YouTube to provide ease of access.

Center staff also began digitizing oral history transcriptions that were only available in paper format in 2004. They had some success using a HP Scanjet 5590 document feed scanner and an early version of Readiris optical character recognition (OCR) software. The software was lost, and the Libraries Systems department replaced it with Readiris Pro 11. Subsequent digitization efforts have been stymied by problems getting good readable OCR text, so the project has been put on hold. Student workers often are tasked with re-keying transcriptions.

In 2007 the Center Director, with the help of the LSU Libraries Special Collections Exhibitions Coordinator, curated a physical exhibition called "Have you Heard?: The Past in First Person from the T. Harry Williams Center for Oral History". The extensive exhibition contained ephemera and narrative relating to more than a dozen oral history collections. The Libraries provided two "listening stations", computers loaded with web-based presentations in the exhibit hall. In addition, exhibit-goers could check out MP3 players with prerecorded narration of the exhibition contents and snippets of oral history interviews. These digital offerings were made available with little cost using spare computers and a staff member as the voice of the narrator. No previous Libraries exhibition had employed technology in these ways. The Center Director counts the exhibition a success, as it led to a few collection development opportunities and awareness of the Center and its mission.

Digitization Station

After attending a digitization workshop at the Oral History Association annual conference in 2006, the Center Director decided that the systematic digitization of at risk and high demand analog collections should become a central focus for the Center. With the idea of "going digital" but with little research in hand they initially purchased two standalone analog to digital Lucid AD9624converters, which are designed to work in a recording studio setting. They realized belatedly that the converter units themselves were not useful without a digitization station, which would cost several thousand dollars. The Center made the all too common mistake of purchasing equipment without a clear plan how the individual hardware or software will interface with existing equipment. Fortunately they were able to later purchase a digitization system that uses one of the Lucid converters.

In order to ensure that in the future the Center made sound investments in technology and established a digitization workflow appropriate to their needs, the Director sought advice from oral history expert Doug Boyd at the University of Kentucky. Dr. Boyd visited LSU in March 2007 to evaluate the Center and conduct an introductory digital audio workshop for the Libraries staff. He generated a seven-page report with recommendations for equipment, collection development, and staffing.

Recommended Analog to digital work station equipment and software

1. Lucid AD9624 A/D Converter
2. RME Hammerfall DSP 9632 PCI Audio interface
3. 2 Yamaha HS50M 5" Active Monitor

4. 1 Tascam 202MKIII Dual Recorder Cassette Deck
5. 4 BP20 20' TRS - TRS Cable
6. 8 DKQR10 10' Dual RCA - TS Cable
7. 1 Furman PL8II 15 Amp Power Conductor w/Light
8. 1 DT770pro Closed Studio Mon Headphone
9. 1 Presonus Cent. Station Audio Control Center
10. 1 Plextor PX-716UF External CD-R/DVD+-RW
11. Sony Sound Forge 8.0 Audio Editing Software
12. Sony Noise Reduction 2.0 Noise Reduction Plug-In

The equipment recommended in the report was purchased with endowment funds nearly a year after Boyd's initial visit. Boyd returned to the Center to help set up the equipment and train a newly hired staff member.

Although not all institutions have the funds to hire a consultant, this less than $2,000 expenditure has proved money well spent for the Center. Without the vetting of the digitization program, the listed recommendations   for   equipment,   and   Boyd's encouragement to pursue positioning the Center as a leader in digitization efforts in the state and the profession, the Libraries administration might not have acted so quickly to support the endeavor. The administration approved reallocating funds to hire a full time staff member for the digitization and in less than two years, the Center has been able to digitize over 700 hours of interviews with their single digitization station.

With the addition of a dedicated digitization station and full time staff member to manage the process, the Center was ready to begin digitizing in earnest. It was immediately apparent, though, that server space and file redundancy would be an issue. The average file size of one hour of digitized uncompressed audio from analog tape is around 1.5 Gigabytes (GB). The Center only had access to a relatively small 74GB drive when digitization began.

Working with the Digital Services Librarian and the Libraries Systems Administrator, the Center temporarily located all digital audio files to a 5TB networked server that primarily serves as storage for TIFF images. In late 2009, a regional corporation donated used storage equipment to the Libraries. The Libraries' Systems Administrator was able to configure four 2TB Raid 5 storage arrays, totaling approximately 8TB, for the Center's long term storage. This unexpected gift enabled the Center to continue digitization efforts, although they will still have to be selective.

The Center exists not just to archive, but to conduct research-based oral history interviews and to educate the community about conducting interviews. To fulfill this mission, the Center keeps a stock of digital audio field recorders to loan for oral history projects. As noted earlier, this equipment is purchased with endowment funds. The Center currently has four Edirol R-09 recorders, two Marantz CDR 310 recorders, and five Zoom H2 Handy recorders for loan. Center staff uses a Marantz PMD 661 for interviews.

The Edirol R-09 and Marantz CDR 310 are portable CD recorders and the Zoom H2 Handy records employ flash memory. Individuals borrowing the equipment are trained and instructed on its use. Digitally recorded interviews are brought to the Center either on CD or on secure digital (SD) flash memory cards. Interviews are saved to the Center's server and eventually processed.

Digitization Workflow

The digitization process is handled by one staff member, although he has recently trained a student worker to help run the digitization station. The staff member samples the audio to determine the optimal hardware and software settings and reformats the analog tape to a lossless uncompressed digital master WAV file. This master file is captured at a bit depth of 24 and a sample rate of 96 kHz in stereo.

The master WAV file is stored on a networked server, which is routinely backed up to a tape drive. This "master file" is not altered after the initial digitization process. Whenever possible, barring any time or funding constraints, a copy of every collection is also stored on an external hard drive as well as burned onto a gold archival CD.

The staff member then creates an optimized file from the master WAV file. Using Sound Forge software, he improves the signal strength and removes distortion from the audio. The optimized file is saved as a WAV file to a different location on the server. He then generates a compressed MP3 file from the optimized file. This MP3 file is the use copy, and it is also saved to the server.

Unprocessed collections are digitized prior to processing to facilitate time stamping of the transcriptions. The Center uses Express Scribe Transcription Playback Software (http://www.nch.com.au/scribe/) and adds time stamps to the transcriptions based on the actual run time. Old transcriptions will be re-audited and time stamps added because the tape time stamps are arbitrary, often reset every time the tape player is used.

Metadata for the entire collection is kept in a Microsoft Access Database. All oral histories entering the center are processed based on a 13 page processing checklist. The processing checklist steps include 1) Accession 2) Transcribe 3) Audit 4) Send to Interviewee 5) Edit. This process is time-tested and thorough. The majority of the oral history collection is cataloged according to AACR2 standards in MARC format in the LSU Libraries online catalog (i.e., OPAC). The Dublin Core metadata in the digital collections is often copied directly from these catalog records.

Implementation and Access

The Center does not currently have a formal collection development policy to determine which oral histories are digitized The interviews that have been digitized thus far were identified as "high risk" on unstable medium or they were considered to be of particular interest to researchers and the public. Materials are also digitized "on demand" for patrons for a fee.

Tapes that were created prior to the Center opening in 1991 and later donated were assessed for deterioration and digitized as a means of preservation. For example, the 60 interviews in the Americans in Vietnam series, recorded between 1974-1977, were identified as at risk and were prioritized for digitization. Because of the content of the interviews, however, the digitized audio will not be offered via the LDL. In this situation, preservation of the materials outweighed the need to provide access.

Particular interviews and/or series of interviews, such as the Hurricane Betsy Series or the McKinley High School Series, were digitized because of their potential value to researchers and the general public. These collections will be uploaded to the LDL as soon as they are fully processed. Patron requested interviews that were digitized on demand for a fee are also candidates for the LDL.

During the past two years the Center staff and Digital Services Librarian have discussed workflows for uploading audio to the LDL. They consulted collections mounted by the University of Louisville (http://digital.library.louisville.edu/), Ball State University (http://libx.bsu.edu/), University of Nevada, Las Vegas (http://digital.library.unlv.edu/), and the University of California, San Diego(http://ceo.ucsd.edu/index.html) to facilitate decision making about the organization and display of online oral history materials.

The LSU Libraries serves all digital library materials via the Louisiana Digital Library, which was developed at the start of this decade by LSU Libraries and the LOUIS Library Consortium. LOUIS staff maintains the LDL for the nineteen participating institutions, including historical societies, libraries and museums. Individual institutions add content to the LDL and all materials are available for public use. The digital library is powered by CONTENTdm software and hosted by OCLC. LOUIS staff assists LDL institutions with customization of the software. LSU Libraries Special Collections maintains over 35 collections in the LDL.

Adding audio collections to the LDL has been a slow process that seems to move in fits and starts. Center staff and the Digital Services Librarian have held many meetings and exchanged numerous emails about serving digitized oral histories online. Debate about the topic centered around how the interviews would be organized and displayed. Many interviews, especially the life narratives, are topically related even though they are in different series. For example, university history overlaps with civil rights history in several interviews. Organizing the interviews both topically and by series can be achieved by using CONTENTdm custom queries to unite items from different digital collections, although this method does require staff to re-create the collection custom queries and topics or series are added.

The CONTENTdm software seems more suited for its original purpose to serve digital images, and the default treatment of audio files is rather clunky. Audio does not play automatically, but instead the text "Access this item" appears at the top of the screen and metadata for the item below it. This presentation of the audio is somewhat confusing, because it is not even immediately clear that it is an audio file. Some institutions using CONTENTdm have devised workarounds that make serving audio in the software more usable.

In order to better group interviews together with the transcriptions and other related content, the Digital Services Librarian began uploading files as "compound objects" or multi-part files in CONTENTdm. Figure 2 illustrates this with the different files, abstract, transcription, and audio, hyperlinked in the left column. This display is not ideal since the metadata for the interview is on a separate screen and the "Access this item" text is still present. In addition to the cumbersome nature of the audio display, patrons wishing to listen to it are forced to download the often very large file to their computer. The Director felt strongly that other options not requiring the patron to download the audio be explored. Copyright would be difficult to manage if the audio was copied to different computers.

After reading about Ball State University development of a user-friendly embedded Windows Media Player above the PDF file within CONTENTdm (Hurford & Read, 2008), the Digital Services Librarian contacted LOUIS about implementing this method. LOUIS staff worked with the LSU Information Technology Services (ITS) department to obtain access to a streaming server from which the audio could be served. MP3 files are uploaded to the server via FTP software and the file path is linked to the item in CONTENTdm in the metadata field "Stream File".

The embedded player facilitates ease of use by providing the searchable PDF transcription to the patron as they listen to the audio. It does not require listeners to download the audio, thus it better protects the copyright of the files. Information about copyright is included in the metadata for each item and future transcriptions may be watermarked with a copyright statement.

To organize the oral history collections in the LDL, the Digital Services Librarian used the "collection of collections" model that CONTENTdm employs to organize user collections on their website (http://www.oclc.org/contentdm/collections/default.htm).   The individual series or collections are cataloged as a whole in the overall Center LDL collection. The series are represented by an image and selecting that image displays metadata taking the patron to the interviews. CONTENTdm software allows the creation of custom queries that will link the different collections and enable patrons to search across them. The individual series can be added to and the interviews and other materials in the collections will remain together, searchable alphabetically by title.

Problems and Some Solutions

Every digitization endeavor has its problems, but it is the individual institution's staffing, resources, and prior experiences that dictate the solutions. The Center, although small, is supported by a large university library. Digitization is a luxury that can be afforded because the Center has endowment money to purchase equipment and to provide staff with continuing education in the field. The time it takes to digitize resources is not a major factor in the continuation of digitization either because digitization is accepted as a part of the overall processing workflow. Digitization at the Center will be funded indefinitely and a full time employee will be dedicated to the effort if at all possible.

The Center is now two years into their programmatic digitization effort. At this point the digitization workflow has been well established and interviews from a few collections have been uploaded to the LDL. This section of the paper details problems encountered, such as legacy digitized collections, prioritizing digitization efforts, storage solutions, staffing, and digital access and display via CONTENTdm software, and how the Center staff and the Digital Services Librarian resolved or did not solve them. Many problems could have been mitigated with more long-term planning, but the degree to which digitization efforts are currently supported and the ramifications of beginning a digitization program were not known at the start of these efforts.

The Center holds some legacy digital collections that do not meet the current standards for digitization. Prior to acquiring the digitization station and hiring an audio technician, Center staff did some preliminary digitization of analog tape using an external cassette tape deck connected to a computer. The sound was collected using a low end sound card to ram (Real Media Player) format in a process like the one that Washington State University Libraries used for their African-American Oral History collections (Bond, 2004). These early recordings were deemed important enough to place in the queue to be re-digitized according to the Center's current standards. For practical purposes, an institution may choose to keep legacy digitized items even if they do not meet current standards because the cost to re-digitize is high. For the Center the lessons learned with early experiments in digitization were important in shaping the future decisions to allocate more funds and staff to the digitization efforts in order to produce better quality sound.

The Center's at risk materials were digitized first, however, some of these materials are not good candidates for online access. The files will need to be stored long term, but because of restrictions they will be largely inaccessible. This falls within the mission of the Center, which includes collecting in addition to providing access to oral histories. Some audio files do not have completed transcriptions, rendered them unacceptable for immediate uploading to the LDL. The interview editing process is very time consuming and there is little immediate results (Bond and Walpole, 2006). Digitization priorities may differ depending on the institutional mission. If the mission is to provide access and preservation is secondary, then more popular or relevant collections should be digitized first. Institutions not supported by a parent institution, such as the Center is by LSU Libraries Special Collections, may not have the luxury to digitize collections just to archive them.

Another ongoing issue is long term storage solutions for the digitized files. The Center hoped to have files saved in at least three different places, a dedicated server in the main library, CD, and offsite storage. Some files are saved to an external hard drive in addition to the networked server, and born digital audio is saved to Gold CD. Ideally a copy of each master WAV file would be stored in offsite storage in a similar set up to the University of Kentucky (Weig, Terry & Lybarger, 2007), but this has not been implemented. The Libraries' server on which all audio files are saved is backed up incrementally to magnetic tape every night. Full backups take 40-120 hours because of the amount of data contained on the servers, so they are conducted once monthly. It is a secure system, but there is always a chance for failure. Future plans call for the Center to assess file storage and redundancy options.

The document "Sound Directions: Best practices for digital audio preservation" provides recommendations for long term preservation storage (Casey & Gordon, 2007), however many recommendations may not be feasible for small centers. The authors emphasize that file redundancy which is neither labor-intensive nor costly in media (e.g., CD or flash memory), should always be implemented. The majority of institutions will likely not have multiple terabyte servers and staff to keep them running, but files can at the very least be backed up to a more affordable storage medium such as portable hard drive or CD. Any storage medium can fail, however, so careful attention to this matter is imperative if an institution is interested in long term storage of files.

An issue that may require further review and assessment is the current standard of capturing audio at the higher sample rate of 24 bit 96 kHz. As server space fills and the Center and Libraries' budgets decrease, however, this standard may be reduced. Capturing audio at 16 bit 44.1 kHz reduces the file size by nearly half, and according to some experts it does not substantially decrease the quality of the WAV file (Weig, Terry & Lybarger, 2007). If the server is filled the Center may elect to save the derivative optimized WAV file to CD rather than the server. File optimization is time consuming, often taking the length of the recording to complete, so deleting these files is not an option.

Before embarking on a digitization project, an institution should estimate the number of files that will be created and storage space needed. An institution may choose to capture audio at a lower and still acceptable rate to expedite the digitization process and conserve storage space. The institution should conduct an assessment of whether file optimization and multiple WAV files are needed before creating additional files that must be saved over the long term. Any derivative files can be recreated, so they should always be deleted or copied to more affordable storage media if server space is at a premium.

Another issue related to the audio capture standards is the Center's lack of written standards and best practices. Workflow principles and digitization methods are generally adhered to, but there is no guide or manual, just institutional knowledge. The workflow is based on recommendations by oral history expert Doug Boyd, who served as an advisor to the Center and also wrote the tutorials and information found on the Oral History Association website (http://www.oralhistory.org/technology/). The Center should apply the same level of detail and documentation to digitization workflow as they have for the processing workflow.

There are only two staff members who work with the Center's digital files, which could pose potential problems if either leave and has often caused bottlenecks in the workflow. At the Center all digitization is handled by one staff member with some student support. Other Center staff members do not have time to perform these duties, so little cross-training has been done. This is a risk because if the staff person leaves it will be difficult to continue digitization efforts. In the same vein, only the Digital Services Librarian currently uploads items to the LDL. This duty is usually shared by graduate assistants, but financial constraints have prevented hiring any additional help. Digitized files often do not get uploaded quickly because they are placed in a queue with all Special Collections digital materials. Cross-training between the digital technician and Librarian is an option that should perhaps be explored. At the very least the two individuals, who are separated geographically across campus should establish better communication and more effective workflows. Information about which collections are ready to be uploaded to the LDL is sent ad hoc via email and there is no current mechanism for tracking the LDL files via the Accession database. Institutions should establish a clear workflow and assign responsibility for different aspects of the digitization process early on in a project. This will alleviate any potential miscommunication or turf war situation.

Before purchasing equipment and hiring staff to digitize audio, an institution should assess the environment where they will be located. At the Center the digitization station is equipped with the right hardware and software, but its location is less than ideal. The Center is located in an 80 year old house that is poorly insulated. The room in which digitization takes place is in the center of the house next to the building air handlers. The sound technician must use headphones while optimizing audio. If the Center is relocated much thought will be put into the location of the digitization station. In addition, Dr. Boyd recommended the Center purchase two digitization stations. When funding is available, the Center will explore this option.

A very important aspect of digitization efforts is providing access. The Center works with the Digital Services Librarian to upload items to the LDL, which uses CONTENTdm software. The software is less than perfect in its treatment of audio files, and efforts to retrofit the software to better serve audio are time consuming dependent on LOUIS staff expertise. LOUIS controls server access so software customization must go through them. The Center benefits from being a part of this consortium environment where an infrastructure is in place and support is offered at all times, but there are some constraints that this relationship brings. Small or not well-funded institutions interested in mounting collections online may be better served entering into a partnership with a larger institution or consortium.

An issue specific to the retrofitting of the software potentially affects patron access and sustainability. The embedded audio player that LOUIS retrofit for audio display does not display a time stamp so patrons cannot skip to a specific section of the interview. The audio player works well in the most current version of CONTENTdm, but the software is scheduled to be upgraded soon. Changes may affect the workflow and change the player functionality. The Center will rely on LOUIS consortium staff to recreate the embedded player in the upgraded software. Some institutions may not be able to expend a great deal of staff time continually addressing the interface when the software is upgraded, so this should be considered when addressing the sustainable access points.

In many ways the process for adding audio collections to the LDL has just begun. In 2008 all processed oral history collections which had been on a cataloging backlog were cataloged in the Libraries OPAC and WorldCat, which facilitates the metadata creation of records in the LDL. Changes in the CONTENTdm software in the past few years have made it more customizable. In 2009 the Center staff began producing audio and video podcasts with images and sound from the collections. The podcasts and information about hem are available on the Center's blog (http://oralhistory.blogs.lib.lsu.edu/). In order to maximize the amount of digitized materials that are available online, key players should outline a digital access plan wherein all materials that are currently ready for public display are listed and other materials are prioritized.

Conclusion

The T. Harry Williams Center for Oral History began a digitization program a little more than two years ago. Since then the Center has acquired digitization hardware and software, hired a full time staff member to perform digitization duties, and mounted several collections to the Louisiana Digital Library. By all accounts, the Center's efforts have been successful, although they hope to develop more sound workflows for digital access to enable them to add additional interviews to the online collections in the future.

Institutions wishing to emulate the Center should consult experts in person or through the literature, follow industry standards set forth by the Oral History Association (http://www.oralhistory.org), and, formulate plans based on best practices such as the CDP Digital Audio Working Group Digital Audio Best Practices (http://www.bcr.org/dps/cdp/best/digital-audio-bp.pdf). It is essential to plan ahead for storage space needs, keeping in mind that what one thinks you'll need is probably less than the reality.

References

Bond, T. J. & Walpole, M. (2006). Streaming audio with synchronized transcripts utilizing SMI., *Library Hi Tech 24*, 452-462.

Bond, T. J. (2004). Streaming audio from African-American oral history collections. *OCLC Systems & Services, 20*, 15-23.

Casey, M. & Gordon, B. (2007). *Sound directions: best practices for audio preservation.* Retrieved from: http://www.dlib.indiana.edu/ projects/sounddirections/papersPresent/sd_bp_07.pdf

Hurford, A. A. & Read, M. L. (2008). Bringing the voices of communities together: the Middletown digital oral history project. *Indiana Libraries. 27*, 26-29.

Integration and the black experience. (2003). Retrieved December 14, 2009 from http://www.louisianadigitallibrary.org/cdm4/ browse.php? CISOROOT=/IBE

T. Harry Williams Center for Oral History Exhibits and Presentations. (2009). Retrieved December 14, 2009 from http://www.lib.lsu.edu/special/williams/ep.html

The Baton Rouge Bus Boycott of 1953. A recaptured past (2004). Retrieved December 14, 2009 from http://www.lib.lsu.edu/ special/exhibits/boycott/index.html

Weig, E., Terry, K. & Lybarger, K (2007). *Large scale digitization of oral history: A case study. D-Lib Magazine 13*. Retrieved from: http://www.dlib.org/dlib/may07/weig/05weig.html

Digitizing a Newspaper Clippings Collection: a Case Study and Framework for Small-Scale Digital Projects

Maureen M. Knapp (John P. Isché Library, New Orleans)

Abstract

How does a small specialty library establish, develop and maintain in-house digital collections? What are the considerations, challenges, and benefits they experience? This chapter describes one library's experience in turning an aging and inaccessible collection of newspaper clippings into a preserved and searchable online collection, which in turn laid a basis for other digital projects. This chapter also discusses considerations, challenges and opportunities observed during their first foray into creating a digital collection.

Keywords: Clippings, Digital libraries, Digital preservation, Digital projects, Digitization, Electronic preservation, Newspaper clippings file, Newspaper clippings, Press clippings.

Background

The John P Isché library is a mid-sized, urban, academic health sciences library serving six schools of health professions at the LSU Health Sciences Center (LSUHSC) in New Orleans, Louisiana. Established in 1931, the library has collected newspaper clippings related to the history and accomplishments of the health sciences institution since its inception, and even today monitors the local papers for pertinent news items. The "newspaper clippings file," as it came to be called, is an astounding 70 year snapshot of the development of the health sciences in Louisiana. Over 6,000 clippings trace development of LSUHSC through the twentieth century, including such topics as: the people, places and events associated with the LSU School of Medicine, the growth of health infrastructure in Southeast Louisiana and New Orleans, and the development of 20th century health sciences education in Louisiana.

Digital Collection Origins

In 2002, access and preservation concerns with some of the earliest newspaper clippings encouraged the library to investigate digitization as a possible solution. Access points to the collection were limited. The only online access consisted of a locally-created subject database containing basic citations to newspaper articles from 1985 to present. Users had to search the local database by faculty name or department, and then locate the physical newspaper clippings in filing cabinets by call number. The remaining fifty-odd (1933-1984) years of the collection was indexed in a card catalog, stored in the library's back offices and only accessible to library staff.

Numerous problems plagued the physical collection. The newspaper clippings had been stored in filing cabinets as they were collected, which allowed the typing paper to curl heavily over the course of many years. The newsprint itself showed signs of age: rust marks appeared where staples and paperclips had once connected pages, and gaps in the collection were apparent.

A lack of funding and staffing was another concern. Any efforts towards creating a digital collection would have to be inexpensive and make use of staff and resources the library already possessed.

However, to truly understand to physical condition of the newspaper clippings file, and the challenges that would arise once digitization began, one must understand the collection process of gathering the original newspaper clippings. While no documentation exists, the library postulates that even back to the 1930s, a library member would skim the daily local papers from around Southeast Louisiana for any mention of LSU School of Medicine, and its faculty, staff or students. Once an article was discovered, it was cut out of the paper, dated, and the name of the paper was noted. The articles were glued to standard 8 ½ by 11 inch typing paper, usually several to a page, somewhat in order by date, and the paper was assigned a numerical call number in the order they were received. Later someone would read the articles, underline named entities pertaining to LSU, and assign a subject heading, which was recorded in a small local card catalog. Finally, the pages of clippings were organized into manila folders by year and placed into filing cabinets until further needed. This entire process continued for 50 years.

So basically, the library had a unique local news collection, spanning the majority of the 20th century, collected and stored under questionable archival methods, with limited access to documents before 1985. In order to increase availability and use of the clippings, the library wrote a grant proposal for a small-scale digitization project to scan the newspaper clippings from 1933-1953, streamline cataloguing, and offer public access to the resource online. The grant proposed using Greenstone digital library software, an open source "suite of software for building and distributing digital library collections" (Greenstone digital library software, 2007), to provide access to the digitized newspaper clippings.

Stops and Starts

Though the grant proposal was rejected, the grant writing process did provide a catalyst for action within the library. The small grant requested $3,000 to purchase a flat-bed scanner, computer and optical character recognition software. Library administration was impressed enough with the grant's digitization plan that they provided funding for a scanner, software and travel to a continuing education class on digital projects in 2003. A library staff member began scanning the clippings. However, the library quickly ran into problems. The Greenstone software would not work properly on their secure intranet, and the library lacked a staff member with enough computer programming experience to install and troubleshoot the software properly. In addition, the image quality of the scanned newspaper clippings was poor, which was attributed to a faulty scanner that did not produce dark enough images. Finally, copyright concerns made library administration hesitant to post the collection online to the general public.

By the time Hurricane Katrina struck New Orleans in August 2005, access, software and image quality issues had put the library's newspaper clippings digitization project on hold. The library's collection was undamaged from this natural disaster. However, it was moved to remote storage for over half a year and the entire library staff was displaced.

During the ensuing hiatus, library staff took several continuing education classes on digitization. "Digitization Fundamentals," a course offered by the Illinois Digitization Institute at the University of Illinois Urbana-Champaign (University of Illinois Library, 2009), was exceptionally useful, as it provided training in digital projects management, standards and organization, as well as an introduction to Photoshop software.

In 2007, an opportunity opened for the library to join the Louisiana Digital library, the state digital library consortium provided through LOUIS: The Louisiana library network (LOUIS: The Louisiana library network, 2009). The library was able to obtain access to OCLC's CONTENTdm platform, which was previously too expensive, as well as the technical infrastructure and support needed to store and access digital assets.

Consortial membership for digital library services addressed many of the problems faced by the library developing an in-house digital collection. The documentation on the technical and operational requirements for participation in the LOUISiana Digital library proved critical. The consortium's style manual for scanning and cataloguing provided guidelines for selecting collections to digitize, scanning practices, post-scanning image manipulation, project workflows, metadata standards, and quality control. Another practical advantage to consortial membership was LOUIS staff support, which provided advice on imaging standards, basic training on the

CONTENTdm software, and a shoulder to cry on when things went awry.

The library began their second try at developing a digital version of the newspaper clipping file in January 2008. As of December 2009, the library has not only met their original goal of digitizing and indexing over 1600 items in the collection from 1933-1953 (LSUHSC New Orleans library, 2009), but also created several other collections.

Work Flow, Image Manipulation and Standards

The format and organization of the newspaper clippings collection created a challenge in regards to digital manipulation and workflow. In order to achieve indexing of items on an individual level, some information that was included only once on a sheet of several newspaper clippings (for example, the name of the newspaper, the date, and most commonly, the clipping's call number) would have to be added to each individual item. Thus, several steps beyond simple scanning and image processing were included in the workflow.

Here are the workflow and standards for creating digital versions of the Newspaper Clipping File:

1. Following consortium standards for creating digital images for the Louisiana Digital library, the full-page newspaper clipping is scanned on an HP Scanjet 8390 flatbed scanner to create an archival black and white image at 300 dpi, 8-bit grayscale and saved as an uncompressed TIFF file on the library server. This creates an archival master version of the original digital image.

2. Using Photoshop, a copy of the archival master version is opened and saved according to file naming conventions for the digital library set forth by the consortium. This creates a duplicate of the archival master that can be manipulated to isolate an individual clipping. This file is the image that will eventually be loaded into the digital collection.

3. The duplicate is cropped to isolate a single newspaper clipping. Pages that have only one clipping on them are also manipulated and cropped to minimize file size.

4. If not visible, the call number, date and newspaper name from the original scan are copied, cut and pasted to the now isolated clipping.

5. Post capture processing is applied. The item is processed for alignment and an unsharp mask filter is applied to correct blurring that might have occurred during the scan process. In addition, the image's histogram is viewed to adjust color intensity.

6. The individual, processed image of the individual newspaper clipping is saved to the server.

7. For pages with more than one newspaper clipping, this process is repeated until all clippings have been isolated.

8. After digital manipulation, the TIFF of the clipping is loaded into the CONTENTdm Project Client. Cursory metadata is entered by a library staff member. The file name, size and location are recorded in a Scanning Log to track progress.

9. The librarian performs Optical Character Recognition (OCR) on the clipping to create an excerpted text field and assigns subject headings. OCR produces an abstract of the first 50 words of the article, which is keyword searchable in the digital library. This takes a bit of time, but it is a good way to review the article and assign the proper subject heading. After a final quality check, the item is approved and uploaded to the digital library. Upon upload, CONTENTdm converts the full resolution TIFF file to JPEG, which is what end-users access when viewing the collection online.

10. CONTENTdm also offers an Archival File Manager, which automatically archives collections in a location specified on our library server as they are uploaded to the online collection. Once a volume is full, it is burnt to an archival quality CD recordable disc, as well as saved on the server.

Cataloging and Metadata

The LOUIS consortium requires collections in the Louisiana Digital library to use the Dublin Core 15 metadata element set (Dublin Core Metadata Initiative, 2008), in addition to non-Dublin core structural and administrative metadata. CONTENTdm allows up to 125 fields per collection. The library decided to add 3 more metadata fields to the newspaper clippings collection: Call number (to locate the item in the physical files), Full Text (for excerpted text) and Contact Information (so users can contact the library). The following lists the metadata fields used in the newspaper clipping collection.

Field Name (in CONTENTdm)	Type of metadata	Metadata Content	Added by
Title	DC	Title of newspaper clipping	LS
Contact Information	A	Contact information for library	T
Creator	DC	Author of clipping	L
Contributors	DC	Contributor to clipping (rarely used)	L
Subject	DC	Institutional controlled vocabulary, MeSH	L
Call Number	D	Call number for the original clipping	LS
Description	DC	"Newspaper clipping"	T
Notes	D	More descriptive information about content of original clipping, if needed	L
Publisher	DC	Newspaper title	L
Date	DC	Date of publication	L
Type	DC	"Text"	T
Format	DC	"TIFF"	T
Identifier	DC	Mandatory field directs users to identifier URL	T
Source	DC	Library name and homepage URL	T
Language	DC	"En."	T
Relation	DC	URL to homepage of Newspaper Clippings Collection	T
Coverage – Spatial	DC	"New Orleans (La.)"	T

Field Name (in CONTENTdm)	Type of metadata	Metadata Content	Added by
Coverage – Temporal	DC	Year of publication	L
Rights	DC	Copyright information	T
Cataloger	D	Initials of librarian	L
Cataloged Date	D	Date of cataloging	L
Object File Name	D	File name of item	LS
Image Resolution (Archival)	A	Dots-per-inch of scanned TIFF i.e.: "300dpi"	T
Image Bit-Depth (Archival)	A	"8-bit"	T
Color Mode (Archival)	A	Grayscale	T
Extent (Archival)	A	Pixel dimensions of image (WWWW:HHHH)	LS
Image Manipulation (Archival)	A	"Crop, alignment, unsharp mask, histogram"	T
File Size (Archival)	A	Size of TIFF image in KB	LS
Hardware / Software (Archival)	A	"HP Scanjet 8390, Photoshop, ABBYY FineReader"	T
Digitized By	A	Initials of library staff member	LS
Digitized Date	A	Date of digitization	LS
Full Text	D	Abstracted content from OCR	L

List of metadata elements used in cataloging items. Meaning of symbols: A is administrative; D is descriptive; DC is Dublin Core 15; LS is added by Library Staff, L is added by Librarian, and T is added by Template.

Many of these fields are inserted automatically via a template in CONTENTdm. The remaining fields are divided among project members. The most tedious data entry was entering the Extent and File Size fields for each item. Each clipping's dimension and size is different, so library staff tends to write these down on a notepad as they scan images for entry, then record them in CONTENTdm and the scanning log later.

Another feature of Content DM is the ability to build a customized controlled vocabulary for the Subject field. This worked to the library's advantage, as the newspaper clipping file possessed a card catalog of subjects. The library uses the newspaper clippings card catalog as a basis to build an institutional controlled vocabulary in the digital library. The card catalog also serves as a reference point to verify names and spellings of affiliated persons. This institutional controlled vocabulary can be shared across digital collections, which is an advantage for future projects related to our institution.

The library soon recognized that other subjects would be necessary to adequately describe the digitized newspaper clippings. Original cataloging varied so much over the years that clippings might only include the name of the person or entity mentioned in the article. The library wanted to add more descriptors, so that articles describing conferences, publications, research grants or other common topics were easier to locate. When applicable, the library consults the National Library of Medicine's list of Medical subject headings (MeSH)(U.S. National Library of Medicine, 2009) for appropriate descriptors in the Subject field. For example, the MeSH term "Congresses as Topic" is used when a clipping discusses conferences, or the MeSH term "Publications" when a clipping mentions a new book or journal article published by one of the institution's faculty. Sometimes, MeSH is not useful, especially when discussing local events such as campus expansion or departmental news. In these cases, a subject heading is created and assigned by the librarian. Clippings in the digital collection can be browsed by year, subject, creator or title. Browsing by date is an interesting way to view the development of institutional history. To further open the collection, keyword searching is enabled in the excerpted text field.

Project Considerations

Storage, standards, documentation, training and staffing were all considerations for this project.

Storage was a huge concern. The deteriorating condition of older newspaper clippings made it evident that storing the physical newspaper clippings in filing cabinets was not conducive to preservation. To address the curling paper, books were used to weight down the paper for several weeks. This did not entirely fix the issue of curling paper, but it did help a little in preparing the clippings for a move to flat storage. After flattening, the files were transferred to acid-free archival folders and placed in clamshell archival storage boxes. Finally, the clamshell boxes of physical files were relocated to the library's humidity controlled Rare Books Room, in order to protect them from humidity and sunlight.

Likewise, the library was heedful of digital storage and the "digital mortgage": how will the library address transfer of archival TIFF files to new formats as software and hardware change? Though the library has yet to encounter a change in image format standards, they did attempt to prepare for this inevitability by storing the collection of archival images in multiple locations, as well as on multiple formats. Having multiple copies also addresses the possibility that some files might eventually become corrupted. TIFF versions of the images are burnt to an archive quality, professional grade CD recordable discs, as well as copied to a location on the library server, which is maintained by our institution and backed up daily to tape at a remote location. This is in addition to the processed JPG file that is available to the public on the Louisiana Digital library. A TIFF of the raw scan of the original newspaper clipping is also retained on the library server.

With multiple storage locations and a complicated workflow, documentation and staff training are also important concerns. The library's consortial membership provided a style manual for scanning, cataloging/metadata standards, and basic workflow suggestions. The library used this as a basis for creating a local workflow policy, which includes detailed directions on image scanning and manipulation as well as step by step directions on how to process the item in

CONTENTdm. A scanning log is used to track size and progress of a collection. The scanning log is simply an Excel file which records the file name, file size, and date of digitization, as well as locations to which the file has been saved.

Regarding training, the library realized it was critical that everyone involved with the project learn Photoshop. The LOUIS consortium takes a 'train the trainer' approach to CONTENTdm, so the librarian was responsible for training local staff on the software after initial training.

This project is staffed with one librarian and two library staff members, who devote about 10 hours a week to this project. Library staff is requested to scan and process 60 clippings per week. Scheduling issues quickly became apparent for the librarian project manager, who has bibliographic instruction and reference desk duties in addition to overseeing digital projects. A supervisor suggested setting aside one day a week to solely devote to digital projects. Friday has since become "Digitization Day" and has worked well in keeping the load of items to be processed and approved by the librarian to a reasonable amount.

Benefits and Challenges

One of the first challenges was software sustainability. The free Greenstone digital library software did not work within the institutional intranet and required higher level technical skills than the library possessed. In addition, problems with the original project scanner resulted in poor quality images that had to be redone.

Support from your institution from inception is critical. Administration has to be on board to provide funding and act as a liaison to other resources, for example, consulting with your institution's legal department about copyright questions. Support from information technology (IT) is also important. Getting our IT department to provide support for open source library software was a challenge that soon put the library's original plans to use Greenstone digital library software on hiatus. One of the benefits of membership in a state digital library consortium is that technical support is provided in an automated timely manner. In addition, the consortium has direct contacts with the software developers at CONTENTdm, so software concerns are quickly addressed.

The newspaper clippings collection is unique in that it collects clippings from many regional news sources. All materials were published after 1923. Therefore, the work may be protected by copyright until 2018. Violation of copyright was a large concern, so the library decided to restrict access to the images within the newspaper clippings collection to the institutional IP address. In order to share the collection with a larger audience, the collection's metadata is searchable and viewable to anyone. This way, any user can find items in the newspaper clippings collection, and if they are not from the institution, the library works with them to get the information or clippings they need.

Funding is a final challenge. Consortial membership to the digital library is about $2000 a year, while hardware and software ran about $1500 in startup costs. In addition, the library director donated a 21" screen won at a library conference raffle for use with the digital projects computer. Digital imaging is much easier with a larger screen. Grants and scholarships are another source of funding. A scholarship from a regional medical library group helped fund attendance at the first continuing education class on digital imaging and metadata for the librarian project manager. An recent Institute of Museum and Library Services "Connecting to Collections" Bookshelf grant (Institute of Museum and Library Services, 2009) allowed the library to obtain a set of conservation resources and books, which was previously non-existent.

The library now has over 10 years of institutional history available online in a searchable database. Visibility and access to this collection has increased. Indexing though OCLC allows results to appear in Google. As a result, the library has received several inquiries about subjects indexed in the newspaper clipping file from the United States and Italy. The clippings file has also acted as a catalyst for change, inspiring library staff to organize the rare books room, research archival storage methods, and apply for grants. One of the benefits the library is proudest of is the mentoring opportunity this created. A library staff member who helped start this project recently completed their library degree and went on to become a Digital Initiatives librarian at another local library.

The library has established a workflow and gained experience in digital imaging and management for future projects. Because of the success in creating the newspaper clippings collection, the LSUHSC School of Dentistry started a digital collection of historic photographs. In addition, the library worked with the LSUSHC Registrar's Office to digitize graduation program records, which are now available in a public, searchable collection. Finally, the library is in the planning stages of creating a digitized version of early volumes of the medical school student newspaper. The library also continues to add items to the newspaper clippings collection.

As one can surmise, it has been a long 4 years to produce this digital collection, but once the library established workflow and standards it was much easier to begin other projects. Support from the state library consortium certainly expedited and streamlined the process, and the library recommends state or regional consortium membership to any smaller institution considering developing a digital project. For all the tedious data entry and malfunctioning software, the creation of an enduring, searchable and accessible source of institutional history made the entire project worthwhile.

References

DCMI Usage Board. (2008). *DCMI type vocabulary*. Retrieved December 9, 2009, from http://dublincore.org/documents/dcmi-type-vocabulary/

Dublin Core Metadata Initiative. (2008). *Dublin core metadata element set, version 1.1*. Retrieved December 9, 2009, from http://dublincore.org/documents/dces/

Greenstone digital library software. (2007). Retrieved December 9, 2009, from http://www.greenstone.org/

Institute of Museum and Library Services. (2009). *Connecting to collections: A call to action*. Retrieved December 9, 2009, from http://www.imls.gov/Collections/

LOUIS: The Louisiana library network. (2009). Retrieved December 9, 2009, from http://appl003.lsu.edu/ocsweb/louishome.nsf/

LSUHSC New Orleans Library. (2009). *LSUHSC New Orleans newspaper clippings collection homepage*. Retrieved December 10, 2009, from http://www.louisianadigitallibrary.org/cdm4/index_LSUHSC_NCC.php?CISOROOT=/LSUHSC_NCC

U.S. National Library of Medicine. (2009). *Medical subject headings - home page*. Retrieved December 9, 2009, from http://www.nlm.nih.gov/mesh/meshhome.html

University of Illinois Library. (2009). *Digital services and development -- training*. Retrieved December 9, 2009, from http://images.library.uiuc.edu/projects/newproj.htm

METRO Grant Success Story: Waterways of New York Project

Claudia A. Perry and Thomas T. Surprenant
(Queens College, CUNY.)

Abstract

The concept of experiential learning is particularly useful when students are required to create database entries as part of an ongoing, real-life, online experience. A METRO grant resulted in an opportunity to use students to create a CONTENTdm database which, with the continued software support from METRO, has continued and evolved until the present. This chapter describes the experience of both faculty and students. Sections include the background, technical issues and implications for teaching, project procedures and workflow, successes and lessons learned, challenges and next steps. Of particular interest is the use of out of copyright postcards and the metadata that has resulted from intensive student study and evaluation of the data contained on these cards. Those contemplating a digitization project of their own will be able to learn much about best practices, project planning, management and the advantages/disadvantages of the CONTENTdm software.

Keyword: Best Practices, Canals, Case Studies, Cooperative Learning, Digitization, Digital Collection Management Software, Digital Collections, Digital Imaging, Experiential Learning, Library Education, Metadata, Postcards, Project Based Learning, Project Management, Project Planning, Quality Control, Standards, Student Developed Materials, Student Participation, Student Projects, Waterways.

Introduction

For many of us, hands-on learning is the best way to integrate an understanding of principles and best practices with a practical grasp of the actual challenges and learning opportunities of a project. This is particularly true for library school graduate students seeking to expand their theoretical, technical and management skills.   As digitization is increasingly seen as a worthy endeavor for even the smallest institutions, it is worth considering the range of approaches available for gaining needed expertise, especially at the novice level. Examining the long-term development of an integrated, semester-long, course-based approach to digitization may be of value for those seeking an inexpensive approach for the creation of small to medium-sized digital collections.

A course entitled "Introduction to Digital Imaging" was first taught at the Queens College Graduate School of Library & Information Studies (GSLIS), City University of New York (CUNY), in the Fall of 2003. In the Spring of 2005, a year-long METRO-funded grant facilitated a co-operative project between the Rosenthal Library and the GSLIS to support student digitization of a portion of the Queens College Rosenthal Library Archives (e.g. see GSLIS, 2005-2009, Digitization projects). The project included a variety of forms and formats. The evaluation of this valuable learning experience identified a strong need to find a single standard format that was information rich and moderate in scope, but which lent itself to more uniform metadata standards and digital specifications. The evolving project, "Waterways of New York", an online digital collection of historical postcards, was created in 2006, and partially supported by METRO through continued access to CONTENTdm. It continues to be extended by GSLIS students each semester the course is taught.

Scope and Format

The most important feedback provided to our team by METRO digitization experts regarding our "Rosenthal Library Archives" initiative was the value of working with a limited number of manageable formats and a relatively focused subject area and time

frame. During the implementation of the grant a serious problem was
the complexity resulting from too many different types of media, the
overly wide range of subject matter, and the challenges these
characteristics presented to the creation of consistent metadata.

One of the GSLIS professors, Thomas Surprenant, has an ever-
expanding collection of Erie Canal and related New York State
waterways antique postcards, which addressed many of the problems
noted in the METRO feedback. In particular, by selecting a single,
simple, information rich format—postcards published before 1923—
copyright concerns were eliminated and only a single set of
digitization specifications needed to be developed.   METRO's
willingness to host the collection on their CONTENTdm server
simplified selection of Dublin Core as the metadata standard, and use
of a subset of the Library of Congress Thesaurus of Graphic Materials
(TGM) for standardized metadata terminology (Library of Congress,
2007).   This greatly aided our ability to develop a manageable set of
project-specific guidelines that could be adequately addressed by the
evolving documentation.

The choice of postcards as the source medium turned out to be far
more interesting to the students than was expected. An initial option
to describe the backs--as well as the front images of cards—was
enthusiastically embraced by virtually all of the students and became
the norm for subsequent classes. Hand-written messages, address
conventions, postmarks, trademarks and other attributes of the cards
were at times as much or even more rewarding to analyze than the
front images themselves. Further, student interest in the varied
aspects of architecture and activities of daily living portrayed in the
postcards led to an expansion of emphasis far beyond the initial focus
of the project on locks, canal boats, shipping, waterways and
transportation.

Background, Technical issues and Implications for Teaching

Any planning for digitization requires a detailed analysis of one's
institution, and an assessment of where the proposed project fits into

its mission and priorities.   Further, consideration of the potential audience(s), project goals and objectives, resources and limitations, oversight and long-term maintenance are among the many issues to be addressed (e.g. see JISC Digital Media, 2008: Project management; North Carolina Echo Project, 2007). These considerations inevitably will shape the nature of the evolving project. It is important that an honest appraisal be conducted, committed to writing, and approved by the appropriate governing bodies. However, the nature of digital projects ensures that adjustments inevitably will be required over time. Changing standards, software and hardware upgrades, technical glitches, and shifts in the growth of a project are just a few of the issues which must be dealt with, often on very short notice. Planning and documentation therefore should be viewed as an iterative process, where ongoing evaluation is used to address and correct for changing circumstances.

Creating a list of stakeholders and intimately involving them in this planning process is critical to success. In our own case, student feedback on procedures and emphasis has been an invaluable aspect of the evolving project.   Each incoming class section serves as a de facto Advisory/ Editorial Board that contributes to the decision-making process.   These contributions include identification of additional TGM terms for our thesaurus, the development of standardized Trademark descriptions, fine-tuning of documentation and lab handouts, and increasingly higher expectations for the quality of the metadata. Within a more traditional library environment, all members of the digitization team, as well as users and other staff members, undoubtedly will have many valuable insights to contribute.

Among the key elements shaping the evolution of a project-based digitization course at Queens College were the following:

Institutional characteristics

- When the initial course was developed it was necessary to have the course proposal cleared with the departmental Curriculum Committee after consultation with the Chair. This required the development of course goals and objectives, specific readings, and course assignments and activities.

- After three semesters teaching the course it was submitted to the GSLIS and College Graduate Curriculum Committees, Faculty Senate and, ultimately, the CUNY Board of Trustees for approval as a permanent course.

- An understanding of the possible pitfalls of the process at every step was important to ensure that all potential hurdles were considered and cleared.

- Even outside of explicitly academic environments, proper attention to obtaining documented approvals and support from key stakeholders--at all levels up to the governing board—will prove invaluable in avoiding challenges and ensuring continued buy-in by the institution and other funding agencies.

Lab facilities (capabilities and challenges)

- For our project we were able to use a 16 workstation Mac lab with direct connections to the Internet. The lab had been expressly designed by GSLIS faculty for digitization-related activities and hands-on learning, in close collaboration with the Queens College Office of Converging Technologies (OCT) and college architectural staff, in conjunction with the development of the course proposal. Appropriate institutional commitment to fund, support and regularly upgrade such a lab was, and is, essential to the continuing success of the project.

- Specifications included an instructor workstation (in addition to student Macs), ceiling mounted projector and wall screen for demonstrations, two (eventually three) flatbed scanners, SilverFast AI scanning software, Photoshop, and the Microsoft Office Suite, particularly Excel.

- A major continuing challenge concerns computer and software upgrades. The OCT staff do not always consider the rhythms of the academic year in making changes to the lab, which regularly causes problems, even after many years of teaching the course. For example, in the Fall 2009 semester alone, new computers were installed during the first week of the semester. This resulted in equipment and software glitches, and a delay in the availability of the lab, as well as the need to test software functionality and then revise/upgrade lab handouts with minimal advance notice.

- While we were grateful for the new equipment (a regular replacement cycle is essential for ongoing functionality), timing issues resulted in a rough start to the semester.

- A major equipment problem for us was solved when Apple changed to an Intel CPU. The new Mac computers are now dual boot (Apple and PC Operating Systems), meaning that they can now run CONTENTdm (CDM) using the Project Client software interface. Previously, lab sessions had to be specially scheduled in a nearby PC lab (CDM Project Client software is not available for the Mac OS). However, dual boot capabilities have created additional problems of compatibility, accessibility and ongoing troubleshooting.

Software

- As noted above, new equipment means software installation and the attendant complications. The specialized nature of our lab, and lack of teaching assistants, necessitates that course faculty test all functionalities and work with OCT staff to address problems. Oftentimes this has meant repeated testing and troubleshooting, frequently a day or two prior to a scheduled class. Such technical malfunctions can wreak havoc on the best-planned teaching schedule.

- While CDM has been sufficient for our needs, and we are extremely grateful to METRO for their continuing support, there are still some issues that cause concern. The biggest is that students cannot directly upload their input into the database due to the administrative rights structure. This situation requires another level of review by the course instructors serving as database administrators/quality control experts, adding substantially to time demands near the end of the semester. In addition, after students submit their data entries for approval, editing ability on their side is extremely constrained, by both time and software limitations.

- More recent upgrades appear to have adjusted this limitation, permitting downloading of materials from the live database for additional editing if errors are detected. However, this creates additional levels of oversight and complexity, and assumes that the instructors will be able to approve the uploads in time for the students to review and make changes. This is simply not readily accommodated within a 15 week course schedule.

- Further, although recent versions have been more stable, in the past CONTENTdm has crashed frequently, causing much frustration on the part of both students and faculty.

- These points emphasize the steep, and ongoing, learning curve of digital project-based courses for faculty, support staff and students.

Support

- Adequate and timely support for equipment and software is essential to any technology-based project. The GSLIS has a number of student computer assistants and a campus-wide Help Desk, but as noted, the specialized nature of our lab sometimes puts it outside of the realm of their expertise.

- It is good practice to fully document and save ALL help desk requests and related support communication. These include emails, screen shots and help desk tickets. These records of ongoing and recurring problems have proved to be invaluable in our efforts to ensure follow-through, and to support our case when requests have not been fully resolved to our satisfaction or when problems repeat themselves.

- CONTENTdm Help seems to work best when we go through METRO. That means that an additional layer of contact needs to be activated anytime is a problem. That said, all relevant staff at METRO, over the years of this project, have been incredibly knowledgeable, supportive and responsive to our needs.

Staffing/oversight

- Experience suggests that having a subject expert for image content is a critical factor. The faculty have, or have developed over time, sufficient expertise to assist students in their metadata and description activities.

- Given the need to protect the postcards and the equipment the lab has to be under supervision whenever anyone is working. This greatly adds to the time burden of both faculty and staff.

- Postcards are stored in archival quality sleeves and students use white gloves when handling the postcards while scanning.

Class size and student characteristics

- The class size is dictated by two elements: the number of work stations and the work volume. Experience suggests that all students need to have access to their own workstations, and two workstations are dedicated to scanning use (a third must be shared between functions). The initial classes scanned, created metadata and submitted for approval six cards (front and back), but many of these initial canal cards were fairly simple rural scenes. Given the amount of detail that has emerged in postcards in later semesters, we have gradually reduced input to three cards (front and back), because the quality and quantity of the metadata has increased substantially. The time spent in quality control by instructors has increased commeasurably, despite having students doing quality control on their partners' work.

- Those involved in the digitization process are best served with at least an intermediate level of computer and software expertise. We have constructed our teaching labs in a step-by-step fashion, and utilize in-class time extensively. This allows the faculty to introduce and demonstrate skills and to detail the various steps of the project.

- In our experience, students who are highly competent in computers and/or relevant software or metadata creation have been more than eager to assist their classmates. This leads to a highly supportive class environment in which all learn from one another, modeling (one hopes) the ideal workplace environment.

- However, a fair number of students have no previous familiarity with the Mac OS, Photoshop, scanning and related software, which complicates the pace at which the class can proceed. The nature of our curriculum and scheduling constraints make it difficult to require pre-requisites beyond the required core courses. Consequently, a teaching assistant to help in quality control, and in the provision of additional technical support in lab sessions, would be extremely desirable for all.

Evolving nature of the target collection

- Initially, the Waterways Post Card Collection consisted principally of cards of the Erie Canal, with collections of additional New York State canals such as the Oswego, Seneca, and Champlain Canals. As demand for the course has remained steady, indeed increased, the diminishing availability of canal-related cards posed a potential problem. (Most cards are currently obtained on eBay, and changing availability in geographic scope is an interesting topic for another paper.) On the other hand, many of those canal-related cards that have become available are increasingly distinctive.

- With the Quadricentennial Celebration of the discovery of the Hudson River approaching in Fall 2009, it appeared to be a logical extension of our collecting scope to extend to another key New York State waterway, the Hudson River. We included in our selection criteria cards depicting New York Harbor and the East River. The first such Hudson River cards were digitized in Fall 2008.

- The expansion in scope of the cards created fascinating but unanticipated challenges. Publishers, trademarks, and the increasing complexity of the images depicted required a substantial expansion of the TGM thesaurus, as well as the development of descriptions of an increasingly diverse set of trademarks, logos, stamp boxes and postmarks.

Consistency and accuracy

- Digitizing any collection over a period of time by a changing group of participants creates somewhat greater consistency and accuracy problems than might apply in a short-term. In spite of the iterative editing of documentation, inconsistencies and errors are regularly emerging in our project. To a large degree, this is due to the pressures of a fast-paced curriculum, a constantly changing panoply of operating systems, software versions, additions to our thesaurus and the ongoing, changing nature of the cards within our purview..

- Our experience has shown us that the students themselves are the best editors in catching errors and inconsistencies. It is obvious that the road to "perfect" metadata, documentation, labs and handouts is continuous, difficult, and perhaps, ultimately elusive. Such is the nature of a work in progress.

- It helps to have students who have a keen eye for detail as well. The project was significantly enhanced when then-student Susan Savage completed an Independent Study project in Spring 2007, that corrected many of our past mistakes, and developed the scaffolding of our current metadata documentation. It is now obvious that outside help in editing is an important part of the process (although not easily achieved).

Key readings and course activities and relevance for the project

- Clearly, carefully selected readings are critical to the success of a digitization project. We provide access to a range of resources in an effort to meet the needs of those at varying levels of familiarity with digitization and related issues. Alumni feedback has suggested the importance to many of providing continued access to the resources once our graduates are working in the field. Once involved in a real world project, many become even more aware of the importance of items that may not have seemed salient at the time of the course.

- Students complete a "Tech Review Exercise" in week seven, to document their understanding of key technical concepts. This reduces the need to cover many basic concepts during lectures, and to focus on practical development of skills and discussion.

- In addition, students prepare a detailed case study of a well-documented digital collection, and present an overview of their sites to class members. Examining the successes and challenges of a substantive collection reinforces the concepts and principles learned and applied throughout the course. Students comment with great pride on the degree of detail of the metadata they have developed for their cards, as compared to some of the case studies examined, including many well-funded projects. For many respondents to our end-of-semester evaluation surveys, the case study is perceived as a high point of the course.

Project Procedures and Workflow

Assignment of cards to students

- Postcards are carefully selected in order to give each student a maximum of exposure to bibliographic richness, varying formats and levels of difficulty.   For instance, at least one card will have writing on it for transcription. Cards also are selected on the basis of color or black & white, as well as postcard era (e.g. divided back; undivided back). In addition, postmarks, publishing information, trademarks and stamps are considered in allocating cards.   A lecture on the history of postcards provides background in understanding the evolution of these standards (e.g. see Smithsonian Institution, n.d.).

- Once selected, each card is given an eight alphanumeric accession number that identifies the subcollection, card number (a total of 9999 entries are available) in that series, the type of image (access or archival), and whether or not it is a front or back view. Early on in the project it was realized that having a related but unique identifier for each side was vital to having both sides of a card displayed together. At this point the Waterways series identifiers are: Champlain (c), Erie (e), Delaware and Hudson (d), Hudson River (h), and Seneca (s). Thus, a card in the Hudson River series available on the Web will have two accession numbers – one for the front and one for the back: e.g. h0062ac1, h0062ac2. Slightly different filing naming schemes are employed for the master archival files (e.g. h0062ar1.tif), so that the nature of the file format is evident even without the file extension.

- We adhere to the ISO 9660 8.3 alphanumeric naming standard to ensure that our files will be compatible across platforms (JISC, 2008, Choosing a file name).

- Stickers with the student names and the accession numbers are printed and attached to the outside of the archival sleeves that contain the assigned postcards. The sleeves are put into a binder so that students can access them, and photocopies of fronts and backs created to ensure a record of assignments.

Scanning and Creating Derivatives

- Once the postcards are distributed to students, they engage in hands-on instructional labs in scanning. Students use SilverFast AI software, in conjunction with the latest version of Photoshop, using the currently available flatbed scanners (these are regularly updated) to create uncompressed Tagged Image File Format (TIFF) scans. The resulting archival files, in the 20Mb range, are stored (and backed up) off line and can be examined by students if extensive detail is needed. These files are the heart of any database because they can be used for non-web purposes

- Using Photoshop, students then create JPEG derivatives at medium compression with a resolution of 150 ppi with 1000 pixels on the long dimension (following the *CDL Guidelines for Digital Images*: California Digital Library, 2009). The "ar" on the archival files are changed to "ac" on the accession numbers to reflect the change in file size and specifications. In this process the archival masters are reduced in size to approximately 200 KB, appropriate for web viewing, and yet still large enough to zoom for some degree of detail.

Assigning Metadata

- The heart of the course is when students assign metadata. A group exercise using different sample postcards for each pair of students, which is then discussed within the class, provides basic experience in assigning subject terms. What is initially thought of as a simple process quickly becomes complex when the students are confronted with the reality of their individual cards.

- Each student is given a thesaurus, based primarily on the Thesaurus of Graphic Materials (TGM), that contains all of the subject terms to be used; an electronic versions also can be used to copy/paste the terms. In addition, detailed handouts with trademark, stamp data, and metadata procedural guidelines are made available in print and digital form. Metadata and JPEG images will be inserted into an Excel template, which lists all of the metadata requirements according to CDM fields (tailored to our project), and the corresponding Dublin Core fields.

- As needed, additional terms from the TGM are added to our project thesaurus to reflect characteristics not previously encountered. For example, the move to using cards depicting New York Harbor required the addition of such terms as skyscrapers, aquariums and ferries.

- Each week, short lectures introduce the students to canal history, lore and terminology. Once the basics are covered students are then given time to insert JPEGS of the fronts and backs o f their first card (the simplest) into an Excel template. They then proceed to select subject terms, develop descriptions, and identify key Dublin Core fields (e.g. Title, Creator, etc.).

- The faculty provides assistance and guidance during this process, and students are encouraged to work with a partner. Initially there is a great deal of trepidation, but as students gain experience and confidence less faculty attention becomes necessary.

Quality control teams

- In order to provide more experience to the students, and to serve as a double check before the metadata is passed on to the faculty, they are paired up with a quality control partner, and required to exchange their Excel metadata files. Each student then reviews his/her partner's metadata, starting with the initial card, and makes any necessary editorial changes and/or suggestions for improvement using a different colored font.   The reviewed metadata set is then forwarded to the faculty for their comments and edits, added in yet a different color font. This provides an iterative record of changes: the input of initial author and control partner, and final corrections by faculty. After receipt of faculty feedback, the teams can then proceed with subsequent cards.

- This staggered approach is recommended because students tend to make the most errors in their first attempts, and to learn from the ongoing feedback. Additional benefits to the project include the identification of new trademarks in the initial set of cards, descriptions of which can then be shared with others on subsequent cards.   Lastly, repeated mistakes may reveal unintended errors or inconsistencies in documentation that can then be revised to reduce future errors.

- While this would seem to be a straightforward process it has turned out to be much more challenging than first envisioned. Yes, the students get, essentially, experience with six, not three cards which is good.   But a number of other problems have resulted. It is almost always the case that the better students pair up and that they turn in metadata that needs little comment. However, it still takes an average of fifteen minutes per relatively error-free file for faculty to review submissions. Weaker students require much more faculty review time either because the editing process is sloppy or submissions are late. In some cases faculty review and editing can take as much as an hour per Excel file. Given time constraints and course deadlines this can get extremely stressful to all parties.

- That said, it continues to surprise the faculty that: 1) the quality of most metadata submissions is so impressive, and that 2) there remain previously unidentified errors in what seems to be a fairly strict process. In this regard the quality control process is working as envisioned.

Below is a transcribed example of the metadata for "1609 • HUDSON-FULTON CELEBRATION • 1909 [front caption] (1front) [h0189ac1]" after it has been uploaded to CDM.

Title: 1609 HUDSON-FULTON CELEBRATION 1909 [front caption] (1front) [h0189ac1)

Creator: Copyright 1909 J. Koehler, N.Y. [indicated on front only]

Subject—Front: Cliffs, Clouds, Flags, Grasses, Portraits, Rocks,   Ropes, Schedules (Time plans), Ship equipment & rigging, Shrubs, Smoke, Smokestacks, Steam engines, Trees, Men, Passengers, People, Color postcards, Sailing ships, Side wheelers, Aerial views , Rivers.

Description–Front: A commemorative postcard celebrating the 300th anniversary of the discovery of the Hudson River, with portraits of Henry Hudson and Robert Fulton superimposed over a daytime aerial view of the Hudson River. Prominently featured are a sailing ship (circa 1609) and steamship (circa 1809) [presumably the Claremont] which together serve to commemorate the passage of time from discovery to the modern day. Soaring cliffs line the far bank and along the near bank; at right, there is a gathering of people (perhaps Native Americans).   An information box titled 1609 HUDSON-FULTON CELEBRATION 1909, lists the following 15 events: Sept. 25 Commencement Day N.Y., Sept. 26 Religious Observance Day N.Y., Sept. 27 Reception Day N.Y., Sept. 28 Historical Parade N.Y., Sept. 29 Commemoration Day N.Y., Sept. 30 Military Parade Day N.Y., Oct 1 Naval Parade N.Y., Oct 2 Naval Carnival Parade N.Y., Oct 3. Religious Day Upper Hudson, Oct. 4 Dutchess Co. Day, Oct. 5, Ulster Co. Day, Oct. 6 Green Co. Day, Oct. 7 Columbia Co. Day, Oct. 8 Albany Co. Day, Oct. 9 Rensselaer Co. Day. COPYRIGHT 1909 BY J. KOEHLER, N.Y. [indicated on front only].

Coverage – Geographic: Hudson River, New York and New Jersey

Date Original: 1909?

Publisher: Graduate School of Library and Information Studies – Queens College (CUNY), New York, New York

Language: eng

Source Height: 3.5"

Source Width: 5.5"

Source: Waterways Post Card Collection of Thomas T. Surprenant: Hudson River

Type: Text; Image

> **Digitization Specifications**: Archive masters were scanned at 600 ppi, 24 bit color using a Canon CanoScan 88800F and SilverFast Ai scanning software and saved as uncompressed TIFFs using Photoshop CS$ and Mac OC 10.5, Derivative access files were saved as medium quality JPEGs, 150 dpi, 1000 pixels on the long dimension. Thumbnails were generated automatically by CONTENT dm.
>
> **Date Digital**: 2009-09-30
>
> **Resource Identifier**: h0189ac1.jpg
>
> **Format**: Image
>
> **Format [Medium]**: Postcards
>
> **File Size**: 218972 Bytes
>
> **Checksum**: 287714794
>
> **Height (of Digital Image)**: 1000
>
> **Width (of Digital Image)**: 637
>
> **Color Space**: sRGB
>
> **Rights Management**: Contact Thomas T. Surprenant, ebeltoms@nyc.rr.com
>
> **Contributing Organization:** Graduate School of Library and Information Studies, Queens College (CUNY), New York, New York
>
> **Digitization Team**: GSLIS 757, Digital Imaging Fall 2009,: Beth Daniel Lindsay, Meg Donabedian
>
> (GSLIS, 2006-2009, *Waterways of New York V. 2.1*).

Uploading to CONTENTdm

- By mid-semester, the students are introduced to the basics of the CDM Project Client software in a hands-on lab. They upload a sample image, are guided through the creation of a "Waterways of New York" banner to be automatically inserted for future uploads, and—following step-by-step directions—use the Template Creator function to input recurring fields (e.g. Source, Digitization Specifications, Digitization Team), and to enable CDM's capacity to automatically capture technical metadata such as Resource Identifier, File Size, Format and Checksum fields.

- They then upload another sample image to demonstrate that these functions are working, and to doublecheck (and correct for) for possible errors in data entry.

- The following week (assuming appropriate progress on early steps in the workflow), they are ready to upload their first postcard JPEG images (front and back, entered as individual files). Early on in the project we decided against uploading the fronts and backs of cards as compound objects, since this would severely limit the amount of detailed metadata that could be made available.

- Students "cut-and-paste" the doubly reviewed metadata from their Excel files into the appropriate fields in CDM. This approach was especially important when we had limited access to the Project Client interface in the adjacent PC lab, and at times of instability in CDM at the client end.

- Following an additional review by faculty for completeness and accuracy at the desktop, students then upload the files to be approved in the Administrative interface.

- It provides tremendous positive feedback to all to see the fruits of many weeks of work appear live in the evolving database, in real time, during this most momentous class session.

- In subsequent weeks, a portion of each class is devoted to additional project work, reflecting whatever particular step each student is addressing.

Timing /scheduling issues

- Given the pressure of a 15 week semester, and the need to respond quickly to student submissions, the entire quality control process takes much more time than initially projected. Yet, there seems to be no alternative to preventing major errors from creeping into the database. And students regularly report, in mid-year and year-end evaluations, that they find the hands-on nature of metadata creation and feedback to be among the best aspects of the course.

- The time constraints on classes (once a week for 2 hours 35 minutes) make it difficult to teach what is needed and to allow students the time to practice. This is particularly true for commuting students, most of whom hold full-time jobs and may come to school only once a week. This is complicated by extremely time-consuming commutes (for students living in Brooklyn, three or more hours round trip is common).

- It is not unusual for a few students to still be attempting to scan (or rescan) their postcards during the seventh or eighth week of class (or to have to redo their derivative files due to lack of attention to digital specifications). This puts the faculty—and student partners--into a real bind when it comes their turn to evaluate student work.

How much detail is enough/too much?

- This question has vexed both the faculty and students since the inception of the course. One of the best aspects of the project is the information rich content of the postcards, both back and front. Students have been particularly diligent in finding, and fighting for, new subject terms and descriptive material. This makes the course an ever evolving environment with an endless series of new things to consider and debate.

- Especially dedicated students have taken the time to research historical events depicted in their cards, leading us to add a "References" field in Fall 2008, where they can add more background and even Web citations.

- Student interests, skills, and insights have made this very much a "student-driven" course, in the best sense of the phrase. Every class has made unique contributions to the quality of the project, and all (both faculty and students) learn from one another. The collective contributions of the myriad participants in this project cannot be understated.

Supervisory issues

- As previously noted, the class inevitably encounters difficulties with students who either are forging ahead or are lagging behind others. In any given class the faculty can expect to see a certain level of frustration as students cope with their individual abilities and challenges.

- The evolving documentation, hardware and software problems sometimes create an illusion that the faculty are not well prepared. It doesn't take much to derail what has been planned for any given class. This adds to the timing and scheduling issues discussed above. On the other hand, as more perceptive students note, this is the way projects function in the real world, and provides insights they can share in future job interviews of how they dealt with unforeseen complications.

Role of independent study students in quality control review and overhaul of documentation

- To date, there have been only two Independent Study students interested in assisting with quality control, one for the METRO-funded archival project (Amy Armstrong), and one for the Waterways project (Susan Savage). They both made extraordinary contributions to the projects in terms of documentation and quality control. There is no doubt that, in the near future, more students and/or faculty will have to be brought into the process of oversight and review in order for existing problems and errors to be addressed, but there are substantial challenges in envisioning how this may be possible in the current economic climate.

- The same difficulties exist with the revision of documentation. Incremental changes have resulted in some inconsistencies, and outright errors, in the documentation. At this point having better documentation has a higher priority than quality control review of the existing database. Better documentation will result in better quality control. During the coming year the faculty intend to make major revisions of the documentation to ensure that it is not only up-to-date but more accurate.

Expansion of the database

- We anticipate that, sometime in the near future, the database will have to expand beyond a personal collection. Two preliminary moves in that direction have already been undertaken. The Ellenville Public Library and Museum permitted its Delaware and Hudson (D&H) postcard collection of 70+ cards to be scanned and inserted into a separate Greenstone database. Similarly, the Erie Canal Museum in Syracuse permitted us to create archival Tiffs of 55 postcards. Students then created derivatives and assigned metadata on these cards, in addition to several they scanned themselves.

- From experience it is, indeed, gratifying to see that a spirit of participation exists within many of the various libraries, museums and historical societies. More needs to be accomplished in this arena and there are plans to work with additional organizations in the coming year.

- Once the collection becomes more mature, enlisting other postcard collectors to contribute to the database is a strong possibility.

- Any future expansion will have to consider moving beyond postcards into other forms and formats. While this is a logical extension, especially with photographs, maps and important historical documentation, the level of difficulty increases. In order to keep students in the process it is likely that the faculty will have to do a great deal of traveling to digitize collections that are all over the state.

Successes and Lessons Learned

The literature of "Best Practices" emphasizes the importance of an "Advisory Council", and the involvement of key stakeholders, to provide feedback and insight into the successes and challenges of an evolving project (e.g. Chapman, 2000). Our students have exceeded every expectation in this regard, and reinforce the importance of input from a variety of stakeholders in the advisory process. Subject headings and description have expanded from an initial focus on canal-specific characteristics (e.g. tugboats, locks), to many attributes of the environment and daily life in early 20th century New York. Detailed rules and guidelines provide standardized descriptions (developed by the students) of trademarks, logos and postmarks and ensure consistency with AACR2 and other standards.

Perhaps most importantly, students have gained an appreciation for every aspect of the overall planning, processes and implementation pertaining to the creation of at least one type of digital collection (images). This practical experience is embedded in an exposure to key readings in the literature, class discussions, and a detailed case study analysis of an existing collection. In particular, they come to understand the enormous demands of metadata creation and quality control, and the tradeoffs that may lead digital collection managers to minimize this aspect of their projects. The role of students as key project participants has been extremely valuable in providing concrete evidence of their experience as they search for jobs in this difficult economy. It has been equally valuable for potential employers seeking qualified job candidates.

At this writing, the project continues, with two course sections scheduled for Spring 2010 and no end in sight. Our students have gone on to excellent positions in the field and the feedback from intern supervisors is consistently positive.   With any luck, our collection will exceed 1,300 images by early 2010.

Challenges and next steps

In addition to many of the future plans outlined above, we are seriously considering migration of the database to an open-source platform, such as Omeka (http://omeka.org/), Greenstone (http://www.greenstone.org/) or other available options. Running such a digital library collection platform in parallel with CDM would present a valuable learning tool for students, while adding to the complexity of the project.

Possible student interest in working on this initiative as an independent study project, coupled with a soon-to-be-completed search for a new lecturer line at the GSLIS, with specializations in digitization and related technologies, provides some basis for optimism as we move into the next decade.   And we remain committed to this labor-of-love that has inspired and empowered so many classes of students.

Yet on the challenges side, for faculty it remains a difficult balancing act. The nature of a project such as this requires continuous updating and editing to ensure consistency and quality in the ongoing development of the project. This process places serious stresses on the competing obligations of supervising faculty for research, publication, service, staying current, and responsibilities for other courses. This is particularly true during a major period of transition within our department. But, some things are very much worth doing, and we hope this example may provide encouragement to others starting out, or expanding their existing initiatives. We look forward to extending the dialogue!

References

California Digital Library. (2009, September). "3.5 Guidelines for access and thumbnail image files." *CDL Guidelines for Digital Images, Version 2.0.* Retrieved December 31, 2009, from http://www.cdlib.org/inside/diglib/guidelines/bpgimages/

Chapman, S. (2000). Section III: Considerations for project management. In M.K. Sitts (Ed.) *Handbook for digital projects: A management tool for preservation and access.* Retrieved December 30, 2009, from http://www.nedcc.org/resources/pubs.php

Graduate School of Library and Information Studies. Queens College, CUNY. (2005-2009). *Digitization projects.* Retrieved January 3, 2010, from http://qcpages.qc.edu/GSLIS/digitization.html

Graduate School of Library and Information Studies. Queens College, CUNY. (2006-2009). *Waterways of New York V. 2.1.* Retrieved January 3, 2009, from http://cdm128401.cdmhost. com/cdm4/browse.php?CISOROOT=%2Fqcgslis_f06

JISC Digital Media. (2008, November 11). *Choosing a file name.* Retrieved September 2, 2009 from http://www.jiscdigitalmedia. ac.uk/crossmedia/advice/choosing-a-file-name/

JISC Digital Media (2008, November 14). *Project management for a digitisation project.* Retrieved December 31, 2009, from http://www.jiscdigitalmedia.ac.uk/crossmedia/advice/project-management-for-a-digitisation-project/

Library of Congress. (2007). *Thesaurus for graphic materials I.* Retrieved December 31, 2009, from http://www.loc.gov/rr/print/tgm1/

North Carolina ECHO Project. (2007). *Project planning. Digitization guidelines, 2007 revised edition.* Retrieved January 2, 2010, from http://www.ncecho.org/dig/guide_1planning.shtml

Smithsonian Institution. (n.d.). *Greetings from the Smithsonian: A postcard history of the Smithsonion Institution.* Retrieved December 31, 2009, from http://siarchives.si.edu/history/exhibits/postcard/chronology.htm

Part II – A Diverse Digital Landscape: Digital Collections in Public Libraries, Museums, Cultural Heritage Institutions, and Knowledge-Based Organizations

Managing Rights in a Medium Scale Audio Digitization Project

Barbara Taranto and Elizabeth Bradley
(New York Public Library)

Abstract

In 2007 New York Public Library received a small grant to digitize a selection of audio recordings of public programs, including lectures, interviews, and panel discussions that took place at the Humanities and Social Sciences Library between 1983 and 2003. This chapter briefly discusses the scope of the project and the institutional reasons for the initiative. The chapter then discusses some of the significant challenges regarding Intellectual Property Rights, faced by the Library and the strategies it employed to deal with the issues. The chapter concludes with a discussion of the policies and procedures the Library has since put in place to manage audio rights.

Keywords: Access, Audio, Copyright, Media, NYPL, Privacy, Public library, Recording, Taping, Transcription.

The Genesis of the Project

New York Public Library has been engaged in digital projects since the mid 1990's when it launched its first public website. In 1998 it published a compilation of digital "reprints" African American Women Writers of the 19thCentury (*Webpage Dodson*, 1998) of out of print, and essentially unavailable 19th century materials from the holdings of the Schomburg Center For Research In Black Culture. By 2000 the Library had established a new unit, the Digital Library

Program, to manage the creation and publication of digitized content from its collections. Within the year an even larger project – the digitization of half a million pictorial items – NYPL Digital Gallery (see *New York Public Library Digital Gallery*, n.d.) - was undertaken and by 2003 the Library was producing approximately 1250 new image files – complete with metadata - per week.

Public domain items were chosen for the first digitization efforts. This allowed the Library to leverage existing bibliographic records for metadata creation without additional research into intellectual property rights. It also allowed the Library to provide a new and exciting online resource for the public.

As the program matured policies and best practices were developed, including how to manage the rare but occasional issue of Intellectual Property (IP). The metadata system was modified to record Intellectual Property rights and access permissions. Processes were established to redact items that were mistakenly digitized and/or published before IP permissions had been received, and new content was being created daily. At the same time the Library began experimenting with new formats such as geospatial data and media files. It also began to look closely at user needs and at new avenues for distribution such as mobile and cellular applications.

As patrons became more experienced web users and their home computing technology improved, user expectations for easy and quick access to rich content increased substantially. Public domain materials were no longer sufficient. Consequently in 2007, the Library decided to initiate a pilot project to determine what was involved in managing rights-encumbered collections in the digital environment. It requested and received a grant from the Metropolitan Library Association to digitize recordings of well-known public personalities and ultimately make them available to the public via the web under the title *24 Hours at NYPL*.

The Scope of the Project

We wanted to test the waters for audio rights management at an institution with a mandate for accessible content delivered at no charge. There were three key goals: 1) discover the issues involved in rights encumbered audio; 2) determine best practices for resolving these issues; and 3) develop a workflow to manage collections with similar issues. A small sample from a contemporary, but relatively high profile collection would be suitable for this purpose since the subjects involved were already rights-savvy performers. It was also decided that to the best of its ability, the Library would seek permission from these rights holders to make these materials freely available to the public without cumbersome access controls.

The Literature

There is a plethora of documentation on Digital Rights Management (DRM) and DRM products available to leverage and control access to digital assets for commercial gain and/or Intellectual Property management (e.g., ARALOC, 2010, Stream Media, 2010 and Discretix, 2010.) Everything from watermarking to anti-cloning technologies is available to "lock-down" content. Likewise there are as many Digital Library resource pages (e.g., Berkeley Digital Library, 2007) detailing these technologies and the consequent policy implications for managing copyrighted and licensed media in a library setting. Furthermore, there is a very lively scholarly discourse in the preservation community around the proper expression (language) of digital rights and the sharing of digital rights information (see Premis, 2010). All of which is exceedingly helpful once the data have been obtained.

There are many practices employed when engaged in digital activities such as national standards for reformatting, file naming conventions, persistence, etc (e.g., Washington State Library, n.d., and North Carolina ECHO, n.d.). However, the process and procedures by which one should manage a Digital Rights project in a library – especially a public library - setting are not thick on the ground. In fact, it is for this reason that New York Public chose to work on these collections – viz. this is relatively new ground.

We chose to digitize a selection of audio recordings of public programs, including lectures, interviews, and panel discussions that took place at the Humanities and Social Sciences Library between 1983 and 2003. The recordings, holdings from the Public Education Program (PEP) represent some of the best of the thousands of public programs offered for a small fee to all comers by the Humanities and Social Sciences Library during those decades. Many of these events were held in a grandly restored space called the Celeste Bartos Forum, a venue that has, as a result, become familiar and beloved to generations of New York City culture-seekers.

The programs chosen for digitization included talks and interviews featuring world-renowned writers, thinkers, and public intellectuals such as Chinua Achebe, A.S. Byatt, Umberto Eco, Christopher Hitchens, Robert Thurman, Oliver Sacks, Esmerelda Santiago, Sarah Vowell, and Wendy Wasserstein, among many others. Permission to record the programs was sought from each subject prior to the event. They were originally recorded live, in analog formats including reel-to-reel and cassette tapes.

When choosing these particular programs, preference was given to those subjects whose dynamic performances were the most in keeping with the goals of the digitization project, and for which permission was anticipated to be negotiated and obtained without too much difficulty or searching. For these reasons as well, single subjects (interviewees) were preferred

Rights Issues with Recorded Programs

For the most part flat art works (as plates or reproductions or original art works) are associated with a wide but manageable universe of rights holders. Even maps which have more "creators" than most print materials – engravers, cartographers, drafters, navigators, colorists, etc. – are fixed. The rights pertain to certain aspects of the creation of the object but do not extend to the subject of the work such as "the State of California" or to all parties that participated in the making of the work such as the oiler who serviced the printing press.

The digitally reformatting of the audiotapes was unexceptional. The tapes files were sent to a reputable vendor and quality control was performed on the files when they were returned to the Library.

Technical metadata was recorded and deposited into a database designed for keeping preservation technical data. The Library's metadata specialists using the in-house utility created descriptive metadata. However, obtaining permission from the speakers on these recordings proved to be an unexpected and ongoing challenge.

The first step in rights process is to determine who is the rights holder. This involved contacting the subjects and in some cases editors, managers and lawyers, to match the audio tapes to their rights holders.   While the subject was clearly known, the rights documentation needed to be created (with the assistance of the NYPL General Counsel's Office) and managed by NYPL staff, in addition to the management of the media asset. In this case, the Library deliberately chose items where the rights were clearly held by a known body, preferably one with a cordial, ongoing relationship to or affinity for the mission and work of the NYPL. Nonetheless seeking and obtaining permission even when the rights holder is undisputed is often tedious and frustrating. In fact, a good deal of time was spent finding and attempting to contact the subject in question. Once contacted, there were many issues to resolve.

Rights holders were often difficult to reach. Sometimes this was due to the age of the information (addresses are out of date, names have changed, etc) or the amount of time that had elapsed since the creation of the content. Sometimes this was due to privacy needs or the sheer number of intermediaries (such as editors, agents, and business managers) that had to be included in the negotiation process. Sometimes there was no one left to contact. The rights may have reverted the estate in the case of an individual's death or passed to another individual without a clear record. In these cases it was nearly impossible to determine the rights.

In a few cases permission was obtained when considerable time was invested. Often rights holders were unfamiliar with the digital environment and needed to be educated by Library staff about the nature and purpose of digitization. This was a slow process and took a good deal of time and patience and to explain everything in adequate detail. It also required a finesse to describe technical processes in a way that was meaningful to non-technical individuals. Sometimes this was successful, sometimes not.

Certain more commercially successful individuals, whose fame had increased in the ensuing years, retained counsel that aggressively challenged the Library's request – sometimes with and sometimes without cause (e.g., An individual may not want to relinquish rights to an unedited version of a performance to avoid the possibility of incurring liability for comments made during the performance.) These individuals seemed to be motivated by one of two factors – control over the distribution of creative content produced at an earlier stage in the performer's career, and/or the possibility of generating revenue from the digitized program.

Certain rights holders were unable to remember the contents of the programs they had recorded. Others were uncomfortable with the idea that their material would be available for free streaming broadcast and download via iTunes University. Despite iTunes' seemingly universal brand, the prospect of an NYPL partnership with a commercial vendor confused and possibly alienated some of the performers (or, as was more often the case, their legal counsel).

One strategic decision made by Library staff was to commission written transcripts of the audio recordings of the events that we wished to digitize, so that we might make the scripts of the events available to anxious authors, publishers and literary agents, many of whom suggested that they could not remember the content of a talk delivered so many years before, and were therefore reluctant to give their approval in advance of reviewing it.

The issues presented as follows:

- Rights holder in dispute
- Rights holder incommunicato
- Rights holder is the estate of a deceased person
- Rights holder unfamiliar with technology
- Rights holder represented by aggressive counsel
- Rights holder unable to remember contents of discussion

- Rights holder uncomfortable with venue

For the most part subjects who participated in these public programs were initially hesitant to grant permission to digitize and republish the program on the web, which for many of them constituted a new and unusual forum for the distribution of their work.   Interestingly, younger performers gave permission with considerably more alacrity and ease than did older performers (or their counsel). As a result of these unexpected challenges, only a limited number of the digitized public programs have been made available to the public. However, the process of negotiating for rights and gathering permissions is still ongoing, and over time many more subjects have been persuaded to participate in the project.

The digitized materials are preserved for posterity and the existence of this trove of live audio material featuring celebrated authors and thinkers (all of whom have book holdings at the Library, and some of whom have deposited their personal papers or manuscripts, as well) is a source of great interest and enthusiasm for Library staff and the users who have learned about them, thus far.

Lessons Learned

Few of the digitized tapes have been made available for public access. However, the project met two of the three key goals: the issues involved in rights encumbered audio were discovered and a workflow for handling similar issues was established.   The third goal - establishing best practices for obtaining permission – can be derived from the case studies in the project.

Many of the subjects were initially reluctant to grant permission for very specific reasons. It leads to the conclusion that addressing these specific concerns can lead to more successful negotiations. By educating the rights holders (and sometimes the counsel) about the new medium of digital audio, many of their material concerns were allayed, or eliminated. By providing written transcriptions as memory aids and evidence to be inspected by counsel, some subjects were able to make a positive, informed decision regarding the Library's request. By being sensitive to privacy issues, ambassadorial about digital content, and above all else, being politely persistent, the Library has been increasingly successful.

New Practices Born From *24 Hours at NYPL*

The entire process of the project is dependent on documentation. Without the proper releases in place these projects are not possible. If releases do not exist then they must be obtained and rights must be clearly spelled out. Furthermore, all records should be managed in a centralized repository so that future uses for these items are possible. The library was able to identify individual rights holders by sheer tenacity and willingness to put in the hours required. The procedure is prolonged and often takes many turns. Clear guidelines and processes are needed in order to track progress and to properly manage the relations established during the negotiations. Without proper record keeping the process breaks down and accuracy suffers. Because of excellent record keeping the Library was able to pursue this project and obtain as many permissions as it has.

The challenges encountered in obtaining rights for *24 Hours at NYPL* highlighted the need for the Library to develop a more robust rights digital management system. While releases had been obtained for the original recordings these releases were paper documents kept in separate files. There was no database to manage these documents and or the relationship the documents had to the assets. All this work had to be done before the work of seeking permission could begin. Furthermore, evaluating the releases to determine the extent of the Library's rights was necessary before any approach could be made.

These preparatory tasks are often considered incidental to digital projects since digital rights are often discussed as a separate case or special case. However, 24 Hours at NYPL underscored the need to tie digital rights management to general collection management. In this case, the relationship was drawn between the previously obtained releases and the audio assets. In the case of the earlier project Digital Gallery the issue was obscured because of the decision to include only items that were either in the public domain or obtained for the specific purpose of being included in the gallery. Nonetheless, the accurate documentation in the bibliographic record was the basis for the management of the digital rights.

This understanding has led the Library to create a robust Digital Rights Application that will manage scanned paper documents such as Deeds of Gift as well as rights information. The data will be managed centrally and tied to both the bibliographic databases and the Fedora Digital Repository. Rights data that is stored in a structured format can be shared with multiple systems and exported for administrative purposes and exposed for OAI harvesting.

Additionally work is being done to educate staff to consider digital rights information as vital as provenance to the acquisition process; and to include these data in any supporting documentation. New guidelines for these managing theses discussions are currently being drafted. The focus is to gather as much relevant information as possible at the time collections are acquired. Protocols such as those listed below are among the suggested practices:

- Identifying all known individuals contained in items in the collection
- Identifying all known authors and/or creators
- Identifying all known third party rights holders
- Identifying permissions and/or releases from third party rights holders
- Identifying documentation related to rights such as releases, contracts, etc.

To the best of its ability the Library is also aiming to secure rights as early as possible in the life of a digital object – or in some cases, the life of a physical object since this informs almost all future decisions. This is a change in practice that is being implemented slowly but successfully in the Research Libraries.

There are many ripple effects to these new practices. In the future the decision to acquire or not acquire a collection may rest of the status of digital rights. Furthermore, the collection development of the entire Library may shift because of thee factors. Certainly, the role of the collection development staff will change.

Summary

The Library's role as a content creator, provider and distributor in the age of podcasts and webinars, wikis, blogs and Twitter is becoming critical. Access to new content areas is challenging especially when intellectual property rights are involved. However, reluctance by rights owners can be overcome by providing written transcriptions as memory aids to help make informed choices. Persistence is key. Often a donor's point of view can be swayed by gentle persuasion and expressed sensitivity to privacy issues.

Obtaining permissions and releases is essential for the success. If not already in hand, the process to obtain these allowances is slow and difficult and can impede the completion of the project.

The lion's share of the work with digital collections with rights that obtain to a party that is not the library is the proper recording and management of that rights information. All parties involved with these collections, including curators, directors, and counsel must share an understanding that rights information is not incidental, but essential to properly manage these collections.

Infrastructure – both technical and organizational - that supports the recording and management of detailed rights data should be implemented in libraries that wish to embark on similar projects. Obtaining these data as early on in the acquisition process as possible is optimal since researching these data is labor intensive and often precludes successful completion of these projects. Staff at all levels should be informed of these best practices and educated in the proper procedures for acquiring and documenting rights.

References

ARALOC. (2010). *Cross platform DRM*. Retrived on May 2, 2010 from http://araloc.com/

Berkeley Digital Library. (2007). *Copyright, intellectual property rights, and licensing issues*. Retrived on May 2, 2010 from http://sunsite.berkeley.edu/Copyright/

Discretix. (2010). *Multi-Scheme DRM client.* Retrieved on May 2, 2010 from http://www.discretix.com/DRM/index.html?source=adwordsCusGdrm-phrase888manufacturers100215&gclid=CKqHsMKX3KACFdlw5QodcyfZBQ

New York Public Library Digital Gallery. (n.d.). Retrieved on May 2, 2010 from http://digitalgallery.nypl.org.

North Carolina ECHO. (n.d.). *Digitization guidelines.* Retrieved on May 2, 2010 from http://www.ncecho.org/dig/guide_1planning.shtml

Premis. (2010). *Preservation metadata maintenance activity.* Retreived on May 8, 2010 from http://www.loc.gov/standards/premis/

Stream Media. (2010). *Streaming Media Hosting is your expert for DRM - Digital Rights Management solutions.* Retrieved on May 2, 2010 from http://www.streamingmediahosting.com/drm.htm?gclid=CMLolpWX3KACFWV75QodEAyXDA

Washington State Library. (n.d.). *Digital best practice.* Retrieved on May 2, 2010 from http://digitalwa.statelib.wa.gov/newsite/projectmgmt/vendors.htm

Webpage Dodson, Howard African American Women Writers of the 19th Century. (1998). Retrieved on May 2, 2010 from http://digital.nypl.org/schomburg/writers_aa19/intro.html

The In-House Digital Laboratory: Possibilities and Responsibilities

Andrea Buchner (Center for Jewish History)

Abstract

The Gruss Lipper Digital Laboratory at the Center for Jewish History has been building sustainable digital collections since 2005. It has worked on more than 100 different projects and digitized a wide variety of materials. This chapter highlights projects that include the digitization of books, photographs, and archival collections. It covers digitization from start to finish, touching upon the selection of materials for digitization, digitization practices and workflows, the management of digital assets, online delivery and users' reactions to digital collections. It concludes with a discussion of the feasibility of an in-house digital laboratory for archives and libraries in general.

Keywords: Digital asset management, Digital imaging, Digital laboratory, Digital preservation, Digitization, Digitization projects management, Digitization standards, Metadata, Sustainable digital collections.

Introduction

The Gruss Lipper Digital Laboratory at the Center for Jewish History was established in 2005 with the generous support of the Gruss Lipper Family Foundation. Today, the lab is at the center of a digital program whose mission is to preserve the digital assets of the Center and its five partner organizations and to ensure long-term access to them. Since 2005, the digital lab has been involved in more than 100 digitization projects and has created more than 68,000 high-quality digital images. It has also created 300 hours of high-quality digital audio files by digitizing oral histories and Sephardic music stored on cassette tapes and reel-to-reel tapes.

The digital lab manages all digital assets via ExLibris' DigiTool, a digital asset management system for libraries and archives (http://www.exlibrisgroup.com). The public interface is CJH Digital Collections (digital.cjh.org). The digital collections are an integral part of the Center's Online Public Access Catalog (catalog.cjh.org). This catalog provides access to the Center's and partners' archival collections and library holdings. If a digital reproduction exists in CJH Digital Collections, the respective catalog record links to them. As of December 2009, 21,000 digital objects were accessible. In 2009 alone, 174,000 users requested digital objects. All materials are accessible to the public free of charge and the collections are constantly growing.

This chapter will examine a variety of projects. They illustrate approaches to the digitization of different types of materials: books, photographs, and archival collections. This chapter will also discuss digital asset management, online delivery, users' reactions to digital collections, and the feasibility of an in-house digital laboratory.

The Gruss Lipper Digital Laboratory

The Gruss Lipper Digital Laboratory (digital lab) is a department within the Center for Jewish History.

The Center for Jewish History is the home of five prominent Jewish institutions dedicated to history, culture, and art. They are the American Jewish Historical Society (AJHS), the American Sephardi Federation (ASF), the Leo Baeck Institute (LBI), the Yeshiva University Museum (YUM), and the YIVO Institute for Jewish Research (YIVO). The combined holdings of the partner organizations bring together the rich variety of Jewish historical experience, ranging from Eastern European Jewry, Sephardic Jewry, German-speaking Jewry, to the American Jewish community.

The collections include more than 500,000 volumes, 25,500 linear feet of archival documents, and thousands of museum objects.

Since its opening in October 2000, over 40,000 researchers have visited the Center and roughly 210,000 patrons have attended various public exhibitions, conferences, and other events that the Center and partners held.

The Gruss Lipper Digital Laboratory, a department of the Center, collaborates with all five partner organizations in numerous ways by digitizing their collections, managing the resulting digital assets, and providing digital consultancy services. During the first two years of the lab's operation it was fully funded through the grant from the Gruss Lipper Family Foundation. When this period ended in 2007, the Center made the digital lab an integral part of its functions and services and continued to offer the lab's digital collections building services to the partner organizations. In order to defray some of the costs, however, the digital lab charges for its services whenever external funding becomes available to the partners. When this is not the case, the lab provides *pro bono* digitization services.

A typical digitization project starts with an idea put forth either by Center or partner staff. This is followed by discussions, examinations of materials, and following established procedures (including the completion of forms) to ensure that materials arrive in the lab that have been thoroughly vetted in regard to their value, physical condition, rights, and available metadata. Once the selected materials have been prepared and arrive in the lab, the process of digitization begins. Projects may involve one or multiple partner organizations.

Projects

When it comes to determining the value of materials, the lab works closely with partner staff. Value lies in the exceptional coverage of a topic, the uniqueness (scarcity) of materials, how well they represent the unique strengths of a partner's collection, and their appeal to the partner's and the Center's audience. Materials must also be in the public domain or be orphan works (i.e., copyrighted works whose owner cannot be identified or located. See *Orphan Works,* 2009), or the partner must have permission from copyright holders to make digital reproductions of them accessible online. Preservation needs also play a role in selecting materials.

Among the materials digitized in the lab are 137 Yiddish and Hebrew children's books from the Yeshiva University Museum (YUM) and the YIVO Institute for Research (YIVO). The books document the development of Jewish children's literature from the turn of the century until the onset of the Holocaust in Eastern Europe. The majority of the books are rare and only available at the Center. They are in the public domain or orphan works and could therefore be made accessible via CJH Digital Collections (digital.cjh.org). The project began as a pilot project funded by the Metropolitan New York Library Council (METRO) in 2007 and grew into a larger project when a private family foundation decided to fund the digitization of additional books. The Center also contributed the digital images to the International Children's Digital Library Foundation which has made them accessible through its website.

In addition to children's books, the digital lab has digitized rare books from the Leo Baeck Institute (LBI). The digital lab has been digitizing rare books since its inception. Funding has come from a variety of sources; originally from the Gruss Lipper Family Foundation, then from METRO and now through a private donor. Most recently, the lab digitized manuscripts from the 15-16th century pertaining to a famous Renaissance controversy between the Christian Hebraist Johannes Reuchlin and the anti-Jewish agitator Johannes Pfefferkorn, who advocated for the destruction of all Jewish books. The digital lab is ideally suited for the digitization of rare books. It is an in-house lab which reduces the risk of loss and damage that can occur during the shipping of books to external vendors. Moreover, the digitization staff is given the time to treat each book carefully and according to its often fragile or tightly-bound condition. This ensures that they are not damaged during the digitization process.

As for photographs, the digital lab has worked on dozens of projects during its first two years of operation, having digitized thousands of photographs (prints and negatives) as well as slides.

Among the highlights are 3,200 photographs of Moroccan and Turkish synagogues from the American Sephardi Federation (ASF).

The digital lab has digitized both portions of archival collections as well as complete collections. From the LBI, it has digitized rare oversize materials. They were selected due to their rarity and fragility. Among the highlights are letters of protection for Jewish communities in Germany from the 18th century. Letters of protection were issued to Jews by local authorities in Europe. These letters gave Jews the right to reside in a town in exchange for a special tax.

The digital lab has digitized a few archival collections in their entirety. The largest collection was from YUM. It consisted of 30 linear feet of materials, mostly fashion drawings by the New York City fashion designer Abe Grubère. However, this collection is an exception and archival collections digitized in the lab are usually small, such as the Raphael Lemkin Collection from the American Jewish Historical Society (AJHS) that consists of 7.5 linear feet. Raphael Lemkin was a scholar who coined the term "Genocide." He was instrumental in the United Nations' adoption of the Convention on the Prevention and Punishment of the Crime of Genocide in 1948. The collection documents Lemkin's lifelong effort to prevent genocide and lobby the United Nations to adopt an anti-genocide convention. In total, the lab digitized the content of 76 folders which translated into 4033 images. The materials were digitized as part of an initiative at the Center that culminated in a conference and an exhibition on genocide in 2009.

Copyright and Fair Use

When materials are selected for digitization the copyright status must be clear. As for the YUM and YIVO children's books and LBI rare books, the books were either in the public domain or orphan works. They could be made accessible via CJH Digital Collections without restrictions.

With regard to the photographs of Turkish and Moroccan synagogues, however, the situation was more complicated. There was a subset of 500 photographs of the 3,000 total, taken in 1989, where the ASF and the photographer jointly held the copyright. The photographer was then consulted for his permission to digitize the photographs and to make the digital reproductions accessible online via CJH Digital Collections. His permission was obtained by means of a license agreement.

As for the Raphael Lemkin Collection, the AJHS had permission from Lemkin's heir to make digital reproductions of the collection accessible. Among the selected materials was much correspondence from third parties. They were letters from various activists to people, committees or organizations that had the power to influence the United Nations or various governments to adopt and/or ratify the convention. The letters were protected by copyright. AJHS and the Center started to contact copyright holders and permission was granted whenever possible. We also reviewed the four factors of "fair use" and concluded that the factual nature of the correspondence and our intended use allow for making the letters accessible to the public for "fair use" (see *Fair Use*, 2009). Each digital folder containing letters was associated with a "click through" copyright notice, outlining the allowed terms of "fair use" such as that no use other than research, teaching, and private study is allowed without prior permission from the copyright owner. Copyright owners not properly identified, or any user with information on the copyright status of a particular work, are asked to contact the Center and AJHS so that appropriate information can be provided in the future. Every user desiring access to the digital materials must agree to these terms by clicking on a button before gaining access to them. The fair use information can also be found in the descriptive metadata record that is attached to each letter and at the bottom of the CJH Digital Collections website.

Image Capture

The Gruss Lipper Digital Laboratory has the following equipment: A BetterLight Super 8K-HS digital scanning camera back and a Mamiya 645ZD 22 megapixel (5,336 x 4,008 pixels) medium format single-shot digital camera. The scanning workstation consists of a motorized AIAXact 3040 DV copystand, four Buhl HID 150W 4k softcube lights as well as two book cradles. The lab also has an Epson Expression 10000 XL Photo flatbed scanner with transparency adapter and a Minolta DiMage Scan Multi PRO AF-5000 multi-format film scanner. The digital lab also has a TEAC 860-R cassette deck, an Otari Mx-5050bII reel-to-reel tape machine, and a Behringer UB502 mixer. This equipment allows for the digitization of the different types of materials found in archives: Bound books, unbound materials, oversize materials, photographs, film, slides, transparencies, cassette tapes and reel-to-reel tapes.

Figure GLDL-1: Gloria Machnowski digitizes a decree from the Leo Baeck Institute with the BetterLight camera. © 2009. Gruss Lipper Digital Laboratory. Used with permission.

When the digital lab receives a collection to be digitized, it tracks the collection, item, and images eventually to be created from the item in a Microsoft Access "tracking" database. For the actual digitization, the digital lab follows standards established by the National Archives

(Technical Guidelines for Digitizing Archival Materials for Electronic Access: Creation of Production Master Files – Raster Images, 2004) which include guidelines for the creation of high-quality archival master images, quality assurance and accompanying metadata. As these guidelines recommend, each image contains a color scale and gray scale as color and tone references and a ruler as a reference for the size of the original document. Depending on the original, the digital lab produces 400 ppi 8-bit grayscale, 400 ppi 24-bit color, or 600 ppi 1-bit bitonal TIFF images with LZW or ITU-T compression. In terms of resolution, photographic prints and film pose an exception. It is determined by the size of the original and a minimum number of pixels needed to produce a high-quality image. 8-bit grayscale images are tagged with a Gray Gamma 2.2 profile, 24-bit color images with an Adobe RGB (1998) ICC color profile.

Recommended technical and administrative metadata that is not embedded automatically during the image capture process in the TIFF image is added to fields in the TIFF header via Adobe's Photoshop software, such as the name and title of digitization staff, scanning facility (Gruss Lipper Digital Laboratory), organization (Center for Jewish History), and contact information.

The TIFF images are not post-processed. The goal is to create a digital archival master file that reproduces the original as closely as possible. During the quality assurance process, the TIFF images are inspected for orientation, sharpness, color, contrast, noise, and dust. Images failing this inspection (images that are skewed, out of focus, over- or underexposed, show digital noise, dirt, or dust) have to be rescanned. Access copies for web delivery are created either in the JPEG2000 or PDF format. JPEG2000 is a format that has an efficient compression rate allowing for the online delivery of high-resolution images into which users can zoom to appreciate fine details. This format works well with illustrated children's books, rare books and oversize materials as well as photographs. At the maximum zoom level, the full resolution and detail of the JPEG2000 image can be appreciated.

For collections consisting of mostly type-written materials, such as the Raphael Lemkin Collection, the delivery format is PDF. The files are small and load quickly and the full text of each type-written document is searchable thereby allowing users to quickly search the content of a digitized folder by keyword.

Metadata

The Gruss Lipper Digital Laboratory records descriptive, administrative, and structural metadata via a variety of community standards. It has adopted MARC 21 (*MARC Standard,* 2010) as the standard defining the structure of a catalog record and AACR2 (*Anglo-American Cataloging Rules,* 2005) as a content standard. The standards are justified since MARC records already exist in the Center's library catalog for many of the items digitized in the lab. They can easily be imported into the Center's digital asset management system using the Z39.50 protocol. The staff of the Center and Center's partners consists of trained librarians who update records when needed.

If records are created from scratch and do not yet exist in the Center's OPAC, the digital lab recommends DACS as a content standard. DACS (see *SAA: Describing Archives: A Content Standard,* n.d.) was not conceived with the space constraints of a library catalog card in mind and therefore eliminates many of the abbreviations present in AACR2, making it a more user-friendly standard in an online environment.

The lab has used MODS (*Metadata Object Description Schema.* 2010) for selected projects, but has not yet officially adopted that standard. The lab has developed cataloging guidelines for a MARC 21 digital collections minimum record and a MARC 21 digital collections core record.

The MARC digital collections minimum and core record are based on the idea of levels of description as put forth in DACS, with the minimum and core record roughly corresponding to DACS' single-level minimum and single-level optimum/added value descriptions. Particularly important is the use of controlled vocabulary. Controlled vocabulary allows for the building of browsing categories in the Center's digital collections portal, CJH Digital Collections (digital.cjh.org). These virtual collections allow users to search for relevant materials across collections and partners. Controlled vocabulary also ensures that a user retrieves all relevant materials when searching by keyword. Subject headings are taken from the Library of Congress Subject Headings (LCSH), Thesauri used are the Art and Architecture Thesaurus (AAT), and the Thesaurus of Graphic Materials (TGM).

The virtual collections in CJH Digital Collections are based on type (the lab uses genre terms to build the "collections by type" browsing hierarchy, such as "children's books," "drawings," "photographs," etc.), repository (the Center and its five partners), and provenance (title of a collection). Most recent research recommends organization by subject (Schaffner, 2009). The lab has begun this type of organization for a selected set of photographs from YIVO (subjects are Holocaust, political life, Yiddish theatre and others).

A "collection by type" to be highlighted is "archival finding aids." CJH Digital Collections hosts 8,200 EAD finding aids, many of them converted from MARC as part of a recently completed project. Our goal is that eventually all finding aids will link to digital objects, if the archival collection has been digitized. These finding aids constitute an additional access point to the digital objects.

Finally, the digital lab also uses OAI-PMH, the Open Archives Initiative Protocol for Metadata Harvesting. The use of this protocol allows for the harvesting of all MARC records in CJH Digital Collections by OAIster, a union catalog of more than 23 million records from more than 1,100 contributors. OAIster records are freely available through WorldCat.org.

Creation of MARC Records

When MARC records already exist in the Center's OPAC, as it is the case for all rare books from the LBI, they are imported into the lab's digital asset management system and adjusted in terms of genre terms and provenance to ensure they appear within the appropriate browsing category in CJH Digital Collections.

For some of the children's books from YUM, MARC records did not exist in the Center's library catalog. YUM, as the only museum among the Center's partners, has its own database that is separate from the Center's library catalog since museum objects follow different rules for description. For these books, a children's book MARC record template was created in DigiTool which was used by the lab's metadata librarian who cataloged the children's books based on the information available in the museum database. For the ASF photographs that were digitized by the digital lab, just as with the YUM children's books, no MARC records existed in the Center's OPAC. In general, not much information was available for them, which is not a surprise since photographs that are part of archival collections are rarely cataloged on the item level. The little information partners usually have about photographs at the point of digitization, call number, dimensions, rights and repository that owns them, is generally transferred to the lab's tracking database. Once digitization is completed, the data is exported from the database and converted into MARCXML and together with the images, ingested into the Center's digital asset management system. These MARC records with minimal description are designed to be enhanced, based on the lab's cataloging guidelines by partner catalogers once they have obtained the missing information, such as title, date, and other added entries.

In addition to descriptive metadata, the digital lab also creates structural metadata. This type of data is necessary for complex objects such as books, archival folders, and archival documents that consist of more than one page. Structural metadata preserves the physical and/or logical structure of such complex/multi-page objects in a digital environment. It allows users to page through a faithful reproduction of the original online. The digital lab uses METS (see *METS Metadata encoding and transmission standard,* 2010) as the standard for structural metadata.

The structure or "structural map" as it is known in METS is determined by the physical and/or logical structure of a physical item. Re-creating structures for books is less complicated and time-consuming since pages are usually numbered and chapters exist. Much more time-consuming is the recreation of the structure of an archival folder. Description usually only exists on the folder level, but a structural map for a folder reaches down to the item level. How detailed the structural map will be depends on how much description is necessary to make the content intelligible to users.

University archivists reported during the *More Product, Less Pixels* session at the SAA Annual Meeting in 2008 that students were frustrated when working with digital archival collections with no item level description. In comparison to a physical folder which can be opened up quickly and paged through, students felt that it was more difficult to determine if the content of a folder was useful to them or not. They complained about an "online microfilm experience." (see *Session 49: More Product, Less Pixels: Alternate Approaches to Digitization and Metadata,* 2008.)

Due to the relatively small size of the Raphael Lemkin Collection, the digital lab decided to facilitate users' experience and to describe the content of each folder not only on the folder level but also the item level. Folder information came from the finding aid but the item level information was supplied by the digital lab's metadata librarian. The results are extremely detailed structural maps. For example, the structural map of a digital folder containing correspondence consists of labels for each letter containing the name of the correspondent and date of creation, and all letters are organized by date.

Moreover, additional information that the lab's metadata librarian gleaned from studying the letters and particularly Lemkin's index cards and research notes was also incorporated. This was done by adding subject headings and added entries to the MARC record that is attached to each digital folder. Finally, AJHS personnel updated the finding aid with links to the digital folders.

File Management and Online Display

The digital lab manages all digital assets via the digital asset management system DigiTool, which has been designed for digital asset management in libraries and archives. It supports a variety of community standards and file formats including audio and video, supports complex objects, assigns unique and persistent identifiers to each digital image and metadata, supports basic preservation tasks such as tracking of changes to objects and metadata, saves this data as well as all other metadata in xml, and allows for digital asset management en masse, all of which reduces the risk of loss or digital obsolescence. The physical infrastructure of the digital repository is provided by a StorageTek FlexLine 210R storage unit. This storage unit currently contains 10 TB of RAID-5 storage, and a tape library system for daily backups to tape. Backup tapes are stored off-site. When it comes to storage and backup, the digital lab works very closely with the Center's IT department.

DigiTool, while primarily a digital asset management system, also powers the Center's digital collections portal, CJH Digital Collections. A variety of viewers allow for the display of all the diverse digital assets described in this chapter, such as simple objects like photographs as well as complex objects like books and archival folders. However, while the viewers are relatively sophisticated (offering zooming and rotation features, browsing by a thumbnail gallery or a table of contents created through METS), the interface cannot be customized beyond color schemes and fonts. External applications can be embedded, such as an Adobe Flash player, and whenever this is done, the Center's web designer is of great assistance. However, one has to keep in mind that DigiTool was primarily designed to manage digital assets and not to create exciting web exhibitions.

User Experience

The digital lab has gained much experience in the creation and management of digital assets. Over the last four years, it has built sustainable digital collections based on its mission to preserve them and to ensure their accessibility for the long term. However, creation and management of sustainable digital assets is only one side of digitization, the other is users' reactions to digital collections. Since early 2009, DigiTool generates reliable usage statistics which the lab started to analyze. At the same time, the lab also joined the photo-sharing website Flickr (http://www.flickr.com/photos/center_for_ jewish_history) and made user surveys available in CJH Digital Collections to obtain feedback.

Usage statistics for CJH Digital Collections reveal that on average in 2009, the site was visited by 14,500 users a month (ca. 470 people a day). Of course, certain collections are requested more often than others. Among the materials discussed in this chapter, the children's book collection ranks the highest in terms of requests, having been requested by users between 30-70 times between March – December 2009. The Raphael Lemkin Collection and LBI rare books rank second, with 20-30 requests per folder or book during the same time period, with one rare book, "Juedisches Ceremoniel" standing out, having been requested more than 78 times. Photographs of Turkish and Moroccan Synagogues are among digital objects least requested (1-10 times during the same period). The discrepancies in requests can be explained by the newness of a project and their availability by several means of access. While the children's books and synagogue photographs are projects that started three years ago, the children's books project was completed only in 2009 when it was incorporated into a bigger children's books digitization initiative. The children's books are currently featured in a virtual collection dedicated to recently completed projects in CJH Digital Collections. They are also accessible through the website of the International Children's Digital Library Foundation and 14 of them are available on Flickr, as is the "Juedisches Ceremoniel."

The Raphael Lemkin materials are accessible online in their entirety only since September 2009. However, the number of requests is high due to the publicity they received in conjunction with the November 2009 Genocide and Human Experience Conference at the Center. In the course of the advertising campaign for this conference, selected materials were featured on the conference's home page and in a dedicated web exhibition.

While the original purpose of joining Flickr was to gain feedback from users (DigiTool does not allow for users to leave comments) it became clear quickly that Flickr is also a great tool to promote the Center and partners' digital collections. The 189 images on Flickr (as of 11 December 2009) were viewed more than 12,300 times over the course of eight months. This means that on average, an image on Flickr has been requested 65 times. This is a much higher average number of requests for images in comparison to CJH Digital Collections. The lab was also contacted and asked if some images could be featured on a personal blog. Moreover, people responded to AJHS' requests to identify unknown people in photographs. Among the people who offered their help was the great-granddaughter of one of the people featured in a photograph. Users tagged images with the occasional "that's a wonderful image" remark. There were no negative remarks. Considering the feedback and number of requests per image, the Center and participating partners deemed the project a success and the uploading of images to Flickr and the administration of the Center's Flickr site has become part of the digital lab's services.

The surveys created to obtain users' reactions to digital collections in CJH Digital Collections indicate that users are generally impressed with the high quality of the images and their delivery. They show that users sometimes get frustrated, citing an inability to find what they are interested in. Users also find it difficult to get a sense for the amount of material online, their content, and how they relate to one another.

From analyzing usage statistics, surveys, and reaching out to users through Flickr we have learned that it will become increasingly important to better promote digital collections, explain more clearly to users what our digital collections are about and how they should be used, and connect with users in new ways.

Conclusion

The Gruss Lipper Digital Laboratory represents an impressive investment on the part of the Center for Jewish History. During the first two years of its operation, a grant paid for the complete refurbishment of a room making it suitable for a digital lab, the purchase of first-rate digitization equipment, and a staff of five people (a director, metadata librarian, photographer, and two part-time digital asset production associates). At this point, the Center supports a staff consisting of two full-time and two half-time positions: one director, one metadata librarian, and two photographers/digital asset production associates. There are additional costs for necessary and continuous upgrades and investment into software, hardware, and data storage as digital collections continue to grow. The cost of continued education for staff as digital technologies evolve also has to be factored in. Finally, technical support that is lent to a digital lab by an institution's IT department must be part of any lab's budget considerations.

Because of these high costs, a state-of-the-art digital lab requires sustained support from stakeholders. These stakeholders have to have an understanding of the challenges that maintaining a digital program brings and an understanding of the basic concepts behind digital preservation. With this support and a professional and standards-based program for digital image capture and digital management as represented by an in-house digital laboratory, the groundwork is laid for the building of a trusted digital repository (RLG/OCLC Working Group on Digital Archive Attributes, 2002), the long-term goal of any digital program.

For the investment it represents, an in-house digital lab like the Gruss Lipper Digital Laboratory brings tremendous benefits. When developing new digitization projects an institution can draw on experienced staff. The digital assets remain under an institution's control, they can be accessed at any time, and there are no access restrictions because rights to the digital images have not been given to a vendor. The high-quality digital images can be used for many different purposes, ranging from web exhibitions to printing and publishing. The professional administration of a digital asset management system ensures that digital assets are managed safely and securely. No file is lost, even years after a project's completion. Strict adherence to community standards ensures that files can be migrated to different formats if the need arises and that data can be exchanged with other systems. The result is digital collections whose hallmarks are usability, portability, and longevity.

There is much more to digitization than just image capture. It includes metadata, standards, digital asset management, online delivery and users' experience, all of which require expert knowledge for creating useful and sustainable digital collections. If long-term preservation of digital assets is part of an institution's mission and if that institution remains abreast of new digitization developments and technologies, an in-house lab is well worth the investment.

References

Anglo-American Cataloging Rules, Second Edition, 2002 Revision, 2005 Update. (2005) Chicago, IL: American Library Association.

Fair use (2009). Retrieved December 11, 2009, from U.S. Copyright Office website, http://www.copyright.gov/fls/fl102.html

MARC standards. (2010). Retrieved December 11, 2009, from the Library of Congress – Network Development and MARC Standards Office website http://www.loc.gov/marc/

METS. Metadata encoding and transmission standard (2010). Retrieved December 11, 2009, from the official web site http://www.loc.gov/standards/mets/

MODS. Metadata object description schema. (2010). Retrieved December 11, 2009, from the official web site http://www.loc.gov/standards/mods/

Orphan works: Statement of best practices (June 2009). Retrieved December 11, 2009, from Society of American Archivists' website http://www.archivists.org/standards/

RLG/OCLC Working Group on Digital Archive Attributes (2002). *Trusted digital repositories: Attributes and responsibilities.* RLG,

May 2002. Retrieved December 11, 2009 http://www.rlg.org/en/page.php?Page_ID=583

SAA: Describing archives: A content standard (DACS) (n.d.). Retrieved on May 1, 2010 from http://www.archivists.org/governance/standards/dacs.asp

Schaffner, Jennifer. (2009). *Metadata is the interface. Better description for better discovery of archives and special collections, synthesized from user studies.* Retrieved December 11, 2009, from the OCLC website http://www.oclc.org/research/publications/

Session 49: More product, less pixels: Alternate approaches to digitization and metadata. (2008). SAA Annual Meeting, August 26-30, 2008.

Technical guidelines for digitizing archival materials for electronic access: Creation of production master files – raster images. (2004). Retrieved December 11, 2009, from the National Archives website http://www.archives.gov/preservation/technical/guidelines.html

Building a Virtual Library – A Case Study at The Library of The Jewish Theological Seminary

Naomi M. Steinberger
(The Library of The Jewish Theological Seminary)

Abstract

The goal of this chapter is to show how a medium-size research library with rich resources in special collections has succeeded in the past decade, in building a digital library. The chapter focuses on building a strategic plan for a digital library and assessing The Library's collections for digital readiness. Planning the digital library includes making many decisions ranging from software, prioritizing collections to digitizing, metadata schemas, and more. Funding for digitization can be grants, gifts in kind where the funder provides the institution with a digital photographer, to funders who want a specific collection digitized. There is a discussion of some of the challenges such as hardware capability and staffing. The important lessons learned through experience and plans for the future of the digital program are discussed.

Keywords: Assessment, Building digital collections, Digital collections, Digital library, Digital project funding, Medium-size academic library, Metadata for digital collection, Strategic planning, Virtual library.

Background

The mission of the Jewish Theological Seminary, the intellectual and religious center of Conservative Judaism, is twofold: to serve as the pre-eminent center for the academic study of Judaism outside of Israel, as one of the pre-eminent centers world-wide, and as a training center to advance that study; and to educate Jewish professionals and lay leaders in the spirit of Conservative Judaism for the total community through academic and religious programs, both formal and informal.

In accordance with the Seminary's overall goals, The Library's mission is to collect, preserve and make available the literary and cultural heritage of the Jewish people. The collection includes 25,000 rare books, 11,000 manuscripts, 400 archival collections, and many other historically significant items. Among the particular strengths of its collection are its 35,000 fragments from the Cairo Genizah (representing the lives of Jews and others in the eastern Mediterranean from the 11th to the 19th centuries), its collection of ketubot (Jewish marriage contracts)—the largest in the world—and its unparalleled collection of Passover haggadot (the traditional text of the holiday, combining narrative and ritual). The Library is also home to the world's largest collection of Hebrew incunabula (early books printed before 1501).

The Special Collections are open to students and researchers from around the country and the world. Scholars of Jewish history specializing in virtually any period or place rely on the Library's unique holdings. Scholars of American Jewry are particularly reliant on The Library's archives. The Library is also the center for scholarly dialogue within The Jewish Theological Seminary (JTS) and the focal point for numerous public events devoted to Jewish culture and books.

Currently, The Library employs 15 librarians, five subject specialists and eight support staff. JTS has 40 faculty and 200 staff serving 500 students. In fiscal year 2010, after budget reductions, The Library's operating budget of $1.7 million plus approximately a half-million dollars in designated funds each year. Budget designated to digital collections is lest than $12,000 per year.

In The Library's 2005 strategic plan, digitization is emphasized as a method of preservation of the original item, because "more damage is done to rare materials through human handling than by any other means." "The more readers can gain access to images of rare materials and forego handling the materials themselves," the document continues, "the better they will be preserved." (Strategic Plan, 2005.)

Large external digitization projects such as The Google Book Project (*Google Book*, 2010) and the licensing of the Otzar Ha-Hochma collection of 19,000 fully-digitized Hebrew Books and HebrewBooks.org are viewed as efforts to take care of the need to digitize modern printed books, allowing the Jewish Theological Seminary library to focus resources on only digitizing materials unique to the library's collection.

Digital Library Strategic Plan

After successfully completing a number of small digitization projects it was clear that a strategic direction for The Library was necessary. In November 2005, we participated in the "Persistence of Memory: Stewardship of Digital Assets" conference presented by the Northeast Document Conservation Center (NEDCC) and partially funded by the Institute of Museum and Library Services (IMLS). At that conference, Tom Clareson, from PALINET, was soliciting libraries to participate in a study funded by the IMLS to assess institutions "digital readiness". JTS volunteered and became one of the sample institutions for this study.

Two members of the project team, Tom Clareson (Program Director for New Initiatives, PALINET) and Richard Kim (then Digital Projects Manager, Metropolitan New York Library Council), served as the project evaluators. The assessment entailed completion of a detailed survey that posed questions about the existing digitization environment, plans, hardware, software, and digital preservation, included was a site visit. During the site visit, discussions were held with people responsible for selection of items for digitization, creating metadata, scanning technicians, conservators, reference librarians and administrators and the JTS IT department. The outcome of the completed survey and the meeting were the basis of a strategic plan for The Library's digital program.

The key interests of the library administration and staff were to determine the best way to manage the existing and future digital assets; evaluate current status of access to digital materials; to develop strategies for future digital projects and funding for those projects; and to begin to look at the sustainability of digital projects within The Library's digitization program.

The assessment report outlined the following recommended (Clareson and Kim, 2006):

- Identification and selection of priority collections to be digitized, including the development of a written "Digital Collection Development Policy."

- Identification of the primary and secondary audiences for the existing and future digital collections of JTS.

- Exploration of existing standards in content creation and metadata.

- Consideration of upgrades to digitization equipment for future projects, as well as exploration of working with digitization vendor services.

- Adoption of a library-wide set of digital procedures.

- Working with a metadata consultant to make sure "retrospective" metadata and the metadata for future projects allows researchers to easily reach the JTS digital collections.

- Exploration of the utilization of a digital asset management system to deliver JTS images to its constituents and to the world.

- Adoption of handling guidelines for materials to be digitized.

- Documentation of current digital preservation practices, and working with a collaborative or third-party digital archiving service.

Implementation of the recommendations began with a document outlining potential unique collections to be digitized followed by guidelines for standards in content creation and metadata and establishment of library-wide digitization procedures. Decisions were made regarding the upgrade of existing metadata. A digital assets management system was licensed and there were explorations regarding digital preservation services.

JTS, as a small academic institution could not support an open sources system, such as DSpace (*About DSpace*, n.d.) or Greenstone (*Greenstone Digital Library Software*, n.d.). Our IT staff is too small and turn over was too high in both the IT department and The Library. We wanted to host our digital assets locally. We had a long-standing relationship with ExLibris, as we run the ALEPH500 system at The Library. A decision was made to license DigiTool (*ExLibris Digitool*, n.d.), their digital assets management system.

One of the significant unique collections identified for digitization were the audio-visual collections. These recordings, in multiple obsolete formats, are completely inaccessible it is therefore imperative for us to digitize. They include musical recording, lectures, films and other unique and unidentified materials.

With recommendations from the digital assessment in hand The Library applied, and was awarded, funding from the National Endowment for the Humanities (NEH) to assess the audio-visual. This assessment conducted by specialists in the field of sound preservation, in combination with cross-training of staff with responsibilities related to the sound collections, has provided the best foundation for conserving primary sound materials and converting them, when necessary, and using the best technology to more contemporary media.

The Library created an inventory of the collection, conducted an assessment of the current status of the collection with sound consultants Chris Lacinak, President of AudioVisual Preservation Solutions, and Kevin O'Neill. An assessment report was produced and staff was trained to handle the audio-visual collections and manage preservation of the collections. (Lacinak and O'Neill, 2008)

With the recommendations of AudioVisual Preservation Services, The Library has moved forward to the next step as laid out in the assessment report. We are seeking funding to gain physical and intellectual control of the sound collections. We have prioritized the preservation of certain collections; and have prepared selected items for reformatting. Once funding is secured we will be able to perform necessary conservation, reformatting, provide for digital preservation and make the recordings available on the web.

One of the most significant issues with which we need to grapple is the recommendation of AudioVisual Preservation Services to develop in-house capability for the reformatting of our sound collections. This will require commitment from The Jewish Theological Seminary to build capacity for reformatting on site in the existing and underutilized sound studio. The institution would need to repurpose the space and commit to allocating funding to acquire equipment and staff the lab. The Report states that it would take eight years to complete the reformatting of The Library's collection.

Subsequent to the funded assessment of the sound collection, The Library received a large gift of a significant ethnomusicological collection and submitted an application for the processing and reformatting of these sound collections.

We received a grant from the Metropolitan New York Library Council (METRO) to digitize a collection of 250 wedding poems, unique poems composed for wedding parties, particularly in Italy during the 17th-19th centuries. One of our staff members was familiar with DigiTool and he was successful in bringing up the system, with the Wedding Poems on schedule in January 2008.

Setting guidelines and standards for the presentation of the digital library generated debate amongst the staff. A standing committee for creation of the Digital Collections met regularly to set guidelines and monitor the development of the digital collections. The committee consisted of the Director of Library Services, Administrative Librarian for Technical Services, Administrative Librarian for Special Collections and the Systems and Digitization Librarian. Guidelines were set for a digital file naming convention; for the quality of the digital image, and the web interface for the digital library. Importantly, decisions were made as to the level of metadata, how the metadata would be presented (DigiTool presents metadata in Dublin core), where the metadata should be created, if none existed, and the extent to which existing metadata needed to be upgraded.

It was determined that The Library would only digitize materials that were not under copyright. The exceptions to this are student undergraduate senior theses and master's theses where we have permission from the students to post their work.

Funding opportunities

Digital project comprise of a number of parts, namely, metadata creation, digitization of the objects, and bringing the objects up as part of the digital library. Each component is labor intensive, and therefore costly. One of the major costs that cannot be carried as part of the library's budget is the actual digitization of materials. As a result external funding and partnerships are required for each special project or collection. Funding has been obtained from various sources, including public funding, private foundations, non-for-profit organizations and individuals.

Two assessments have been completed and a third in process with grants from public sources. The digital readiness assessment was funded by an IMLS grant awarded to the NEDCC. The NEH funded the assessment of the audio-visual collection. Currently we are evaluating the effectiveness of the use of our digital library with funds from METRO who receives the funding from New York State.

Individuals have donated funds to digitize specific collections such as the bookplate collection, the Solomon Rosowsky Field Recordings fro pre-state Israel (1936 and 1938) and the recordings of Cantor Samuel Hallegua from Cochin, India (1967-1968). This was all achieved through unsolicited funds. Each of the individuals either had a connection to the collection (the Hallegua recordings) or were interested in the subject areas (book plates and field recordings).

Funding has been received in exchange for "in kind" services. The Library's entire collection of 35,000 fragments from the Cairo Genizah, literally a hidden treasure. These documents are a storehouse of documents found in a synagogue Cairo at the end of the

19th century. They were digitized through an international project, the Friedberg Genizah Project, where photographers were sent to The Library to work on site, but were paid directly by the external project.

A private foundation had particular interest in digitizing specific "treasures" from The Library's collection. This enabled us to digitize a number of The Library's most valuable and important illuminated Hebrew manuscripts including the Esslingen Mahzor (Ashkenaz, 13th century), subsequently loaned to the Metropolitan Museum of Art during 2008-2009 and the Rothschild Mahzor, (Florence, 1490).

Funding for specific projects enable us to select the materials and scale the project accordingly. When we began digitization in 2000 we selected materials that could be digitized on a flat bed scanner. The National Foundation for Jewish Culture awarded funding to digitize items related to Jewish American culture. With two grants we digitized 350 newspaper clippings from the US press from the 18th and 19th centuries and 100 unique pamphlets from the late 18th and 19th centuries. With funding from METRO in 2008 we digitized 250 wedding poems. With current funding from METRO we are digitizing diaries, in 25 volumes, belonging to the great Jewish theologian Mordecai Kaplan.

Building Digital Projects

The "NINCH Guide to Good Practice in the Digital Representation and Management of Cultural Heritage Materials" (The NINCH Guide to Good Practice in the Digital Representation and Management of Cultural Heritage Materials, 2002) served as a guide for planning specific projects. It emphasizes the many components necessary to create a successful digital project. Over the past decade, The Library has learned through experience to improve the methodologies, workflows, image and digital file formats and minimum metadata necessary to create a successful and sustainable for digital projects. Each project has served as a building block for improvement.

A medium-size academic library cannot sustain a full service digitization lab with cameras, scanners, audio conversion equipment, that quickly become obsolete. The acquisition and maintenance of technical equipment fell outside our core mission. Our collection includes extraordinarily rare materials that cannot leave the premises. Items on parchment cannot leave the temperature and humidity controlled environment of the rare book room and special reading room for extended periods of time.

We did purchase a flat bed scanner, a digital camera with lights and a book scanner. Most of this equipment is out of date but still serves us well for in-house work.

Libraries are experienced in creating metadata for bibliographic description of books and other materials. We need to apply those methodologies to the digital object and learn how descriptions of digital materials differ, or do not, from description of the physical object. We have retooled and learned different metadata schemas commonly used for digital collections such as Dublin Core (Dublin Core Metadata Initiative, 2010) and MODS (Metadata Object Description Schema, 2010).

Prioritizing Projects

Because of the rarity and research value of the collections, many institutions approach JTS with invitations to participate in collaborative digital projects. Some funding sources have approached the institution about specific digital projects. While prioritizing which collections should be digitized funding organizations and individuals approach The Library with their projects and request our participation.

The following questions need to be asked before partnering: Would a project provide complimentary materials to JTS holdings? What collaborations are possible? How important and useful are the items to users? How does one assess usefulness?

The physical condition of the item, the ease and method of digitization all play a role in prioritization. Do you digitize the "popular" favorites of The Library or do you make little know, hidden and inaccessible collections available? When approached by a funding group with a specific project how do you evaluate the project in relation to overall library priorities?

The Library's goal is to present a broad range of digital materials reflecting the breadth of its collection. To date we are presenting books, manuscripts, musical scores, sound recordings, archival finding aids, flat items, pamphlets, and little know and inaccessible collections such as the wedding poems and bookplates.

Early Projects

The Library's early digitization projects were flat objects (newspaper clippings), pamphlets which were saved as .pdf files (American Judaica pamphlets from late 18th and 19th centuries) or digitization from slides and transparencies (ketubbah—marriage contract – collection).

Funding was secured for the digitization of the newspaper clippings and the pamphlets and for the purchase of a flat bed scanner. The files were all saved as .pdfs. Metadata existed in The Library's ALEPH500 catalog. The .pdf files were loaded onto the ALEPH server and links were made within the bibliographic record utilizing the MARC 856 field.

Access to unique visual materials was a high priority. The ketubbah (Jewish marriage contract) collection comprises of more than 500 contracts, many of which are illuminated or illustrated. 35 mm slides or 4 x 6 transparencies were available for about 450 of the contracts, all were cataloged. A slide and transparency adapter was purchased for the flat bed scanner and they were easily scanned in three sizes, thumbnail, medium and large. Each of the three files were saved on the ALEPH server and then linked to the bibliographic record. Users have access to the small, medium and large sized of each of the marriage contracts.

Partnership Projects

Partnership projects give us the opportunity to have large collections digitized with external funding and to utilize technology that is not available in The Library. Crafting a partnership agreement has been one of lessons learned over the past five years. One of the important issues emerging from these partnership projects, is control of the images. The partner may have a copy for use, generally on their site, but JTS must own the images. Quality of the images is also an area of concern with partnership projects.

We have participated in three major partnership projects each with successful outcomes but not without challenges.

Genizah fragments: A partnership agreement was signed with The Friedberg Genizah Project (FGP) to digitize the 35,000 fragments from the Cairo Genizah owned by JTS. These documents, discovered at the end of the 19th century are "a collection of fragmentary Jewish texts stored in the loft of the ancient Ben Ezra Synagogue in Cairo, Egypt between the 8th and 19th centuries. These manuscripts outline a 1,000-year continuum of Middle-Eastern history and comprise the largest and most diverse collection of medieval manuscripts in the world." The FGP was established to facilitate and transform Genizah research by identifying, cataloging, transcribing, translating the fragments, rendering them into digital format (i.e., photographing) and publishing them online. (Genizah Project, Executive Summary, n.d.)

FGP hired digital photographers with state of the art digital cameras to produce 600 dpi color images of the 35,000 fragments in The Library. They funded staff to prepare the material for digitization, work with the digital photographers, re-shelve the material and document the work. The photographers shot images for about four months. All the fragments were shot with targets that included their local identification number. The digital images were delivered in "dng" format for the repository copy and in .jpg format for access. They are available, with registration, on the FGP site. JTS holds an internal access copy but has not made it public because of the limited metadata accompanying the image.

Lessons learned from this first partnership project: In order to successfully complete a major digitization project one must seize an opportunity. This was an outstanding opportunity to digitize the 35,000 Genizah fragment. The project was driven by the funder. They determined the items to be digitized, the method of digitization, the choice of photographer, the rate of digitization, etc. There was no specific budget for the completion of this work nor was there a designated time-frame. Work commenced and continued at a swift pace until it was completed. The funder's representative wanted to be involved in The Library's internal workflow. Often work was rushed and not adequately planned. The most significant issue is that there is no metadata for the Genizah fragments and the material is not freely available. Only scholars who register, and are accepted by, the FGP may search the information.

Library "treasures": There was another funder who selected items which he was interested in digitizing, supplied the photographer (who was approved by The Library) and delivered digital images in TIFF format. While this project was funder driven, it supplied The Library with images of some of its greatest manuscripts such as the Rothschild Mahzor (MS 8892) from Florence, 1490. A separate site, Special Treasures from The Library of The Jewish Theological Seminary (http://jtslibrarytreasures.org/) with turning the page technology was launched. Only 50 of the 450 leaves are on display on this site. The site also includes other digitized manuscripts from the collection, which are available with full metadata, on The Library's digital library in 2008.

Rare book digitization: A project to digitize very rare books, incunabula and 16th century books, was completed during the fall of 2009. This project reaped the benefits of our experience. As this was not a comprehensive project, books needed to be selected, posing a more complicated workflow. The goal was to digitize only unique books that had not been digitized by other libraries. Once they were identified, the condition of the book was checked with guidelines from the paper conservators. The books were digitized on a Zeutschel OS12000 book scanner in black and white. Each book needed to have a wide enough opening so that the image could be shot. A ruler was placed on each page. All the books were cataloged and the file name for the digital image was the ALEPH (our ILS) system number for the book. The bibliographic records were retrieved from ALEPH. Hebrewbooks.org, the organization that was performing the digitization, delivered the digital images in tiff and pdf formats. We loaded the pdf files to our server and are now in the process of loading them to digital library. We exported the metadata and delivered it to

Hebrewbooks.org as they are loading the pdf files and metadata to their collection of full text religious books in Hebrew which to data total more than 40,000 titles.

Lessons learned: We took far more control over the steps of this project. The external funder did however chose the equipment used, we would have preferred to digitize the books in color, utilizing a digital camera. At the beginning of the project the digitization technician was trained by The Library's paper conservator in order to ensure careful handling of each book. Greater control over the choice of materials, the way the materials were handled and preparation of the metadata made this a successful project. During November 2009 92 rare books were digitized.

Outsourcing

We have no capacity to digitize sound at JTS. We have digitized two musical collections working with two external sources. One collection was digitized by a private sound engineer and the other project went to the lab at the Center for Jewish History, a non-for-profit organization that had until our request, not digitized for other institutions. This proved to be beneficial for them as it provided them with some income during a "down" period in their digitization lab. Plans are underway to send an archival collection, comprising volumes of diaries, to the studio of a digital photographer that we have worked with on numerous occasions.

The output of the digitization of the 252 Solomon Rosowsky Field Recordings collection was in .mp3 format. We requested an archival output. This resulted in a raw and sometime difficult to hear output. The metatdata for this collection, created in an Excel spreadsheet, was created at the time of digitization and is not part of the catalog as they are a subsection of an archival collection.

The quality of the sound the Hallegua collection, digitized in 2009, proved to be far more successful. Partnering with the Center for Jewish History and utilizing their digital lab we accepted their recommendations and created archival .wav copies and access .mp3 copies. The quality of the work completed in the second project is clearer than the first project. Metadata is yet to be created for this collection. Once it is available we will make the collection accessible.

Library initiated project:

When we have the luxury of planning and implementing a digital project on our own terms we have learned that this is the ideal situation for us. The digitization of manuscripts from a pre-selected list has been the most successful project, from a digitization point of view, that we have embarked on. We selected important manuscripts that had no surrogates. The processes of the project were reviewed by a project team who included: paper conservators, conservation assistant, curator, special collections reading room staff, systems and digitization librarian, heads of technical services and special collections and director of library services as chair. The goal was to look at the entire scenario of bringing in a digital photographer to shoot 4,000 manuscript leaves over a two-week period. We planned the space for digitization, the spreadsheet of targets, the physical targets, workflow for pulling items and reshelving them, assistance for the digital photographer, metadata for the manuscripts, and plan for bringing up the digital objects in the digital library.

The planning meeting raised questions from all the stakeholders. If there were any outstanding questions, all stakeholders were later updated on the answer or resolution. Meeting with the entire group enable everyone involved to know exactly who had a stake in the project. It allayed any fears and anxieties. Bringing the team together enabled a smooth process for the preparation of the materials for digitization, the actual digitization and the preparation of the metadata. The final piece, bringing the digital objects up in the digital library posed other problems regarding staffing.

Challenges

Much has been accomplished but not without challenges. Hardware and software capacity, staffing and funding are all issues that we continue to grapple with.

Capacity issues

The capacity of The Library's server that stores digital objects and the capacity of the library's license for its DigiTool installation are both limited. Issues related to capacity entail actual storage of the digital images. Often one has different manifestations for a single image or multiple images for a single document – for example, for a five-page document that was shot as a RAW file there are TIFF images, which in turn may generate JPEG files and also a PDF.

The number of version of the same document that one needs to keep is determined by capacity. There is the repository server where one stores the images. The number of manifestations that are saved there may be determined by the institution's capacity. One must work with those responsible for the institution's servers.

Staffing

Staffing is key to the success of each digital project. The key to building a successful team for the digital library is for each team member to be cognizant of their specific role in the project.

The team consists of **curators** who select materials for digitization. The selections are determined by funding, importance, fragility of the item, value of material, or by other criteria.

Once the items are selected they need to be assessed by the **paper conservators** (for items on paper and parchment). They look at the physical stability of the item. They can recommend if an item can be digitized, with recommended equipment (scanner, book scanner, photographer). They can also recommend if an item needs to be encapsulated in Mylar before digitization, and/or if an item needs to have a conservation assistant working with the photographer throughout the shoot.

Special collections staff is responsible for pulling and shelving books. They need a complete and accurate list of the items to be scanned. For a longer-term project, they need to prepare materials each day to be digitized and materials that need to be reshelved. If the project is based on a list of items found in a certain collection, they may often need to search for the item.

Digital photographer or scanner. Generally, this person is not part of The Library's staff, but is an outside contractor or a temporary worker hired to do the specific work. They need to be integrated into the working environment of The Library, which may include the physical location of the equipment, the rules and hours of the special collection reading room.

Technical assistant to assist the photographer with turning pages, preparing the shoot, and other needs surrounding the shoot.

Cataloger and metadata librarian needs to review the current metadata for the object and make appropriate adjustment to the metadata for the digital library based on the standards established. Some of the metadata added include genre, collection, and location of digital object. In some cases the metadata needs to be upgraded, but this is subject to great debate amongst library staff. In most cases it depends on the amount of existing metatdata and the object in hand.

Systems and digitization librarian – Needs to export metadata and deliver it to the cataloger and metadata librarian and needs to prepare the materials for ingest into the digital library.

Since the existence of the JTS digital library, in January 2008, we have had three systems and digitization librarians. Because of the staff turnover, it has been challenging to complete many of our digital projects and make them available online. Since October 2009, with a new person in this position, new workflows are being documented and the actual ingest of digital objects is being completed by other members of the staff under the guidance of the systems and digitization librarian, rather than by the person holding that position. The position has evolved, with the initial incumbent successfully building and launching the digital library. The digital library was launched and there were initial documents added to the collection, there was no documentation of the processes used which left the second person in a difficult situation. There was little activity in loading objects during that year. With the third person hired in the fall of 2009 it was clear that the first step was to create workflows and to clearly document them for others to follow and for The Library to have in order to successfully maintain the digital library. Lessons learned: stop and document what you are doing and share the documentation and the work.

From Digital Projects to a Digital Program

As we move into the second decade of digitization these are some of the strategic directions that we need to address.

Assessment: With funding from METRO, The Library will assess the effectiveness of its digital collections in DigiTool. A survey is currently being built and will be posted on the site and sent out to a wide group of constituents. The plan is to implement recommendations from the survey, add new collections to the site, most notably the Mordecai Kaplan diaries, and then survey the effectiveness at the end of the grant period. We hope that this assessment will help guide us in our work.

Documentation: We are documenting the workflows that we are establishing for the creation of digital collections. With the documentation, and with adequate funding, we will be able to hire staff to work on building the digital collections.

Digital preservation: In the winter of 2008 we participated in the Sustaining Digital Preservation workshop funded by the IMLS. We also attended a METRO meeting in the fall of 2008 focused on digital preservation. Conversations have begun with ExLibris about their new digital preservation software. We need first and foremost to obtain the commitment of the JTS administration to invest in digital preservation. This is challenging, considering the serious nature of the institution's finances in wake of the economic downturn in the US. Little work has been done at JTS to address these needs.

New projects, improving workflow, increasing capacity, increasing staff to enrich with metadata are all necessary aspects of a successful digitization program. Our hope is that with creativity, imagination, thoughtfulness and good luck, organizations drawn to the uniqueness and richness of our collections will continue funding The Library of The Jewish Theological Seminary in this important work.

References

About DSpace. (n.d.). Retrieved March 9, 2010 from http://www.dspace.org/about-dspace/introducing/

Clareson,Tom and Kim, Richard. (2006). *Digital Program Survey Final Report from April 5, 2006 Visit.*

Dublin Core metadata initiative. (2010). Retrieved March 30, 2010, from http://dublincore.org

ExLibris DigiTool. (n.d.) Retrieved March 9, 2010 from http://www.exlibrisgroup.com/category/DigiToolOverview

Genizah project, executive summary. (n.d.) Retrieved March 30, 2010, from http://www.genizah.org/about-Executive_Summary.htm.

Google Books. (2010). Retrieved March 13, 2010 from http://books.google.com/

Greenstone digital library software. (n.d.). Retrieved March 9, 2010 from http://www.greenstone.org/

Lacinak, Chris and O'Neill, Kevin. (2008). *Sound Recording Consultation Final Report,* June 26, 2008

Metadata object description schema. (2010). Retrieved December 11, 2009, from the official web site http://www.loc.gov/standards/mods/

Strategic Plan. (2005). *The Library of The Jewish Theological Seminary. 2005.*

The NINCH guide to good practice in the digital representation and management of cultural heritage materials. (2002). Retrieved May 9, 2010 from http://www.nyu.edu/its/humanities/ninchguide/

Local Objects, Local People, Local History: Creating the Wisconsin Decorative Arts Database

Emily Pfotenhauer (Wisconsin Heritage Online, Wisconsin
Historical Society and the Chipstone Foundation)

Abstract

The Wisconsin Decorative Arts Database is a digital collection of three-dimensional artifacts from the collections of historical societies and museums throughout Wisconsin, hosted by the Wisconsin Historical Society and supported by the Chipstone Foundation. Since 2006, the project has documented nearly 1,000 examples of furniture, ceramics, textiles and other decorative arts made by early Wisconsin craftspeople and held in the collections of over 40 institutions throughout the state. This case study examines the genesis of the project, the photographic standards and metadata specifications established for object documentation, and the unique challenges of developing a diverse digital collection of museum artifacts from a wide variety of local and regional institutions.

Keywords: Artifacts, Collaboration, Historical societies, Local history, Metadata, Museums, Photography

In the past decade, the work of state- and regionally-based digitization programs across the country has resulted in an explosion of local history resources available online. These initiatives are collaborative efforts among libraries, archives, and museums to make their collections freely available to a broad audience of students, teachers, historians, and genealogists. Some of the earliest and most influential of these programs include the Maine Historical Society's Maine Memory Network, the Minnesota Digital Library, and the Colorado Digitization Project (now known as the Collaborative Digitization Program at the Bibliographic Center for Research). For the most part, programs such as these have focused on what some museum professionals refer to as "the flat stuff": photographs, books, manuscripts, and other two-dimensional materials. This focus on the digitization of archival materials belies the fact that three-dimensional artifacts form the core of the collections of most local historical societies and museums. Moreover, the everyday objects people create and consume (for example, furniture, clothing, and tools) are considered by many scholars to offer significant evidence for historic research, as much if not more so than historic photographs or original manuscripts. Yet most institutions participating in collaborative digitization programs have not made their collections of three-dimensional objects available online at the same rate as their two-dimensional holdings.

Case studies of statewide and national digitization programs reveal the challenges common to most collaborative digital endeavors, regardless of the types of material being digitized. Roberto (2008) describes the lack of consistent standards in place for describing collections among even the largest and best-staffed museums in Great Britain. When collaborations are expanded to include small, local historical societies and museums, the creation of consistent collections data becomes even more challenging due to a lack of available staff, resources, and expertise (Rowe & Barnicoat, 2009). These obstacles are compounded when working with three-dimensional objects, which require more space, equipment, and technical expertise to photograph and more research and subject expertise to catalog.

This chapter examines the development of one digital collection of three-dimensional objects from multiple institutions: the Wisconsin Decorative Arts Database (http://content.wisconsinhistory.org/decorativearts). This project was initiated in 2006 by the Wisconsin

Historical Society and the Chipstone Foundation of Milwaukee, a private foundation for the study of American decorative arts and material culture. Chipstone and the Society had three goals in mind at the outset of the project: 1) to bring to light objects held in the collections of Wisconsin historical societies and museums and share them with a broader audience, 2) to document examples of furniture, ceramics, textiles, and other decorative arts made by nineteenth and early twentieth-century Wisconsin craftspeople in order to reveal settlement patterns and the persistence of handicraft traditions in the state, and 3) to add the first three-dimensional artifacts to Wisconsin Heritage Online (http://www.wisconsinheritage.org), a research portal that brings together a diverse range of digital collections from Wisconsin libraries, archives, museums, and historic sites.

The Wisconsin Decorative Arts Database is founded on the work of a multitude of "real world" individuals—the staff and volunteers at local historical societies and small museums throughout Wisconsin who work to preserve and share their collections, as well as the men and women who built the chairs, stitched the quilts, and threw the pots that are recorded in the database. In addition, the story of the Wisconsin Decorative Arts Database is a highly personal "real world" story for me, as the project grew out of my interest in the material culture of my home state.

The seeds were planted in 2005 while I was a graduate student studying American furniture and decorative arts in the Department of Art History at the University of Wisconsin-Madison. The time had come for me to choose a subject for my master's thesis research, and I wanted the opportunity to study objects hands-on and up close. I decided to focus on furniture made in the community of Mineral Point, an important early trade center in southwest Wisconsin—as well as the town where I grew up. During the year I spent researching and writing my thesis, I unearthed a surprising amount of locally-made furniture still surviving in both public and private collections and met numerous Mineral Point residents dedicated to preserving their community's distinctive history.

This search for furniture made in Mineral Point caught the attention of the Chipstone Foundation of Milwaukee. In 2006, Chipstone approached the Wisconsin Historical Society with the idea to create an expanded fieldwork program that would include furniture, ceramics, textiles, and metalwork made by craftspeople throughout Wisconsin between 1820 and 1920. From the beginning, a central focus of both Chipstone and the Society was to make these findings freely available to the public in digital form. Both institutions were already leaders in the digitization of cultural heritage materials — Chipstone with its *Digital Library for the Decorative Arts and Material Culture* (http://digital.library.wisc. edu/1711.dl/DLDecArts), developed in collaboration with the University of Wisconsin Digital Collections Center, and the Society with a number of innovative digitization efforts including the award-winning *American Journeys* (http://www.americanjourneys.org) and *Turning Points in Wisconsin History* (http://www. wisconsinhistory.org/turningpoints)—so a digital database of museum collections was a natural extension of both institution's missions.

I was appointed as Chipstone's Charles Hummel Fellow to manage all aspects of the initiative—fieldwork, photography, research and writing as well as the structure and organization of the digital collection. As my background was in art history, not digital collections, I had a great deal to tackle in order to create an effective online resource. What kinds of materials would be included and how would they be located? How would each object be imaged? How would users search the database? What kinds of metadata should be included? And what exactly was metadata, anyway?

Fortunately, a few pieces of the puzzle were already in place. The Wisconsin Historical Society would host the collection in CONTENTdm, a content management system already in use by the Society's Library-Archives division. Wisconsin Heritage Online (WHO), a developing statewide digitization program, would also harvest the collection into its central web portal. WHO's *Metadata Guidelines* (2006) provided a useful introduction to creating and organizing digital content, as did the Collaborative Digitization Program's *Dublin Core Metadata Best Practices* (2006). However, these guidelines were established specifically for images and text-based materials, not three-dimensional artifacts.

Translating information about chairs, quilts, and pots into the standardized fields recommended by existing guidelines was a bit like trying to fit square pegs into round holes. Developing a crosswalk or a systematized data import process was impossible, because no two museums or local historical societies handle cataloging in the same way. In fact, many institutions do not even use a digital collection management system, instead relying on typed index cards or handwritten ledgers to catalog their collections.

I developed a standard set of metadata elements based on WHO recommendations, mapped them to the fields defined by the Dublin Core (http://dublincore.org/documents/dcmi-terms), and assigned customized local field names. For example, the Dublin Core Creator element became a local "Maker" field, while Dublin Core's Format.medium became a field called "Materials and Techniques." In addition to providing images and physical descriptions of each documented object, a central focus of the project was to place each artifact in its historical context by conducting research on the biographies of makers and owners as well as design influences and cultural meanings. This goal called for the creation of multiple Dublin Core Description fields: one for physical description, one for historical information, and one for the citation of research sources.

Another key cataloging decision was the selection of a controlled vocabulary appropriate to the database content. Because it is built into PastPerfect Museum Software, a popular content management system, *The Revised Nomenclature for Museum Cataloging*, aka *Chenhall's Nomenclature* (Blackaby, Greeno, and the Nomenclature Committee, 1995) is used by many local historical societies and small museums in Wisconsin. However, the Getty Research Institute's *Art and Architecture Thesaurus* (http://www.getty/edu/research/conducting_research/vocabularies/aat) provides more nuanced and specific terms for decorative arts objects. A significant level of granularity is required to accurately assign object names and subject headings in the database. Using *Chenhall's Nomenclature*, a chair can be described primarily according to function, e.g. "Chair, Dining" or "Chair, Side." The AAT allows for more precise descriptions of form and style. For example, a chair can be distinguished as a bow-back Windsor chair, a fan-back Windsor chair, or a sack-back Windsor chair. While the differences may appear minute to a general audience, these kinds of distinctions are essential to the work of decorative arts scholars and collectors. — A revised and updated edition of Chenhall's Nomenclature, Nomenclature 3.0, offering a greatly expanded vocabulary for the description of museum artifacts, was released in late 2009. Future subject headings provided in Wisconsin Decorative Arts Database metadata may incorporate terms from this new edition.

One major question remained before any fieldwork could begin: how to create quality digital images of objects that not only varied widely in size and format but were scattered across the state? Just as few institutions could offer detailed digital catalog records for their collections, few had the resources or expertise available to image their collections extensively, if at all. In addition, as with its metadata guidelines, the WHO *Digital Imaging Guidelines* (2006) addressed the scanning of two-dimensional materials almost exclusively and offered little support for photographing three-dimensional objects. Much of the available documentation on imaging museum artifacts, such as Stanford University's Digital Michelangelo Project (Levoy & Garcia-Molina, 2000) and the work of the Graphics Lab at the University of Southern California's Institute for Creative Technologies (Hawkins, Cohen, & Debevec, 2001) centered on the creation of complex three-dimensional digital renderings using multiple cameras and laser scanning.

It was necessary to develop a simple, portable imaging approach so that photography could be completed quickly (to adapt to the limited schedules of volunteers and busy staff) and unobtrusively (to accommodate the often cramped storage quarters of small institutions). I arrived at my photographic process through a combination of consultation with professional photographers and on-site trial and error. Jim Wildeman, a photographer based in Madison, provided a basic introduction to artifact photography. Selecting the right equipment for the job was essential. The Chipstone Foundation funded the purchase of a Canon Rebel XTi digital SLR camera as well as a tripod, a remote shutter release, a neutral gray paper backdrop and backdrop stand, and two stationary tungsten lights on adjustable stands. Indispensable incidentals included a long extension cord, tape measures (both fabric and metal), white cotton gloves for handling items, and cloths and brushes for removing dust from artifacts. The entire photography kit could be packed into the trunk of a car and quickly set up on location. Participating institutions need only to provide an electrical outlet and suitable working space.

After the framework of the digital collection was laid out and procedures for photographing and cataloging artifacts were determined, on-site work could begin. Based on my experience with local historic sites and individual collectors in Mineral Point, I knew that putting out a general call for material via an email listserv would yield minimal results. It was much more effective to contact each potential contributor directly, usually with an introductory email or letter and then a follow-up phone call to discuss possible objects before scheduling an in-person visit. Once on site, objects were selected for documentation based on the availability of documented provenance, oral history associated with the item, or stylistic similarities to other known objects.

I began my fieldwork with two familiar sites from my graduate research: the Mineral Point Historical Society and Pendarvis, the Wisconsin state historic site in Mineral Point. Starting with these sites gave me the opportunity to refine my documentation techniques in a comfortable environment. I could take as long as I needed to make minute adjustments in lighting or re-measure the dimensions of a chair or flowerpot. I connected with the next three participants, all mid-sized regional museums, via word-of-mouth recommendations: the Neville Public Museum of Brown County in Green Bay, the Chippewa Valley Museum in Eau Claire, and the Sheboygan County Historical Society.

After working with this handful of pilot institutions, it was clear that the phrase "decorative arts," while a common academic term, was something of a stumbling block for potential participants. Some possible contributors read the phrase too narrowly, expressing concern that the objects in their collections were not "decorative" enough, while others interpreted it too broadly, hoping to include items manufactured outside of Wisconsin but used locally or objects that lacked any known history whatsoever. At the same time, I was discovering many artifacts that did not fit my original parameters but were of compelling historical significance.

Although the title of the database remained the same, the selection criteria were adapted to accommodate objects that offered important evidence of Wisconsin craft practices and industrial development, even if they did not fit into an academic definition of the decorative arts. For example, the staff of the Historic Blooming Grove Historical Society in Madison contacted me about their collection of materials from the Frank J. Hess and Sons Cooperage, one of the last manufactories in the nation to produce hand-hewn white oak beer barrels. While not "decorative arts" in the traditional sense of the term, the Hess barrels reveal a fascinating story of an immigrant craftsman who brought a traditional European craft practice to Wisconsin, adapted it to the local environment, and passed it on to a second generation (Holland, 1966).

Although I received a number of word-of-mouth recommendations and direct contacts, most database participants were located through the Wisconsin Historical Society's *Directory of Wisconsin Local History Organizations* (http://www. wisconsinhistory.org/localhistory/directory). The Society's local affiliates include more than 350 county historical societies, local historical societies, community museums and historic house museums. The vast majority of these institutions are run by volunteers or a tiny cohort of part-time staff. Many are open to the public seasonally and for limited hours, sometimes as little as one or two weekends each month. This meant that arranging access to collections hinged on flexible scheduling and the willingness of staff and volunteers to open their doors during non-public hours.

The fieldwork process, an in-person visit to select, photograph, and document individual objects, is the most rewarding, yet also most exhausting, part of the project. From September 2006 through June 2009, I logged over 10,000 miles traveling to sites across the state. I sifted through all manner of collection storage facilities, some meticulously organized and others packed to the gills with artifacts piled on shelves and stuffed in boxes. I handled thousands of artifacts and toured all kinds of historic buildings. Most excitingly, I met dozens of people who were passionate about their work, dedicated to preserving the history of their communities, and eager to share their collections with new audiences.

Depending on the number of items selected for documentation, a site visit can last from a few hours up to two or three full days. Preparing the material to post online takes much longer. A series of graduate and undergraduate interns from the Material Culture Program and the School of Library and Information Studies at the University of Wisconsin-Madison have helped support this phase of the project. Basic editing procedures, including cropping, sharpening, and color balancing, are performed on each image using Adobe Photoshop or ACDSee. Images and corresponding metadata are uploaded directly to the Wisconsin Historical Society's CONTENTdm server.

A central mission of the database is to establish an historic narrative for each artifact by investigating the history of the object's maker and owner as well as its cultural significance and formal influences. Due to the myriad of primary source documents and other historic material now available online, a major portion of this research has been conducted solely in the digital realm. The most useful sources for biographical and genealogical information proved to be the Wisconsin Historical Society's *Genealogy Index* (http://www.wisconsinhistory.org/vitalrecords), offering pre-1907 birth, death, and marriage records for the state of Wisconsin, and the full-text-searchable *Wisconsin County Histories* (http://www.wisconsinhistory.org/ wch). The commercial website Ancestry.com was also valuable for searching federal census records.

Participating institutions are required to sign a Memorandum of Understanding that authorizes the Wisconsin Decorative Arts

Database to photograph objects and publish those photographs and associated metadata online. Each institution receives an archival-quality CD containing the image files and retains full rights to those images. (A second CD, along with any paperwork generated during the research process, is archived at the Wisconsin Historical Society and the digital images are backed up on the Society's servers.) For the most part, participants have readily agreed to these terms. However, a few have expressed concern about making material from their collections freely available online, citing either a desire to retain control over digital images or a fear of theft of the physical collection. In most cases, these fears were abated with the argument that the benefits of participation—particularly the increased opportunity for exposure and publicity—outweigh the risks.

Participation offers historical societies and museums the important benefit of an increased online presence. Most participating institutions maintain their own websites, but many lack the resources to fill these sites with substantive information about their collections. To increase online exposure, each contributor is clearly identified at several points in the database. The metadata for each catalog entry includes an "Owner" field as well as a rights statement with a link to the institution's own website. The opening page offers users the option to browse the database by selecting a specific participant's collection. Another page functions as a directory of content contributors, with an image and description of each institution as well as a link to their own website.

Two popular free web features—a blog hosted by WordPress and a gallery on the photo-sharing site Flickr—supplement the database and extend its presence online. I use the blog, Wisconsin Object (http://wisconsinobject.wordpress.com), to chronicle my travels and announce when new content has been uploaded to the database. It also provides a venue for more lengthy examinations of selected artifacts and makers. The Wisconsin Decorative Arts Flickr gallery (http://www.flickr.com/photos/wisconsindecarts), which is linked from the blog, presents examples of recently uploaded database content. While not numerous, user comments on both the blog and the image gallery have provided an important window into the audiences for this material and the types of objects they find most compelling. For example, the most-viewed image on Flickr is a colorful beaded bandolier bag made by Great Lakes Indians in the late nineteenth century, now in the collection of the Wisconsin Historical Museum. A corresponding blog entry on the cultural significance of bandolier bags is one of the most popular posts. Users who have commented on the blog or added the image to their own Flickr galleries include craft hobbyists and collectors—two major audiences that were not considered at the outset of the project.

The Wisconsin Decorative Arts Database's regional approach to material culture research is nothing new. Since the 1970s, researchers throughout the United States have worked to document decorative arts made locally and held in local collections. Most notably, the Museum of Early Southern Decorative Arts (MESDA) in Winston-Salem, North Carolina established a fieldwork program in the 1970s and 1980s, supported by the National Endowment for the Humanities, to locate artifacts made by craftspeople working in seven southern states before 1820 (Niven, 2001). This research yielded a vast paper-based archive of photographs and files that now serves as an indispensable resource for scholars studying the material culture of the American South.

While modeled on the work of MESDA and other statewide fieldwork initiatives, the Wisconsin Decorative Arts Database is the first program of its kind to be created entirely in digital form. An online database of regional artifacts offers a number of advantages over a paper archive or a published catalog. New content can be added continually, revisions can be made in response to new research, and related materials can be brought together via hyperlinks. Moreover, making collections available digitally helps small, local cultural heritage institutions remain relevant to students, historians, and other audiences whose research is grounded in the ready availability of online resources.

Since 2006, nearly 1,000 catalog entries have been added to the Wisconsin Decorative Arts Database, representing artifacts from the collections of 40 historical societies and museums throughout

Wisconsin. In September 2009, the database was recognized with an Award of Merit from the American Association for State and Local History. With financial support committed by the Chipstone Foundation and the Kaufman Americana Foundation through June 2011, the program will continue to unearth important evidence of early craft production in Wisconsin. In addition to adding new content, explorations are underway to develop creative ways to expand and promote the project, including both online and bricks-and-mortar exhibitions and publications.

References

Blackaby, J. R., Greeno, P., & The Nomenclature Committee. (1995). *The revised nomenclature for museum cataloging: A revised and expanded version of Robert G. Chenhall's system for classifying man-made objects.* Walnut Creek, CA: AltaMira Press.

Bourcier, P., Rogers, R., & The Nomenclature Committee. (2009). *Nomenclature 3.0 for museum cataloging: Third edition of Robert G. Chenhall's system for classifying man-made objects.* Walnut Creek, CA: AltaMira Press.

Collaborative Digitization Program Metadata Working Group. (2006). *Dublin Core metadata best practices* (version 2.1.1). Retrieved from http://www.bcr.org/dps/cdp

Hawkins, T., Cohen, J., & Debevec, P. (2001). A photometric approach to digitizing cultural artifacts. In *Proceedings of the 2001 Conference on Virtual Reality, Archeology, and Cultural Heritage*, 333-342. New York: Association for Computing Machinery. doi: 10.1145/584993.585053

Holland, R. (1966). The last wooden beer barrels. *Wisconsin Tales and Trails 7*, 12-16.

Levoy, M., & Garcia-Molina, H. (2000). *Creating digital archives of 3D artworks [White paper submitted to the National Science Foundation's Digital Libraries Initiative].* Retrieved from http://graphics.stanford.edu/projects/dli/white-paper/dli.html

Miller, S. J. (Ed.). (2006). *Wisconsin Heritage Online metadata guidelines* (version 2.0). Retrieved from https://wiheritage.pbworks.com

Niven, P. (2001). Frank L. Horton and the roads to MESDA. *Journal of Early Southern Decorative Arts, 27*, 1-147.

Roberto, F. (2008). *Exploring museum collections on-line: The quantitative method.* In J. Trant and D. Bearman (Eds.), *Museums and the Web 2008: Proceedings.* Toronto: Archives & Museum Informatics. Retrieved from http://www.archimuse.com/mw2008/papers/roberto/roberto.html

Rowe, P., & Barnicoat, W. (2009). *NZMuseums: Showcasing the collections of all New Zealand museums.* In J. Trant and D. Bearman (Eds.), *Museums and the Web 2009: Proceedings.* Toronto: Archives & Museum Informatics. Retrieved from http://www.archimuse.com/mw2009/papers/rowe/rowe.html

Digitizing the Rare Book Collection of the Leo Baeck Institute

Renate Evers (Leo Baeck Institute, New York)

Abstract

The article focuses on typical problems encountered during the establishment of a digitization program for rare books at a small special library – from finding the best solutions for rare book cradles to organizational and technical challenges and pitfalls.

Keywords: Digitization, Judaica Collection, Rare Book Collection, Special Library

The Library of the Leo Baeck Institute: A Medium-sized collection

The Library of the Leo Baeck Institute (LBI) in New York is internationally recognized as the most comprehensive repository for books documenting the history and culture of German-speaking Jewry. Over 80,000 volumes and 900 periodical titles provide important primary and secondary material. Most of the collection deals with central European Jewry during the nineteenth and early twentieth centuries. It also includes material dating back as far as the 16th century and is as current as the Jewish population in Germany today. The focus of our collection is on the diverse culture of German-speaking Jewry, especially in the arts, sciences, literature, philosophy, and religion. The Institute was established in New York in 1955, one of the largest centers of the exiled German-Jewish community. In 2000 the Leo Baeck Institute became part of the Center for Jewish History, an umbrella organization for 5 Jewish research institutions.

The Rare Book Collection of the Leo Baeck Institute

The Rare Book Collection of the Leo Baeck Institute (LBI) consists of ca. 2,000 volumes primarily in the field of German Judaica, dating from the earliest period of printing in the 15th century and continuing through the annihilation of European Jewry under the Third Reich. Rich in rarities ranging from early 16th century writings to Moses Mendelssohn and Heinrich Heine, first editions and dedication copies of works by more recent prominent writers, many of its volumes were salvaged from famous Jewish libraries that were confiscated and dispersed by the Nazis. In many cases these primary sources cannot be found anywhere else in the world. An important part of the rare book collection is a collection of illustrated and art books. Among them are many limited editions of twentieth century artists' portfolios and several illustrated eighteenth century books on Jewish customs. The Institute also has a significant collection of books dealing with "Science of Judaism" (Wissenschaft des Judentums). The emergence and establishment of modern Jewish scholarship in the 19th and 20th century in Germany and Europe became the cornerstone and predecessor of Jewish Studies.

Project: Digitizing the Rare Book Collection of the Leo Baeck Institute:

The goal is to digitize the rare book collection in order to make these exceptional primary sources easily available to researchers on and offsite, and to minimize use of the originals. To begin, the focus is on titles which are in highest demand.

We started a pilot project with a selection of 38 books in 2005 when the Leo Baeck Institute was awarded one of the first grants in the newly established Metro Digitization Grants Program. The experience gained in this project enabled us to continuously enlarge our digital rare book collection. Working closely with scholars in the field and using feedback from our users in order to identify a meaningful selection, so far we have successfully digitized 167 rare books (about 22,000 pages) from our rare books collection. Among those books are 33 illustrated and art books which were funded by another Metro Grant awarded in 2008. By now we have worked out the technical details and workflows for our digitization program and are identifying new funding sources in order to continue the process. Newly digitized books are continually being added to our digital management system and made available on the Internet.

Future projects: in 2008 the Archives at the Leo Baeck Institute embarked on an interesting new project - "DigiBaeck," which is destined to put all LBI archival holdings onto the World Wide Web in close cooperation with the Internet Archive. In this framework we consider to digitize parts of our book collection as well. Besides, we are collaborating with other libraries and have applied for shared digitization projects.

Web interface and Examples

The digitized books are accessible through the web interface of our digital management system Digitool (*Ex Libris the Bridge to Knowledge, 2010*). The books can be retrieved via a search interface or can be browsed by various categories. Searchable are the bibliographical data and the full-text, most of the books underwent OCR (optical character recognition).

Additionally we reference the digital objects in our online library catalog records by adding the URL in MARC field 856 (see *856 - Electronic Location and Access*, 2003.)

Challenges

This chapter focuses on the challenges faced and solved mainly during the implementation of LBI's digitization program in 2005/2006 as well as during follow-up projects. The problems were typical for projects which engage in new technologies, ranging from technical to organizational hurdles. Some of the difficulties which we encountered were connected to the special medium rare books.

Challenge 1: Outsourcing a Digitizing Project

Choosing the right vendor, developing a set of criteria for finding the right vendor including testing of sample files, negotiating a contract, monitoring and testing the results proved to be a very challenging endeavor.

During the selection process for a digitization vendor, we developed the following set of criteria and asked vendors to submit a proposal with information and price quotes for the following areas:

- Master files (TIFF) 300, 400, 600 ppi in bi-tonal, grayscale and color
- Derivatives (jpeg, jpeg 2000) 300, 400, 600 ppi in bi-tonal, grayscale and color
- Scanning oversized materials, foldouts
- Technical and structural metadata
- File naming
- Cameras used
- Book cradle
- File storage and delivery
- OCR (Optical character recognition)
- Insurance
- Security (handling of books, security of lab area, book tracking system, etc.)
- Shipping and delivery
- Quality control
- Other costs
- References

We provided vendors with samples from our collection and asked them to provide us with scanned images and metadata. The scanned images underwent a quality check, the metadata was checked against standard recommendations. The best thing to do would have been to load the sample files into our digital management system, but at the time of our vendor negotiations our digital management system was not yet fully implemented.

Overall we compared the vendor proposals and the samples very thoroughly, especially the price quotes for different scanning scenarios, the setups of the scanning labs, the quality of the scanned images, and the vendors' ability to produce structural metadata for our digital management system. The determining factors were the book cradle solutions and security features (e.g.: handling of books, security of lab area), the quality of the scanned images, the ability to provide complex metadata as well as the price differences.

During the negotiation process we encountered variations of important technical details (e.g. file types, file naming, cameras used, technical and structural metadata, OCR) which helped us to make decisions which we then incorporated in the final contract. The contract spelled out our decisions in the listed areas. We learned that it is very advisable that the contract describes as many technical details as possible.

Challenge 2: Medium Rare Bound Books from Previous Centuries

One of the biggest challenge to digitize rare books from previous centuries is the fact that flatbed scanning is usually not an option since bindings cannot be removed for the scanning process. Rare books in our collection are usually treated as artifacts, the content is as important as the bindings and physical appearances. Older books are often very tightly bound and cannot be opened 180 degrees, it is very common that they can only be opened 90 to 120 degrees.

Many of the scanning services which we approached were only equipped for flatbed scanning and declined to take on projects with bound books. Commercial solutions explicitly for rare book cradles do not seem to exist. Those few vendors we encountered which also scan bound books usually built or customized their own solutions for rare book cradles. Some used commercial book cradles for modern books which can be opened 180 degrees and added features to make them suitable for books which cannot be opened 180 degrees. Others vendors constructed adjustable boards to hold the books in place without applying pressure during the scanning process.

The Gruss Lipper Digital Laboratory at the Center for Jewish History designed and uses two book cradles, one cradle has a fixed 90 degree angle, the other one a 120 degree angle. The cradles are made of acrylic and covered with black velvet. Velcro straps keep the book in place. The use of 2 "fixed" angle cradles turned out to be a simple, but successful solution.

The different book cradles which we encountered represent different solutions for accommodating books which can only be opened at an angle less than 180 degrees. It is hard to make a general recommendation for a best solution. Depending on the type of books and condition of their bindings some cradles are better or less suited for the task of supporting fragile bindings and spines and of exerting as little pressure on the books as possible. For some books it is possible to use glass plates, but glass plates put too much pressure on most of the books. It is a trade-off - if glass plates cannot be used it very often results in shadows which often cannot be removed through the adjustment of the lightning. Overall those solutions which had a support for both front and back bindings were better suited for our specific collection.

Rare books require additional manual handling time in securing the volume after each page is turned which makes the process more costly than scanning regular books.

Challenge 3: Technical and Structural Metadata for Compound Objects:

Not all scanning vendors are capable to provide the necessary technical and structural metadata for compound objects. During our search for a scanning service in 2005/2006 we realized that digitization vendors came from different backgrounds – photographers, microfilming companies, library services, bookbinders, etc. – and were thus often not aware of or capable of adjusting to emerging library best practices and standards. Many of them were able to deal with single digital objects and equipped to deliver the technical metadata, but not able to provide ready-to-go structural metadata in order to build complex digital objects.

Our digital management system DigiTool (Ex Libris) requires the use of METS (Metadata Encoding & Transmission Standard, 2010) for storing structural metadata along with descriptive, administrative, technical and other kinds of metadata in an XML "wrapper." During our vendor search in 2005/2006 we found out that at that time many vendors were not aware of or capable to provide this type of metadata with the scanned images. If the scanning process is outsourced it is very advisable that the vendor provides structural metadata at the same time, otherwise it becomes a very tedious and time-consuming endeavor to match the digital objects to a structure map afterwards. During the testing phase we asked the vendors to supply us with metadata, preferably METS. During our initial project we could only find one vendor who could provide us with METS files. During the first phase of our project we additionally discovered that we needed a translation code between the METS ALTO version that the vendor could create and the METS ALTO version that our digital management system understood.

Challenge 4: Organizational Parameters & Limitations of Digital Management Systems

We had the "problem" that we had to use a digital management system which was chosen by our umbrella organization and which was not fully implemented at the time when we started our digitization program. The challenge was to bridge shortcomings of the system and shortcomings of what digitization vendors could provide, a typical problem when a technological field has not yet developed mature and commonly accepted standardization guidelines. The first versions of our digital management system did not accept structural METS files in METS ALTO standard, so we had to find additional funding for developing a translation code between METS ALTO (what Vendors were able to produce) and the METS "dialect" that our system understood, which resulted in higher costs.

Organizational set-ups and the choice of the technical system have a great influence on the direction and the outcome of a project. These factors cannot be underestimated and they influence the timeline and the financial framework of a digitization project.

Challenge 5: Keeping up with Evolving Digital standards

One of the challenges we faced in follow-up projects was to keep up with evolving and maturing guidelines for digitization. One of the lessons learned was that it is necessary to spell out technical requirements in detail in a contract and to make sure that they are applied, and not to take them for granted. General formulations can lead to ambiguous interpretations.

Example 1: An area of dispute in one of our project was if it is "allowed" to enhance or sharpen master files during the scanning process.   Many labs follow the NARA guidelines (see National Archives, 2004) and do not apply ANY sharpening or other "enhancements" during capture or to master files.   If errors are detected during the capture, then the camera is calibrated. One of the vendors enhanced the master files instead of calibrating the camera. Our contract read: "Quality of image: Files will be inspected for sharpness, image contract, density and faithfulness to original and improved if necessary."   - that should have only be allowed for derivatives, and not for master files. The master files should be true to the original materials; colors and contrast of the digital files should represent accurately the original pages. Many of the master images had too much contrast (visible in bad histograms) which probably came from sharpening during the scanning.   In that respect our contract was not specific enough, we did not specify that only derivatives could be altered, but not master files.

Example 2: It proved to be necessary in our 2008 project to spell out in the contract to check regularly if the calibration of the camera results in an accurate image. In our contract we had specified that the images produced should be "faithful to the original" materials. The colors and contrast of the digital files should represent the original pages accurately.

Our first vendor calibrated the camera only once at the beginning of the scanning process to the "default" NARA guidelines. The results were aggravating: the majority of the image files had extensive color bleeding, a severe image quality problem. Ultimately we had to rescan our books at another digitization facility.

Our contract was sufficient in the sense that we could rightfully claim that the bad image results were a breach of contract. But we had to rescan all our books – something which is definitely not advisable for rare books. A line in the contract about periodic camera calibration could have prevented this dilemma. We should have also done quality checks periodically.

Lesson learned: The contract texts for projects in emerging technological fields are often vague and only give a narrative description of the wanted outcome since various schools of thought exist in terms of technical specifications.

In many cases a narrative formulation in the contract about the desired outcome is the only possible way to address an area of concern, but in some cases it is not sufficient. The more hardcore technical details can be specified in a not ambiguous way the better. It is also very advisable to control the project frequently, to do several test phases, and not to rely on past vendor performances.

Conclusion

The successful implementation of our digitization program was and is based on a combination of persistence, serious initial testing, vendor comparison, ongoing testing of results, questioning of vendors, collecting of technical information, balancing of outside factors, changing of vendors when the outcome did not meet our expectations. The most challenging aspect of our rare book digitization project has been the steep learning curve of getting into the technical intricacies of creating digital content, and balancing outside factors to get the project on its way and moving. The most rewarding aspect has been to make hitherto relatively unaccessible books accessible to a broader audience.

An important lesson learned was that is necessary to keep up with evolving and maturing guidelines for digitization – and to make sure that they are really applied, and not to take them for granted. Even established workflows have to be reevaluated from time to time, since the field changes all the time, and the technical details become more detailed and sophisticated. Digitizing of rare books is a very manual, labor, and ultimately cost intense work.

References

856 - Electronic Location and Access. (2003). Retrieved May 9, 2010 from http://www.loc.gov/marc/bibliographic/bd856.html

Ex Libris the bridge to knowledge, Overview. (2010). Retrieved March 15, 2010, from http://www.exlibrisgroup.com/category/DigiToolOverview

Metadata Encoding & Transmission Standard. (2010). Retrieved May 9, 2010 from http://www.loc.gov/standards/mets/

National Archives. (2004). *Technical guidelines for digitizing archival materials for electronic access: Creation of production master Files - raster images*. Retrieved May 9, 2010 from http://www.archives.gov/preservation/technical/guidelines.html

The Caprons of Paris: A Digitization Project in a Small Library System

Misty De Meo (County of Brant Public Library)

Abstract

The County of Brant Public Library set out with the goal of documenting the history of the founder of the town of Paris by digitizing a collection of his original papers. By building contacts within the community, the Library was able to successfully complete its initiative and open new avenues for future projects. The equipment and digitization methods used are described, with a special emphasis on the methods in which the Library was able to circumvent its small budget. The Library's complementary local history wiki, and the project's methods of promotion, are also described.

Keywords: Digital collection, Digitization, Historical society, Local history, Marketing, Web 2.0, Wiki

Introduction

One of the key goals of the County of Brant Public Library is to act as a gateway providing the most accessible routes to information. The County of Brant Public Library Digital Collections was envisioned as a means by which local historical information which was currently unknown or inaccessible to most members of the community could be made easily and publicly available. The goal of this project was not merely to provide information, but to provide the means by which the community could interact with history and share information.

The County of Brant, located in southern Ontario, is a diverse collection of unique communities, each with its own history. It has a modest population of 34,415 divided among 30 distinct communities, formerly separate municipal entities, spread out over 843 km² (Statistics Canada, 2006). The Library has five branches spread throughout the County. It was impossible for a single project to document the County as a whole. This digitization project was designed as the first part of an ongoing digitization program which would eventually represent the entire "community of communities" that makes up the County. The short-term goal was to document the history of the town of Paris, the largest community in the County of Brant, through its founder Hiram Capron; the long-term goal was to build an ongoing program documenting all of the communities in the County, using the Capron project as a method to open doors and create momentum.

The keys to the success of this project have been *technical flexibility* and *innovation*, which enabled success within a modest budget, and community engagement, which provided the support, contacts, and materials necessary to grow a small project into a pair of ongoing initiatives.

Project selection

The Library evaluated a number of potential project partners when planning this project, from communities across the County. Unfortunately, for various reasons, we were not able to work with all of the local historical societies we approached.

Most importantly, we needed a critical mass of original materials – a body of materials large enough to form a hypothesis as the basis of a project. Local history is exponential – pursuing a sufficiently large collection of materials leads to new collections and new potential partners. While many potential projects had seemed promising, a number proved to be unsuited to this project on examination; some collections were small and lacked that force behind them which we felt was necessary to give us an "in" to the community, while others proved to contain many inauthentic items and reproductions which were unsuited to this project, which was focused on original primary historical documents.

An ideal project was eventually found in the Paris Museum and Historical Society, whose archives hold a large body of original documents. Hiram Capron, the town's founder, is an important figure in the history of Paris and is almost unusual in that his legacy is by and large authentically supported by the documents the museum holds. The museum was willing to consider a partnership, and provided the Library with open access to its Capron collection. At the time of the agreement, approximately 50 items were identified for digitization in the project. The "critical mass" criteria proved apt: at the time of writing (March 2010) the Library has digitized a collection of over 425 items, provided by the museum and by new contributors, as a part of the Hiram Capron project and further projects. By beginning with the founder of Paris, we have been able to broaden the perspective to provide a wide variety of materials about the town's history and to forge partnerships with new donors.

Several historical societies have expressed concern of retaining ownership and control over their items. One of the necessary keys to developing partnerships was to show potential project partners that digitization could enhance the value of their collections and their services, rather than replace them. Our partners at the Paris Museum and Historical Society have reported that their visits have increased since the launch of the digital collections websites.

Management and staffing

The project involves three key members of the Library. The Library's CEO, Gay Kozak Selby, originated the project and secures funding from outside sources; she performed initial project planning, research, and hiring with the library's e-resource librarian, Christine MacArthur. Christine was also responsible for day-to-day management and co-ordination of promotion. Scanning, technical management, and design of promotional materials was the job of the professional archivist, Misty De Meo.

In addition, the project has made use of shorter-term student workers in order to handle particular extra tasks and features. In the summer of 2009, the Library employed a university student using funding from Young Canada Works to provide transcriptions of a large number of handwritten documents in the Capron collection in order to make the full text searchable online. Other projects of this nature are anticipated in the future.

Funding

Funding was provided through the Library Strategic Development Fund, an ongoing grant operated by the Ontario Ministry of Tourism and Culture with the goal of assisting innovative projects and community development. The Library was one of the recipients for the 2008-2009 grant, receiving $18,405. This grant was critical to the success of the project; it could not have gone forward without external funding. It provided for equipment costs, the hiring of a professional archivist to supervise and perform digitization, and some of the project's operating costs. The total operating budget was $35,000, with the remainder of the budget paid by the Library. Summer student work has been funded though Young Canada Works, a program operated by Canadian Heritage. The Library's primary website was provided by a grant from Knowledge Ontario.

Content Management System

A number of factors influenced the selection of the content management system used by the host for the digital collection. These included ease of use and intuitiveness of user interface; advanced user interface features; searchability; and accessibility through external search services, such as Google. While the Library holds a license to use SirsiDynix Hyperion, we felt that it was insufficient for our needs after evaluating a neighboring institution which had used it (King Township, 2008). Its interface is somewhat cumbersome and simplistic; we decided that its "look" would turn off a large number of visitors. It also lacks advanced features for object descriptions or supplementary viewing options, such as contextual maps or "zoomable" image views. Perhaps most importantly, its results are not available through Google – we recognize that most of our potential visitors will be using tools other than our own built-in search engine to discover content, and so leaving our content out of Google needlessly keeps our content away from interested visitors.

In the end we selected a website toolkit called VITA created by the Our Ontario division of Knowledge Ontario, a local organization which provides a variety of digital services and content. Our Ontario, which focuses on providing access to digitized historical materials, provides grants to small organizations and so we were able to obtain use of the software and hosting free of charge.

Our visitors have generally been impressed with the advanced features VITA makes available. One of the most popular features is its Google Maps integration. Each item can be tagged with a set of coordinates that will cause a Google Maps widget to display below the item. We have used this extensively with items such as historical maps, which allows us to display a modern image of the town centered on the same location as the map. Another popular feature is the integrated "Zoomify" software, which allows the user to zoom in to an oversized item at greater levels of detail, or to pan and rotate. An item which demonstrates both of these features is available at http://images.ourontario.ca/brant/details.asp?ID=68322

VITA is also designed around modern Web 2.0 search methods; consequently, in addition to its own built-in search, it makes all of its content available via Google and permits material access and sharing through RSS and social networking sites (Knowledge Ontario, 2009). Thanks to this, our VITA site features prominently on the first page of Google results for key terms such as "Hiram Capron". Our site makes significant use of user-interaction features, encouraging users to comment and contribute information. Many items contain "mystery questions" inviting users to submit information that is missing about an item.

Our Brant: local history, local voices

The project, as originally planned, comprised only one digital history site displaying primary documents. Since then, we have made the decision to launch a second local history website at the same time as our primary site, currently available at http://ourbrant.wikia.com/ As materials and contributions for our primary site were being prepared, it became clear that a great deal of information would not be appropriate for inclusion in the primary site. As is almost certainly the case with most established communities, much of the history of Paris has by this time become a matter of tradition which is not entirely substantiated by the remaining documentation.

The goal of the primary Digital Collections site was to provide original historical documents, photographs and other items in a digital format, both for the purposes of historical research and to allow people to learn about the town's history. For this second audience, it was especially important to provide peripheral materials which slotted each item into the "narrative" of historical events in order to build understanding, which was achieved both through item descriptions and through explanatory photo essays. However, because the site is focused on the documents and historical evidence more than the story, it has been considered very important that the narrative presented is not at odds with the historical documents and that it does not make assertions which are not supported by the documents. We were further interested in enhancing interaction with our users and clients; we felt that the Web 2.0 style interactive features in the VITA website software was one of its greatest strengths, and we looked for further opportunities to enable this kind of interaction within our communities.

As a result, it was decided to add a second site to the project. The goal was to provide an appropriate location for people from the County to document the area's history as they personally understood it. With a focus less on hard historical facts and records, it would provide an appropriate place to record these popular anecdotes of local history. Hence, we defined the primary goal of this site as providing a place for anyone from the county to share their personal histories.

Based on this goal, we decided to provide spaces for the following types of content: (1) Personal memories and life stories; (2) Family histories; and (3) Profiles of notable local residents, buildings, and organizations.

The wiki format was judged to be most appropriate for this application due to the ease with which it facilitates collaboration and open contributions with a relatively low barrier of entry for new users. The wiki format was also judged appropriate due to the abundance of services which provide free hosting, such as Wikia (http://www.wikia.com/), as this would eliminate a financial barrier to the creation of the site.

While we have found other local history wikis during the planning process, we have not found another site with the same focus and consequently much of Our Brant's design is entirely original. Many sites we have found focus on locations as grounding points for memory, such as Placeography (http://www.placeography .org/) and Zurbu (http://zurbu.net/), while a few others, such as the Wagga Wagga Local History wiki (http://waggalocalhistory. wetpaint.com/), focus on events. Furthermore, a number of these wikis are not open to the public for editing, such as the Alexandrina Local History Wiki (http://alexhistory.pbworks.com/) or the Montana History Wiki (http://montanahistorywiki.pbworks.com/). Our Brant differentiates itself from these other services by providing open access for editing to any registered or anonymous users, and by placing a strong focus on individual history and personal memory rather than using the anchors of locations and subjects.

Input Methods

Ease of editing was considered to be one of the most important features. Many of the residents in Paris and the County who are interested in sharing local history are not very comfortable with computers. Despite the familiarity of Wikipedia, it is not simple to create pages without using a special markup language (Baker, Hoover & Rose, 2009); given our probable audience, this was not considered acceptable. While Wikia includes a rich text editor which abstracts markup language from the user on individual pages ("Rich Text," 2009), it does not automate elements such as page structure or link structure. We chose to adopt the forms-based input system used by Baker et al. on Placeography, which presents the user with a simple set of input boxes and checkmarks using software called Semantic Forms. Once submitted, the result is an attractive, professional-looking page without requiring the user to employ any markup language.

Another benefit of the Semantic Forms software, and the Semantic MediaWiki software on which it is based, is the ability to perform queries on the information entered in form fields (Semantic MediaWiki, 2009). Our Brant uses this extensively to build the index pages which allow users to browse the site's content. Because these indices are based on queries, they update in real time to include newly added content; this has simplified page creation by eliminating the need for users to create links to their pages (e.g., see Figures PARIS -1 to PARIS-3).

The community pages provide the central browsing interface to the site's content, using queries to aggregate together all content which is marked as belonging to this community. Each community page also contains links to the forms for creating new pages, and each individual page contains an "edit with form" link which allows it to be altered using the same form interface.

Participation

Baker, Hoover and Sherman (2009) note the importance of building a community in order to create a successful wiki, and we took their lessons to heart when preparing Our Brant. We approached local community members about contributing to the site prior to its launch; these included the president of the historical society we partnered with as well as stakeholders in the area's history, such as the owner of the historic Asa Wolverton House in Paris. In addition, we drew on our own resources and digitized transcripts of oral history interviews that the Library had conducted in the 1970s and 1980s. This allowed us to present the site at launch with a significant amount of content to attract users and to provide examples of what they could contribute.

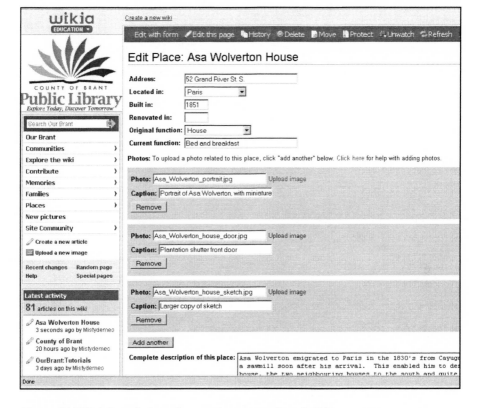

Figure PARIS-1 Sample form for creating a page for a building

Figure PARIS-2 The result page

Memories	People
▪ John Anderson	▪ Syl Apps (hockey player and Conservative MP)
▪ Mrs. Ernie Buck, Marge McCorkindale, Mr. & Mrs. Andy Leishman, Alice & Andy Scott	▪ Hiram Capron (founder of Paris)
▪ Edith Carnie	▪ Walter Capron (Hiram Capron's nephew)
▪ Tom Cocker	▪ Alma Duncan (artist)
▪ Clara Farr	▪ Ron Eddy (current mayor of the county)
▪ Gord Gibson, councillor	▪ Hugh Finlayson (first mayor of Paris and tanner)
▪ Eleanor Hardie	▪ Norman Hamilton (prominent early businessman)
▪ Bob Hasler, president of the Paris Museum and Historical Society	▪ John Penman (owner of Penman's Mills)
▪ Margaret Laing, librarian	▪ Ted Reader (television chef)
▪ Norma Leighfield, reeve	▪ Jay Wells (hockey player)
▪ Muriel and Jack Pickell, owners of the Paris Star	▪ Robert West (boat renter, entertainer, and eccentric)
▪ Corydon C. Randall	▪ William West (poet and owner of the Nith Navigation Co. boat rental company)
▪ Jackie Remus	▪ Charles Whitlaw (miller and mayor)
▪ Kay Riddolls, nurse	▪ Paul Wickson (artist)
▪ Dale Robb	Click here to add a person if you don't see someone on the list.
▪ Foster Scott, teacher	
▪ Mel Sharpe, mayor	
▪ D.A. and Isobel Smith	**Places**
▪ James Thomson, Penmans employee, and wife	
▪ Police Chief Watts	**Churches**
▪ Shirley Williams, from Qua family	▪ Paris Baptist Church
▪ Leonard Wise, owner of Harry Wise Menswear	▪ Paris Presbyterian Church
Click here to add your own memory about this community!	▪ Sacred Heart Roman Catholic Church
Family histories	St. James Anglican Church
▪ Patton family, owners of Kilton Cottage	

Figure PARIS-3 The browse index for Paris. (Shortened, as the complete list is too long to be shown.) The lists of memories and of people are generated by queries and are updated automatically whenever a new page is created.

This proved to be a success; when examining our statistics, we found that visitors had discovered our site even before the launch and were sharing links to our content online (Qua, 2009). In addition to complete content, we have also seeded the site with a large number of "stub" pages – short articles with only a minimum of content, which contain invitations to the reader to complete them.

In order to help promote usage of the site to an audience that may not have access to the internet, we have also started a program to accept site contributions on paper; this ensures that those who do not own computers or who do not feel comfortable with computers can still contribute to the site.

Digitization standards

Our digitization standards were based on those recommended by a number of sources, primarily the U.S. National Archives and Records Administration (2004), and the Canadian Museum of Civilization (2007). Due to the size of our organization we were not able to completely adhere to these conditions; very specific standards pertaining to digitization room design and monitor calibration are not realistically achievable using the budgets of most small organizations. Our standards include both a web display format and a preservation format, which is meant to remain accessible and usable in the long term.

	Preservation masters	Display copies
Format	8-bit TIFF (from scanner) DNG camera raw (from camera)	8-bit JPEG
Resolution	600dpi (from scanner)	Minimum 1000 pixels along longest end; higher when necessary
Colour space	sRGB IEC61966-2.1	sRGB IEC61966-2.1

We selected the Digital Negative (DNG) format as a master format for camera images instead of TIFF because of the increased flexibility it offers (Adobe, 2009). While proprietary "raw" formats are archivally unsound, because of their closed specifications, DNG offers a manufacturer-neutral format for this data. Adobe has made the specification publicly available, which ensures that it can be supported by future software. There is no archival consensus on the use of DNG as a preservation format (Hess, 2009), but we feel that its benefits outweigh any risks. When storing preservation copies on media without significant limitations on storage space, such as the County's central hard drives, we also store uncompressed TIFF copies of camera images.

Our standard workflow is as follows:

- Import image from scanner or camera raw into Photoshop as 16-bit RGB, using the sRGB profile
- Perform any necessary colour correction and cropping
- Convert image to 8-bit colour depth
- Enlarge image by 0.5 inches or 1 inch
- Type item number in lower right corner, and partner information (if appropriate) in lower left corner
- Save preservation TIFF
- Resize item to display size and perform sharpening
- Save web JPEG

Books

A special note should be made of our standards in digitizing books. Many digitization projects, such as Google Books, use computer processing to flatten pages, remove bindings, and recolour pages to a bitonal, or pure black and white, format. We chose to use a different presentation method. This digitization project is primarily archival in nature, and most of the bound material selected was chosen for its archival qualities as much as its informational qualities. A guiding rule of archives is that context is as important as content in reading meaning from an item (Van Ballegooie & Duff, 2001), so our standards are designed in order to ensure that the context of a book's usage is evident in our digitized version.

A good example of this is our digitized copy of Frederic A. Holden's 1859 *Genealogy of Banfield Capron*, a family history of the Caprons. The copy available to us was Hiram Capron's personal copy, which was later owned by a succession of other Caprons who have made extensive annotations and additions to the book.

CAPRON FAMILY.   107

[901]

SARAH M. CAPRON, daughter of Otis and Polly, was born August 22, 1796, and married Samuel Boyden, July 19, 1824.

CHILDREN. — VI. GENERATION.

977 Samuel Boyden, Jr.; born May 28, 1825; died young.
978 Sarah Curtis; born August 7, 1827.
979 Martha Maria; born November 11, 1829.
980 Samuel, Jr.; born April 28, 1831.
981 Benjamin Franklin; born September 4, 1833.
982 Mary Elizabeth; born May 24, 1835.
983 Edmund Capron; born September 1, 1838.

---

[980]

SAMUEL BOYDEN, Jr., son of Samuel and Sarah, married Ellen L. Morse, October 17, 1855.

---

[981]

BENJAMIN FRANKLIN BOYDEN, son of Samuel and Sarah, married Maria Louise Kingsbury, November 28, 1857.

---

[903]

JUDITH CAPRON, daughter of Otis and Polly, was born Dec. 13, 1801.   She married Nicholas Cook.

CHILDREN. — VI. GENERATION.

984 Lucina Cook; married Alvin Cass.
985 Polly; married Amos Ingalls.
986 Martin; married Mary Martin.
987 Hannah; married George Randall.
988 Martha Jane; married Lovell Pickering.
989 Nicholas, Jr.
990 Judith.

Figure PARIS- 4 Page 107 from Google Books's edition

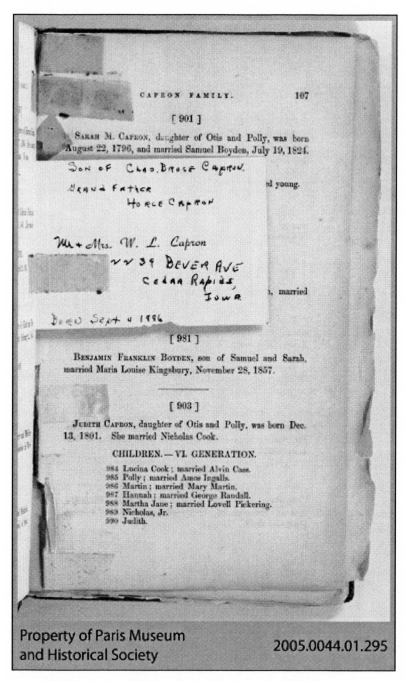

CAPRON FAMILY.   107

[901]

SARAH M. CAPRON, daughter of Otis and Polly, was born August 22, 1796, and married Samuel Boyden, July 19, 1824.

Son of Chas. Bruce Capron.
Grand Father
Horace Capron

Mr + Mrs. W. L. Capron
~~ 39 Bever Ave
Cedar Rapids,
Iowa

Born Sept 4 1996

d young.

, married

[981]

BENJAMIN FRANKLIN BOYDEN, son of Samuel and Sarah, married Maria Louise Kingsbury, November 28, 1857.

[903]

JUDITH CAPRON, daughter of Otis and Polly, was born Dec. 13, 1801. She married Nicholas Cook.

CHILDREN. — VI. GENERATION.

984 Lucina Cook; married Alvin Case.
985 Polly; married Amos Ingalls.
986 Martin; married Mary Martin.
987 Hannah; married George Randall.
988 Martha Jane; married Lovell Pickering.
989 Nicholas, Jr.
990 Judith.

Figure PARIS-5: Our edition of this page, showing the original book's condition. The page behind the attached card was also digitized separately

These annotations are as important for our purposes as the original book. They identify some of its owners, and provide contextual information on how this family history was used and why it was important to them. For that reason, we have chosen to digitize these archival books in full color with any annotations or additions, maintaining the full size of the page and bindings.

Metadata

To simplify metadata collection given our resources, the Library has focused on using the VITA software's metadata for our digitized items. Metadata is entered at the time a record is prepared for display in VITA, and is preserved by saving local copies in the VITA and Dublin core formats. VITA's metadata is stored in an XML-based format, which allows translation into other formats as needed in the future. Metadata is standardized using a number of mandatory and preferred fields, and supplemented with any additional relevant fields per item.

Mandatory:	Preferred:
Contributing Partner	Citation
Copyright Status	Collection
Language of Description	Copyright Date
Media Type	Copyright Holder Name
Title	Copyright Statement
	Creator Name
	Date(s) of Original Donor
	Earliest Year
	Latest Year

Preservation

Both the preservation master copies and the web copies are preserved, along with metadata and any OCR/transcription data. Two physical copies are created on archival quality DVDs; one set is kept by the Library, and the other by our project partner. In addition, supplemental preservation copies are stored on the County's servers.

Equipment

The original project plan called primarily for the digitization of flat documents, which consisted primarily of single pages or a small number of pages, and the project's equipment and software was purchased with these types of documents in mind. The original equipment purchased for this project consisted of one computer workstation, with Adobe Photoshop CS4 software; two scanners; and general archival supplies.

Scanners

The Epson GT-20000 (Epson), the first scanner purchased, is advertised primarily as a workgroup scanner, and its primary purpose is scanning large size documents. It supports documents of a size up to 11.7" x 17", at a resolution of 600dpi. It was purchased on the recommendation of our partners at Our Ontario.

The V500 (Epson) is intended primarily as a photo scanner; it was purchased as a secondary unit. It supports resolutions as high as 6400dpi, with documents up to 8.5" x 11.7" in size, and unlike the GT-20000 it is able to scan photo negatives – this was the primary reason it was chosen. Both scanners support colour depths of up to 48-bit colour.

Book scanning

As the project progressed, new material came forward and it became clear that bound books and book-shaped materials would also need to be scanned. The majority of these items were Hiram Capron's personal account ledgers dating back to 1828, and were very fragile. It was clear that their brittle spines would not survive the bending necessary to flatten the book for use in a flatbed scanner. In addition, the natural curvature of ledger and book pages when laid out flat on a scanner would produce sub-optimal images, especially when performing OCR (Clements, 2009). Another concern was the scanning of oversized objects, as many items in the collection included elements which were larger than the 11.7" x 17" size that the largest scanner could image.

We decided to use photographic imaging for these items, which would free us from physically fitting items into a flatbed scanner. While we were familiar with commercial book scanning cradles, such as those produced by Atiz (Atiz) and Kirtas (Ristech), our equipment budget for this project did not permit a purchase of this expense. Consequently, we constructed our own simple cradle at a low cost.

The only supplies required for the cradle itself were:

- Two white foldout foam presentation display boards: Presentation boards proved to be ideal because they are segmented and naturally fold out. This allowed the longest ends to be raised at a 90-110° angle from the surface of the table, providing the surface for a V-shaped cradle.

- Weights to hold the boards in place: The boards need to be held in place using physical weights of some sort, both to provide support to hold the body up at an angle and to prevent slippage from the weight of the book or artifact being digitized. Weights were easily produced from salvaged supplies. Binders were initially used, but these proved insufficiently heavy to guard against heavy objects slipping. Boxes of books from storage were ultimately the ideal solution, and certainly plentiful in any library.

- One camera, with an SD card: A discussion of the selection of the camera is contained in the next section.

- One tripod

- One plate of glass to hold down pages (optional): The use of glass permitted curling pages to be held flat while being photographed. However, because a polarizing filter was not available, glare prevention is a challenge. The plate of glass was taken from an unneeded spare picture frame.

- Two large sheets of black paper, providing a scanning surface for items to rest on

Figure PARIS-6: The book cradle.

The total cost of the supplies needed came to less than $700, and many of the supplies were already available at the Library. The only parts which needed to be newly purchased were the camera and its memory card, at a cost of approximately CAD $550.

The photograph above depicts how the setup functions. The book or artifact being digitized is placed in the centre of the cradle. Next to it, the camera is placed on the tripod and angled facing down at the page. Because only one camera was used, only the even or odd pages are digitized at a time; after completing one pass, it is necessary to flip the book and photograph the other pages. After photographing, the images can be transferred to the computer for processing. The use of a consistent angle and book positioning means that the images can be automatically processed using Photoshop batch processes, so it is not necessary to manually crop individual pages.

The cradle provided significant advantages when compared to other options. It allowed books and ledgers to be digitized clearly and legibly while providing pages which are flatter in appearance than those scanned using a flatbed scanner. The use of a camera also meant that capturing each individual image was significantly more efficient than using a flatbed scanner, because camera imaging is much faster than flatbed scanners. In addition, the use of presentation boards meant that the size of documents could be very large – as large as 36" x 24". The greater limit on item size was camera resolution. The use of such a large surface meant that the cradle was also useful for digitizing other oversize archival records which could not fit in the flatbed scanners.

When selecting a camera for use with the cradle, a number of criteria were considered. The criteria which guided our decision were:

Resolution. While most high-end digital cameras have more than sufficient resolution to digitize average-sized books and items, the collections being digitized included some very large objects containing fine-grained detail such as a 19th century atlas that measured 15" x 17.5". These items necessitated a camera with a very high megapixel count in order to produce legible images.

Raw compatibility. The "raw format" is a type of "digital negative" (Toborg, 2009), which allows cameras to record information exactly as received by the sensors; this enables more advanced post-processing (Canon, 2008). The most valuable feature this permits is quick and accurate colour correction.

Cost. Any camera selected had to fit within the equipment budget remaining for the project, which eliminated DSLR cameras of a high resolution.

Compatibility with professional book digitization equipment. If a future budget permitted the purchase of professional book digitization equipment, it would be most beneficial to be able to use the camera which had already been purchased in order to reduce costs.

DSLR (Digital Single-Lens Reflex) cameras are popular choices for book digitization (Torborg, 2009), particularly because of their high imaging quality and higher dynamic range (Wan, 2008). However, for this project another camera was selected which better met our needs. In particular, the requirement of a high megapixel count ruled out most entry-level DSLR cameras. Based on these criteria, we selected the Canon PowerShot G10, at the time the highest-end "prosumer" Canon PowerShot camera available. With its 14.7 megapixel sensor [1] (Canon, 2008), it was capable of capturing sufficiently fine detail in large items such as the atlas. It also met the other criteria because it supported the raw format. There were no DSLR cameras within the budget available with a comparable resolution; the resolution was considered an acceptable trade-off for image quality and benchmarks indicate that, for the purpose of this project, the G10 is within an acceptable quality range compared to similar DSLRs (DxO Labs). It provides excellent image quality for digitizing books and documents even in non-ideal lighting conditions.

Lessons learned from the cradle

While the cradle has been very successful for imaging documents unsuited for flatbed scanners, determining the best shooting methods has been an ongoing process and both materials and practices have been amended as the project progresses. We have switched to a carefully configured camera setup instead of its uncalibrated default settings, and have improved the cradle's design.

---

[1] The G10 has recently been replaced by the Canon PowerShot G11, which has a significantly reduced resolution of only 10 megapixels – a 33% reduction (Butler, 2009, p. 1). While the reduction in resolution was for the purpose of reducing the amount of noise in images and increasing detail at lower resolutions (p. 17), the G10 performs better and produces more detail at the lowest film speed (pp. 11, 14, 19) used in digitization. While the G10 was a suitable replacement for a DSLR for this project, the G11 would not be.

There have been some minor tweaks to its physical construction, which have helped to significantly improve quality. The presentation boards work very well as an inexpensive, readily available material. White presentation boards were initially used because they were the most readily available medium. However, the Canadian Museum of Civilization (2007) recommends using black or neutral grey backgrounds for photography. In our testing, we determined that using a black background does produce superior results, with lower noise levels and a superior contrast ratio.

More detailed accounts of our findings, and those of others, can be found at the DIY Book Scanner website at http://www.diybookscanner.org/ and at the archivist's personal blog, located at http://www.mistydemeo.com/ .

Software processing

As Wan (2008) notes, the G10's image tends to be noisy direct out of the camera, and this is especially noticeable when the camera is shooting in its JPEG mode. In our experience, noise can be minimized and detail maximized by shooting using the raw format in well-lit environments; using appropriate exposure settings; using the lowest ISO ("film speed") level available; and by using Adobe's Camera Raw software for noise removal (included with Photoshop) in place of the Canon Digital Photo Professional software bundled with the camera. As with the white balance settings, software noise correction processing can be automated and hence does not adversely add time to the processing workflow.

Promotion

Both of our sites have been promoted using a variety of methods, including traditional methods such as print and through special events, and through non-traditional online methods.

Online

Our passive advertising methods have been primarily focused online and have centered around findability – ensuring that both of our sites can be located using search engines such as Google, and in other places where users may be looking for related information. Our sites are linked and indexed in a variety of relevant locations, including our primary library site and the sites of local historical societies. These have helped to increase its Google ranking, ensuring that key terms such as "Hiram Capron" and the names of individuals for whom we have memories appear among the first search results. As well, we have included links on highly trafficked online resources which do not contribute to our Google ranking, such as the Wikipedia articles for Hiram Capron, Paris, County of Brant, and others. Our statistics show that, in the month of November, approximately 10% of our visits came through Wikipedia and 20% came through search engines.

Interlinking between our two sites has also helped to direct visitors to our other materials; 25% of our visits on one site in the month of November came through links from the other.

Press

Press releases were distributed to the local media at various stages of the project, beginning shortly after the digitization work began; a new press release was distributed every month or two months. They provided ways of announcing the project and providing the community with short updates on progress, and also provided ways to communicate project events to community members. A week prior to the project's official launch, we also purchased a set of advertisements in all of the area newspapers.

Local community newspapers were the most amenable to working with us. All of our press releases were printed by the local County newspapers, and the community newspaper from Paris sent out a photographer to document our Digitization Days event. Unfortunately, obtaining coverage and advertising in the larger newspaper from a bordering city proved more difficult; not all of our press releases were printed, and advertising space was substantially more expensive.

We have found that the rumors of the death of the newspaper are greatly exaggerated. Print was one of our most effective advertising methods. Through informal questioning, we determined that most of those contacting us about the project had read about it through newspapers. Our advertising space has also proven to be effective. Our Google Analytics report on the site's first week available to the public showed a substantial spike of traffic, representing our highest daily visits to date, immediately after our newspaper advertisements were printed.

Close to the time of our launch and after it, growing interest in the project has enabled us to take part in local television and radio; this has helped promote the project and generated further interest.

Advertising handouts

In addition to our print materials, we prepared a number of advertising materials to distribute to our partners and directly to community members.

To advertise our website and specific events, we designed three eye-catching posters. Two are permanent posters, designed to generate ongoing interesting the project, while one is a one-time poster intended to advertise a specific event.

The permanent posters were created to advertise both of our websites. The primary poster was intended as a project-neutral advertisement for the site; consequently, it was designed to avoid specific references to the Capron or Paris projects and image selection was necessarily constrained to images which were not distinctly Parisian. The second poster is intended to solicit contributions to the Our Brant site, and specifically targets an audience which is less familiar with computers. In both cases, we were able to draw from photographs in the collection in order to obtain attractive design elements which could generate further interest in the collection itself.

Due to the expense of having posters professionally printed, we opted not to design complex posters for most one-time events such as the Digitization Days event. However, we judged our launch to be important enough to warrant a professionally printed poster. In addition to relatively wide distribution to generate interest in the launch event, it was especially valuable for the purpose of distribution to the agencies which provided our grant.

The three posters were displayed in all of the branches of the Library. In addition, they were also distributed widely to project partners and other locations such as local genealogical societies, museums, and businesses.

We also produced a set of promotional postcards to be distributed directly to Library patrons. Both the front and backs of the cards contain information on the websites with their URLs. The cards are prominently displayed at the circulation desks of all Library branches as well as our project partner, and clients are invited to take as many as they would like.

Events

The Library has held two special events in order to help build interest in the project. The first was a community event called Digitization Days, which was held on November 13th and 14th, 2009. It was conceived for the dual purposes of sounding out any additional material for our project which might be held by community members, and project promotion by digitizing individual families' photographs and documents to build interest in digitization and our website. During this event, community members could bring in their personal photographs or documents to be scanned and, for a small fee, could take home the scans on an archival CD.

Much to our surprise, we found that the majority of the contributors were not interested in taking home any personal digital copies of the photographs they had brought to be digitized. They had brought their material specifically for the purpose allowing it to be included on our website. In total there were eight contributors over the two days of the event; of these, five brought material specifically for our website, and one other was willing to allow his photographs to be posted after its purpose was explained. A total of 22 new items were obtained for our two websites during the event. The largest number of contributions came from one family who brought 15 original historical land leases, 9 of which have been included on our website.

This revealed a flaw in our planning. While volume of contributions had been considered, it had seemed very unlikely that there would be a surfeit of relevant materials for inclusion on our website. Consequently, our planning had focused on limiting the number of contributions per person. Fortunately, contributors were evenly spread across the day; in the future, we will ensure that all relevant material can be digitized in the event that the number of contributors exceeds capacity.

The Digitization Days event proved to be a success. The most valuable outcome was a new contact who owns a large untapped collection of original historical documents.

Our project's launch event was held on December 6, 2009. We invited members of the community to attend and see an introduction to our two digital collections websites. As entertainment, we provided a slide show with photographs from the collection. In addition, the president of the historical society we partnered with came in full 19th century costume in character as "Hiram Capron." We sent Victorian-styled invitations to a wide variety of recipients, and attracted visits from our Member of Provincial Parliament and the County's mayor.

Conclusion

While the two Digital Collections sites have now officially launched, development is very much ongoing. The materials available have acted as catalysts for community interest and involvement. Based on the current interest the project has generated, the Library has continued its work with the Paris Museum and Historical Society for additional projects and partnered with new organizations to document the history of other communities in the County. By digitizing the wide body of materials described, and opening doors within the community, the Capron project has helped lay the foundation for a digitization program which can document the history of all of the County's communities.

References

Adobe. (2009). *Digital Negative (DNG)*. Retrieved Dec 8, 2009, from http://www.adobe.com/products/dng/

Atiz. (n.d.). *Atiz BookSnap: It's a book ripper*. Retrieved from
http://www.atiz.com/brochure/booksnap.pdf

Baker, T., et al. (2009). *Collaborative history - Creating (and
fostering) a wiki community*. In J. Trant and D. Bearman (eds).
*Museums and the Web 2009: Proceedings. Toronto: Archives &
Museum Informatics*. Retrieved from
http://www.archimuse.com/mw2009/papers/baker/baker.html

Butler, Richard. (2009, December 16). *Canon PowerShot G11 Review.
Digital Photography Review*. Retrieved Dec 16, 2009, from
http://www.dpreview.com/reviews/canong11/

Canadian Museum of Civilization Corporation. (2007). *Digitization
Standards for the CMCC: Scan and Artifact Photography*.
Retrieved May 17, 2009, from
http://www.chin.gc.ca/ATutor/bounce.php?course=29

Canon. (2008). *PowerShot G10 Camera User Guide*. Japan: Canon.

Clements, Maureen. (2009). *The secret of Google's book scanning
machine revealed. As a Matter of Fact Blog: NPR*. Retrieved from
http://www.npr.org/blogs/library/2009/04/
the_granting_of_patent_7508978.html?sc=fb&cc=fp

DxO Labs. (n.d.). *Compare cameras. DxO Mark*. Retrieved Dec 11,
2009, from http://www.dxomark.com/index.php/eng/Image-
Quality-Database/Compare-cameras/(appareil1)/247|0/
(appareil2)/334|0/(appareil3)/319|0/(onglet)/0/(brand)/Canon/(
brand2)/Canon/(brand3)/Canon

Epson. (2009). *Epson GT-20000*. Retrieved Nov 3, 2009, from
http://www.epson.com/cgi-bin/Store/consumer/consDetail.jsp?
BV_UseBVCookie=yes&oid=63075503

Epson. (2009). *Perfection V500 Photo Color Scanner*. Retrieved Nov
3, 2009, from http://www.epson.com/cmc_upload/0/000/142/
325/V500_InfoSheet.pdf

Hess, Richard L. (2009). *Re: NEF images*. Aug 13, 2009. ARCAN-L.
http://www.mailman.srv.ualberta.ca/mailman/private/arcan-
l/2009-August/006136.html

Holden, Frederic A. (1859). *Genealogy of the Descendents of Banfield Capron*. Retrieved Dec 8, 2009, from http://books.google.ca/books?id=qLHTscb_XEwC

Holden, Frederic A. (1859). *Genealogy of the Descendents of Banfield Capron*. Boston: Geo. C. Rand & Avery. Paris Museum and Historical Society, 2005.0044.02.

King Township Public Library. (2008). *Timeless king online*. Retrieved Dec 14, 2009, from http://www.king-library.on.ca/heritage.php

Knowledge Ontario. (2009). *VITA [3.3] user manual (Version 1.0)*. Retrieved from http://our-ontario-contributor-network.near-time.net/files/vita3-3_usermanual.pdf

Qua, George. (2009, October 12). *Qua family name. Ulster ancestry genealogy & ancestry forums*. Retrieved Dec 10, 2009, from http://www.ulsterancestry.com/forums/viewtopic.php?t=2801

Ristech. (2009). *Kirtas APT BookScan 1200. Ristech*. Retrieved Nov 3, 2009, from http://www.ristech.ca/kirtas-apt-bookscan-1200.html

Semantic MediaWiki. (2009). *Help:Inline queries*. Retrieved Dec 1, 2009, from http://semantic-mediawiki.org/wiki/Help:Inline_queries

Statistics Canada. (2006). *2006 community profiles – Brant*. Retrieved Dec 14, 2009, from http://www12.statcan.ca/census-recensement/2006/dp-pd/prof/92-591/details/page.cfm?Lang=E&Geo1=CSD&Code1=3529005&Geo2=PR&Code2=35&Data=Count&SearchText=brant&SearchType=Begins&SearchPR=01&B1=All&Custom=

Torborg, Wayne. (2008). Manuscript digitization at the Hill Museum & Manuscript Library: Building on the legacy of microfilm. *Microform & Imaging Review. 37*, 1, pp. 17–27, ISSN (Print) 0949-5770, DOI: 10.1515/mfir.2008.002, Winter 2008

U.S. National Archives and Records Administration. (2004). *Technical guidelines for digitizing archival materials for electronic access: Creation of production master files – raster images*. Retrieved from http://www.archives.gov/preservation/technical/guidelines.html

Van Ballegooie, Marlene, and Duff, Wendy M. (2001). *RAD revealed: A basic primer to the rules for archival description*. Ottawa: Canadian Council of Archives.

Wan, Don. (2008). *Canon PowerShot G10 review. Digital Photography Review*. Retrieved Dec 2, 2009, from http://www.dpreview.com/reviews/CanonG10/

Wikia. (2009). *Help:Rich text editor. Wikia*. Retrieved Nov 27, 2009, from http://help.wikia.com/wiki/Help:Rich_text_editor

Zurbu. (2009). *Local history and development forums on Zurbu*. Retrieved Dec 4, 2009, from http://zurbu.net/

The Mass. Memories Road Show: A State-Wide Scanning Project

Joanne Riley and Heather Cole
(University of Massachusetts Boston)

Abstract

Running a state-wide digital history project on a shoestring budget and staffed primarily by volunteers is not only possible, but brings immeasurable rewards for the contributors, volunteers, organizers and staff while gathering priceless documentation of their communal heritage. The Mass. Memories Road Show (http://www. MassMemories.net) is a public scanning project based at the University of Massachusetts Boston which partners with local communities to digitize family photographs and stories at public events with the goal of creating a digital portrait of all the 351 cities and towns in the Commonwealth. This article describes how the project works to ensure broad participation in the planning and execution of the project, as well as a detailed description of the logistics of a Road Show event, which could be replicated in other communities.

Keywords: Archives, Community history, Community, Digital collection, Digitization, Family, History, Libraries, Local history, Massachusetts, Memories, Multi-cultural, Partnership, Photos, Place-based, Public history, Public, Scanning, State studies.

Introduction

The Mass. Memories Road Show (MMRS) is an ongoing, on-the-spot public scanning project in the Commonwealth of Massachusetts, sponsored by the Joseph P. Healey Library at the University of Massachusetts Boston and Mass Humanities, the state humanities council. The MMRS documents Massachusetts people, places and events through the contributions of individuals who bring their photos and stories to be digitized at public events throughout the state. Over the next few years, the project will partner with hundreds of local organizations to visit each of the 351 communities in Massachusetts, gradually building up a self-portrait of the Commonwealth through the contributions of its residents. The MMRS is online at http://www.MassMemories.net.

Project Background

The MMRS grew out of the place-based education initiatives of the University of Massachusetts Boston's "Massachusetts Studies Project" (MSP), which provides resources for Massachusetts teachers and students in the areas of local history, culture and environmental studies. A series of casual brainstorming sessions with librarians, MSP board members, teachers and local historians coalesced in a vision of a public history project inspired by elements of PBS's Antiques Roadshow (people bringing their personal treasures to a local event for professional perusal) and the Library of Congress' American Memory Project (a library organizing digitized images from a common heritage to be shared on the World Wide Web, see The Library of Congress, n.d.) The subsequent development of the MMRS project was guided by the work of Daniel Cohen and Roy Rosenzweig (2005), Stuart Lee and Kate Lindsay (2009) and by the writings of Robert Putnam and others about the nature of civic engagement. We have borrowed elements from a number of superb online digital history projects, among them the Maine Memory Network (Maine Historical Society, 2009), for its richly productive collaborations with partnering organizations across the state, The Organic City (*The Organic City*, n.d.) for its place-based communal storytelling approach, the Coney

Island History Project (*Coney Island History Project*, n.d.) for its effective application of social web tools, the Charlestown Digital Story Project (*UMBC Digital Story*, n.d.) at UMBC for its engaging multimedia oral histories created through student-elder collaborations, the Worthington Memory Project (Worthington Public Library, 2002) for its transparent application of best practices in indexing, and Orlando Memory (Orlando Memory, n.d.) for its solicitation of public contributions to a community history project.

The MMRS project was originally designed to meet two goals: collecting digital surrogates and personal annotations of locally held primary sources that document people, places and events in Massachusetts; and developing a searchable online repository of sources that could be used for educational purposes at all levels. As the project developed, we discovered that it met another important need that has been incorporated as a key goal of the project: community building. Road Shows have turned out to be deeply engaging community events that connect people within the community to each other and to others throughout the state, and have proven to be meaningful in lasting ways to the people who contribute and to those who volunteer. At its best, the MMRS seems to generate both of the types of productive social relationships that Robert Putnam describes in Bowling Alone: the Collapse and Revival of American Community (Putnam, 2000); that is to say, bonding social capital (holding together people who see themselves as being similar in social identity) and bridging social capital (bringing together people who consider themselves to be "unalike" in some aspect of social identity.) In the words of a Road Show volunteer and contributor:

> *"[The Road Show] brings the community together... [It] acknowledges to people that they are a part of the history-making... It brings people to understand and respect different cultures in their town through the old and new pictures... I think it is one of the great community programs to encourage the whole family to be involved."* (MMRS Letters of Support, 2008).

Since its launch in the fall of 2004, the MMRS project has organized Road Show events across the state, in the process digitizing thousands of photos and stories, collaborating with dozens of community organizations and generating the practical lessons we will share in this essay.

Guiding Principles

The following key principles have guided the development of the MMRS since its inception:

First, we believe that everyone who lives or lived, works or worked in a given community is equally representative of that community. Thus, the Road Show's on-the-ground events and the resulting digital collection are intended to reflect as realistic a picture as possible of the community, based on demographics past and present. For example, for a community that was predominantly Irish in the early 20th century and is now largely Vietnamese, the event attendees and the photos and stories in the digital collection should reflect both of those cultures.

A second guiding principle of the MMRS project is the idea that we are not creating a comprehensive archive of Massachusetts' (or a given community's) history; rather, we are creating a self-portrait of the state based on the photographic artifacts that are held in individuals' personal photo albums and scrapbooks. Thus, the photos that individuals bring to the event reflect their choices of how they want to represent themselves and their families in the project archive, as opposed to meeting a predetermined collecting standard. This leads naturally to the project protocol that contributors caption and describe their photos in the first person, rather than in impersonal archival language. For instance, one Road Show image's caption and description read:

> *"The Reading Theater Circa 1924: This is the second theater in Reading built by my great uncle, Ed Turnbull. He also built the first in 1913. My father, Arthur Kelley, was a popcorn boy. We moved to Reading because my father loved it after spending so much time here."* (Mass. Memories Road Show, 2010; Image ID 41.106.1).

Another guiding principal is that the Road Show events themselves play a vital role in creating an understanding of communal history. Particularly in large, diverse cities, individuals and organizations may not be aware of the larger historical and contemporary context of their community. Yet all of the people arriving at their local Road Show with photos in hand have in common their connection to that physical location and its history, regardless of their age, ethnic, economic or religious background; all "belong" simply by virtue of their involvement (present or past) in this place. At the Road Show events, each person's connection to the community is formally acknowledged through their presence there. The events help build connections between contributors and contributing organizations and the digital collection serves to mirror a community back to itself. This principle of inclusion informs all planning processes and influenced our early decision to arrange the public events so that all participants could observe and share in the contributions of others. For example, we project all photos on a wall screen as they are being scanned, and arrange seating so that contributors can listen to others' stories as they are being recorded.

A final, later-adopted guiding principal of the MMRS is that the contributor is as worthy of documentation as the contribution. We hope that our digital collection will serve as a resource of primary source material well into the future. As such, we came to understand that the participation of Road Show contributors and volunteers was also worthy of documentation. Each person who takes part in a Road Show has shown a commitment to their community history that we realized should be captured and preserved. Thus, we include "Keepsake Photos" (described below) and staff / volunteer group photos in the dataset for each Road Show.

These principles formed the foundation for the development of the MMRS project and are, we feel, responsible for the extraordinary atmosphere of cooperation and community that participants have mentioned in describing the Road Shows:

"The Road Show connected people of all ages to the past, resulting in a deeper understanding of the present. [The] Road

Show modeled for youth how to work together to share the history of everyone's history. Through involvement in the Road Show, a torch was passed to [our] youth, the torch of stewardship of their community's history." - a Road Show organizer/contributor (Letters of Support, 2008).

"Many participants stayed and shared their photographs with those sitting next to them, watched others being videotaped, or watched the images being projected onto the overhead screen. The interactive nature of the event allowed participants to share stories and learn about other communities in their city." - a Road Show organizer (MMRS Post-Event Participant Survey, 2009).

The Massachusetts Model

From the beginning, we aimed to create a model project that could be replicated beyond Massachusetts. In the second year of the project, we consulted with archival, legal and information technology specialists to ensure that the database structure and metadata collection forms met accepted standards and best practices for digital history projects and that the online resources would available for educational use. These specialists' recommendations were compiled in The Mass. Memories Road Show Handbook: Procedures and Protocols for a Public Scanning Project (University of Massachusetts Boston, 2006), available on the project website. They guided us in creating an open-source database system that stores the information from the Contributor and Photo forms in fields that are compatible with the Dublin Core metadata set, and in ensuring that the images collected may be made available online on a non-exclusive basis for non-commercial uses.

Road Show Logistics

Funding

The early years of the MMRS project's development were partially supported by grants from the Massachusetts Historical Records Advisory Board, the Mass. Foundation for the Humanities, and a

Professional Development grant program at the University of Massachusetts Boston. These grants, totaling approximately $30,000 over three years, covered some initial equipment, student work, and expenses for pilot Road Shows. The majority of the project's support in its early years was in the form of extensive contributions of time and equipment from the project director, volunteers and community collaborators. Thanks to the track record built up through the early Road Shows, the project reached a turning point in 2006, when it was brought under the umbrella of the University of Massachusetts Boston's Joseph P. Healey Library as a community outreach initiative, a step which allowed for the hiring of a public historian as a project manager (.5 FTE) to focus on growth, stabilization and outreach.

In 2008, the state humanities council, Mass Humanities joined with UMass Boston's Healey Library to co-sponsor a "mini-grant" program to expand the Road Show. The program accepts applications from interested communities who are required to assemble a local planning team and outline how they plan to achieve a realistic community portrait through their outreach and marketing. If accepted for funding, the planning team handles local outreach and provides volunteer staff, translators, non-technical equipment and refreshments on the day of the event, while the grant funds professional videography, stipends for event staff and post-production of images, data and videos. The Healey Library provides technical equipment and in-kind staffing for preparation, volunteer training, website application support, consultation with the University Archivist, running the Road Show event and follow-up.

Planning

Planning for a Road Show begins as much as a year in advance of the event. Because our goal is to make these events and the materials collected a realistic self-portrait of the community, we involve as many local organizations as possible in the planning process: public libraries, historical societies, public schools, cultural and ethnic organizations, youth groups, historic preservation organizations, business people, government officials, genealogists, senior citizens and others.

Ensuring participation by those who are sometimes under-represented in local history projects (young people, non-English-speakers, new arrivals and other minority members of the community) is most dependably accomplished when the local planning team is comprised of persons representing the same range of backgrounds as the community at large. While this representation is critical for the Road Show's success, it is equally important that local planning team members share a genuine interest in cultural heritage, archives, genealogy, family history, community history and community building. Too often, "diversity" in planning committees is arrived at by requesting the participation of municipal or organizational representatives who are routinely tapped to represent their communities in all sorts of projects, regardless of their personal interests. We have learned that putting extensive effort into finding true kindred spirits across a community's various subgroups - those whose eyes light up at the mention of "old pictures" or "family stories" or "local history" - can pay huge dividends in the overall ease of encouraging broad participation in the eventual Road Show.

The local planning team is responsible for outreach to the community to recruit contributors to the event. We have found that the best-attended Road Shows were invariably the result of person-to-person outreach by the local organizing team which, while time-consuming, was much more effective than general publicity or postings around town.

One community member described her participation in a local planning team as valuable both personally and professionally:

"The Mass. Memories Road Show is a vehicle not only to showcase communities but helps to bring them together. I was able to observe how members of various and diverse institutions came together to put on a community event. I met leaders of the Asian community, historic/cultural institutions and veteran neighborhood organizations" - MMRS local organizing committee member (MMRS Letters of Support, 2008).

Staffing

The permanent MMRS staff consists of a part-time project manager who oversees all aspects of the project, and the MSP director who serves in an administrative and advisory capacity. Both positions are located within the Digital Library Services Department of the Healey Library at the University of Massachusetts Boston.

In addition to the permanent MMRS staff, each Road Show event is staffed by 15-20 people: a combination of experienced "Roadies" (people who previously volunteered at a Road Show in their own community) and local volunteers. Roadies receive a small stipend (ca. $50) for each subsequent Road Show they work; in other words, staff are not paid to work in their own community but are compensated to bring their experience and expertise to another Road Show in the state. Local volunteers are recruited by the local planning team and need not have any professional experience in archives, local history or digital projects. We have been pleased to have skilled amateur photographers, genealogists, librarians, teachers, historians and computer buffs among our volunteers and Roadies.

One of the many unexpected outcomes of this project has been the camaraderie built up among Roadies across Road Shows, and the cross-fertilization that occurs through the activities of people from different communities traveling to help others document their community heritage. Some Roadies have been with the project for several years, and the number grows with each event, since all contributors and volunteers are routinely invited to help staff subsequent Road Shows.

Staffing an event is apparently equally rewarding for the Roadies, who often speak of feeling privileged to bear witness to the stories shared by event contributors:

"Once the event began, I was touched in many ways. Some stories brought a tear to my eye, like one woman's description of how her brother was a prisoner of war for six months in World War II, and the hurt and pain she felt, but the comfort his picture brought her... Working on the project is by far the most rewarding venture I have been involved in so far." – MMRS

volunteer, Roadie and videographer (MMRS Letters of Support, 2008).

Training

All of the Road Show functions aside from videography - i.e. photo scanning, metadata collection, still photography and customer service - are performed by amateur Roadies and volunteers who are trained just prior to the event. The MMRS staff provides written instructions and conducts the training for all Roadies and volunteers.

In the past, volunteer training had been scheduled two days before the Road Show, which allowed time to run the training along with an interim day to fix any problems that might be identified during the training session. However, it proved difficult to assemble all of the volunteers in advance of the event, so subsequent Road Shows have incorporated an hour-long training immediately before the event, when all volunteers for the day are present. While this worked reasonably well, we are developing a series of self-paced multimedia training materials for all volunteers to work through well in advance of the event. This will improve the efficacy of the training process and will also bolster the confidence of inexperienced local volunteers as the day of the Road Show approaches.

AT A ROAD SHOW

Each Road Show is held in a public space, most often a local public library, historical society or community center. Most Road Shows are scheduled to last about four hours, with an additional two hours in advance for setup and an hour for breakdown and cleanup. Each Road Show consists of "stations", which are tables devoted to specific Road Show functions. Road Show participants move from one station to another, providing information, having their photos digitized and their stories recorded.

Contributors are invited to drop in at any time during the event. We have found it works best to have a loose and casual atmosphere. If a contributor arrives under great time pressure, we squire them quickly through the process. But for the most part, people arrive at the event, go through the process, and then linger to listen and watch as others go through the process. Even when the crowds have been heavy, there has never been any impatience but only excitement and goodwill. Said one contributor: *"I could have spent two hours with all my photos and stories. I really had a good time"* (MMRS Post-Event Participant Survey, 2009).

Below are details about each of the seven Road Show event stations, offered in hopes that those who choose to undertake a similar endeavor may benefit from lessons learned in this project's early years.

Welcome Station

The Welcome Station is the first stop for all contributors to the Road Show. Locating the Welcome Station in the corridor or anteroom outside the event space helps manage crowds and can also serve as a visual invitation to the event for passersby. The station is staffed by two "Greeters", generally one experienced Roadie and one local community member. As contributors approach the table, the Greeters welcome them to the event, briefly explain the station layout and give them a numbered nametag and a Registration Form to complete. The number on the contributor's nametag and form is used to match each contributor to his/her photos, stories and metadata. Greeters accept and review the Registration Form, and then invite the contributors to proceed to the Info Station to complete paperwork on their photos. If any of the contributors need assistance with translation, mobility or other challenges, then a floating volunteer is summoned to assist them as they proceed from station to station.

Equipment: 4-6' table and chairs; pre-numbered stick-on nametags; registration forms; clipboards; pens (all forms must be signed in pen.)

Info Station

At the Info Station, contributors complete paperwork on each of the photos they are contributing to the MMRS digital collection. The Info Station is staffed by three to five "Reviewers." Their role is to assist contributors in selecting a few photos that represent themselves, their family and/or their community, and assist them in completing a Photo Form for each photo. Reviewers encourage contributors to select photos that best fit one or more of the following categories: an original photo (rather than a printout or photocopy), a photo where they know some identifying details (where taken, when, people photographed, etc.), a photo that has particular meaning to the contributor, a photo that is unusual in some way, or a photo that has people in it (rather than a scenic shot).

Contributors are encouraged to complete the Photo Form as best they can, using a first-person approach in providing the "who, what, when, where" of the photo. The Reviewer then reviews the Photo Form and may prompt the contributor to clarify or add more information (last names, additional details, etc.) Reviewers can add more information derived from conversation on the back of the form, if necessary. Once each Photo Form is complete, the Reviewer assigns a sequential number to each of the contributor's photos, writing that number on the relevant Photo Form. Finally, the Reviewer invites the contributor to take their photos and Photo Forms to the Scanning Station, accompanying the person there if necessary. If there is a waiting line at the Scanning Station, the contributor may visit any of the other stations in any order.

Notes: In our experience, reviewers need to actively encourage contributors to use first person ("I, Me, My, Our...") in photo captions and descriptions. Frequently contributors will bring in an entire album of photographs and it can take some time to help them sift through them to select two or three to share with the project. Contributors frequently do not fill out the Photo Forms completely at first; it often takes additional coaching or asking questions to encourage the contributors to share more detailed information about their photos.

Equipment: Two 6-8' tables 10-12 chairs; Photo Forms; Clipboards; Pens

Scanning Station

At the Scanning Station, the contributor's photographs are digitized on a flatbed scanner. This station is staffed by two volunteers/Roadies: a "Scanner" and a "Reviewer." The Reviewer collects the Photo Forms and performs another quality control check for completeness, legibility and correctness of the ID number. The Scanner scans each photo at 300 DPI and saves as a TIF file named using the format RoadShow#.Nametag#.Photo#.tif. This filename is also recorded on the Photo Form. The scanning process is projected live on a wall screen for all event visitors to see, which enhances the spirit and enjoyment of the event. After the photos are scanned, they are immediately returned to the contributor, while all of the paperwork is collected by the Reviewer and stored in a large envelope at each station.

If the photo is too big or unwieldy to fit on the scanner, or if, as sometimes happens, the contributor brings a three-dimensional object (we have seen aprons, clocks, weavings, jewelry and more) those contributors are sent to the Keepsake Photo Station where the digital camera is used to photograph the oversized object.

Notes: Each Scanning Station can handle between 70 and 100 photos within the event time. For most Road Shows to date, this has meant setting up two Scanning Stations.

Projecting the scanning process onto a wall screen not only helps to build community, but also is an engaging way for those waiting their turn at one of the stations to pass the time. There have been a number of exciting moments in Road Show where someone recognizes a person or place that flashes on the screen and adds their story to the mix.

Equipment: laptop computer; scanner (capable of scanning letter-sized documents and photographs as tiffs at 300 DPI) and necessary drivers to connect scanner to laptop; LCD projector; portable projection screen; paperclips; blank CDs for backup; two 6-8' tables and chairs; large envelopes to hold collected photo and contributor forms and backup CD.

Keepsake Photo Station

The Keepsake Photo Station is staffed by a "Photographer" and a "Paperwork Manager." The Photographer snaps a photo of the contributor holding one (or more) of the contributed photos, from a distance of about four feet, and framing from the waist up. The Photographer then prints out the photo as a souvenir for the contributor to take home with them, while the digital version is saved for later incorporation into the online database. The Paperwork Manager is responsible for completing the Keepsake Photo Log with the name, nametag number and other relevant information which is transferred to the image file of the keepsake photo after the event.

Notes: The Keepsake Photo Station also serves as the station for photographing images and objects that are too large to fit on the scanner. Because the printing process can be slow, contributors are invited to visit other stations while their keepsake photo is being generated. Printed photos are posted onto a bulletin board for later pickup.

Equipment: digital still camera; tripod; keepsake photo log; rich colored backdrop; photo printer with paper and ink (capable of printing 4x6" prints from digital camera onsite); bulletin board and thumbtacks; table for printer; chairs

Video Station

At the Video Station, contributors are asked to share a 3-5 minute story about the photo(s) that they contributed to the project. At the Video Station there is a Videographer and an Interviewer, although these can be the same person, depending on the experience of the staff. The Interviewer begins by asking the contributor to state their name and nametag number on camera for data quality control purposes, and then asks the contributor to share a three to five minute story about one or more of the photos that they brought with them. Clarifying questions may follow, in a casual, conversational style.

Notes: While trained amateurs can achieve high quality scanning results, videography is still best left to professionals, or at least those with extensive experience in videotaping in public settings under time and quality pressures. Public access television stations in each community have provided experienced staff for this important function.

Equipment: digital video camera; appropriate lighting, lavaliere microphone and other equipment for recording interviews; photogenic chair with armrests for interviewees to sit in; backdrop, preferably one reflective of the community.

Preservation Station

The Preservation Station includes a display and handouts on how to care for family photos and documents, both contributed by volunteers from the New England Archivists. Contributors can stop by this table to peruse the displays, pick up information and ask questions of the archivists. Road Show volunteers direct contributors to the Preservation Station if they notice that a contributor's artifacts are delicate or in poor condition, or in response to questions from contributors about preservation, valuation or potential repositories for their artifacts.

Notes: Despite the Preservations Station's alluring display of "Archival Evils" showing the dramatic effects that mold, moisture, heat, glue, etc can have on precious family artifacts, contributors have tended to pass by this station, perhaps because it is not directly related to the digitization processes. To mitigate this, we now place the Preservation Station closer to the scanning action, and encourage the archivists to wander the room and offer advice as moved to do so by what they see among the contributions.

Equipment: 6-8' table and chairs; display materials and handouts about photo preservation, preferably supplied by professional archivists

Local History Station

The Local History Station provides consultation and resources on local history. This station is usually staffed by representatives from the local historical society or reference librarians who are broadly knowledgeable about the history of the area and its residents over time. The Local History Station includes a display on local history and local history resources (books, pamphlets, maps, etc.) Local historians/librarians also keep an eye out for any photos that they may want to solicit as a donation to their archives.

Notes: The volunteers at the Local History Station are able to answer local questions, and identify persons, places and dates in contributors' photos. These are also the people who will be carrying on aspects of the project into the future. Usually the local groups who staff this station come away with new member signups to their organizations.

Equipment: 6-8' table and chairs; brief written history of the town in pamphlet form; other relevant local history information (books, maps, etc.)

Post-Event Processing

Based on our own experience and the recommendations of professional consultants, we developed a routine for managing the wealth of information gathered at each Road Show. At the end of each event, we back up the digital images onto a portable hard-drive and make photocopies of all the paperwork. Within a few weeks of each event, MSP staff members perform the data-entry and image processing necessary to include the images and metadata in the online database. Once data entry is complete, we send digital copies of all materials to each partnering organization for that event. We also send out a brief survey to participants, send contributor contact information to all partners, and finally, notify all participants when the photos and videos have been mounted on the project website at www.MassMemories.net.

351 and Beyond

In its first five years of operation, the MMRS has visited only a fraction of the 351 cities and towns across Massachusetts and has collected just a portion of the millions of photos and stories that still lie in the basements, attics, scrapbooks and photo albums of its residents. We have a long way to go and, like many other projects, continue to seek ways to reach a broader audience, ensure long-term sustainability, and reduce operational costs. To that end, we are in the process of converting the project's current database and website into a web-based data-management system to streamline data- and image-processing procedures.

At Road Shows we have seen high school students and retirees share stories about how their common childhood neighborhood has changed over time. We have heard former residents from opposite sides of what had been a racially-segregated housing development recall overlapping events from their childhoods. Parents have come to Road Shows with their children to share photos of their immigrant ancestors. After the events, we see communities continuing the connections and conversations that were started at Road Show events through local history exhibits, extended documentaries about local residents, and new partnerships among local organizations. The ultimate lesson learned? Running a state-wide digital history project on a shoestring budget and staffed primarily by volunteers is not only possible, but brings immeasurable rewards for the contributors, volunteers, organizers and staff while gathering priceless documentation of their communal heritage.

In closing, here are words from some of those who have participated in the Mass. Memories Road Show to date:

"The students said they learned so much from the families and individuals who showed up to share photos and tell stories of the old days... Students began to realize that they will someday be the elders, the caretakers of their city's, their family's, their culture's history." - Middle school teacher whose students participated in a Road Show as contributors and volunteers

"I met many new people and heard many interesting stories about the history of the community in which I live that I would have otherwise never heard. I have left the experience of my involvement with the Mass. Memories Road Show with even more interest in my community and the tapestry of people that populate it." - Road Show volunteer/contributor.

"I have only worked in three Road Shows and can't wait for more!" - 8th grade student who worked as a Roadie during his summer break.

"We heard the story of the lamplighter in North Quincy, learned that a Quincy resident was Jimmy Dolittle's wingman, and that people still remember the smell of fresh bread at the Sumner

Bakery. These footnotes don't appear in standard histories, but now they are on record for all to share." – Local history librarian and Road Show organizer.

"Having spent my entire career in the field of public history, I cannot think of a project that contributes more to a broader public reflection and appreciation of the past. The Road Show has developed a creative, innovative and, perhaps most importantly, an effective approach to engaging a community in documenting its own history." - State humanities council representative and Road Show attendee

The authors would like to thank the following supporters who helped shape the Mass. Memories Road Show in its earliest days: Ron Adams, Phil Byrnes, Celeste Finison, George Hart, April Hagins Johnson, Elizabeth Clancy Lerner, Cagen Luse, Marisa Luce, Mary McCarthy, Paul McCarthy, Elisabeth McGregor, Hoa Mai Nguyen, Daniel Ortiz-Zapata, Frances Pollitt, Frank Poon, Barbara (Bobby) Robinson, Ellen Rothman, Sequoia Stenlund, Emily Sweeney, Earl Taylor, Rebecca Withers.

References:

Cohen, Daniel J. and Roy Rosenzweig. (2005), *Digital history: A guide to gathering, preserving and presenting the past on the web.* University of Pennsylvania Press. Retrieved March 23, 2010 from http://chnm.gmu.edu/digitalhistory.

Coney Island History Project. (n.d.). Retrieved March 23, 2010 from http://www.coneyislandhistory.org/

Lee, Stuart D. and Kate Lindsay. (2009). *If you build It, they will scan: Oxford University's exploration of community collections.* In *EDUCAUSE Quarterly, vol 32,* 2009. Retrieved March 23, 2010 from http://www.educause.edu/EDUCAUSE+Quarterly/ EDUCAUSEQuarterlyMagazineVolum/IfYouBuildItTheyWillScan Oxford/174547#TB_inline?height=400&width=630&inlineId=side bar1&modal=false

Maine Historical Society. (2009). *The Maine Memory Network, a project of the Maine Historical Society*. Retrieved March 23, 2010 from http://www.MaineMemory.net.

Mass. Memories Road Show. (2010). *Mass. Memories Road Show - Your family's place in Massachusetts History*. Retrieved March 23, 2010 from http://www.massmemories.net.

MMRS Letters of Support. (2008). *Letters of support submitted for MMRS nomination for NCPH Public History Award*. Unpublished documents. (January, 2008).

MMRS Post-Event Participant Survey. (2009). Unpublished data.

Orlando Memory (n.d.). *Homepage*. Retrieved March 23, 2010 from http://dc.ocls.info/.

Putnam, Robert D. (2000). *Bowling alone: the collapse and revival of American community*. Retrieved March 23, 2010 from http://www.bowlingalone.com/

The Library of Congress. (n.d.). *The Library of Congress: American memory*. Retrieved March 23, 2010 from http://memory.loc.gov/ammem/index.html.

The Organic City. (n.d.). *Homepage*. Retrieved March 23, 2010 from http://www.theorganiccity.com/wordpress/.

UMBC Digital Story. (n.d.). *Digital stories from Charlestown*. Retrieved March 23, 2010 from http://www.umbc.edu/oit/newmedia/studio/digitalstories/ctds.php

University of Massachusetts Boston. (2006). *The Mass. Memories Road Show handbook: Procedures and protocols for a public scanning project*. Retrieved March 23, 2010 from http://www.msp.umb.edu/MassMemories/handbook/MMRSHandbook.pdf.

Worthington Public Library. (2002). *Worthington memory*. http://www.worthingtonmemory.org/index.cfm.

Picturing the Museum: Education and Exhibition at the American Museum of Natural History

Kelli Anderson, Barbara Mathé, Eric Muzzy, Stacy Schiff
(American Museum of Natural History Research Library)

Abstract

The Research Library of the American Museum of Natural History received funding from the Metropolitan New York Library Council in 2007 to produce a web exhibit of 989 historic images. *Picturing the Museum: Education and Exhibition at the American Museum of Natural History* served as the prototype for a comprehensive database for the Research Library's extensive Photographic Collection. In the larger context of the history, development, and use of the Library's Photographic Collection, this article describes the project's conception through a self-published book produced for the Trustees' Library Committee, the funded project and the ongoing development of the larger database. One of the internal goals and results of the Picturing the Museum project was to analyze, codify, and document local practice, policies and workflow for more efficient delivery of images to the web.

Keywords: Cultural metadata, Digital imaging, Digitization, Exhibition, Libraries, Museum, Museum education, New York, Photograph, Photographic collection.

The American Museum of Natural History
Photographic Collection

Founded in 1869, the American Museum of Natural History (AMNH) is one of the nation's preeminent institutions for scientific research and public education. Throughout its history, the Museum has pursued joint missions of science and education. The Museum's power to interpret wide-ranging scientific discoveries and convey them imaginatively has inspired generations of visitors to its grand exhibition halls and educated its visitors about the natural world and the vitality of human culture.

The Museum collections include over 32 million objects and specimens relating to anthropology, zoology, paleontology and the physical sciences. From the collected stories, clothing and material culture of the peoples of the Pacific Northwest Coast to the dinosaur eggs unearthed in Mongolia, from meteorites brought back from Greenland on a wooden sailing ship by Robert Peary to one of the most comprehensive sets of fossil horses ever assembled, the breadth and variety of the collections is astonishing.

Illustrating the work of the Museum scientists and staff are over 1.5 million black and white negatives, color transparencies, lantern slides and photographic prints held in the AMNH Research Library. The majority of these photographs were taken by Museum explorers and scientists who documented their field work. At the same time, they photographed the local environment and the people who lived there. The physical growth of the Museum was recorded by staff photographers who also photographed the work of the exhibition and education departments. These images are requested by researchers, students, educators, and professionals from around the world for academic and general publication, educational broadcast and distribution, artists' reference and personal use.

The dissemination of this extraordinary Photographic Collection can be traced directly to Museum founder Albert Bickmore, one of the earliest and most enthusiastic advocates of visual education. Bickmore's lantern slide lectures were so successful that a new and larger theater was built in 1900 to accommodate the lines of teachers awaiting admission. To expand the Museum's educational mission beyond its walls, Bickmore created a lantern slide lending library of over 140,000 slides. The slide library formed the basis of the Natural Science Study Collections that were delivered to schools throughout New York State. (see Figure AMNH-1)

Figure AMNH-1: Image 37244, Teachers selecting lantern slides; Image 313944, School Delivery, American Museum of Natural History Photographic Collection.

In addition to the slides, the Museum delivered specimens and, later, model dioramas accompanied by lectures prepared by the Museum's educational and scientific staff. Bickmore's initiative foreshadowed the digital distribution of images by over a century. It is now possible to create worldwide access to the Collection and the public has come to expect to be able to find images online. Organizing, describing and digitizing a photographic collection of this size, however, is an enormous undertaking.

Picturing the Museum

To develop internal support within the institution for digitizing the Photographic Collection, the Library staff selected 50 appealing images related to the Museum's history and designed a small print-on-demand photo book to distribute at the January 2007 meeting of the AMNH Trustees' Library Committee (see Figure AMNH-2).

Figure AMNH-2. Front and back covers of Picturing the Museum (© 2007), American Museum of Natural History, produced using Blurb.com (www.blurb.com).

At the same time that the book was being developed, the Library used a similar theme, *Natural Science Education and Exhibition at the American Museum of Natural History*, as a digitization project proposal for METRO's Regional Bibliographic Databases and Interlibrary Resources Sharing Program. This choice was made because the parameters of the grant proposal indicated that the subject matter should relate to the New York City Metropolitan Area. While most of the AMNH photographs were taken in distant places on every continent, the images of the Museum and its work were made in New York City and the surrounding area.

The METRO funded project, *Picturing the Museum: Education and Exhibition at the American Museum of Natural History* (URL: http://images.library.amnh.org/photos/index.html) was created to showcase nearly 1000 images from the Photographic Collection, and to act as a prototype for developing a larger more comprehensive image database that would grow over time. The photographs in Picturing the Museum illustrate how the Museum staff presented natural science to the New York City public and the reactions of that public, particularly the school children. The pictures have been used by scholars studying education, museology, visual representation and local history. An NYU professor e-mailed the Library describing how the web site generated a new research topic, an article entitled "Exhibiting the Exhibit-Makers" about the history of the photographs of exhibition preparation at the AMNH. She is presently researching the Museum Archives to find more about the long-neglected Museum staff photographers in order to define their role historically within the institution. The pictures on the web site, documenting dinosaurs to fashion history, also tell a story about the people of New York City as the twentieth century emerged.

Building upon Albert Bickmore's prescient vision of distributing images as an educational resource, the long term goal of the project is to make more images in the Collection readily available to researchers, scholars, students and the general public. Online access to the Photographic Collection will expand Bickmore's initiative exponentially, vastly increasing the numbers of those who will use the images for research, publication, broadcast and personal use. Students will be able to use these images in their class presentations and more individuals will be able to find pictures of their family from previous generations, like the Ainu woman from Japan, whose grandfather's photograph from the 1904 St. Louis Exposition is in the AMNH Photographic Collection. Online access will also help to preserve the original materials. Before scanning was institutionalized at the Museum, negatives would be repeatedly pulled from the collection for printing in the Museum's photographic studio. Now they are scanned once and left undisturbed, preserved in a climate controlled environment.

Perhaps the most exciting potential of digital access to the AMNH Photographic Collection is that it offers the possibility of restoring provenance to many of the images in the Collection. With negatives filed numerically upon accession and prints arranged by subject to facilitate teaching, many collections were disassociated from their history. Study of historical photographic evidence is infinitely more valuable when examining a series of photographs instead of a single photograph out of context.

Sources for the Image Metadata

The basic records for the *Picturing the Museum* database were derived from 23 typed logbooks that had been created when the negatives were originally added to the Museum's collections. The logbook data reflects but does not consistently duplicate the data on the negative envelopes or on the photo print file cards that have been used to provide access to the images (see Figure AMNH-3).

As part of a previous Mellon funded digital library project, the logbooks were scanned and then triple-keyed (a process by which the data was entered by hand three separate times and compared for discrepancies), an outsourced task. The result was 186,000 raw legacy records. Despite over a century of errors, anomalies, and abbreviations, using the legacy data as a source and editing and correcting that data is much faster than new cataloging. The verbatim legacy data itself is maintained in a separate field in the record. While all the data for Picturing the Museum came from the logbooks, it was important to plan the database design and write cataloging rules to consistently accommodate the larger Photographic Collection in all its variety. Fields not necessary in Picturing the Museum and later added to capture additional data for other collections included English translation, common name, scientific name, and cultural context. Images from rare books, expedition photographs, and images of artifacts would have this information associated with them.

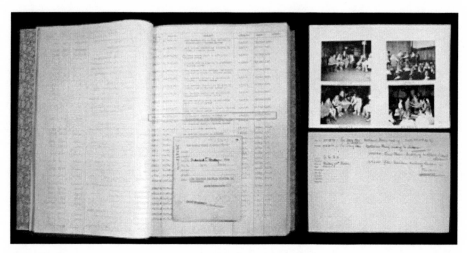

Figure AMNH-3. Data sources: logbook, back and front of photo file card, and negative sleeve, American Museum of Natural History Photographic Collection.

Staffing and Workflow

The METRO grant enabled the Museum to employ a part-time cataloger and a scanning technician for the project. Already on staff, the AMNH digital services librarian created a prototype web site for the image repository using Ruby on Rails and MySQL and the digital photographer created the web site's graphic design and styling. The Museum archivist managed the project and staff - consisting of volunteers, project employees, interns, and regular staff working on the project. The acting director provided expert direction and oversight. A library school intern with experience working for a stock photo agency did the image selection by reviewing the photo file cards and contributed greatly to the organization of the four themes chosen for the site: Dioramas, Education, Exhibition, and Exhibition Preparation. Workflow was planned so that scanning began approximately four weeks before cataloging to maintain the arrangement of the materials as organized for the project. The team met regularly to exchange materials and discuss the ongoing development of the database.

Selection and Staging of Materials

The intern choosing the images reviewed the photographs on the photo file cards and chose the most compelling. The negatives were scanned and uploaded to match the logbook data which had been imported into the database. Lastly, the cataloger edited the logbook data using the additional information found on the photo file cards and negative envelopes.

Retrieving the negatives and staging the physical materials for Picturing the Museum required detailed planning and careful record-keeping. Several individuals worked with the materials to select, retrieve, scan, catalog, and re-file the images at different times. Project staff members in teams of two retrieved the negatives from the film storage room and grouped them by format to expedite scanning. Digitizing, describing, organizing, storing, and building a database for approximately 1000 images and their metadata was a large and complicated undertaking with a sizable team and many detailed procedures. The experience gained will be crucial for the ongoing digitization of the larger Photographic Collection.

Equipment and Technical Specifications

The funding received from the METRO grant allowed for the purchase of new equipment and software. For the project, the Library purchased the Epson Perfection V750-M Pro flatbed scanner, a MAC Pro work station, Eizo CG211: ColorEdge Color Calibration LCD Monitor with hood, and the Eye One Calibration hardware. Later in the project, due to an issue with moiré patterns appearing on 26 images, an anti-newton ring glass was purchased to rescan the problem images. Protocols on how to maintain a consistent color-managed environment, in order to ensure the tonal fidelity of the scanning and post-processing work were developed. An initial monitor profile was created with the Color Navigator software and the

Eye-One Calibration device and the monitor was measured against the profile monthly to ensure that the calibration had not drifted.

Most of the negatives scanned for this project were glass plate. The black and white negatives were captured in 16-bit grayscale TIFF files at an archival size equivalent to those recommended in the National Archives and Records Administration's manual, Technical Guidelines for Digitizing Archival Materials for Electronic Access: Creation of Production Master Files – Raster Images. All archival images were scanned to leave film borders and glass plate edges intact. The scans were corrected conservatively to make available as much of the information from the original negatives as possible. Manual dust and scratch removal was carried out when these interfered with image viewing. After the tone and texture correction, all images were converted to 8-bit grayscale and saved as TIFF files with borders cropped for web presentation on the Museum's SAN. The JPEG web derivatives are automatically uploaded and sent into storage alongside the TIFFs.

The post-processing work procedures, based on the National Archives and Records Administration's best practices, are documented on the Picturing the Museum web site. Additionally, the technical information section of the project web site includes a detailed guide created by the Library's digital photographer, http://images.library.amnh.org/photos/imageworkflow.html.

Conditions of Use

The American Museum of Natural History endorses a policy that makes images in the Photographic Collection freely available to the research community to the fullest extent and as soon as possible. At the same time, it is recognized that access to some images must be restricted to protect the privacy of individuals and to respect various cultural traditions. An individual's image will be removed from the site upon request from that individual. Non-commercial users may download the files for their own use provided that they cite the Museum as the source of the image. No one may alter or modify the content without written permission from the Museum.

Terms for commercial use of the images are detailed on the Picturing the Museum web site. These terms were written and subsequently approved by the Museum's General Counsel and composed so that they would refer to the Museum's Photographic Collection as a whole not just to the Picturing the Museum site.

Development of the Database System

The database for Picturing the Museum was designed to include search and browse features and an efficient cataloging interface, and to enable sharable metadata for interoperability. Metadata values and collection tables for the Picturing the Museum database were loosely modeled on the DSpace version 1.41 database schema. This design offered an opportunity to create multiple collections with distinct metadata schemas. Because the Library had different fields for different collections, instead of creating separate tables, metadata values were appended to a single table with a unique key to identify the field names for each collection. This design offered streamlined storage and a simple approach to dealing with repeating fields. The Library used MySQL to manage the images and metadata because it is a widely used database environment in the open source community, and was, at the time, the primary production database for Ruby on Rails web sites.

Preliminary data clean-up of the logbooks was conducted using SOLR which is based on Lucene, a Java implementation of an enterprise search and retrieval library (*Welcome to Solr,* 2010). The Ruby-based SOLR framework was meant to be used as an advanced search mechanism across all collections, but the time to implement this feature became an issue. The web, however, is just one aspect of the Picturing the Museum image repository; Ruby is the language used to develop the computer workflow and image processing.

Since the Library had extensive existing descriptive metadata comprising the bulk of a cataloged record, a scripted workflow was created with the Ruby language to ingest this metadata into corresponding collections, with a field indicating each specific logbook for each image. Metadata for these collections was ingested into the database prior to images being uploaded and a separate workflow was created in Ruby to upload images into the repository. During this upload, images were associated with a collection and a TIFF image and corresponding service master copy, a cropped original, and three derivative thumbnails were processed. Embedded rights and technical metadata using Harvard's open source Jhove were then extracted. Finally, an external library was created in Ruby to manage the retrieval and display of records in the web presentation environment.

Cataloging Procedures and Metadata Documentation

Editing and producing the photo book helped to refine the scope of the digital project and revealed some descriptive cataloging issues that would have to be addressed in the creation of an image database. For example, when producing the book we found that the original captions from the logbooks often did not translate into a good descriptive title. Images such as 22847, Mr. Albert with loan collections for school use, had no logbook caption at all. Images such as 274856, now reads Two boys collecting turtles, Trailside Museum, but was originally, Two boys collectors bring ing in turtles, including the grammatical errors and typos. Titles were composed to be as descriptive as possible using key words to increase retrieval.

The descriptive data fields were formed according to DACS (*SAA: Describing Archives: A Content Standard*, n.d.) and mapped to Dublin Core (see *DCMI Metadata Terms*, 2008), unqualified, for future interoperability through OAI web harvesting. The descriptive fields for Picturing the Museum include the following:

- Image Number
- Medium (Source Format) (drop down based on the Thesaurus of Graphic Materials)
- Size
- Original Caption
- Title
- Original Photographer (drop down)
- Copy Photographer (drop down)

- Date
- Geographic location (based on the Thesaurus of Geographic Names)
- Person
- Institution
- Permanent Hall
- Expedition
- Temporary Exhibition

Roughly based on the VRA Core Element Description (see *Welcome to VRA Core 4.0*, n.d.), syntax rules for the title field were crafted to be brief and consistent. Writing a new title but retaining the original caption helped maintain integrity to the original data and the history of the Collection, while allowing for a broader search. For example, an original caption of "Corean hats" would be edited to "Korean hats" in the title. A search by either spelling would yield the record. Also, original captions reflecting social and political realities of the time of the photography would be retained while a more accurate or culturally sensitive title could be crafted. For example, the larger database includes many images of artifacts from the Congo; Congo is retained in the source data, while the geographic location field now reads Congo (Democratic Republic), as it appears in The Getty Thesaurus of Geographic Names (i.e., TGN, see *Getty Thesaurus of Geographic Names Online*, n.d.,) which was used to create the standard names of places in this field. Similarly, cultural names such as "Indian" would be changed to "Native American", "natives" to "people" or "people of ...." Researchers can therefore find information by both historical and present-day terms retaining the original documentation.

Considering the size of the AMNH Photographic Collection as a whole, the records were designed for easy and fast data entry that would comply with documented standards for interoperability.

The geographic location field wasn't as much of a challenge during Picturing the Museum, but when the database was expanded to include field photographs and images of artifacts, the metadata became more complex. For example, a 19th century figure of Burmese jadeite carved in China required a repeated field for geographic data (as well as an updated geographic name of Myanmar for Burma).

Because there are so many more place names in the AMNH Photographic Collection than appear in the TGN, the cataloger uses the broadest term in the string in the Geographic Location field and references the specific site or place name in the title or note field. However, the AMNH Library plans to contribute these place names, such as Hopetown, British Columbia, to the TGN in the future as the Photographic Collection contains images from many smaller villages and localities worldwide.

Information that isn't suitable for any other field and that isn't found in the TGN or the Library of Congress Authorities but is necessary for describing the image is placed in the title or note field so that all data is captured and will appear in search results.

Working on the book also highlighted the need for local authorities for photographer's names, permanent halls, temporary exhibitions, and Museum expeditions. The first developed was the photographer list. Using SOLR, the programmer produced a unified list of the many name variations in the 23 logbooks. Names were validated in the catalog and files of the AMNH Research Library as well as through the Library of Congress Name Authority Headings then inserted into a drop-down box on the cataloger's interface.

For over a century of photographs, there were over 262 photographer names, including celebrated individuals such as Roy Chapman Andrews and Edward S. Curtis. For many images, no photographer was listed at all and "Unknown" was entered. Authority lists are also required for temporary exhibits, permanent halls, and expeditions. Not only are these terms unique to the American Museum of Natural History, but they have changed over the years prompting discussions about whether to use current Museum terms or historic ones to reflect the Museum the way it is today, or the way it was when the images were photographed.

Choosing metadata fields and creating a data dictionary that reflects the content in all collections as well as in Picturing the Museum requires planning and flexibility.

Database Growth

Because the image database continues to grow, continuity in staffing and procedures has proven valuable. A guide to cataloging procedures is available on the web site (see *PTM Cataloging Procedures*, n.d.) Expanded examples and data fields for other Collections are documented internally. The cataloger recorded issues throughout this entire process allowing the programmer to make improvements to the interface to accommodate the metadata needs of different collections. Documentation also helped to prepare for the training of student interns and volunteers to catalog in the database.

The cataloging interface for the project evolved over time and continues to change as additional image collections are digitized and cataloged. For example, a 1928 hand-colored lantern slide from a Museum expedition to Mongolia will require different metadata than images selected for Picturing the Museum due to medium, the need for additional local subjects, and a field for Museum expedition, and there are many such items in the Collection.

Fields added to the database after Picturing the Museum include the following:

- Artist (drop down)
- Publication
- Catalog/Specimen Number
- Object/Specimen Location
- Department/Discipline (drop down)
- Cultural Context
- Common Name
- Scientific Name
- Local Subject (drop down)

Drop down lists are used for ease and consistency in fields like original and copy photographer, artist, department/discipline and local subject. This last term allows for a somewhat standardized vocabulary that can be searched for often used subject terms. For example without this data field searching for "birds," would not yield an image titled "Cardinal." Images of dinosaurs often don't use that word in the title e.g. "skull of Tyrannosaurus Rex," would not be found by searching "Dinosaur." This approach will yield a large if not comprehensive data set for the general researcher. More precision will result from geographical headings and fields with authority controlled vocabularies. Drop down lists will be added when the authority work is completed for Permanent halls, Temporary exhibits and Museum expeditions.

Lessons Learned and the Future of the Database

The type of images in Picturing the Museum — historical documentary photographs generally taken in the Museum and the New York City area — are a subset of the AMNH Photographic Collection. Other kinds of pictures coexist within that larger collection: field photographs taken on Museum sponsored expeditions, images of specimens and artifacts, and portraits of individuals. Authority work is a current priority, particularly for names of Museum halls and Museum expeditions. Lists are nearly completed for permanent halls and temporary exhibits but creating authorities for Museum expeditions is a larger and more complicated task and will require some time.

Picturing the Museum is the only portion of the Image Database available to the public at this time but the entire database is searched frequently by the Library staff to fulfill research requests from both inside and outside of the Museum. This AMNH Image Database combines the logbook data, another smaller color database as well as sets of data specific to collections that were not integrated into the larger numbering scheme. The staff continues to make documentation of procedures and data standards a priority, especially as the database grows to include the metadata fields for other types of collections, e.g. specimen or artifact numbers, artists' names and the names of culture groups. Work is proceeding with the help of volunteers. The part time image cataloger for the METRO project, now a permanent staff member, is developing a training program for volunteers and interns to edit the catalog records based on a similar plan using volunteers to scan and process images. The AMNH Library has close to 60,000 images scanned and over 200,000 largely unedited records.

Researchers request photographs on a routine basis and even though most of the records are unedited the database has become an indispensible time saving tool to search for an image and then determine whether or not it has been scanned. Providing individual images for use in books, articles, classroom projects and videos is a mission related service of the Library. However, it is also important to recognize that this is a photographic archive and for scholarly research projects, it is essential to view the images together in their historical context. Despite a century long tradition of item level description, one of the major opportunities provided by the Image Database will be to recollect the collections of images that have been dispersed in the Museum collections over time and place them in their historical context.

The Library has begun a prototype of a web template to be used as an interface to contextualize collection specific information. By identifying and grouping the images, e.g. by the name in the expedition field, it will be possible to retrieve a preselected group of images from that expedition and link to a select dataset as the container list on the web site. The other text, e.g. site overview (scope and content); biographical notes, historical notes, bibliographies, other resources map can be easily encoded into an EAD (see *Encoded Archival Description Version 2002 Official Site*, 2009) finding aid. As more of these special photographic collection web sites are developed, the Library will create a separate interface on its home page for direct access to these collections. As part of that effort, it will also integrate the means for viewers to comment on the images, members of originating cultural communities, scholars, students and others will be able to correct and add to the information currently associated with the images, expanding the knowledge surrounding their history. Mapping to EAD and at the same time making the collection level records for the web sites harvestable by OAI, will also increase the possibility of retrieval of these collections.

In a world of technological change and seemingly limitless possibilities for communication, the AMNH Library is expanding on Bickmore's vision for sharing visual resources and knowledge for the people for science, and for education, now and in the future.

References

PTM Cataloging Procedure. (n.d.). Retrieved May 1, 2010 from http://images.library.amnh.org/photos/PTM_CatalogingProcedures.pdf

DCMI Metadata Terms. (2008). Retrieved May 1, 2010 from http://dublincore.org/documents/dcmi-terms/

Encoded Archival Description Version 2002 official site. (2009). Retrieved May 1, 2010 from http://www.loc.gov/ead/

Getty Thesaurus of Geographic Names Online. (n.d.). Retrieved May 1, 2010 from http://www.getty.edu/research/conducting_research/vocabularies/tgn/

SAA: Describing Archives: A Content Standard (DACS) (n.d.). Retrieved on May 1, 2010 from http://www.archivists.org/governance/standards/dacs.asp

Welcome to Solr. (2010). Retrieved March 30, 2010, from http://lucene.apache.org/solr/

Welcome to VRA Core 4.0. (n.d.). http://www.vraweb.org/projects/vracore4/

Part III – The Digital Campus: Digitization in Universities and Their Libraries

Developing an Institutional Repository at Southern New Hampshire University: Year One

Alice Platt (Southern New Hampshire University)

Abstract

In 2008, Southern New Hampshire University was awarded a three-year, $500,000 national leadership grant from the Institute of Museum and Library Services to create a digital repository using DSpace open source software. Events from the first year of the repository's development are presented and discussed. Key elements addressed include the challenges involved with customizing the DSpace infrastructure, creating standards for access and master files, implementing metadata standards, and developing digital preservation policies. The value of cross-departmental participation is shown, and the importance of planning for digital preservation is presented.

Keywords: Best practices, Digital library, ETD, Electronic, Interfaces, Institutional repository, Open source, Scans.

Introduction

In 2008, Southern New Hampshire University was awarded a three-year, $500,000 national leadership grant from the Institute of Museum and Library Services (IMLS) to create a digital repository using DSpace open source software. The inspiration for the project was a collection of student theses and dissertations from the School of

Community Economic Development (SCED). SCED is a unique program with participation from all over the world, particularly the United States and Tanzania, and also countries such as Uganda, Peru and the Philippines. Like many thesis collections, the projects were printed using consumer-grade equipment, and only one copy was bound and saved for the library. The international nature of the projects, in addition to the danger of losing them to deterioration, made them an attractive collection for beginning a digital repository. Faculty papers from the International Business program were also included in the grant project, to make papers once only accessible from a professor's office available to the world.

Many institutions lack the financial and human resources to build a successful digitization program. The gap between resources available versus resources required can often be bridged by a grant; a search for IMLS grants from 2004-2008 using the keyword "digitization" shows that at least 57 IMLS grants were provided to libraries and museums for digitization projects (IMLS, 2009). Like most institutions, the repository at SNHU's Shapiro Library could not have come to fruition without grant assistance.

The following pages share the Shapiro Library's experiences during the first year of repository development.

The People Involved

Digitization programs need a strong level of organization and administrative support to succeed. Programs that only live within the walls of the library without buy-in from administration and other departments are at risk of failure for lack of support. The Shapiro Library's digital repository is managed by a Digital Initiatives Librarian, who receives support from the Digital Content Specialist, two graduate assistants, and two cross-departmental committees: the Implementation Committee and the Policy Team.

The Digital Initiatives Librarian is responsible for managing the repository, including creation of metadata standards, scanning workflows, policy development, and quality control. The Digital Content Specialist creates descriptive keywords, and writes abstracts for the theses. Two graduate assistants were hired to execute the scanning, optical character recognition (OCR), and access file creation.

The Implementation Committee was initially organized to prepare the grant application, and after the grant was received, organized the necessary infrastructure. Represented on the committee are the Library Dean, the Electronic Resources Librarian, the University Webmaster, the Dean of the School of Community Economic Development, and both the head of the IT department and the IT programmer committed to the project. The committee hired the Digital Initiatives Librarian and a Digital Content Specialist, who both subsequently joined the committee. The Implementation Committee continues to meet on an as-needed basis to monitor the repository's development.

While some members of the Policy Team are consistent with the Implementation Committee, the focus for this group is to determine policies for the repository and discuss other questions that might arise, whether they are related to file format, collection development, or metadata. Because of the nature of the team, there are more librarians represented: the Electronic Resources Librarian, Technical Services Librarian, and the Access Services Librarian are all part of the team, as well as the Digital Initiatives Librarian, Digital Content Specialist, and the Library Dean. Also on the team are the IT programmer and the Associate Dean of the Faculty. The associate dean's participation is effective in keeping the university administration informed on the progress and policies of the repository. The Policy Team initially met every two weeks, and continues to meet at least once a month.

Developing the Technical Infrastructure

After identifying the initial collections for the repository, the Implementation Committee selected the digital repository software and the hardware on which it would reside. Oya Y. Rieger (2007) explains that when selecting software, a number of factors should be considered, including matching your institution's needs to the software's features, considering what resources will be required to install and maintain the software, and assessing the overall usability for both staff and end-users. Often the question might arise: to open source, or not to open source? While using open source software is the current trend, institutions should look closely at their resources to determine if they can support the technological and human resources required to work with open source software packages.

The grant awarded to SNHU included funds to hire the Digital Initiatives Librarian and the Digital Content Specialist. It also financially supported time spent working on the grant by other positions already in place, including IT. Assessment of these resources determined that enough support was available to consider open source software. DSpace stood out as the most widely-used open source institutional repository software package available for academic library use, with an active user community and a wide array of resources available (DuraSpace, 2009, Resources).

The differences between implementing open source versus proprietary software quickly became apparent. While DSpace is advertised to be useful "out of the box," this is not a realistic assertion (DuraSpace, 2009, About DSpace, para. 1). A certain level of programming skill and time is required in order to customize the software. In DSpace, the level of programming needed to make customizations beyond changing the color scheme of the website can be daunting for someone without experience in both programming and website design. The Digital Initiatives Librarian's web design skills and the IT programmer's skills were both needed to make most of the necessary customizations to the user interface.

Community support - While the DSpace community is very active, with a well-populated wiki and listservs for general and technical questions, it is also a complex community. Users vary by what platform they work on (Linux vs. Windows) and what version of DSpace they use. During the time of SNHU's installation, most of the user community was working with either DSpace 1.4 or 1.5. To further complicate things, some users of 1.5 were using what is known as the JSP user interface, while others used the XML user interface – each involving different programming methods for customization. Therefore, not all questions and answers posted by the community are relevant to one's needs. One example encountered was a DSpace wiki entry explaining how to change the DSpace code to enable linking authors in a simple item record. When the code did not function properly, the question was posted to the DSpace tech listserv. Another community member explained that the encoding described in the wiki had changed in version 1.5 (Platt, 2009). Additionally, answers to questions regarding installation varied widely depending on if the user was on Linux or Windows. While DSpace does have a large user community, that community requires some careful navigation.

Professional development – In early June 2009, the NITLE consortium presented a timely DSpace workshop (NITLE, 2009). The variety of sessions provided a strong background to DSpace's capabilities. One session in particular, "Developing Interfaces and Interactivity for DSpace with Manakin Workshop" by Eric Luhrs of Lafayette College, was extremely helpful, providing tools and the know-how necessary to make customizations to the XML user interface (Luhrs, 2009). Without the benefit of this interactive instruction, the learning curve involved would have been much more difficult to transcend.

The experience at the DSpace workshop points to the importance of this type of professional development in the rapidly-changing digital library environment. Conferences such as the Open Repositories Conference and the Joint Conference on Digital Libraries have both included specific DSpace sessions and workshops in the past. A simple search of the web reveals user groups and workshops available for other digital library platforms, including proprietary software such as OCLC's CONTENTdm. Providing funding for librarians and IT staff to attend these types of educational events should be a priority for any institution embarking on a digitization project.

From Paper to Electronic

Creating an electronic record for access involves metadata authoring, scanning, and access file creation.

Metadata – Metadata standards should be determined before the first item is ever added to the repository. Because qualified Dublin Core is installed with DSpace by default, and because Dublin Core is the leading schema for describing digital resources, it was selected for the schema. Determining which elements to make available in the DSpace submission form was more challenging. Not every element should be used to describe a digital object – not all are appropriate for all collections. Besides, the time-consuming nature of metadata entry requires that standards be chosen with efficiency in mind. Michael Boock and Sue Kunda (2009) explain how creating a metadata record for both the DSpace repository and MARC catalog can take up to an hour per record, even when students create the majority of the descriptive metadata (p. 300-302). While it is important to consider descriptive, administrative, structural, and preservation metadata, these elements must be chosen carefully to achieve thorough, but cost-effective item description.

The CDP Metadata Working Group's "Dublin Core Metadata Best Practices", the DCMI Usage Board's "DCMI Metadata Terms", the Scholarly Works Application Profile as described by Julie Allinson (2008), and the Networked Digital Library of Theses and Dissertations' metadata standard (Atkins, Fox, France, & Suleman, 2008) were all examined. From these best practices, 32 qualified Dublin Core elements were selected, with the intention that any item added to the repository could be appropriately described using some or all of these elements. Approximately 20 of these are used to describe the SCED thesis projects in particular.

Scanning – During the development of the DSpace infrastructure, the scanning workflow was also launched. The initial collection of student theses and dissertations from SCED proved to be challenging to scan. Part of the purpose of the SCED thesis project is to document work completed by the student in the field, outside of the classroom. To that end, most of the theses, collected from 1984-

present, include large appendices of documentation including letters, financial statements, marketing materials, photographs, architectural plans, and even a wall calendar used as a fund-raiser. Additionally, students were given the opportunity to be creative in their presentation, often using color, graphs, and decorative fonts.

Sample theses were selected and scanned by the graduate assistants to test how the scanner and OCR software would handle the diverse materials. These initial scans immediately raised questions. There were not yet policies in place for how much information should be captured in the scans, causing uncertainty when incidental color was encountered, such as flyers printed on colored paper. Additionally, there was confusion surrounding the fact that the digitization process includes preserving master files, saved in traditional TIFF format, in addition to the PDF files created for access. The IT staff was not prepared to store and preserve this large collection of master files, and panic arose about their massive size – the files, scanned at 600 dpi in grayscale or color, were 30 to 80 megabytes each. This "megabyte shock" is not unusual, particularly at small institutions; Stacy Nowicki (2008) also noted problems with large TIFF files at Michigan's Kalamazoo College.

After much discussion, the Policy Team agreed to scan the papers for their intellectual content only. Best practices from the California Digital Library (2008) and the CDP Digital Imaging Best Practices Working Group (2008) were consulted to determine digitization standards: a 600 dpi setting for black and white pages, and 500 dpi for grayscale or color pages. This 500 dpi setting resulted in a minimum of 4000 pixels on the largest side of the scan, in accordance with these recommendations (California Digital Library, 3.6.1; CDP, p. 8). It should be noted that if the pages were significantly a different size, the dpi setting would be adjusted to meet this parameter. Master files are saved in TIFF format (California Digital Library, 2008, 3.2). Grayscale and color are only used when necessary to preserve the intellectual content of the document, leaving most of the pages to be scanned as black and white. As a result, the master files are much smaller; the black and white scans are approximately 4 megabytes each.

The solution to the color question requires a certain amount of human judgment, but is viable because the Digital Initiatives Librarian and the graduate assistants conducting the scanning are located in close proximity to one another, facilitating an environment for quick decisions. David Lowe and Michael Bennett (2009) state that the Internet Archive chose to scan all their documents in color, eliminating the need for human judgment (p. 210).

Access File Creation – After creating master TIFF files, it is necessary to convert them for public access. The Portable Document Format (PDF) format, processed so that full-text searching is possible, is ubiquitous among subscription and open access academic databases. It was the obvious solution for our collection.

To enable full-text searching, the TIFs were processed using optical character recognition (OCR) software. ABBYY FineReader 9 Professional was selected, based on a review in PC Magazine (Mendelson, 2008). This feature-rich software enables OCR recognition and error-checking in multiple languages, and performs well with most text, including text printed with a dot-matrix printer, and text formatted in blocks, such as in newsletters and flyers.

From FineReader, the graduate assistants are able to save the PDF with an option called "text under image," saving the corrected OCR text in an invisible, searchable layer under the scanned page image. In order to keep the size of the file reasonable, the PDF images are saved at 300 dpi; to enhance accessibility, the option for creating a tagged PDF is selected (Johnson, 2004).

After the PDF is created, it is opened in Adobe Acrobat, and additional metadata is added to the file's properties, including title, author, and copyright status.

Information in the repository should be not just available, but accessible to all. This includes maintaining file sizes to enable faster load times, ensuring that even users with dial-up modems can download the files in a reasonable amount of time. According to a survey led by John Horrigan at the Pew Internet & American Life Project (2009), seven percent of Internet users in the United States are using dial-up services at home (p. 7). While seven percent sounds small, it is equal to approximately 9 million households in the United States, out of the 129 million counted by the U.S. Census by July 1, 2008. International user statistics vary widely, but it would be best to avoid frustrating any users with unnecessarily large file sizes, thus increasing the viability of the collection.

Therefore, nearly all of the projects are split into two PDFs. Because the bulk of most of the thesis projects is the supporting documents in the appendix, the papers and their appendices are saved as separate PDF files. Of the first 88 student projects scanned, the average file size of the project paper by itself was 2.33 megabytes, with a median of 1.73. The appendices' average was 8.29 megabytes, with a median of 5.2. Both the main paper and the appendix PDFs are available from the same item record in DSpace.

To improve the access files' longevity and accessibility, the PDFs are saved as PDF/A when possible. Roger Reeves and Hans Bärfuss (2009) explain the International Standards Organization's (ISO) goal for PDF/A is that it "provides a mechanism for representing electronic documents in a manner that preserves their visual appearance over time, independent of the tools and systems used for creating, storing or rendering the files" (The Goal of PDF/A). One example of the advantage of PDF/A is ensuring that elements such fonts are embedded in the file, so they display properly even if the user does not have those particular fonts already loaded on his computer. The utility provided in Adobe Acrobat Professional 9 was used to save the files in PDF/A format.

The Often-Missed Point: Digital Preservation

While all of the decisions involved with customizing the DSpace user interface were being addressed, one major component of the digitization program was not addressed: the concept of digital preservation. While it was understood that digital preservation was an issue, it was uncertain how preservation would be accomplished.

The ICPSR Digital Preservation Workshop at the University of Michigan was an excellent opportunity to learn more about digital preservation. This five-day, in-depth workshop made it clear that if an institution presents digital documents online, there is an assumption that they will be preserved there forever – much like a book on the shelf is expected to be readable ten, fifty, or even hundreds of years after it is bound. However, digital files are fragile in their own way, and are susceptible to obsolescence, storage media problems, and other issues (Cornell, 2007, Tutorials, chapter 3: Obsolescence & Physical Threats).

While digital preservation is a complex topic with many components and considerations, the primary concern was how to adequately care for the master TIFF files. Each image must be preserved in the event that the access PDF file becomes corrupted, or when PDF is superseded by a new access file format. The Digital Preservation Tutorial developed by Cornell makes it clear that institutions can not burn files to CDs, put one CD on the shelf, another in someone's garage, and believe they have preserved their files (2007). According to the tutorial, even CD standards have changed over the years, and early formats are now obsolete (Chapter 3: Obsolescence, Chamber of Horrors, Disk Media). It is also apparent that backing up files without including any descriptive information is still not adequate preservation; how many of us have opened a floppy disk and wondered, "What the heck is all this stuff?" Master files must also have their own metadata associated with them to describe what they are. But learning how to preserve these files, as well as adequately preserving the access files and their associated metadata in these early years of digital preservation, is a challenging process that has not been adequately addressed during the first year of repository development at the Shapiro Library. It is probable that many other institutions have also not addressed their own digital preservation questions, or even asked them.

The problems with file obsolescence and data backup are just one small component of creating a digital preservation program. The guidelines presented by the ICPSR workshop are a helpful resource in determining how to ensure that digital preservation at the Shapiro Library is compliant with standards described by the Reference Model for an Open Archival Information System (OAIS), an industry standard. Much progress is anticipated for the second grant year.

Conclusion

The myriad of details involved with creating a digital repository at Southern New Hampshire University were more complex than anticipated. Learning and implementing standards for metadata, master files and access files was time-consuming, but taking the time to establish standards in the beginning doubtless saved a great deal of trouble for the future. Even so, it will be necessary to keep up with developing industry standards, and it would not be surprising if further adjustments are needed down the road. A digital repository is much like a physical building; periodic maintenance, remodeling, and wear and tear should be anticipated and expected.

The Shapiro Library's digitization program has strong administrative support, participation from several university departments, and strong financial resources. The repository will become a successful program for the university long after the grant period concludes.

References

Allinson, J. (2008). Describing scholarly works with Dublin Core: A functional approach. *Library Trends 57*(2), 221-243.

Atkins, A., Fox, E., France, R. & Suleman, H. (2008). *ETD-MS: an interoperability metadata standard for electronic theses and dissertations*, ver. 1.00, rev. 2. Retrieved from http://www.ndltd.org/standards/metadata/etd-ms-v1.00-rev2.html

Boock, M., & Kunda, S. (2009). Electronic thesis and dissertation metadata workflow at Oregon State University Libraries. *Cataloging & Classification Quarterly, 47*(3/4), 297-308. doi:10.1080/01639370902737323.

California Digital Library. (2008). *CDL guidelines for digital images*. Retrieved from http://www.cdlib.org/inside/diglib/guidelines/bpgimages/reqs.html

CDP Digital Imaging Best Practices Working Group. (2008). *BCR's CDP digital imaging best practices version 2.0. BCR*. Retrieved from http://bcr.org/dps/cdp/best/digital-imaging-bp.pdf

CDP Metadata Working Group. (2006). *Dublin Core metadata best practices: version 2.1.1. BCR*. Retrieved from http://www.bcr.org/dps/cdp/best/dublin-core-bp.pdf

Cornell University Library. (2007). *Digital preservation management: Implementing short-term strategies for long-term problems*. Retrieved from http://www.icpsr.umich.edu/dpm/

DCMI Usage Board. (2008, January 14). *DCMI Metadata terms*. Retrieved from http://dublincore.org/documents/dcmi-terms/

DuraSpace. (2009). *DSpace*. Retrieved from http://dspace.org

Horrigan, J. (2009). *Home broadband adoption 2009. Pew Internet & American Life Project*. Retrieved from http://www.pewinternet.org/Reports/2009/10-Home-Broadband-Adoption-2009.aspx

Institute of Museum and Library Services. (2009). *Search awarded grants*. In Grant Search. Retrieved from http://imls.gov

Johnson, D. (2004). *What is tagged PDF?* In *Accessible PDF Learning Center*. Retrieved from http://www.planetpdf.com/enterprise/ article.asp?ContentID=6067

Lowe, D. B. & Bennett, M. J. (2009). A status report on JPEG 2000 implementation for still images: The UConn survey. *Archiving 2009*, 6, 209-212.

Luhrs, E. (2009). *NIS Camp: Developing interfaces and interactivity for DSpace with Manakin*. Retrieved from http://nitlecamp.pbworks.com/f/manakin-workshop-slides.pdf

Mendelson, E. (2008). *ABBYY FineReader Professional 9.0. PC Magazine*. Retrieved from http://www.pcmag.com/article2/0,2817,2305621,00.asp

NITLE Information Services. (2009). *Nitlecamp*. Retrieved from http://nitlecamp.pbworks.com/

Nowicki, S. (2008). *Using DSpace for institutional repositories*. Retrieved from http://hdl.handle.net/10090/4522

Platt, A. (2009, Oct. 6). *Two theme modification questions. Message and responses*, archived at http://sourceforge.net/mailarchive/forum.php?forum_name=dspace-tech

Reeves, R. and Bärfuss, H. (2009). *PDF/A – A new standard for long-term archiving*. PDF/A Competence Center. Retrieved from http://www.pdfa.org/doku.php? id=pdfa:en:pdfa_whitepaper

Rieger, O.Y. (2007). Select for success: Key principles in assessing repository models. *D-Lib Magazine, 13*(7/8). doi:10.1045/july2007-rieger

U.S. Census Bureau. (2009). *Annual estimates of housing units for the United States and States: April 1, 2000 to July 1, 2008 (HU-EST2008-01)*. In *Housing Units: State Housing Unit Estimates: 2000 to 2008*. Retrieved from http://www.census.gov/popest/housing/HU-EST2008.html

Digitization of the Yale Daily News Historical Archive

Kathleen Bauer, Ian Bogus, Karen Kupiec
(Yale University Library)

Jennifer Weintraub (UCLA Library)

Abstract

The Yale Daily News is Yale University's independent student run newspaper. Founded in 1878 it is the oldest continuously published daily newspaper at a United States university. From the initial print volumes until digital versions started in 2000, the entire run of the printed paper consists of 122 volumes and approximately 100,000 pages. In 2007, Yale University Library was asked to create a pilot project to digitize and make available an initial set of ten years of the newspaper with a $50,000 start-up budget. In this article, we will discuss how the project began, and issues that developed during the process related to copyright, interface design, workflow, quality control, and fundraising. This project helped Yale University Library, a large, strongly hierarchical institution, to develop workflows that allow its staff to develop new skills and work across traditional departmental boundaries. Library staff that have traditionally performed tasks related to our print collections or for smaller digital projects have developed new skills and methods for workflow, metadata creation and quality control for a large-scale digital project.

Keywords: Campus newspaper, Copyright, Newspaper digitization, METS, Quality control, Yale, Scanning.

A newspaper digitization project is one that every library, public or academic, can undertake. It is often not hard to get the rights to a local or small paper and an academic or public library has a built-in audience for this type of project. Local researchers will love having it online and genealogists from further afield will bless you. And yet, newspaper digitization, while having recently come into its own, has been somewhat difficult for libraries. Newspapers are crucial to research, providing detailed local and international accounts of events; these incredibly important primary source materials are made of poor quality material that will last a relatively short period of time. Newspapers are hard to digitize because they are published daily with hundreds of issues a year, comprised of various individual sections, and then individual articles, oversized, delicate, and contain thousands of words and pictures that require careful quality assurance. In addition they have unusual layouts, and articles often are split across two or more nonconsecutive pages. There can be numerous contributing authors, syndicated cartoons, advertisements, supplements, and even the occasional joke issue.

Fortunately, newspaper digitization is not new. Many organizations have taken on newspaper digitization and the major national and regional newspapers are now available for licensing by libraries. While many projects focus on digitization of newspapers from microfilm, there is also an increasing number of digitization projects that begin with the original paper. One important clearinghouse for information and best practices for newspaper digitization is the National Newspaper Digitization Program (The Library of Congress, 2009). This program, a joint effort between the Library of Congress and the National Endowment for the Humanities uses the power of grant dollars to enable proper newspaper digitization, research in newspaper digitization and access to the digitized papers through a central resource.

The Yale Daily News, Yale University's student run newspaper, is 132 years old and is the oldest continuously published daily newspaper at a United States university. In 2007, Yale University Library (YUL) was asked to create a pilot project to digitize the newspaper with an initial $50,000 start-up budget provided by the

Yale Daily News's parent foundation (the Oldest College Daily Foundation) and YUL. In this article, we will discuss how the project began, and issues that developed during the process related to copyright, interface design, workflow, quality control, and fundraising.

This project helped YUL, a large, strongly hierarchical institution, to develop workflows that allow its staff to develop new skills and work across traditional departmental boundaries. Staff across the Library who have traditionally performed tasks related to our print collections or for smaller digital projects have developed new skills and methods for workflow, metadata creation and quality control for a large-scale digital project.

The Yale Daily News (YDN) is staffed and produced by student volunteers. The paper is not owned by Yale University, and the student reporters and editors are advised by the independent Oldest College Daily Foundation (OCD). OCD is comprised of former YDN staffers and Yale graduates. In 2005 the OCD came to the YUL with an idea for a project to digitize the Yale Daily News archive and provide access on the Internet. The OCD realized the complexity of the proposal especially considering they did not own a complete run of the newspaper. They asked the YUL to partner with them as OCD owned the rights to the content while YUL had the expertise and the means to make it accessible. To start the pilot project, OCD and YUL contributed $25,000 each to finance a pilot project. YUL decided that for the pilot project we would not digitize anything for which there was an existing digital edition (the YDN has been available online since 2000). Thus, we still had to choose a small amount of material from 120 years of print issues, or a fraction of the 100,000 pages in the entire run, for our initial digitization pilot.

This type of partnership, between an external group owning copyright and the campus library, can be useful for both parties. It is a good way for library staff to gain experience with a complex digitization project and digital collection building, it provides useful material for fundraising for technology projects, it enables the library to provide a useful resource to the campus community, and it enables both the newspaper and the library to create an online product with research value freely for a product that may not have a large sales market.

Several basic principals helped guide the development of the Yale Daily News Historical Archive. Open or commonly used standards for our digital files were important in the event content needed to be migrated to new interface software in the future. We wanted to digitize each newspaper in its entirety, thereby preserving the historical context provided by editorials, cartoons and advertisements. Therefore it was important that we capture the images on each page, not only the text. Another key principle was our requirement that the Yale Daily News be freely available on the Internet. Finally, we wanted the newspaper to be fully searchable, browsable, and to include advanced search features such as byline and title searches. These principals are similar to those elucidated by NDNP and other newspaper digitization projects.

The Initial Decisions

Our first decisions concerned how we would scan the images and what the quality needed to be. Scanning from original source materials will almost always provide the truest digital image but depending on the format of the source there may be undue complications. The physical copies of the Yale Daily News held in the Library's Manuscripts and Archives department are tightly bound which hinders how well the volumes can be opened. Tightly bound materials pose a few risks for digitization projects. Not only can they be damaged during scanning but they can also inhibit producing quality digital images. Microfilm is easy and inexpensive to digitize but by nature is already a derivative format; it will always appear as a black and white photograph of an original document. Microfilm can also be of poor quality, out of focus, smeared, scratched, or otherwise unreadable. Pictures that have been microfilmed often have lost much of their detail.

Luckily, the Yale Club of New York had a complete copy of the Yale Daily News and was willing to donate it to the project. This third copy allowed us to avoid the difficult decision of inexpensively scanning microfilm, scanning bound volumes at a high cost, or disbinding our only physical copy, which would balance the cost and the quality but would leave us with individual leaves to box and store. We were able to disbind, scan and discard these volumes without compromising library collections.

The question of how much storage space would be required for the thousands of images we would receive impacted a number of basic technical decisions. Bitonal scanning would not represent the photographs adequately so grayscale or color images would be required. We felt confident that JPG2000 as a reliable file format for these kinds of materials. Though the Yale Daily News is an essential part of research at Yale, we were not undertaking a scanning project to replace the print and microfilm versions of the YDN, but merely to provide access. JPG2000 allows large amounts of information to be stored in a compressed form, without the compression artifacts and other data losses inherent to JPEGs.

Other universities digitizing complex text and newspapers were using METS (The Library of Congress, 2010b) along with ALTO (The Library of Congress, 2010a). The METS files enable the program to understand the structure of a document, such as a newspaper issue with 16 pages. These files were considered "required elements" for our projects, as they would enable us to search within the issues. The ALTO files provide technical metadata for optical character recognition. The combination of the METS files which describe the issue of the newspaper with the ALTO files which describe the layout, enable full text searching and the highlighting of search words within the display of text. The user sees a representative image (a digital photograph) of a page. The searchable text created from OCR is a stored in a different file, in essence creating a layered document. The METS/ALTO links these two such that when a portion or zone of the image is highlighted it is associated with the text it represents. Users can then search for phrases and see the matching term highlighted on the page image. They can also select and copy the text directly from the image.

Yale was not in a position to write software to provide access to METS/ALTO files for their full functionality. Instead, we decided use CONTENTdm, a commercial product that would suit our needs and fully utilize the METS/ALTO structure. In order to streamline the process as much as possible, we decided to employ vendors to provide as many of these services for us as much as possible. The creation of the METS/ALTO files were included in our request for proposal (RFP) as "Highly Desirable Elements" allowing us to see potential solutions our scanning vendors could perform without totally rejecting a proposal if a vendor could not provide them.

In choosing the issues to digitize it may have seemed obvious to start with the first issue. However, since the OCD and the Library were going to need to fundraise to continue the project, both the Library and the OCD felt it would be best to do a range of interesting time periods to generate interest with potential donors. In addition, an interesting grant funded project that was already underway was digitization of World War 1 posters and pamphlets held in the YUL collection. We decided to tie into that project and digitize issues from 1913-1919. In consultation with Manuscripts and Archives it was discovered that archivists there use the Yale Daily News frequently in answering reference questions and particularly beginning when A. Bartlett Giamatti was President of Yale. The records of Yale's President, and many university offices, were closed to researchers for thirty-five years. The YDN thus provides the best available material for historical research on Yale activities between 1978 and 1981. Finally, we decided to digitize a very exciting time period that is always in demand amongst students, 1967-1970. During this time Yale and New Haven experienced student protests, a murder and resulting controversial trial of a member of the Black Panthers, and a move toward co-education.

The pilot batch consisting of 800 issues from 13 years, or approximately 8000 pages. We were fortunate to be included in a gift from the Yale Class of 1945W, which is the class of students from 1939-1945 whose initial Yale education was interrupted by World War II and completed their degree in an accelerated program upon returning. This provided another 6 years of material bringing the total number of pages to 24,000.

Selection of Vendor and System

In July 2006 we sent the RFP to four vendors and received responses. Most of the vendors were able to fulfill our required and desired elements using similar technology. The RFP process and careful evaluation of the samples supplied by the vendors was illuminating. Through this process, we were able to learn more about the way different vendors work and we had a chance to test drive the solutions to our problem and evaluate different scanning techniques.

All of the vendors used DocWorks software to OCR the files, zone the articles, and create the METS/ALTO files. Then they prepared the package of files for loading into CONTENTdm, using a special loader developed by CCS, the company that created DocWorks. We were able to provide access to the newspaper by using CONTENTdm. This software package, used by many academic libraries, enables users to do full text searching on an issue or across all of our newspapers. The functionality not only allows viewing images of each page but also permits the user to click on an article to view the complete article by itself. The recognized text is also accessible, useful for cutting and pasting. CONTENTdm can automatically create PDFs of the issue on the fly for printing. Finally, because of the zoning and the ALTO files, when an article goes on to another page, CONTENTdm pulls all of the parts of an article together into one screen, making for easy reading

We chose to work with Digital Divide Data, a nonprofit company based in New York City. Digital Divide Data employs young people in third world countries. Their employees not only learn IT skills but also attend classes part time in an effort to break the cycle of poverty.

Digital Divide Data gave us several options for scanning the newspapers. Because they are old, the newspapers had a yellowish tinge. We chose to scan the newspapers in grayscale, which provides a smaller file size and quicker loading of CONTENTdm. We also chose to process the text so that the background and text have a high contrast, while leaving the images in grayscale. The result is easy to read, easy and quick to print, and true to the original intent of newsprint

Workflow

For strategic reasons, YUL does not scan the newspaper issues chronologically, making tracking the project complicated but a high priority so that the various participants could at any time see the status of the project and if any part was held up. A database was created for each volume of the newspaper. Fields were added including a pull down list for the status of each volume. Because various personnel throughout the library were working on the project this database helps everyone know what the status is of every volume.

When volumes have funding designated the status is changed so staff knows to prepare those volumes next. The volumes are collated and a manifest is created that includes basic information such as the volume, number, date, and page count in each issue. Missing volumes, printing errors in the enumeration, and possible inhibitions to scanning are also recorded. The volumes are then disbound with the manifest in hand. Pages missing a significant amount of text are removed with the rest of the issue it belongs to. These issues are recorded in the database under "Issues Needing Replacement." Microfilm will be used to scan missing issues and in order to keep a visual consistency entire issues are scanned from the same sources. For efficiency sake, missing issues are gathered and microfilm is sent and scanned in batches.

Once a volume has been disbound the manifest is printed and tied with the volume. Preparing volumes is frequently performed in batches between shipments. This allows us to have a number of batches ready and waiting until the shipment is due making deadlines easier and less harried.

Regular shipments are usually sent to Brechin Group, a digitization vendor subcontracted by Digital Divide Data, at the beginning of each month. After Brechin scans the volumes, the digital files are then stored to hard drives and sent to Digital Divide Data's Cambodia office for processing where the images are zoned, metadata is created, and the CONTENTdm files are created. Once processing is complete the hard drives are then sent back to Yale where the files are upload directly into our CONTENTdm test server for quality control.

Quality Control

Given the quantity of items in every shipment, it is not possible to check every page. Instead sample issues are checked from every batch returned by the vendor using the ANSI/ASQ Z1.4-2003 (American Society for Quality, 2003) standard quality control procedures. This standard clearly defines how many items need to be sampled, the acceptable error rate, and when to accept or reject a batch based on the number of errors discovered. This standard was developed based on, and is almost identical to, an old military standard (i.e., MIL-STD-105E, Department of Defense, 1989) for inspecting shipments.

This method is based on the idea that there is a level of error one is willing to tolerate but if the error rate is too high the entire batch will be rejected and reprocessed. The Yale Daily News Project identifies four separate areas that need to meet specified quality rates: Image Quality, Zoning, Headlines & Authors, and OCR. If a particular area fails the vendor only has to redo that particular area, not reprocess the entire batch from the beginning. This helps zero in on particular problems for our vendors, though it complicates how we select the samples. Ideally, the sample would be totally random, but this is not feasible considering the samples are based on the particular units being checked; so the image quality is based on each page as a unit, but the zoning error rate is based on each article as a unit. It isn't reasonable to line up all the pages, let alone the articles, and randomly sample them considering complete issues are loaded into CONTENTdm. To get around this, a system was created to convert article and pages into whole issues to be checked.

A quality control tool was created that helps staff through the process that is based off the ANSI standard. The manifests for each batch are added and the inspection level is chosen. The tool then determines how big the sample sizes are as well as the rejection thresholds. A random number generator selects the issues that will comprise the sample. The sample issues are searched in the CONTENTdm test server where the batch was loaded. Errors are recorded in the tool as well as notes such that it can be easily found again if needed. Once complete the tool calculates the results and tells staff appropriate actions. Once a batch is approved it is moved from the test system to the live system.

Copy Right

When we started the Yale Daily News Historical Archive, the copyright situation seemed straightforward. Copyright of the YDN belongs to the Yale Daily News Publishing Co., Inc. This company is run by the student officers of the YDN, under advisement of a professional manager. The project was conducted in close collaboration with the officers of YDN and the Oldest College Daily Foundation, and we had their permission to digitize and make material freely available. Early in the project we concentrated on the earliest material from the 1880. This material was mainly text written by students, with some advertisements. There were no photographs. Subsequently material from World War I was digitized, but material was pre-1923 and again consisted mainly of text written by students, although a few photographs began to appear.

It was not until we started work on material from the 1960's that we grew concerned that we might have a problem. In the 1960's the YDN began to run comic strips, some of which were produced by Yale students. Most notably, a strip called Bull Tales first appeared in September 1968 written by an undergraduate named Garry Trudeau. After Mr. Trudeau graduated he changed the name of the strip to Doonesbury which was then syndicated nationally, including in the YDN. Peanuts also regularly ran in the YDN throughout the 1960's, 1970's and later years. The inclusion of these popular and copyright protected comic strips raised red flags for us: were we allowed to include this material, and did we need to seek permission to do so? We worried that we would need to excise this material from the digitized copies of the papers.

The comic strips were not unique material that could not be found elsewhere, but it did seem that at a time of social and political upheaval at Yale and the entire nation, the YDN staff included the strips for a purpose, and they did play a part in the tone of the YDN. Doonesbury was often overt political comment on current events: Peanuts less so, but still was part of a social commentary. The digitized YDN would not be complete without the inclusion of the strips as they first ran in the paper. We decided that a safe course of action would be to contact the rights holders, Trudeau and the estate of Charles Shultz. In both cases, permission was given to use this material.

We were lucky that this issue was a problem for other projects as well. In June 2008, at the same time we were granted permission by the authors to run both strips, the 11th circuit court of Appeals in Atlanta rendered a decision in the case of Greenberg v. National Geographic Society siding with the NGS. Greenberg had sued NGS for including in a digitized version of the magazine material written by Greenberg and originally published in the printed magazine. Greenberg claimed that NGS only had permission to use his material in the original publication, and in reusing his work in the digital version had violated his rights under Section 201c of the Copyright Act. In siding with NGS, the court found that the use of Greenberg's and other's work was permissible because the magazine was faithfully reproduced and presented as the original, with material presented in its original context. This was in contrast to the 2001 finding in Tasini v the New York Times Co., where the Supreme Court found that the rights of freelancers were violated because in the digital product in question individual articles could by viewed individually, without the original context of surrounding material. The difference between these decisions ultimately lays in how the digitized content is displayed. The publisher has the rights to the issue as a whole and can repackage it as a whole, but they cannot split out the parts and make them into a different product. In our presentation of the YDN, each issue is presented in its entirety as a faithful and full reproduction of the original. While searches will indicate individual articles (and occasionally comic strips) the user always finds that material in the context of its original issue. This decision meant that although we did get permission from Garry Trudeau and Charles Schultz to use their strips it was not required that permission was specifically granted to include them.

Challenges involving Workflow and Data Correction

Anytime a new project starts, especially with a new vendor, there is a period of adjustment and problems are expected. Vendors work with numerous customers with various expectations. It is extremely important for customers to be as clear about their expected outcomes and requirements as possible. Good vendors will make every attempt to satisfy those requirements.

In earlier volumes of the Yale Daily News it was not common for authors to be named in the articles. During a batch of later years, when it became common to name authors, it was discovered that the authors' names did not display with other metadata in the header bar in the pop up window. This was recorded as an error as it was our understanding that fields tagged as "authors" would show up with the title of the article. In discussing this with the vendor they were in fact tagging them correctly and gave us a short list of issues to check in our CONTENTdm installation for why author names were not being displayed.

Other problems were found before the material left the library. As we started disbinding older volumes there was some damage to the pages. Examples of types of damage were photographed and sent to the project staff so decisions could be made on where the cut-off of acceptable versus unacceptable damage would be made. It was ultimately decided that some minor loss of text was acceptable as long as the user could still surmise the lost text and it was not in an area that may be in a targeted search, such as the title of the article.

Other challenges have come up during the course of the project but because of our good relationship with the vendor we can work out solutions easily.

Funding and Sustainability

The project was originally funded with contributions from the YUL and the Oldest College Daily Foundation. In addition the YUL matched its original funding amount for one additional year. At the same time the Library Development Office added the YDN digitization project to its priority list and began actively seeking contributions. The Yale Class of 1945W (the World War II years) signed on quickly to fund the eight academic years covering 1940-1948.

As we moved the project from the pilot phase into production we faced challenges brought about by the depressed economic climate of early 2009. This became the most important factor in determining how the project would continue. Decreases in the Library budget resulted in the elimination of additional library funds. Therefore, digitization of additional content is currently being funded entirely by donor contributions.

The Library's Development Office continues to prioritize this project on its development list and actively works with potential donors to identify time periods that may be of individual interest and are available for funding. Contributions are publicly acknowledged on the   Library's   website   (http://images.library.yale.edu/digitalcollections/ydnAcknowledgments.aspx).

As we move forward issues for digitization will be selected based on a variety of criteria. Donor funding may be given for specific years. These years will be given the highest priority in the digitization queue. Next, if donors do not select specific years for digitization, priority will be given to years that are in demand by researchers at Yale. Specific years or eras are requested repeatedly – including the 1960's. Identification, digitization and availability via CONTENTdm of these specific years can improve services to researchers by providing them immediate access to the information they require while at the same time increasing staff productivity by avoiding repeated copying of the same articles. Once we have digitized all content identified as highly desirable by researchers we will fill in remaining year gaps beginning with the oldest content.

Conclusion

The Yale Daily News digitalization has been a challenging and rewarding project. It has been a partnership with organizations outside of the library, such as the OCD Foundation, and also a great opportunity within the library for various departments to work together. The core team within the library comes from five separate departments: Cataloging and Metadata Services, Electronic Collections, Library Access Integrated Services, Preservation, and Usability & Assessment. This group meets regularly and work out issues that each department have interests in finding collaborative solutions, many of which were able to move into other fledgling projects. In addition, Preservation department staff performs the tasks of preparing the newspaper for digitization and for checking the quality of the digital files as they return. This process utilized skills the department already had, expanding them for newspaper digitization.

On the fundraising side it has proven to be a great springboard. Yale graduates tend to be quite loyal and they have frequently been very interested in looking back into the digitized YDN content that has been created. Not only are they giving back to help complete the project but it has also been an eye catching project where other potential projects can be discussed and funded.

Finally, digitizing the Yale Daily News has enabled the library to produce a free, highly useful, and unique digitized resource for both Yale University and other researchers. The expertise gained in this project has enabled YUL staff to build on this success with other, more complex, digital projects. YUL staff can now successfully digitize varied material such as maps, annotated manuscripts and books. Mass digitization of books may free libraries to concentrate on high quality digitization of unique material that is present in nearly all public and academic libraries. A newspaper digitization project can be an excellent springboard for digitization of this diverse set of material.

References

American Society for Quality. (2003). *ANSI/ASQ Z1.4-2003: Sampling procedures and tables for inspection by attributes.* Milwaukee: American Society for Quality.

Department of Defense. (1989). *Military standard. Sampling procedures and tables for inspection by attributes.* Washington, D.C.: Department of Defense.

The Library of Congress. (2009). *National digital newspaper program.* Retrieve May 20, 2010 from http://www.loc.gov/ndnp/

The Library of Congress. (2010a). *ALTO: Technical metadata for optical character recognition.* Retrieve April 10, 2010 from http://www.loc.gov/standards/alto/.

The Library of Congress. (2010b). METS *Metadata encoding & transmission standard.* Retrieve April 10, 2010 from http://www.loc.gov/standards/mets/

New Jersey Digital Legal Library

Wei Fang (Rutgers University)

Abstract

The New Jersey Digital Legal Library (NJDLL) was launched in 2003 and it's been up and running since then. NJDLL has sixteen collections with about 500 video clips and 20,000 electronic documents. It has served over 300,000 visitors and is popular among legal professionals and researchers. The goal of this project is to create a Web-based digital library where patrons can browse and search for previously unavailable New Jersey legal information. In this article, the author presents the background history of the NJDLL, how it was constructed, workflows, and how problems were solved in depth. Future development suggestions are also discussed.

Keywords: digital library, legal library, XML, LAMP, repository, Supreme Court, oral arguments.

Introduction

As part of the Rutgers University School of Law, the Rutgers University Law Library – Newark with its more than half a million volumes of printed books is the largest law library in New Jersey. Its collections include state and federal statutes and court decisions, federal and New Jersey regulations and administrative decisions, federal and New Jersey legislative history materials, the codes of ordinances for many New Jersey municipalities, Anglo-American legal periodicals, the primary materials of international law, extensive historical materials on English law, and a special collection of criminology and criminal justice materials. The library has served the law school and the surrounding legal community for more than a century. Our law librarians wanted to share the unique collections that the law library had with others in the world and the only way to do it was to convert the collections into digital documents and host them online via the Internet.

The NJDLL project focuses on legal materials related to New Jersey. The target audience groups are legal professionals, historians, researchers and the general public. After more than five years of development, its collections include electronic legal documents as well as New Jersey Supreme Court oral arguments archives. The NJDLL project was first proposed in the fall of 2000 by Paul Axel-Lute, the collection development librarian, and was initialized in spring of 2002 with hardware and software funded by Rutgers University. In April 2003, the digital library was inaugurated with three collections: 1) New Jersey Administrative Reports 2) New Jersey Executive Orders and 3) New Jersey Attorney General Opinions. In 2005, the law library negotiated with the Supreme Court of New Jersey to be the host of its Oral Argument video clips using Microsoft Windows Media Video technology. We are also hosting the digital collection of the New Jersey Council On Affordable Housing's decisions. The NJDLL has now grown to become a popular digital library with sixteen collections ranging from year 1779 to present (see table below).

Collection	Description
Holmes v. Walton	Case file transcriptions (1779-1783) etc.
New Jersey Administrative Reports	First Series; Covers 1979-1991
New Jersey Attorney General Opinions	Covers 1949-1998
New Jersey Council on Affordable Housing (COAH)	Decisions, 1986-Present
New Jersey Department of Human Services, Administrative Orders	Orders from 1977 forward
New Jersey Executive Orders	Covers 1941 - January 1990
New Jersey Governor's Code of Conduct	Text of Code

New Jersey Affordable Housing Archive	Various resources relating to affordable housing in New Jersey
New Jersey Legislative Counsel Opinions	Opinions Since 2004
Supreme Court of New Jersey Oral Arguments	Video Archive of Arguments since 2005
The Law of Slavery in New Jersey	Bibliography, Statutes and Cases
The Mount Laurel Material of The Affordable Housing Archive, New Jersey	History and Selected Documents
Miscellaneous Documents	Topical Legal Documents
Mercer Beasley & Univ. of Newark Law Reviews	Digitized versions of select Law Reviews
Statute Compilations	Compilations of New Jersey Statutes
Weintraub Lecture Series	Selected lectures from the law school's annual lecture series.

NJDLL Collection List

System Architecture

After the project was started, a new position was created and the library hired Kevin Reiss in October 2003 as the digital services librarian who served the library till March 2006. He played a major role in setting up the overall architecture of the site. Meanwhile, the library purchased a new server that has two Intel Xeon processors, two 74 GB hard drive in RAID 1 configuration, two 100 MB network interface cards and 8 GB internal memory. The server was set up in an air-conditioned, secure room with automatic fire extinguisher. It was then connected to a high-speed network for the best user experience. The library decided to use as much open source software as possible. The best part of the open source software is that it is free. Also, unlike most of the commercial software, users can look through all the source codes to make sure it is safe to use if necessary. As a result, the entire project was built with Redhat Linux, Apache server, MySQL database server, PHP and XML parser. We also used Swish-e search engine (Swish-e, 2009) for the searching functionality. Operating system, server software and supporting software were installed within a month. A tape-based system performs full backs up of the server once a week.

Usability and Accessibility

The library administration identified three collections to get the project started. After law librarians selected documents in these three collections and the server was tested, the digital services department of the law library received go-ahead signal to start building the site. The first and critical step was to determine the digital documents' formats. There were many digital document formats that we could choose from, including Adobe PDF, Microsoft Word, Corel WordPerfect, etc. After some careful evaluations and tests, we chose Adobe PDF and DjVu as the formats for our digital documents of the collections. Adobe PDF and DjVu are widely supported by the open source community and they both have free readers available for PC and Mac users to download. For all scanned materials, we defined a protocol that requires all the documents to be saved in 300 DPI monochrome in both TIF format and JPEG format. We also performed Optical Characters Recognition (OCR) on scanned documents. Depending on the size of the collection, the library outsourced boxes of documents to an outside digitization company. The library would contact a digitization company and provide specifications for the company to follow. For smaller sized and consistently updated collections, instead of outsourcing, the library purchased a high speed sheet scanner and an overhead book scanner to scan all the documents in house, since this method would cost less and provide the most convenience in the long run. After converting paper-based documents into digital documents Adobe PDF, Djvu, and plain text, XML files for the metadata of the documents were composed manually.

The site was built using PHP language with item information stored into a MySQL database. A menu system was designed and it used XML file to generate the menu on the fly. For instance, when a patron visits the site, the PHP language will produce the page layout and extract item information from the database while the XML parser generates the menu for that particular page. This provides the system manager with flexibility and accessibility to manage the site.

User interface could be the most critical element when designing a Web site. Digital libraries have traditionally been regarded as difficult to use (Borgman, 2000). When the site was constructed in 2003, most people used computers with dial-up connection and low resolution monitors. The library, therefore, designed the NJDLL with a fixed resolution at 800 pixels in width. To reduce the network load and provide a faster speed, the site used only one graphic, the New Jersey logo, on most of its pages. We also designed a simple interface with an interactive menu list – just to make the uers to be comfortable with (Markri S., etc al., 2006).

Workflows

As described in the System Architecture section, the library uses as many open source tools as possible. However, this does not mean that the library objects to using commercial software. We use Adobe Acrobat Professional (Adobe Acrobat Professional, 2009) to generate PDF files and use Any2 Djvu Server (Any2DjVu Server, 2002) to generate DjVu files from PDF files. The Adobe Acrobat costs about one hundred dollars per university license and the Any2 DjVu service is free of charge. Similarly, work study students use commercial software Abbyy Finereader to perform OCR tasks and use open source software, Notepad++ (Notepad++, 2009), to compose metadata files. For video files, work study student use Windows Movie Maker from Microsoft (WMM, 2004) to convert video clips. Although the WMM is not open source, it is freely available.

Throughout the years, the library has developed and improved three protocols to process digital objects based on the types of the resources as well as the scale of the resources (Figure RU-1).

Internal Resources

The library defines internal resources as collections over which the library has total control. Reference librarians are in charge of identifying each and every item to be scanned. Depending on the size of the collection, the library administrators decide whether to scan the documents in house or to outsource them. When a collection is scanned in house, work study students, hired from the law school and other departments of the university, are assigned to scan the documents using the high-speed sheet scanner for loose leaf pages and using overhead book scanners for rare documents. They also generate all metadata files associated with each item. When a collection is outsourced, the library contacts the outside vendor to provide digitized documents using CDs or DVDs. The digital services librarian will do a quality check and verify the quantity. If everything meets the requirements, work study students will be assigned to compose metadata for the documents.

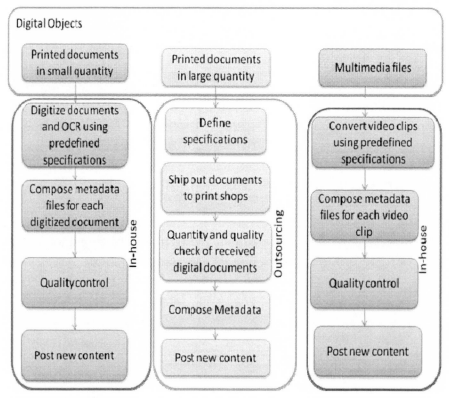

Figure RU-1: Workflows

When the content is ready to be updated, the digital services librarian uploads metadata and digitized documents to the server and runs a UNIX script to generate database records and item information based on the metadata file. Librarians and IT personnel use SSH to upload files and run UNIX commands. To simplify daily work, they also use Webmin and phpAdmin to manage the site and the database.

External Resources

External resources are the resources that the library has to acquire from outside of the library and the library has no or very limited control over the quality of the resources. The NJDLL has two collections that use external resources: New Jersey Supreme Court Oral Arguments (NJSCOA) and legal documents from New Jersey Council On Affordable Housing (COAH).

The library uses the in-house protocol to scan materials for the COAH collections. For the NJSCOA, the library assigns work study students who are law school students for their capability of interpreting legal materials. Work study students are trained to produce metadata and video clips for this collection based on the files received from the IT office of the New Jersey Supreme Court. As a procedure jointly developed by the Court and the library, after the case is argued, the IT office will transfer video recordings in standard broadcast resolution along with transcripts and detailed argument information to a FTP server. When we decided to host the NJSCOA video archives, we developed a new database and procedure to convert the original high resolution video clips received from the Court into low-bandwidth and medium-bandwidth video clips. For each and every video recording, work study students will produce two video clips for medium and low bandwidth, metadata in XML format. After a month of the argument date, cases will be uploaded to the server and posted by the digital services librarian using a UNIX script.

Quality Control

Quality is a very important element of any successful Web site. As the matter of fact, if one site does not provide a good quality expected by the visitors, it will soon lose credit, attract no visitor and dry out quickly. Using existing standards is very important in quality control, product usability and documents preservation. Work students will encode metadata records for each digital record by following the standards listed below:

1) METS: Metadata Encoding and Transmission Standard (METS, 2009)

2) EAD: Encoded Archival Description (EAD, 2002)

3) Text will follow the Text Encoding Initiative (TEI) P5 guideline (P5, 2009)

New work study students need to be trained before they can work on any assignment. The library has composed many procedures for the students to follow. Before the metadata records can be used to generate web pages and shared online, the digital services librarian will check them for quality.

Backup Strategy

A modern library should provide two basic functions: preserve and serve. As important as serving knowledge to the people, our library also has long history of preservation. All master scan images in NJDLL project are stored in uncompressed TIFF format. Metadata files are composed using XML formats, and we have a well-oiled backup strategy to ensure that we don't lose these important digital assets when disaster strikes.

A mirrored RAID 1 hard drive array is used as the first tier of backup. The IT office controls an external tape drive that backs up the entire server every week. To save tapes, the IT office recycles tapes after two months of the last backup. The digital services department also backs up the server remotely by using a server-grade external hard drives as the third tier of the backup. Each tier holds a full set of backups, including normal backup sets and incremental backup sets.

Frequency of backups: One normal backup would be performed monthly. Every week, an incremental backup would be performed. Two physical locations are assigned for the first tier and third tier backup devices.

Problems Encountered and Counter Measurements

During the past five years, the biggest technical problem we had was security. We started the Web site and made it public in 2003. The site did not have any protection initially since we thought that we are an organizational site and it is on a state university's network. The site was hacked within a month. After the incident, the server and the site were restored and we installed firewall and trapwire on the server. The site was also readjusted to accept administrative connections from Rutgers University IP addresses only. Both the IT office of the law school and the library monitor the activities on the site consistently and update server patches as soon as they are available.

Structurally, the site was built by grouping small collections one at a time. Each collection had its uniqueness in terms of materials and focus scope. The site had to be fine tuned each time there was a new collection to be added. When we added the Supreme Court Oral Argument into our collection, one big issue was that we had to use the Court file name schema that is difficult to use and understand by our work study students. For instance, a dash and an underscore may make no difference to the student workers, but the UNIX server will treat them differently. We had to communicate with the Court and adjust the naming schema between the library and the Court.

Another thing which may not be as obvious as the name schema was the technical documents that the site management team has to compose. When the server was installed and the site was built, everyone involved focused on their work and paid little attention to writing down technical notes and documents. When some of the staff members left for other positions, the successors had a lot of difficulty in understanding why the script or the system was designed in its way. We now require all staff members to write technical documents on a regular basis and new staff members have to read those documents before performing any work on the server or the system.

The technologies we have used are becoming obsolete gradually. One example is that the library has been using the Windows Media Video for years and keeps getting phone calls from Mac users complaining that they are not able to view the contents. Considering the fact that more and more students and attorneys are using Mac computers, this is something the library has to address. We are building our own Youtube-like video repository to host copyrighted video recording (Fang, 2009) and we may use the same video repository to host the Supreme Court oral arguments in the future.

One issue that is hard to get around is that the inconsistent quality of work study students. Every semester the library has to hire students to scan documents, compose metadata, and convert video clips. As required by the Rutgers University, the library can only choose students within the university. Students may come from the law school or any other department of the university. Generally, undergraduate students perform tasks with the lowest quality. They have no idea about legal documents and make errors all the time. On the other hand, law school students perform all the tasks the best. They get their hands on quickly and enthusiastically. However, they are always on a busy schedule especially during the exam session. In order to solve this issue, the library composes protocols and asks new work study students to memorize them. This can reduce errors in some degree though it cannot completely eliminate them.

The project has been up-and-running for more than five years. We would like to track website activities. Apache web server provides a log file and the server has software that can analyze the log file. However, it does not provide many details on each page or file viewed by the visitors. We tried other new methods on the site, including Web analytic software and some online Web analytics providers. Not all these methods were reliable. In one particular case, the Web site stopped responding since it was waiting to load tracking codes from the tracking provider. After deploying Google Analytics (Google, 2009) on the library's main Web site, we got positive results (Fang, 2007). The library finally decided to use Google Analytics on the NJDLL site for its functionality and reputation. Now, after two and half years of using the Google Analytics to track our site, we are satisfied with the results.

Important skills learned from doing this project

1. Security always has the top priority: the server should be behind a hardware or software firewall and set up in a way that administrators can only log in from the Intranet. Just in case something bad happens, a fully tested backup plan and equipments should be used.

2. Use uniform name schema: when collaborating with another organization to develop a new collection, it is extremely important to go through naming schemas before starting coding. Every detail has to be thought about thoroughly or later on the smallest hole can grow unmanageable.

3. Document everything: Spending five minutes writing a short note may save you a day of work later.

4. The last day of old technology is better than the first day of the new technology: Five years may seem to be a short period in the technology field, but we've seen a lot of new hardware and software faded away. Our take on the technology is that we stick with a time-proofing reliable platform as long as it meets our requirements and visitors' expectations.

Future development

As of now, we have about 500+ video clips and about 20,000 electronic documents on the site. The site attracts about 40,000 visitors annually, which is just enough for our hardware to handle. The law library will keep maintaining and adding new items to the site every semester. New collections will also be added once they are digitized. The biggest goal for the next few years would be merging our video content from Windows Media Player format to the more popular Adobe Flash Video format.

Currently the entire site is being indexed by the Swish-e search engine on a weekly basis. We have some good experiences with this free search engine, but it is hard to be reconfigured and needs some workaround procedures to get the XML files indexed correctly. We are planning to replace the Swish-e search engine with Google's Custom Search, with which the university has contract.

When the time comes to replace our current server's software platform, we will use Ubuntu server edition (Ubuntu, 2009) and Drupal (Drupal, 2009) as the new platform and merge over all the existing contents. Ubuntu server edition is a Linux based LAMP ready operating system. Drupal is an open source content management system, which has been used by thousands of Web sites, including government Web sites such as the whitehouse.gov.

References

Adobe Acrobat Professional. (2009). *Adobe and PDF*. Retrieved from http://www.adobe.com/products/acrobat/adobepdf.html

Any2 DjVu Server. (2002). *Welcome to the DjVu Any2Djvu Server*. Retrieved from http://any2djvu.djvuzone.org/index.html

Borgman, C. (2000). *From Gutenberg to the global information infrastructure: access to information in the networked world*. Cambridge, MA, USA. MIT Press.

Drupal. (2009). *About Drupal*. Retrieved from http://drupal.org/about

EAD. (2002). *Encoded archival description version 2002*. Retrieved from http://www.loc.gov/ead/

Fang, W. (2007). *Using Google analytics for improving library website content and design: A case study*. In *Library Philosophy and Practice, Annual Vol. 2007* (Special Issue Libraries and Google) Retrieved from http://www.webpages.uidaho.edu/~mbolin/fang.pdf

Fang, W. (2009). Online law school video repository: The flash way. *Computers in Libraries, Vol. 29*, No. 6.

Google. (2009). *About Google Analytics*. Retrieved from http://www.google.com/analytics/

Makri, S., Blandford, A., & Cox, A. (2006). Studying law students' information seeking behaviour to inform the design of digital law libraries. Paper presented at the Alicante, Spain.

METS. (2007). *METS schema, & documentation*. Retrieved from http://www.loc.gov/standards/mets/mets-schemadocs.html

Notepad++. (2009). *About Notepad++*. Retrieved from http://notepad-plus.sourceforge.net/uk/site.htm

P5. (2009). *TEI: P5 guidelines*. Retrieved from http://www.tei-c.org/Guidelines/P5/

Swish-e. (2009). *About Swish-e*. Retrieved from http://swish-e.org/

Ubuntu. (2009). What is Ubuntu. Retrieved from *http://www.ubuntu.com/products/whatisubuntu*

WMM. (2004). *Windows Movie Maker 2.1 Download*. Retrieved from http://www.microsoft.com/windowsxp/downloads/updates/moviemaker2.mspx

Pratt Institute: A Historical Snapshot of Campus and Area

Paul Schlotthauer (Pratt Institute Libraries)

Abstract

The chapter discusses the planning and procedures for two digitization grants received from METRO in 2005 and 2006 by the Pratt Institute Libraries. Despite the creation of a timeline, unexpected issues necessitated adjustments. Selection of materials was more labor intensive and time consuming than expected. Our collection consisted of different formats, which required managing significant differences in metadata content and interpretation. OAI-compliancy was problematic with our image management software. Also, we had modified the Dublin Core fields, which created compatibility issues with OAI gateways. In 2006, we planned for potential pitfalls based on our previous experiences, but still encountered delays and problems, such as color management. In 2008 we mounted our images on Flickr and saw a marked increase in use.

Keywords: Archives, Best practices, Bookplate, Color correction, Compliancy, Digitization, Historical images, Image management software, Imaging, Intellectual control, Metadata Template, Negative, Pratt Institute, Preservation, Project management, Selection criteria, Selection guidelines, Special collections.

Introduction

In 2004, when we applied for the METRO grant for digitization, the library at Pratt Institute's Brooklyn campus had a Visual Resources Center that, since 1997, had been digitizing its collection of over 160,000 slides for teaching and research purposes. We had staff and student workers with training and experience in digitization, as well as dedicated space, equipment, and technical support. Our digitized images were available online, so we had some acquaintance with the issues surrounding online collections.

For us, therefore, it was not so much a question of beginning a digitization initiative as it was beginning a new phase in our already-existing digitization program. Our hardware was no longer state of the art. The evolution of metadata schemas and best practices, such as *Western States Digital Imaging Best Practices* (later revised by the Bibliographic Center for Research as *BCR's CDP Digital Imaging Best Practices*) (Bibliographic Center for Research [BCR], 2008), meant that our own protocols were inconsistent if not out of date: they worked for us, but they were not truly in step with the most current professional standards. We envisioned a METRO grant as an opportunity to update and tighten our practices, and believed that the resulting increase in efficiency would generate momentum to expand our digitization program in order to better meet the increasing expectations of our users.

Determining the Team and the Project

When we applied for the grant, we began to assemble the team. For project manager our Director of Libraries selected our Visual Resources Curator, who had managed Pratt's digitization program for over a year and had a background in photography, metadata, and technology. As the Institute's archivist, I had devoted considerable effort to researching, organizing, and preserving the archives' large image collection, and was therefore asked to serve as the selector and conservator of the materials to be digitized.

Throughout the course of the project, both the project manager and I took several of the digitization training courses offered by

METRO, including Digital Imaging, Digital Project Infrastructure, Preserving Digital Materials, Metadata for Digital Collections, Introduction to XML, Basic Copyright Issues, and Using Adobe Photoshop for Image Quality Control. These classes provided us with a firm foundation in various aspects of digitization that enabled the project to proceed more efficiently.

For our scanning technician we selected a graduate student from the School of Information and Library Science who possessed considerable knowledge of imaging, metadata, and Web content management issues, and who had prepared, scanned, retouched, and cataloged many images in the Visual Resources Center. We also began to draft a job description for a project cataloger.

In determining the experience and training needs of the project team, we adhered to the guidelines of the North Carolina Exploring Cultural Heritage Online (ECHO) initiative and addressed four principal issues: conservation, digitization/encoding, metadata/cataloging, and technical development/support (NC ECHO, 2007). We also planned to use a graduate student from Pratt's Communications Design Department to develop the Website for this project. As with our scanning technician, we involved both our School of Information and Library Science and our School of Art and Design in a truly collaborative effort, which gave weight to our assertion that digitization was relevant to the entire Institute, not just the Libraries.

As the image curator, I was faced with the problem of what to select from the archives and Special Collections for digitization, given the embarrassment of riches at the Institute and METRO's limit of five hundred images per institution. As Janet Gertz (2007) has stated, "In selecting well, institutions of all sizes and types concentrate on the parts of their collections that are best suited to digitization, make the most effective use of the technology, and meet their clients' needs. . . . Good selection decisions come through carefully assessing the physical nature and content of the original materials, the intellectual property rights connected with them, and the requirements for a technically sound, well-described, and cost-effective product that serves both users' need for access to the content and the institution's need to preserve the materials" (Introduction, paras. 1 and 2). I therefore decided to make an eclectic selection from several collections rather than focusing on one format or theme.

I based my broad criteria on subject matter and quality of image. My goal was to illustrate the breadth and diversity of the collections while emphasizing various facets of the Institute as an academic institution, a presence in the local community, and an important influence in the fields of art, architecture, fashion, design, and education. Our archival image collection existed in a variety of formats, including photographs, slides, and negatives, and focused primarily on such aspects as the architecture and grounds of the campus and the Clinton Hill section of Brooklyn in which it is located; student work in art, architecture, fashion, and design; and campus life and activities. I selected a number of historical photographs of Pratt's buildings, some of which date from the nineteenth century and are well known for their architectural features.

The campus, a twenty-five-acre oasis in the historic district of Clinton Hill in northern Brooklyn, was also represented, in part because early images of the campus afford views of surrounding Brooklyn streets and include long-demolished buildings and structures. There were also photographs of classes in session and students at work dating from the early decades of Pratt's history.

These were significant from the standpoint of the history of education. They depicted the state-of-the-art studios and equipment used for classes in such fields as drawing, woodworking, engineering, and physical education. Also important from a socioeconomic standpoint was the presence of women and minorities in many of these photographs, demonstrating the Institute's progressive outlook in an era when racial and gender discrimination were the norm in the United States. I included images of the founder and his family, as well as some of the mansions they built, as comprising an important part of Brooklyn's history. Finally, I chose examples of student work, such as architectural models and drawings, designs for clothing and interior decoration, sculpture, prints, and posters, which illustrated the outstanding body of work produced by Pratt students during its existence. Many of the examples in this category came from negatives dating from the 1950s through 1970s, and all gave evidence of the creativity fostered by the Institute's faculty.

From Special Collections I selected prints of hand-colored stenciled fashion plates from *La Gazette du Bon Ton,* considered the most influential French fashion magazine of the early twentieth century, as well as representatives of Pratt's collection of nineteenth- and twentieth-century bookplates. The fashion plates could serve as resources for fashion students and designers, while the bookplates were outstanding examples of period book art and typography.

We were gratified to receive a one-year grant from METRO to digitize this selection. We first created a timeline incorporating all the major activities, which allowed us to track our progress and, at the mid-point, enabled us to make the adjustments necessary to complete it in time (Figure PRAT-1).

Imaging took place on an iMacG5 (20-inch, 1.8 GHz, 1 GB RAM, 250 GB hard drive), an Epson Expression 10000XL scanner, and Adobe Photoshop Creative Suite software, all made possible through the METRO grant. The raw and enhanced TIFF files were saved to Gold Mitsui CD-Rs and a 1.6 TB LaCie external hard drive (the LaCie drive not only allowed secondary storage and backup but at times became a shared drive for the various computers used for this project). The resolution had to be determined by the format: the photographs, bookplates, and fashion plates were scanned at 600 dpi, whereas the negatives were scanned at 1,200 dpi.

Once we received the grant, and while the initial scanning was taking place, the project manager, scanning technician, and I formed a search committee to recruit a digital archive cataloger. This person's ability to capture the descriptive and technical metadata would be a crucial element in the success of this project, so we insisted that candidates possess experience and knowledge of MARC21, AACR2, Library of Congress Subject Headings, Dublin Core, and emerging descriptive metadata standards.

Original Timeline

	02/05	03/05	04/05	05/05	06/05	07/05	08/05	09/05	10/05	11/05	12/05
Images Scanned/ Edited	100	200	300	400	500	Edit	Finish				
Records Catalogued		40	80	160	240	320	400	480	Edit	Finish	
Website Design				Begin Plans	Start Design	Refine Design	Create Site	Create Site	Create Site	Launch	
Promotions									Create	Create	Send

Revised Timeline

	02/05	03/05	04/05	05/05	06/05	07/05	08/05	09/05	10/05	11/05	12/05
Images Scanned/ Edited	100	200	300	400	500	Edit	Finish				
Records Catalogued				60	150	300	400	500	Edit	Finish	
Website Design							Start Design	Refine Design	Create Site	Launch	
Promotions									Create	Create	Send

Figure PRAT-1. Schedule for the 2005 Grant.

We also expected knowledge of authority control in the online environment, as well as experience using bibliographic utilities and assigning metadata to digitized materials for Web-based display and searching. During the interviews, in addition to asking the usual questions, we gave the candidates several images and asked for on-the-spot descriptions; this was an effective means (with considerably varied results) of determining the candidates' observation powers and the kind of descriptive information they would be likely to provide. The search committee's diligence was rewarded with a candidate who produced outstanding work.

Descriptive metadata was to follow the Dublin Core elements of title, creator, subject, description, date digital, date original, format, digitization specifications, resource identifier, rights management, contributing institution, publisher, contributor, type, source, language, relation, and coverage. Technical metadata was to include resolution, size in Kilobytes, height and width in pixels, bit depth, and color space. Library of Congress Subject Headings, as well as LC's Thesaurus for Graphic Materials, were to provide the controlled vocabulary for cataloging content.

Challenges

Scheduling

Despite our careful planning, we encountered a variety of challenges, several of which affected our schedule and required adjustments. Perhaps the greatest problem was maintaining a consistent workflow. All the team members except for the cataloger took on the project in addition to their usual responsibilities, which impeded the conducting of regular meetings and delayed weekly or monthly goals. Because we were spread rather thin at times, it was difficult to maintain good communication within the group. We all recognized how quickly we would lose control if the team were disjointed, so we made special efforts to touch base regularly and keep each other informed through e-mail exchanges and periodic meetings. Thus, when the project director left before the project was completed, it was relatively easy for me to step in and take her place.

Selection and Scanning

Because we did not focus on a specific theme or collection, I needed to employ multiple criteria in my selection process, including artistic quality, historical significance, and research or special-interest potential, to assemble a collection both unique and engaging on various levels. I tried to operate within the parameters set forth in several resources on this issue (Gertz, 2007; Hazen, Horrell & Merrill-Oldham, 1998; Southeastern NY Library Resources Council [SENYLRC], 2004), but even so, freedom of choice made it difficult to adhere to the maximum number of images mandated by METRO without omitting something I thought especially interesting, and in fact I had to pare down the number of selections several times. This was more labor intensive and took up more time than anticipated, and thus a certain amount of haste was required given the time frame. Even so, I was late in delivering the final selection. For future projects, we knew we would have to begin the selection process sooner and allow more time for its completion. Of course, focusing on one theme or collection would also ease the problem.

Another important reason for the delay was the fact that only the negatives had pre-existing unique identification numbers. The bookplates, fashion plates, and most of the photographshad no identifiers at all. We had to devise a system for these at the time of selection. The simple act of numbering all these images, especially for those in fragile condition, was extraordinarily laborious and time consuming, even with the aid of student workers, yet it would have been disastrous not to have done it. Given the time constraints for this project we had no choice but to plow ahead, but, based on this experience, I can certainly endorse the view that, whenever possible, one should avoid digitizing materials lacking a minimal level of intellectual control.

The project's wide range of materials also made the development of a systemized workflow and management of the digital results difficult. The scanning process required a tremendous amount of patience, especially with the negatives, for which the time needed to correct the images was considerably longer than for the prints and plates. The negatives, being film, showed dust and scratches much more prominently than the other formats, especially at the high resolutions we were using. Our Epson scanner had no Digital Image Correction and Enhancement (ICE) functionality for filtering, and we chose not to use the dust-removal feature native to the Epson scanner because we feared it was insufficiently robust. That meant depending on the tedious and time-consuming process of editing out dust and scratches by hand via Photoshop's clone stamp tool. In retrospect, it might have been better for us to use Epson's dust-removal feature—sophisticated or not—for the sake of saving much-needed time.

The bookplates in particular presented problems regarding accuracy of tone and color reproduction. Following the National Archives and Records Administration's recommendations in Guidelines for Digitizing Archival Materials for Electronic Access (Puglia, Reed & Rhodes, 2004), we included a Kodak Q-13 gray scale target with each scan, which improved the accuracy and consistency of color and tone reproduction. We also used ICC color profiles, converting the ColorSync Workflow profile (standard for Epson scanners) to the Adobe RGB 1998 workspace for post-processing in Adobe Photoshop. We were not entirely satisfied with the results, and realized that color management software would have been useful for profiling and calibrating our scanners and monitors. In addition, the presence of several large windows in the Visual Resources Center meant that lighting was highly variable and rendered difficult the comparison of the originals against the digitized images to check quality and accuracy for color, brightness, and tone. The process was less consistent and more subjective than we would have preferred, but that was a drawback of being housed in a building constructed in 1896 with windows intended to provide as much natural illumination as possible.

Another obstacle was the condition of many of the items, especially the photographs, some of which dated from the nineteenth and early-twentieth centuries and suffered from cracks, brittle paper, peeling emulsions, and other damage. They were housed in archival polyethylene or Melinex sleeves for protection, which meant the scanning technician had to remove and replace the images from the sleeves carefully to avoid inflicting further damage. The technician, after scanning, made attempts in Photoshop to minimize some of the visual imperfections that appeared in the scans because of the condition of the originals. This was a time-consuming process. However, this project was as much about preservation as it was access and outreach. Several images were chosen precisely because they would not last much longer.

One positive result of these problems was the creation of standards for imaging workflow and various file-management issues such as naming conventions and folder hierarchy systems. In one way, the scanning issues we had to confront were beneficial (albeit annoying), because they provided us with a solid foundation of practical experience working with a variety of formats that would allow us in future projects to anticipate potential problems and enable us to construct schedules that would accommodate them. They also gave us a greater understanding of the logistics involved in the deceptively simple and clear-cut process of "digitization," which increasingly has become, for the uninitiated, a buzzword for quick-and-dirty reproduction and document delivery.

Metadata

The nature of our project also contributed challenges for metadata creation. The diverse nature of the items required the cataloger to quickly gain expertise in cataloging bookplates, fashion plates, and historical photographs and negatives. Research performed in one subject area did not usually apply to another; for instance, knowledge of the history of Pratt Institute, necessary for the prints and negatives, had no bearing on the fashion plates and bookplates. As Pratt's archivist, I was the main source of information for questions about the historical images, but researching the bookplates and fashion plates was a bit more complicated. The cataloger had to consult resources at Columbia University to obtain background information on the bookplates, their creators, and the historical techniques used to create them.

The cataloger had to use a slightly different approach for each type of material. The format differences across collections were a given, but the interpretation of the creator, description, and subject fields often varied as well. For example, the description field for a fashion plate with printed text in French required a different format and style than that for a photograph of an architectural drawing. In hindsight, it would have been more efficient and cost-effective had we focused on the metadata for one type of material at a time.

As they did with color reproduction, the bookplates proved especially problematic. Many of the artists were identified by only a monogram or other symbol, and a large number were undated, but the cataloger simply lacked the time to research and identify each plate more thoroughly. The techniques used to produce the plates (such as etching or engraving) might also have been determined for many of the plates had there been additional time or cataloging resources, though the cataloger was able to do this for some of the plates. There were issues at the quality-control stage as well. For example, we initially entered the bookplate owners' names in the format Firstname Lastname. When we realized that this produced idiosyncratic sorting in our image presentation software, however, we changed the order to Lastname, Firstname—a relatively small change in the metadata template that proved time consuming because it had to be implemented in each individual record.

We also had to modify the Dublin Core metadata template in order to provide more effective descriptions of the bookplates' unique elements. For instance, the person for whom a bookplate was made is as important as the artist who created it, and the motto, when there is one, becomes a major means of identification. We had to accommodate these features by creating the elements Owner and Motto, and we changed the Creator field to Artist because we felt many people might misinterpret Creator to refer to the printer of the physical object rather than the artist who designed the plate. Additional modifications were also made (Figure PRAT-2).

Simple Dublin Core Fields	Modified Dublin Core Fields for Bookplates
Identifier	Identifier
Source	Source
Date	Date Original
	Date Digital
Creator	Artist
Title	Owner
Coverage	Place
Description	Description
Subject	Subject
Language	Language
Format	Format
Type	Type
Rights	Rights
Contributor	Contributing Institution
Publisher	
Relation	
	Motto
	Keywords
	Digitization Specifications
	Digitizer
	Cataloguer

Figure PRAT- 2. Basic and Modified Dublin Core Metadata.

Access to Our Digital Collection

Although many of the grant recipients for METRO's 2005 initiative used CONTENTdm as their image management and presentation software, Pratt had made a decision, prior to and independent of the grant, to purchase Luna Insight software, which was used by the Getty Museum and other important art institutions. The reasons for this had to do with numerous organizational and storage features deemed necessary for the needs of our faculty and students: unlike some institutions, Pratt's primary and overarching digitization concerns had to focus on the continuing research and pedagogical needs of art, design, and architecture programs at both the undergraduate and graduate levels. This decision was not without consequences when it came to creating access to our METRO collection.

To begin with, implementation of Luna Insight into the browser environment was a slow, difficult process; a significant learning curve was required to resolve issues surrounding Insight's interface and layout, which was new to everyone. Our greatest difficulty, however, was making the collections OAI-harvestable. Our systems librarian joined us at this point to provide assistance, and he discovered that Luna Insight's databases were not fully compliant because they were unable to allow selective harvesting based on a specific date stamp— that is, they could harvest repository files that were static but not dynamic. Even achieving this level of compliancy was frustrating and time consuming because OAI harvesting was naturally not Luna's responsibility (in fact, Luna's support staff told us that Pratt was its first client utilizing OAI harvesting for Insight collections). Therefore, it became our sole responsibility to generate the files, intermediate them with a gateway, and register them with a harvester, although no member of the team had done this before.

With some difficulty we were able to generate static repository files with the Luna Insight software, after which we had the collections registered and intermediated through the Los Alamos National Laboratory's (LANL) open-source experimental OAI Static Repository Gateway software (Srepod). This was not an easy process because our inexperience with OAI gateway software resulted in a steep learning curve. Once we had gained sufficient mastery of the software, however, we chose to register our collections with OAIster, though here, too, we encountered difficulty, because our attempts were met with persistent error messages. Eventually we had to contact a member of the OAIster team at the University of Michigan, who was able to assure us that our collection had been registered successfully.

What made the OAI harvesting process so challenging was the fact that it comprised three distinct steps and was supported by three independent systems: Luna Insight, Srepod, and OAIster. Luna was unable to help us with Srepod and OAIster, Srepod was unable to help us with OAIster, and OAIster was unable to help us with Srepod, yet the three steps of the process had to mesh with one another in order to achieve success. Moreover, as open-source systems, Srepod and OAIster understandably could not provide extensive personalized technical support.

We also encountered compatibility issues because, as mentioned above, we modified the Dublin Core template when cataloging the bookplates. During the harvesting process, we discovered that OAI gateways and harvesters require strict compliance of metadata with the simple Dublin Core schema (i.e., the basic fifteen fields). We were able to solve this problem by retaining our specialized, bookplate-specific fields while adding the standard fields we had previously excluded. We thus ended up with two metadata templates—the specialized fields and the standard Dublin Core fields—in the same record, with duplicated values in some of the fields (for example, the values in our specialized Artist field were duplicated exactly in the Dublin Core Creator field). In our Luna Insight presentation, only the specialized fields were displayed; when we harvested for OAI, only the Dublin Core fields were harvested.

Perhaps no other problems encountered during this project were as perplexing and complicated as those surrounding OAI compliancy. Confronting these issues provided us with a greater understanding and appreciation of the complexity of the process, but it also brought home the fact that, without considerable personalized technical support, it was difficult to fulfill an important requirement of the grant initiative. We also understood that it would be unfair to expect any system to be able to provide that level of guidance. It was very much a learning experience, and our systems librarian documented each step of the process, from the generation of the static repository files with the Luna Insight software to the final registration of the collection with OAIster.

2006 and Beyond

As we approached the completion of the 2005 project, our director urged us to apply for another grant in 2006 to maintain our momentum. This time, we focused on only one theme. One advantage of our previous metadata research was the discovery that our bookplate collection included work by several important American bookplate artists, and we also recognized the general research value of bookplates for librarians, antiquarian booksellers, and genealogists, as well as their beauty, creativity, and technical achievements. Therefore, we decided to digitize the remaining 1,100 plates in our ex libris collection, anticipating that the digital dissemination of the plates would serve not only the Pratt community but also the increasing number of individuals and organizations, both national and international, dedicated to the study of ex libris. When METRO awarded us our second grant, we were delighted with the opportunity to digitize an entire collection—and one, moreover, that had lain hidden in Special Collections since the late 1970s. For almost three decades no one had known about or been able to access these bookplates; now, anyone with Internet access would be able to.

Although several individuals on the 2005 team had left, a few remained and, with me as project manager, formed the nucleus of the 2006 group. Despite the personnel changes, however, this project proceeded more smoothly than the previous one, partly because we applied the lessons learned from the 2005 project and partly because we were dealing with only one collection (for which we had already worked out metadata issues) and therefore did not have to cope with multiple formats and approaches. Despite our allowing more time to import the images and metadata, we once again found it necessary to readjust our timeline because it was not easy to calculate accurately the amount of time necessary to digitize, enhance, and catalog the plates, even though we knew in advance how many there were. Also, we initially thought we could jump start the cataloging by initiating metadata creation before scanning, but we soon were forced to reverse the order, because the cataloger needed to zoom in on many images to determine certain details for the metadata (for instance, whether the plates were etchings or engravings). In addition, some of the scanning problems described for 2005 had not been completely corrected at the time we began the 2006 project, and so it required additional time to resolve them finally. Fortunately, thanks to the cushion we had built into our original timeline, the schedule modifications did not affect the completion of the project (Figure PRAT- 3).

Once our online collections went live, we publicized them throughout the Institute and held an open house to provide instruction and hands-on demonstrations.

ORIGINAL DIGITIZATION PROJECT TIMELINE

	01/06	02/06	03/06	04/06	05/06	06/06	07/06	08/06	09/06	10/06	11/06	12/06
Preparation	▓	▓										
Metadata	▓	▓	▓	▓								
Scanning/Imaging					▓	▓	▓	▓				
Web Design									▓	▓		
Promotion											▓	▓

REVISED DIGITIZATION PROJECT TIMELINE

	01/06	02/06	03/06	04/06	05/06	06/06	07/06	08/06	09/06	10/06	11/06	12/06
Preparation	▓	▓										
Scanning/Imaging	▓	▓	▓	▓								
Metadata					▓	▓	▓	▓			▓	
Content Import										▓	▓	
Promotion												▓

Figure PRAT-3. Schedule for the 2006 Grant.

We also notified various American and international organizations dedicated to the study of bookplates, such as the International Federation of Ex Libris Societies (FISAE), because we anticipated (correctly) that our collection would attract considerable long-distance interest, and hoped that scholars more knowledgeable than we would contact us with additions and corrections to our metadata. Several sites posted our announcement, and we were especially pleased to hear from the Australian Bookplate Society, which noticed that Australia was not represented in our collection and actually offered us a donation to fill that gap!

In 2008 the Pratt Institute Libraries chose to become a participating institution in ARTstor, which meant, for us, discontinuing Luna Insight. Our art, design, and architecture images would be hosted as a local collection through ARTstor, but that was not an appropriate repository for those from Special Collections and the archives because of their unique and (in the case of the photographs and negatives) proprietary nature. The limitations on our financial resources meant that whatever image management software we selected would have to be open source, but time constraints prevented us from thoroughly examining the variety of available systems, so our Visual Resources Curator suggested we post them on Flickr. This turned out to be an excellent idea, because we very quickly saw a marked increase in visitors, some of whom supplied information that, for our bookplates, allowed us to expand or correct our cataloging, which was precisely what we had been hoping for. The collection logged over 300,000 views in the first nine months on Flickr, and not a single image has been viewed less than nineteen times! Clearly our presence on Flickr allowed individuals to discover us serendipitously in a way not possible when they were required to navigate our Website.

I noticed, too, that staff from the Institute's administrative branches, such as the Public Relations and Communications Office and the Office of Alumni Relations and Annual Giving, more frequently browsed the collections before making requests for historical images, with the result that they knew exactly what they wanted and were even able to provide us with source and identifier numbers. This has increased the efficiency of our workflow and document-delivery capability enormously.

The only drawback with Flickr is its inability to support OAI-compliancy. We are hoping to acquire an open-source image management system that will correct this. Meanwhile, we continue to digitize archival images as needed, and have even begun digitizing important historical publications frequently used by researchers, which we are planning to post on the Archives page of the Libraries' Website. There is no question but that we have experienced a sea change in our digitization efforts as a result of our two grants, and our story vividly illustrates not only the old maxim that success breeds success, but also that long-term impetus can be generated from a single opportunity.

Acknowledgments: The success of our projects was achieved only because of the dedication and expertise of the members of the project teams, whose members included Amanda Schriber, Brian Cross, Lorraine Smith, Vernon Bigman, Stephen Klein, and Michael Nolasco. I am particularly grateful to Lorraine Smith, until recently the Visual Resources Curator at the Pratt Institute Libraries, who was our image cataloger for the 2005 project and supervised the digitization process in 2006 as Acting Visual Resources Curator. She was responsible for coping with many of the technical issues described above and reviewed this chapter to make sure my explanations were accurate.

References

Bibliographic Center for Research [BCR]. (2008). *BCR's CDP digital imaging best practices, version 2.0*. Retrieved from http://bcr.org/dps/cdp/best/digital-imaging-bp.pdf

Gertz, J. (2007). *Preservation and Selection for Digitization* [Northeast Document Conservation Center Preservation Leaflet No. 6.6]. Retrieved from http://www.nedcc.org/resources/leaflets/6Reformatting/06Preser vationAndSelection.php

Hagen, D., Horrell, J. & Merrill-Oldham, J. (1998). *Selecting research collections for digitization.* Retrieved from http://www.clir.org/pubs/reports/hagen/pub74.html

NC ECHO. (2007). *NC ECHO guidelines for digitization 2007 (Rev. ed.).* Retrieved from http://www.ncecho.org/dig/digguidelines.shtml

Puglia, S., Reed, J. & Rhodes, E. (2004). *NARA technical guidelines for digitizing archival materials for electronic access: Creation of production master files—raster images.* Retrieved from http://www.archives.gov/preservation/technical/guidelines.pdf

Southeastern NY Library Resources Council [SENYLRC]. (2004). *General collection criteria guidelines for HRVH.* Retrieved from http://www.hrvh.org/about/selectioncriteria.htm

Scaling Back for an "Experimental" Collection

Mark F. Anderson (The University of Iowa Libraries)

Abstract

Digital Library Services (DLS) at the University of Iowa Libraries has progressively worked toward coordinating more large-scale digitization projects both within the libraries and across campus, moving away from model of web exhibits that were often created before the department was formed in 2005. However, a variety of situations still call for small-scale projects. This chapter, describing the design and production of the "W9XK Experimental Television Digital Collection", shows that small-scale digitization projects can bridge that gap, and yield collections that rise above the level of web exhibits in their usefulness to scholars and the general public by limiting exclusive selection and promoting comprehensiveness. While mirroring this approach of mass-digitization, digital librarians can also use curatorial decisions and software functionality to further assist users of these small-scale collections.

Keywords: Archives, Digital collections, Digital libraries, Digitization, Web exhibits.

Introduction

Henry Wadsworth Longfellow wrote, "Most people would succeed in small things if they were not troubled with great ambitions." Even if the poet was not referring specifically to digital initiatives in libraries, it's an appropriate sentiment at a time when so much institutional effort is directed toward mass digitization projects such as the agreement between Google and the Committee on Institutional Cooperation (the consortium to which The University of Iowa belongs) to digitize no less than 10 million volumes from among members' collections (Committee on Institutional Cooperation, n.d.). At the same time, it has become common for institutions, or units within institutions, to work on building small, narrowly-focused collections as an initial foray into digitization, while securing funding for the necessary resources to ramp up to large-scale scanning projects and mass digitization, or to expose exceptional materials. This chapter will discuss one of these small digital collections, but will begin with the development of the digital library at the University of Iowa to which it belongs.

Digital Initiatives at the University of Iowa

The earliest digital collections hosted by The University of Iowa Libraries date back to the mid-1990s, and were a combination of small web exhibits and larger efforts to digitize materials from flagship collections. The web exhibits were considered "virtual versions" of exhibits displayed in the library's exhibit hall and which combined highlight images with essays and other supporting text provided by library staff and campus scholars (University Libraries. University of Iowa, 1999). In 1997, the Libraries were awarded Library of Congress/Ameritech National Digital Library Competition funds, which supported the digitization of nearly 8,000 talent brochures from the papers of the Redpath Lyceum Bureau, an agency that represented performers on the Midwest Chautauqua circuit. In many ways, this was the Libraries' first mass-digitization project (The Library of Congress, 2003). Other scholarly digital collections created at the time included the Center for Electronic Resources in African Studies and the International Dada Archive.

In 2005, a new department, Digital Library Services (DLS), was formed to manage digital initiatives. Since that time, DLS has progressively worked toward coordinating more large-scale, "left-to-right" projects both inside the Libraries as well as with faculty and scholars on campus, moving away from the highly selective model of the early web exhibits, which tended to contextualize the digital materials for the user. Conversely, the model of comprehensive digitization aims to allow users the freedom to repurpose digitized materials for the creation of new knowledge and insight. This requires not only a thorough approach to digitization on the part of the library, but also the availability of tools to facilitate new uses for the items, especially tools that link, overlay, and share data. Unfortunately, many of these tools require extensive development and are not yet available as turn-key solutions.

Situations such as the anniversary of an important institutional event or a specific user-driven request have still led libraries to undertake small- and medium-sized digitization projects. The challenge for libraries is to create smaller digital collections that are valuable for scholarship. Small-scale digital collections may provide the same research potential as the entire physical collections from which they are drawn.

Within the University of Iowa Libraries, DLS has cultivated a particularly close relationship with three content providers: Special Collections, Iowa Women's Archives, and University Archives. With the first two units, digitization projects are becoming more large-scale and left-to-right in their approach, but less so with the latter. This is mostly due to that fact that University Archives subscribes to the "principle of provenance", the archival practice of organizing collections by creator rather than subject, and collections are often selected for digitization based on a topic of interest rather than contributing entity, making it difficult to consider left-to-right scanning. For physical exhibits of University Archives materials, this has long led to "artificial collections" that pull from many different record groups, according to University of Iowa Archivist David McCartney. More recent digital collections from the archives are no exception. (D. McCartney, personal communication, October 27, 2009). This kind of intermediation by the selector is a major difference between the small-scale "boutique" digitization model and mass-digitization.

In "Shifting Gears: Gearing Up to Get Into the Flow," the authors direct libraries to stop obsessing about items and making curatorial decisions about what to digitize since the selection has already been done (Erway, R., and Schaffner J., 2007). Arguing that if items were important enough to acquire originally, they are important enough to digitize, the authors advocate a more programmatic approach of digitizing items as they are accessioned, rather than thinking of digitization in terms of discrete projects. Is it possible to work within these provocative guidelines and still develop small-scale digital collections that are "in the flow"? Yes. For example, libraries can push the decision making process from the item level to the collection level. After all, with so much catching up to do, there's no way all existing collections can all be scanned at once. Small collections can be selected for digitization, and worked through left-to-right, even if that means scanning hand-written grocery lists on backs of dry-cleaning receipts (a real-world example from an Iowa Digital Library collection). In this way, DLS has operated with the understanding that a digital collection, even a small one, should be a comprehensive surrogate of a physical collection, regardless of size or scope, which attracts not only general interest, but promotes new scholarly activities as well. Also, for text items, the combination of brief metadata and optical character recognition (OCR) can provide access without the need of extensive, handcrafted records.

Selecting the Collection

At a time when video is so easily accessible through websites Hulu, Netflix, Boxee.tv, and YouTube as well as thousands of cable and satellite television stations, it's hard to imagine the technical and organizational challenges facing engineers and technologists involved in the infancy of television. Were these pioneers of a century ago similarly considering the scale of their new experimental medium? If so, then the small digital collection described in this chapter is particularly appropriate: "W9XK Experimental Television at Iowa" (http://digital.lib.uiowa.edu/w9xk).

February 2009 was seen as an excellent opportunity to promote the history of the W9XK experimental television station on the University of Iowa campus by means of digitizing related archival materials, both because of the congressionally-mandated conversion to digital broadcast television, which was set to take place that month, and the 75th anniversary of the station the year before. W9XK, the first educational TV station in the U.S. went on the air January 25, 1933, with a weekly or twice-weekly schedule of lectures, music, and drama. Reception was reported back to the university from as far away as Oklahoma, Kentucky and New York (University Libraries. University of Iowa, 2009). Appropriate materials were gathered from throughout the archives including correspondence and newspaper clippings from faculty and electrical engineering department subject vertical files, still photographs from a prominent campus photographer, articles from a campus engineering journal, WPA federal writers project papers, and a student thesis.

With no single collection to process in a left-to-right manner, this project is a departure from DLS's more recent production model described earlier, and runs somewhat contrary to the challenges in "Shifting Up," but it is unlikely that these materials would be scanned together in any other way short of a heroic effort to mass-digitize the entire University Archives. The collection is small, containing just over 50 digital objects (although some of the objects are composed of several items grouped together, their organization to be discussed below), but it tells an important story of the station's development and operation in the broader context of early advances in television technology, using the variety of formats listed above. Unfortunately, no video or film footage of W9XK's broadcasts could be included in the collection since none is known to exist today.

Building the Collection

From 2005 to 2007, digital initiatives at the University of Iowa Libraries were completed mostly by staff in DLS in "in-house" production. Scaling up to support larger digitization efforts has required production tasks to occur in other library departments with both the staffing and expertise to process not only more materials, but also address unique handling and cataloging issues that invariably arise from digitizing entire collections. Metadata is now mostly applied by cataloging staff, except in cases where collections come to the library already packaged with existing records, which requires more in the way of reorganization and standardization rather than creating new records from scratch, which as a brand new collection, is the way metadata for the W9XK collection was handled.

In a similar way, the scanning that had been done by staff and students working directly under DLS has mostly moved to the Preservation and Reformatting department. However, scanning for the W9XK collection broke from this workflow model. A staff member in University Archives was interested in learning about scanning and image editing, especially the operation of a new top-down book scanner the Libraries had just purchased. The potentially small size of the digital collection presented a good opportunity for that. In this way, small-scale digital collections afford opportunities to deviate from established workflows for staff to develop new skills. But with other parts of production spread out, it may not make a considerable difference in time to do just part of the production "in-house". The time for an item in the W9XK collection to be completely processed and added to the digital collection was neither considerably faster nor slower than other collections.

The University Archivist selected and pulled appropriate materials from the physical collections listed above and prepared them for the staff member who scanned them on either an 11x17 flatbed scanner or the newly acquired top-down scanner, which accommodates items up to 24 x 36 with a book cradle for bound materials. Scans were then edited and display files derived by DLS staff who then uploaded the images to CONTENTdm, the digital library software that the Libraries use for many of its digital collections. Lastly, cataloging staff added descriptive, administrative and technical metadata to the objects. Metadata is almost always applied to the digital items following upload to the digital content management system in order to take advantage of software functionality that allows for easier batch cataloging processes, increasing efficiency.

Collection highlights and sample searches were selected for a collection homepage, and the university archivist provided an introductory paragraph, which takes the place of the more contextual and interpretative writing that used to accompany web exhibits directly alongside images. A lingering concern about small-scale digital collections is packaging them in beautiful, but deep, web portals that users must navigate to find the information they seek, rather than letting digital objects live in a large repository with thin logical collections built around them. A compromise is to maximize collection exposure to search engines and aggregators. The Libraries use Google Sitemaps to help assure collections are crawled and ranked highly by Google. OAI harvesting of collections is enabled for outside service providers, and the Libraries also implemented a next-generation catalog that brings together records from the traditional catalog as well as online books and journals, local web pages and digital collections such as W9XK.

One recent change in how DLS delivers large-scale, left-to-right digital collections is to use folder-level organization of the digital objects. The digital library software used for most collections in the Iowa Digital Library, CONTENTdm, uses "compound objects" to deliver multi-page items, from the two sides of a postcard, pages of a document, a monograph, or an entire folder's worth of materials arranged hierarchically. This decreases the number of items for users to browse through up front, or consider in results sets. While the W9XK collection did not fit the folder-structure organization model since its items came from many different archival collections, one of the digital collection-delivery decisions made was to display correspondence items (letters between engineering faculty, university administrators, government authorities, and the public) so that letters and their replies were in the same compound objects, rather than as separate objects. One could argue that this mediation is too much along the lines of a web exhibit, but it was thought to be helpful in navigating the correspondence. Feedback from users would help to support whether this is a good decision. In any case, digital librarians often have to make organizational decisions based on software functionality and with the intention of assisting users and researchers.

Use of the Collection

The W9XK Digital Collection was officially launched on February 17, 2009 through press releases and library blogs. While we must expect that our users will tend to find our digital collections through the back doors of search engines and aggregators rather than our finely-crafted web portals, only 10% of visits have come directly through Google, while more than half of all users are referred to the collection from promotion on university and library pages as well as the library catalog, although the search engine could have sent users to these local pages first. Over 75% of page views to date occurred during the first two months, owing much to the initial publicity (Figure IOWA-1).

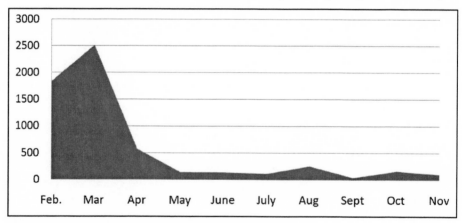

Figure IOWA-1. W9XK Pageviews by month (2009)

While somewhat discouraging, most early use may have just been casual interest, and it may take longer for research and scholarly use to increase. Owing to Lally and Dunfords assessment of the impact of Wikipedia in directing users to library digital collections, links to the W9XK collection have recently been added to Wikipedia articles on experimental television and may have an effect on traffic over time. In "Using Wikipedia to Extend Digital Collections" (Lally, A. and Dunford, C., 2007), the authors note that Wikipedia is "a prime candidate for ... efforts at pushing information about the Libraries out to where users conduct their research," as their server statistics indicate it is indeed driving a significant amount of traffic to their collections.

65% of visits to the W9XK collection home page have come from within the state of Iowa, a higher percentage of local visits than for two other small-scale digital collections in the Iowa Digital Library, which were prompted by high use and requests for reproduction from unique physical collections, especially where appeal went beyond the local area (Figure IOWA-2).

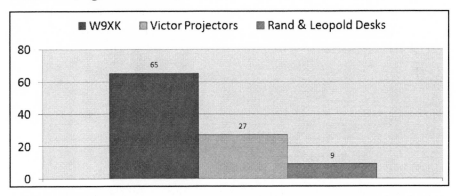

Figure IOWA-2. Percent collection use from Iowa networks

Two examples of these are the Victor Animatograph pamphlets (http://digital.lib. uiowa.edu/victor) and the Rand and Leopold Desk catalogs ((http:// digital.lib.uiowa.edu/desks), both with fewer than 30 items each. The Victor Animatograph Corporation of Davenport, Iowa made the world's first 16mm motion picture projector, and was a leader in the area of film technology throughout the 20th century. People in possession of one of these projectors would often contact the Libraries requesting copies of the product pamphlets, which contain detailed schematic diagrams and operating instructions. This collection was built before resources allowed for left-to-right digitization, so rather than digitize the entire collection of papers from the Victor Corporation, just the 21 highly-requested pamphlets were scanned. Since launching the collection, 20% of visits to the collection have come from outside the United States, and over 70% of visits to the collection have come from outside the state of Iowa according to site statistics.

The Rand & Leopold Desk Company was an office furniture manufacturing firm which operated out of Burlington, Iowa for 102 years before closing in 1990. Furniture collectors had always been interested in the Libraries' collection of 27 original product catalogs, and there were many requests for reproduction. After scanning them and making them available through the Iowa Digital Library, only 7% of site visits to the digital collection have come from outside the US, but over 90% have come from outside the state of Iowa. Perhaps more so than the W9XK collection, these two small collections meet the goal of facilitating information needs of users who cannot easily travel to the UI Libraries.

Difficulties in Tying a Bow

Even when original goals are met, small-scale digital collections don't often stay "done" for long. Scope-creep is a common danger, for even when items haven't been cherry-picked for a digital collection, the source collection almost always logically connects with more collections. In trying to connect users with a broader universe of resources, libraries are compelled to extend the scope of their digital collections. In an example of how digital collections never seem to stay finished, a collection of an artist's papers in the Iowa Women's Archives were digitized to complement her digitized artwork. When discussing publicity of the collection, IWA staff noted that they had found several audio oral histories and also a video made about the artist. Even when those multimedia materials are digitized and added to the collection, it's possible that the archive will acquire additional items that would need to be added to the digital collection in order for it to remain comprehensive.

Conclusions

Even as mass-digitization projects begin and are sustained at libraries through funding and organizational commitments to scaled-up scanning workflows, requests for creating small-scale digital collections will persist. This is because many unique collections, especially those with preservation issues or spread out in archives will not be included in mass-digitization workflows. Likewise, the needs of libraries' clientele and donor relationships do not necessarily coincide with broad institutional objectives. Responding to these requests can help strengthen relationships inside and outside of the library and build support for digitization programs. Even one-off collections should fit within programmatic guidelines, although in the case of the W9XK collection, some liberties were taken in its creation. Small-scale digital collections can be useful to researchers and the general public, but they have to be accessible. Once found, the collections should be complete to the point where users can be confident that they have the entirety of a collection's information at their disposal. Although the W9XK digital collection required the hand-selection of items, steps were taken to ensure the fullness that is necessary in today's digital libraries.

References

Committee on Institutional Cooperation. (n.d.). *CIC-Google agreement*. Retrieved from http://www.cic.net/Home/Projects/Library/BookSearch/CIC-Google.aspx

Erway, R., and Schaffner, J. (2007). *Shifting gears: Gearing up to get into the flow*. Retrieved from http://www.oclc.org/ programs/publications/reports/2007-02.pdf

Lally, A., and Dunford,C. (2007). Using wikipedia to extend digital collections. *D-Lib Magazine, 13* (5/6).

Library of Congress. (2003). *Library of Congress and Ameritech Competition (1996-1999): Awards and collections*. Retrieved from http://lcweb4.loc.gov/ammem/award/collections.html

University Libraries. University of Iowa (1999). *Keeping our word / North Lobby exhibit / University of Iowa*. Retrieved from http://www.lib.uiowa.edu/exhibits/keeping/intro1.htm

University Libraries. University of Iowa. (2009). *Iowa city town and campus scenes*. Retrieved from http://digital.lib.uiowa.edu/ictcs

University Libraries. University of Iowa. (2009). Victor Animatograph
     Company Pamphlets. Retrieved from http://digital.lib.uiowa.edu
     /victor

University Libraries. University of Iowa. (2009). *Map/diagram of
     Midwest, 1930s.* Retrieved from http://digital.lib.uiowa.edu/
     u?/w9xk,67

University Libraries. University of Iowa. (2009). *Rand and Leopold
     Desk Company Catalogs.* Retrieved from
     http://digital.lib.uiowa.edu/desks

From Confusion and Chaos to Clarity and Hope: Reorganization of Work Flows, Processes, and Delivery for Digital Libraries

Jody L. DeRidder (The University of Alabama Libraries)

Abstract

Digitization support within an institution may be fractured across several departments, only partially funded, and may suffer restraints imposed by delivery software which seriously hamper progress. Most digitization is undertaken with little thought for the future; the result is digital file chaos and confusion. Without clarification of file identities and relationships, preservation and migration to new systems are seriously hampered. Additionally, low funding for archival staff may preclude the creation of valuable item-level metadata. The University of Alabama Libraries leveraged the expertise available across the library to build a cross-departmental collaboration with which to face our challenges, recognizing that obstacles become opportunities for creative solutions. We are involved in a series of pilot projects to explore how to address the gap in archivist staffing to create item-level metadata. This chapter shares our discoveries and solutions.

Keywords: Cross-departmental collaboration, Digitization, Digital file organization, Metadata creation, Open source software.

The first few years of most digital library initiatives are marked by 'boutique' collection development, in which the standards,

333

organization, methodology, metadata, file names, and consistency vary considerably. At the time of my arrival at the University of Alabama in mid-2008 as head of the new Digital Services department, over thirty such digitization projects had been completed. Each collection had its own file-naming system and metadata fields, with inconsistencies throughout; nothing was standardized. Metadata in the delivery software did not retain in any predictable fashion a reference to the related archival files, and could not be exported in full. Digital Services staffing was minimal, requiring time from the Cataloging and Metadata Services for subject headings and upload, from archival staff for preparation of content and descriptions, and from Web Services to manage the interface and software support.

The scope of the task ahead was to expand heavily on the scanning staff and equipment, develop a feasible set of systematic work flows for supporting a large increase in scanning, build a cross-departmental team capable of supporting digital library development, and to create an organized and reusable set of digital content that is not dependent upon resident knowledge for continuation or restoration. Challenges included a simultaneous reduction in archivist work hours, minimal space for expansion, difficult relations between some departments, and insufficient time available from Web Services.

As in many smaller organizations, our digitization effort is tremendously dependent upon cross-departmental collaboration. Programming assistance and web delivery, metadata services, archivist expertise and a regular influx of well-chosen content are all critical to the development of our online research collections. A previous gift from EBSCO Industries to the libraries supports digitization and the development of technical infrastructure, but it does not support the processing, arranging, and description of archival collections. Our need for content creates a demand on the archivists that they simply do not have the resources to meet.

Recognizing the need for improved cross-departmental communications and teamwork, our dean (L. A. Pitschmann, personal communication, August 25, 2008) called together lead representatives (including two associate deans) from Library Technology, Web

Services, Collection Development, Cataloging and Metadata Services, Special Collections and Archives, and Digital Services, to form an ongoing Digital Programs group which would meet regularly to hash out problems, develop alternatives, research opportunities and assign priorities. The creation of this group was a stroke of brilliance. By forming this framework for participation, setting forth a strategic goal and providing clear administrative support, our dean laid the groundwork for success. Given our multiple operational and relational challenges, we could only succeed by seeking solutions with the assistance of all impacted parties.

Against this backdrop we are working through four major problems: digital file chaos, the inability to reunite metadata with the archival content, software restrictions on the number of collections, and a lack of archivist time to create item-level metadata.

Problems and Solutions

Digital File Chaos

Managed, efficient production and expanded growth of collections requires standardization, not only of work flows and procedures, but also of storage and file naming conventions. Delivery systems become outmoded; migration into replacement software requires consistency of legacy content. Consistency of file names and storage patterns can also support cost-saving automation.

As mentioned, we already had over thirty digitized collections, each with different file naming systems and metadata in various states of disarray across a completely disorganized file system. What little documentation existed was scattered. Collections had been digitized for years with no road map, and with no concern beyond getting the content onto the web. We needed a clear methodology for file organization.

I consulted with the archivists to gain a greater awareness of the scope of current and future digital content. After much debate, we determined that it was most important for us to store content in such a way that we could retrace the material to the archival analog collection. Digital collections are transitory and overlapping by their very nature; we decided that the perception of a digital collection must be determined by metadata, not by origin (searching on a shared value can retrieve all components of a digital collection). Together we developed a file naming scheme to encompass all our holdings and projected digitization plans for the next few years. We created hierarchical levels of organization: first by holder, then by collection within those holdings, then by item within that collection, and finally by sequence for delivery (Figure ALAB-1). Each hierarchical level is concatenated with an underscore in the file name, so that provenance and location, as well as sequence for delivery, are automatable and clear.

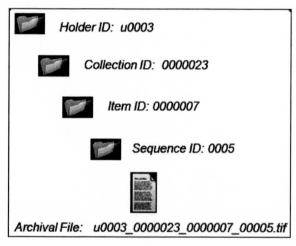

Figure ALAB-1. [University of Alabama Libraries Digital File Naming Scheme. (©2009, University of Alabama Libraries. Used with permission.)]

A "holder" is construed loosely, as we could not incorporate all the variant hierarchies of our organization feasibly into a file name. Supporting metadata clarifies identity and relationships. It was important for us to prefix each identifier with a letter so it can be used as an ID attribute within XML files (W3C, 2005). The n groupings are non-profit agencies, the p is for patron holdings, and u is for content from holdings areas within our university. We grouped content by format, as each format requires different handling and metadata description. For example, u0001 is the still image collections from the

Hoole Special Collections; u0002 is rare books, u0003 is manuscript collections, and so forth. Any of these holdings areas may have multiple collections.

For the collection number, which composes the second segment of an identifier (concatenated with an underscore separator), we echoed the existing collection numbering system whenever possible. Thus, MS 1980 will be the collection number ending in 1980, for example.

As an example, u0003_0000252 is the identifier for the digitized manuscript content of the collection known to our archivists as MS 252. Items and their subsidiary pages, however, are numbered sequentially. Item numbers follow the collection number, again, concatenated after an underscore. For example, the fifth digitized letter in the MS 252 collection would be identified by u0003_0000252_0000005. If it's a multi-page item, there will be a fourth set of numbers here, one per page, to identify the sequence for delivery. The image for page 4 of letter 5 would be identified by u0003_0000252_0000005_0004.

Thus, every part of every object has a defining and unique identifier which relates it to every other file in some fashion. We struggled with all the different anomalies we currently had and could foresee, simplifying this identification system as much as possible while still retaining the generic flexibility to apply it to all of our digitized content, regardless of the form or treatment. We then expended a great deal of effort to bring all legacy content into the new file organization scheme, gathering what information was still available to make sense of the chaos of files that remained from previous projects. Because of this system of file naming and organization, we are now able to automate much of our quality control. We have scripts that locate missing sequences, incorrectly named files, or files in the wrong place. We even have scripts to repair file names when large quantities of file names are in error. This has already saved us hundreds of hours.

Given that each level of the organization scheme contains or relates information which applies to each level below it, our associate dean (Thomas C. Wilson) decided it made sense to echo this file naming scheme in the directory organization for storing files. Everything from a particular holder should be together in a directory named for that holder. Everything from a particular collection should be in a directory named for that collection. Thus, in our storage directories, all of the Hoole manuscript collections will be within the same directory (u0003). This is an intuitive use of the file directories to provide clarity and simplicity of organization.

For example, within the u0003 directory is a subdirectory 0000159, which contains information about all digitized content from MS 159. Within this collection directory exists a subdirectory for each item, named for the item number. The storage directories thus echo the file naming scheme, providing clear, simple, automatable organization. Drilling down through the file system to the logical depth locates the digitized archival file (Figure ALBA-2).

Metadata and documentation are stored at the levels to which they apply. Thus, metadata about the collection is in the Metadata folder at the collection level, metadata about an item at the item level, and metadata about a specific page is at the page level. Each sub-file inherits the information available at the levels above it. Thus, provenance documentation added at the collection or holder level clearly applies to all files in the directories below it. If some information only applies to page 4 of a letter, it is stored in that file's directory.

An organizational patterning such as this (Figure ALAB-3) retains the item structure, both physically and nominally, through the file identifiers. The simplicity, systematic numbering, sequencing, and clear documentation stored at the level applicable makes the digital content resurrectable for future delivery systems, without complex metadata schemes or database dependence. The organizational scheme is built to be scalable and extensible enough to manage digital content into the foreseeable future. In addition, because the directory structure echoes the file names, we were able to automate the storage of content and the creation of attendant LOCKSS (LOCKSS, 2008) manifests.

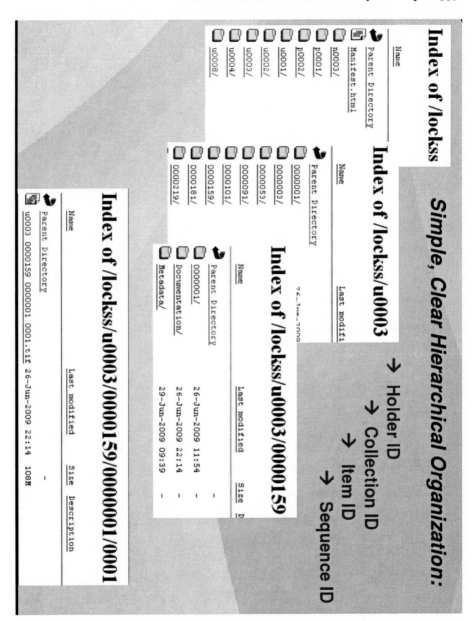

Figure ALAB-2. University of Alabama Libraries LOCKSS Content Organization. (© 2009, University of Alabama Libraries. Used with permission.)

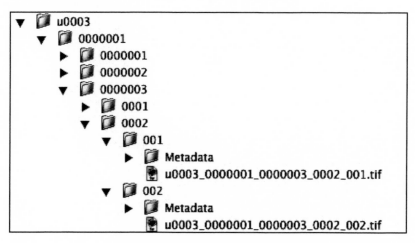

Figure ALAB-3. University of Alabama Libraries Digital File Naming Scheme: Sub-page numbering. (© 2009, University of Alabama Libraries. Used with permission.)

The manifest pages (Figure ALAB-4) link all files to be harvested for duplication across the Alabama Digital Preservation Network (Network of Alabama Academic Libraries, 2009), which is to date the lowest-cost model of digital preservation.

To secure our content further, we capture MD5 checksums upon deposit in our storage system, and verify them weekly prior to full-tape backups. This enables us to ensure that the original file is unaltered over time, and can be restored from a good backup should any corruption occur.

Reuniting Metadata with Archival Content

Software systems come and go, and successful transition between them is dependent upon standardized and coherent content and metadata. Most of our metadata had been altered or added after upload of content into our delivery system, and did not exist with the archival files. Upon examination of the exports from our software delivery system, we found that no single export contained all the metadata for a given archival object. Even in the most complete export option, there was no page-level metadata apart from the title and transcript, and archival file references were sometimes altered, often missing, and always contained reference to the upload directories, which no longer existed.

Tom S. Birdsong paper
u0003_0000159 Manifest Page

Administrative Information

- u0003_0000159.v1.xml

Collection Level Metadata

- u0003_0000159.v1.txt

Content

- u0003_0000159_0000001_0001.tif
- u0003_0000159_0000001_0002.tif
- u0003_0000159_0000001_0003.tif
- u0003_0000159_0000001_0004.tif
- u0003_0000159_0000001_0005.tif
- u0003_0000159_0000001_0006.tif
- u0003_0000159_0000001_0007.tif
- u0003_0000159_0000001_0008.tif
- u0003_0000159_0000001_0009.tif
- u0003_0000159_0000001_0010.tif
- u0003_0000159_0000001_0011.tif
- u0003_0000159_0000001_0012.tif
- u0003_0000159_0000001_0013.tif
- u0003_0000159_0000001_0014.tif

LOCKSS system has permission to collect, preserve, and serve this Archival Unit

Figure ALAB-4 University of Alabama Libraries LOCKSS Manifest example. (© 2009, University of Alabama Libraries. Used with permission.)

In the metadata, if indeed there was an identifier, it was stored in multiple different fields in different forms. Sometimes there was nothing at all to indicate what the original file name had been.

We studied the file naming schemes used in all the 30-some existing collections, working out how to rename the files to retain the ordering of delivery, the intended organization of complex files, and the relationships between related items. Analyzing the metadata in the CONTENTdm (OCLC, 2009a) database, we matched up what information we could locate with what little had been retained with the archival files, and slowly filled in the gaps. Whatever sorting and matching could not be scripted was done by hand, often requiring research and investigation.

During this time we explored the use of 7train (Fogel & Hetzner, n.d.) for transforming exported CONTENTdm Standard XML metadata into METS (Library of Congress, 2009b) files, which reordered and clarified the relationships between complex objects. Based on 7train's method of using the first Dublin Core (DCMI, 2009) identifier field in the export as the file name for the resultant METS file, we selected this field for our file identifier, and tagged it the same in every collection. Our metadata librarian (Mary Alexander) has worked hard to remediate the metadata, entering the correct unique file identifier in the specified location in all records. Only by repairing the descriptive metadata to consistently reference the correct identifier, can we match our exported metadata to the appropriate archival files.

The benefits of using this process are that the Dublin Core metadata assigned to the object at the top level is retained, the organization of the complex digital object is retained, and the transcripts or Optical Character Recognition (OCR) content are included in the resultant METS file. However, what is lost includes any metadata which does not map to Dublin Core, value-added labels which clarify the content in the fields, and page-level metadata beyond the title and transcript. If no archival file was used in upload, it is not referenced in the METS; those referenced may have their file name altered, and always refer to the upload directory. If the location of this directory is not corrected after upload to reference the actual location of the archival file, this is useless for reuniting metadata and archival content.

This version of METS was designed for web delivery, not for preservation. California Digital Library created 7train to enable repositories in the state that were using CONTENTdm to participate in their state-wide digital federated search service (Fogel, 2006), which requires METS (California Digital Library, 2009). The METS file contains links into the CONTENTdm software for access to the thumbnails and service derivatives. For preservation, these links will be useless, as delivery systems change rapidly, if indeed the content is still online. Additionally, the 7train METS contains no technical or preservation metadata, as none was created by, or exported from, CONTENTdm.

Seeking to make our METS files more useful, we determined how to add technical metadata, and analyzed the database structure and storage directories to identify the actual location and name of thumbnails and service images. Scripting to replace the derivative links and archival file reference with full path links to the actual files proved to be more trouble than it was worth.

However, as our storage system began taking shape, another option emerged. Our storage structure reflects the compound file structure, creating an unambiguous arrangement which will survive any delivery software. A digital archivist of the future should have no trouble reconstructing our content. The METS file itself may be redundant. Rather than altering the 7Train METS file to meet our preservation needs, we decided instead to leverage our organizational scheme to meet the challenge. All we really need to do is to create the technical metadata, name it correctly, and drop it in the right directory (Figure ALAB-5). Then we will compile the metadata and content links for an item via script into a preservation-ready METS file for long-term storage.

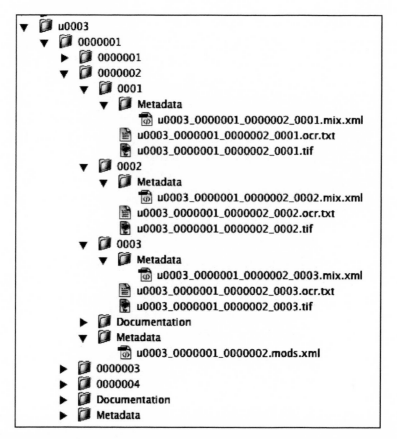

Figure ALAB-5. University of Alabama digital file organization for preservation. (©
2009, University of Alabama Libraries. Used with permission.)

Software Limitations on the Number of collections

The expansion of Digital Services had a major impact on Hoole
Special Collections. Archivists were scrambling to find sufficient
content to digitize at first; small collections were easiest to pull
together, so we suddenly were digitizing many tiny collections. What
an archivist considers a collection is determined by provenance, not
by quantity.

However, CONTENTdm (version 4.3) was designed to support no
more than 200 collections. It was clear that we could no longer define
our collections the same way our delivery software did. Therefore we
needed to reorganize our content in a way that provided the user

access desired by our archivists, while meeting the constraints of our current delivery system.

We met with the archivists to ask what kind of grouping made sense to them. After much debate, they finally selected date ranges for most of our content, which corresponded to particular eventful periods in American History. Access to each of the digitized analog collections would be managed by canned links searching for the analog collection name in the Dublin Core relation:isPartOf field. Archivists assigned each collection to a time period, and the metadata librarian and I began to sort out how to merge multiple collections and split combined ones.

When merging collections in CONTENTdm, the two collections being merged must have identical metadata fields. It was during this process that we realized the depth and variety of our metadata across all those 30-odd collections. It is far more than can be captured in Dublin Core, and we realized that we wanted to retain the value-added labels. Knowing that a person is a photographer or a lyricist or a composer or a performer is far more valuable than can be conveyed by Dublin Core "creator."

Our metadata librarian combined all our metadata fields into a single spreadsheet, so that all the CONTENTdm "containers" could handle any of our collections. Since each label requires a different spreadsheet column for ingest, we found we needed 87 columns. However, by hiding the columns that aren't needed, this becomes manageable. Different versions of this spreadsheet are used for each type of material, simply with different hidden columns. Since all the containers have the same metadata configuration, this streamlines uploads. The metadata librarian need only unhide the columns and export the spreadsheet for upload. Recognizing the value of the many tags in use, we decided to map all the fields to MODS (Library of Congress, 2009c) to discover if that metadata standard would be capable of retaining all our descriptive information; and indeed it does.

My associate dean recognized the possibilities for further leveraging our current file organization for better user access and delivery, sidestepping many of the restrictions placed on us by CONTENTdm. He procured the services of a talented programmer (Tonio Loewald), who proceeded to write a translator, which, given a template, can translate any Unicode tab-delimited spreadsheet into separate XML records of the desired schema. His Archivists Utility (Loewald, 2009b) reads in our 87-field spreadsheets and creates a MODS XML record from each line. This enables us to capture all of our metadata, not just the Dublin Core elements, outside of the delivery software for preservation storage.

We added scripts using open-source software such as ImageMagick (ImageMagick Studio LLC., 2009), LAME (Cheng et al., 2009), and Tesseract_OCR (Google, 2009) to generate derivatives from the archival files. These are placed into web-accessible directories that mirror our archive structure. By adding the MODS, and now our newly emerging EADs (Library of Congress. 2009a) we now have all the components for an open, modular delivery system. Under my associate dean's direction, the programmer has built an XML schema-agnostic delivery system, Acumen (Loewald, 2009b), that reads the XML where it lives in a live directory. Metadata and derivatives can be accessed easily and changed at any time without going through any software system. Web agents and web search engine crawlers can easily access our online content also, as it is not buried in a back-end database. Relationships between files are inferred by the file naming system, so that all components of an item are retrieved together, and all items in a collection can also be retrieved by using the collection identifier. In addition, since the file name communicates the hierarchy and relationships of files, digital content can be reorganized according to work flow or even moved between servers while keeping unchanging URLs.

We're very excited about the possibilities this modular methodology offers. By bringing digital content up to the level of the web, we are setting the stage for semantic web applications and the development of user-friendly tools for access and reuse of our content.

Staffing Gap for Creation of Item-level Metadata

Shortage in funding support for archivists is widespread. With the current attention to digitization of archival content, and the lack of funding for archivists, a critical gap is created. The archivists are well-versed in the knowledge of the time periods, issues, relationships, and people related to the archival content we seek to digitize; they are the personnel best suited to describe the material in a way which will enable users the best possible access. A knowledgeable archivist will be able to identify important personages of the time, particular buildings and locations, and can provide biographical, historical, and cultural context which gives meaning to the documents we seek to digitize. Since the metadata provides the necessary information for successful retrieval, correct descriptive information may be the most valuable knowledge capture we could provide. However, the archivists are hard pressed to provide even minimal processing to the burgeoning mass of incoming content. In order for us to move forward in digitization without more funding for archivists, we began to devise pilot projects to seek out alternative possibilities.

Our first pilot project involved students creating item-level descriptive metadata as they digitized content. The collections chosen were small image collections containing a little over 200 photographs. To test for consistency, we assigned only one student to one of the collections, and four different students worked on the second collection. Within a few days it was clear that our careful instructions to the lone student were clearly insufficient. Her metadata spreadsheet was rife with errors; the primary focal person in the collection had his name misspelled seven different ways, and many words were abbreviated (and usually incorrectly). In 56 entries, we located 217 spelling and abbreviation errors. Grammar, punctuation, capitalization and spelling errors were abundant, and the captions and descriptions created were vague and unhelpful.

In the jointly described collection, each student had his own methodology and focus, and the variations between the choices for descriptions and captions were sufficient to impair search and retrieval even within the collection itself. Where one student might use the terms "infant" and "woman," a second student would use the terms "baby" and "lady." While the errors and misspellings were far less frequent, it was clear that for consistency, we needed either stricter guidelines and controlled vocabularies, or to limit the number of employees assigned to create metadata for any one collection. Additionally, since the students had no background information on the context of the collection, the time period, or the content, they were unable to identify well-known buildings, well-known personages, or other significant content of interest. This point became extremely clear when our students could not identify such historically important figures as Governor George Wallace or the locally beloved Paul "Bear" Bryant.

A second pilot project involves the reuse of existing MARC metadata for sheet music which had been cataloged over a period of years by various catalogers. After extraction of the MARC records and analysis, we were dismayed at the variations in how the MARC fields were used. For example, we found the first line of text in fields 590, 500, 740, and 246, along with other types of content. The arranger, lyricist, musician, and composer names were interspersed in field 245c with various textual prefixes, preventing a systematic method of separation. Without remediation, transformation to another metadata scheme would not be recommended, as we cannot safely crosswalk these fields. Metadata librarians and catalogers are currently involved in repairs to the original records.

A third pilot project involves having an archivist and metadata librarian each developing their own version of item-level metadata for the same photograph and correspondence collections. Each worker gathered time measurements, and neither party was allowed to view the others' descriptions until finalized. Both versions of each collection will be put online in the same web interface, and usability tests will determine to what extent the differences impact user experience. Questions for users will be derived from the known metadata in the finding aid, since the information in the series description would lead the user to expect success in searching for the item-level material that fit the description. If, for example, the series description mentions letters about boarding schools prior to 1900, a query in the usability study would be to locate a letter about boarding schools written prior to 1900. This method of creating queries was not communicated to the metadata creators, so it could not skew the results. It is possible that neither metadata version will provide helpful results to the queries. In the final analysis, the level of usability for each version will be weighed against the time cost and availability of the personnel in the department that created it. We hope to be able to relieve the archivists of the burden of item-level metadata creation. While archivists know more about the content, and provide more detailed and informed metadata, their available time is very limited. Over the years, we have assumed that the expertise of the metadata creators is of primary importance, but new findings by Paul Conway (Conway, 2008) have thrown doubt on that belief. Since "the proof is in the pudding," we will determine if it is to our advantage to reduce the quality of metadata in order to get more of our content online.

A fourth pilot project will depend solely upon EAD finding aid descriptions at the series and sub series level to provide findability and context for digitized items. Our Archival Access Coordinator (Donnelly Lancaster Walton) suggested that we seek to recreate online the experience of a patron exploring material in the reading room: a folder is opened, and the patron goes through the documents one at a time. No other information is available to describe the material. This methodology will enable archivists to focus on EAD finding aid descriptions, and our digitization team will take box after box and simply digitize content in order for web delivery. As content is digitized, links will be added to the online finding aids from the folder level, out to web directories which contain the digitized items, ordered as they were encountered in the folder. In this manner, we will be able to provide online access to huge collections for which we have insufficient resources to provide item-level descriptions.

We have just been funded by NHPRC to demonstrate this low-cost, scalable model (University of Alabama Libraries, 2010a). Already we have developed scripts (University of Alabama Libraries, 2010b) to add links into the EADs and create minimal MODS records as quantities of scans become available. The software we develop to support this mass digitization method will be made available open source. As soon as the content begins to appear online, we will conduct usability studies to compare the user experience between accessing content via the finding aid, versus item-level search and retrieval, and will publicize the results.

The fifth pilot project we expect to undertake in the coming months will involve users in tagging our materials online. To the extent possible, we will repurpose available open source software, capturing the tags and free-text descriptions in a database for vetting by our metadata librarians. Tags may be made automatically visible in the web interface and included in indexing for search and retrieval. After review, acceptable entries will be added to the to the descriptive metadata record on file. Our first foray into this venue will be with photograph collections for which we have almost no descriptive metadata. Hence, any apparently valid contributions will be accepted. In this manner we also hope to build user interest and support as we build interaction into our interface.

Summary

In the real world, digitization support within an institution may be fragmented across several departments, only partially funded by donor gifts, and may suffer seemingly arbitrary restraints imposed by delivery software. Some of the departments upon which success depends may be understaffed and unable to meet the demands for digitization support. In addition, most digitization is undertaken with little thought for the future, either in terms of transitioning to alternative delivery software, or long-term access to digital content.

Obstacles are opportunities for creative solutions. We leveraged expertise available across the library to build a successful cross-departmental collaboration. We are developing open source software support for an open, scalable, modular digital content delivery system with consideration for long-term preservation. Our file organization patterns alone may prove to be a life raft for digital content which funding cuts have left unsupported. This or a similar patterning will make reconstruction of digital content far easier. By possibly adding a BagIt manifest (Boyko, Kunze, Littman, Madden & Vargas, 2009), it becomes potentially feasible to zip up entire digital archives for long term storage in a safe repository or LOCKSS until such time as funding support returns.

The delivery system we are developing will be free and open source, requiring minimal technical expertise. An underfunded institution will be able to use it to raise their content to the level of the web where search engines can promote their materials and web agents can provide greater usability. Since the actual metadata and delivery content is not ingested, but left in the web directory, it can be changed as needed, without risk of harm to the online delivery. Metadata schemes change regularly, and this XML schema-agnostic, modular solution is a low-cost, scalable, simple approach to building online digital libraries with the future in mind.

Thus far, we still use CONTENTdm for participation in multi-site search systems that depend upon this software, such as our state-wide Alabama Mosaic (Network of Alabama Academic Libraries, n.d.). However, the winds of change are blowing. During an open discussion at the 2009 AlabamaMosaic Annual Meeting in Montgomery, Alabama, the director reported a conversation with an OCLC technician who stated that FirstSearch would replace the CONTENTdm Multi-Site server. Thus, continued support of the CONTENTdm Multi-Site Server (OCLC, 2009c) is suspect, as OCLC moves toward FirstSearch (OCLC, 2009b) for cross-database search support. Many small collaborative digitization efforts depend upon CONTENTdm, but they need not be held hostage by a proprietary system. Acumen could potentially fill the gap, offering a low cost option providing much of the same functionality without the constraints.

We continue to explore how best to fill or reduce the gap created by the apparent need for item-level metadata for access and retrieval, and hope that the solutions we adopt in that area will help others as well. We have certainly found that working together with mutual respect and consideration has brought both challenges and unexpected benefits. By bringing everyone to the table, struggling together with the chaos before us and facing the same goals, we have unleashed passion and creativity, enabling us to make astounding strides into clarity, organization, and hope for the future.

References

Boyko, A., Kunze, J., Littman, J., Madden, L. & Vargas, B. (2009). *The BagIt file packaging format* (V0.96). Retrieved November 14, 2009, from http://www.cdlib.org/inside/diglib/bagit/bagitspec.html

California Digital Library. (2009). *Online Archive of California (OAC)*. Retrieved November 15, 2009, from http://www.cdlib.org/inside/projects/oac/

Cheng, M., Taylor, M., Hegemann, R., Leidinger, A., Tominaga, T, Shibata, N., et al. (2009). *The LAME project*. Retrieved November 14, 2009, from http://lame.sourceforge.net/index.php

Conway, P. (2009). The image and the expert user: a qualitative investigation of decision-making. Paper presented at Archiving 2009, Arlington VA. In *Archiving 2009, Vol. 6.* (pp. 142-150). Society for Imaging Sciences and Technology.

DCMI. (2009). *Dublin Core metadata initiative*. Retrieved November 15, 2009, from http://dublincore.org/

Fogel, P. (2006). CDL 7train Profile – *CONTENTdm simple and complex objects in METS Metadata encoding and transmission standard*. Retrieved November 15, 2009, from http://www.loc.gov/standards/mets/profiles/00000010.html

Fogel, P. & Hetzner, E. (n.d.). *7train METS Generation Tool*. Copyright the University of California Regents. Retrieved November 15, 2009, from http://seventrain.sourceforge.net/

Google. (2009). *Tesseract-ocr*. Retrieved November 14, 2009, from http://code.google.com/p/tesseract-ocr/

ImageMagick Studio LLC. (2009). *ImageMagick*. Retrieved November 14, 2009 from http://www.imagemagick.org/script/index.php

Library of Congress. (2009a). *EAD Encoded archival description (Version 2002)*. Retrieved November 14, 2009, from http://www.loc.gov/ead

Library of Congress. (2009b). *METS Metadata encoding & transmission standard*. Retrieved November 14, 2009, from http://www.loc.gov/standards/mets/

Library of Congress. (2009c). *MODS metadata object description schema*. Retrieved November 14, 2009, from http://www.loc.gov/standards/mods/

LOCKSS. (2008). *What is the LOCKSS program?* Retrieved November 14, 2009, from http://www.lockss.org/lockss/Home

Loewald, T. (2009a). *Acumen*. Retrieved November 15, 2009, from http://acumen.lib.ua.edu/

Loewald, T. (2009b). *Archivists utility*. Retrieved November 15, 2009, from http://lb-416-003.lib.ua-net.ua.edu/notes/?f=Archivist%20Utility.txt

Network of Alabama Academic Libraries. (n.d.). *Alabama Mosaic*. Retrieved November 14, 2009, from http://www.alabamamosaic.org/

Network of Alabama Academic Libraries. (2009). *The Alabama Digital Preservation Network (ADPNet)*. Retrieved November 14, 2009, from http://www.adpn.org/

OCLC. (2009a). *CONTENTdm Digital collection management software*. Retrieved November 15, 2009, from http://www.contentdm.com

OCLC. (2009b). *FirstSearch Online reference*. Retrieved November 15, 2009, from http://www.oclc.org/firstsearch/

OCLC. (2009c). *Multi-site server*. Retrieved November 15, 2009, from http://www.oclc.org/firstsearch/

University of Alabama Libraries. (2010a). *Septimus D. Cabaniss Papers digitization project*. Retrieved March 9, 2010 from http://www.lib.ua.edu/libraries/hoole/cabaniss

University of Alabama Libraries. (2010b). *UA libraries digital services planning and documentation.* Retrieved March 9, 2010 from http://www.lib.ua.edu/wiki/digcoll

W3C. (2005). *XML:id Version 1.0.* Retrieved November 15, 2009, from http://www.w3.org/TR/xml-id/

Digitizing Colorado State University's Historic Photograph Collection: A Case Study

Beth Oehlerts (Colorado State University Libraries)

Abstract

This chapter discusses the experiences of creating a medium-sized digital collection of the earliest photographs from Colorado State University's Historic Photograph Collection. The entire collection of 500,000 photographs chronicles the history of Colorado State University, the city of Fort Collins, and Rocky Mountain National Park. Digitizing the first phase of this vast collection included capturing 5500 images from glass plate negatives, 750 images from magic lantern slides, and 7500 images from gelatin nitrate prints. These formats were chosen because they are the oldest and most fragile. The project was not without challenges, including utilizing untrained staff and students, coping with equipment problems, and creating avenues of communication to more than 40 people involved in the creation of the collection. This chapter will discuss these challenges and how we worked to resolve them.

Keywords: Archives, Digital collaboration, Digital collections, Digital projects, Digital scanners, Gelatin nitrate prints, Glass plate negatives, Magic lantern slides, Photograph collections.

Introduction

Beginning in the late 1990s, Colorado State University Libraries (CSUL) started large-scale digitization activities in partnership with the Colorado Digitization Project (CDP). The first of these was the *Warren and Genevieve Garst Photographic Collection* of wild animal photographs donated to CSUL and digitized with CDP funding (http://lib.colostate.edu/wildlife/). *The Sidney Heitman Germans from Russia Collection* was another early digitization project (http://lib.colostate.edu/gfr/index.html) funded by the CDP. These projects, and a series of smaller ad hoc projects over the next three years, were created following the CDP's best practices guidelines and gave a few staff the opportunity to learn digitization.

In 2006 CSUL received the University Historic Photograph Collection (UHPC) a collection of 500,000 photographs documenting the history of Colorado State University, Fort Collins, and Rocky Mountain National Park. The collection came from the University's Office of Instructional Services and was given to CSUL's Archives and Special Collections Department with the understanding that it would be preserved and access given to a wider audience through digitization. Planning for the digitization of the first phase began in early 2007, as did creation of a finding aid for the earliest images in the collection, which included glass plate negatives, magic lantern slides, and gelatin nitrate prints from cellulose nitrate negatives. These photographs are also the most fragile materials in the collection. The goal was to digitize approximately 5,500 glass plate negatives, 750 lantern slides, and 7500 gelatin prints.

Although we had no budget line dedicated solely for digitization, our work did have the support of both the Colorado State University (CSU) and CSUL's administrative teams. Funds were provided by the Libraries' administrative team to purchase digital scanners, including an archival-quality overhead scanner used for later archival digitization projects. Administrative support provided extra funding in the project when we needed to hire students and acquire additional server space to house our digital master files.

Literature Review

Of the recent literature addressing digitization, the focus is often on the technical and preservation-related issues that arise following the creation of a digital collection; less of the recent literature focuses on the staffing issues encountered when creating digital collections. Boock and Vondracek (2006) found that when institutions begin digitization activities they often add these tasks to staff responsibilities rather than hire new staff dedicated to digitization. In a 2005 survey of ARL libraries, they found a majority of the responding institutions capitalized on the existing knowledge and skills of staff, encouraging current positions to evolve rather than hiring new digitization staff, as was the case at CSUL. Boock continues the discussion, focusing on how the Oregon State University Libraries (OSUL) reassigned several staff positions to a new digitization production unit, initially using staff for scanning, quality control reviews, and metadata creation using a metadata schema (Boock, 2008). OSUL relies on student employees for almost all of its digital imaging and metadata assignment, performing no quality control reviews on their work. In examining the organizational implications of digitizing, Sutton (2004) recalls how early digitization efforts were seen as temporary endeavors, requiring the temporary re-assignment of staff.

D'Andrea and Martin (2001), reporting on digitization workflows at Temple University, discuss utilizing part-time student staff to supplement the work of digitization staff. D'Andrea and Martin note, and our experiences confirm, there are positives and negatives in hiring students to work on digitization projects. The authors recommend hiring students whose interests match the project, not just those who apply for the job, and fully informing students about the nature of the work.

Establishing Best Practices

In 2005, in response to the growing need for local standards and procedures to guide the creation of CSUL's digital collections, CSUL created the Digitization of Local Collections Task Force and charged it to review existing national and international standards and best practices, and to recommend the steps necessary in building high-quality local digital collections. Among its findings, as reported in the final report, *Digitization of Local Collections* (Digitization of Local Collections Task Force, 2005), the Task Force identified a lack of formal project management, a need to prioritize projects, and the need to determine the impact in-house digitization would have on staffing. Based on the Task Force's final report and the Western States Digital Imaging Best Practices, version 1.0 (Western States Digital Standards Group, 2003), CSUL then created a series of local best practices covering all aspects of the digitization process, starting with guidelines on how to handle and care for materials to be scanned. Our policy is to capture an image that is a true representation of the original. To do this all the objects in the UHPC digitization project were digitized as archival objects, with no alteration made to the master image.

With some of the glass plate negatives, lantern slides, and gelatin nitrate prints more than 100 years old, including glass plates that are cracked or chipped, we scan an object once to reduce the chance of damaging fragile materials by repeated handling. Master images are created as TIFF (Tagged Image File Format) files. The glass plates were scanned at 1200 dpi, the magic lantern slides at 2400 dpi, and the gelatin nitrate prints at 1200 dpi. The master images were deposited in a project folder on a central server prior to the application of metadata and ingest into our digital repository.

Our best practices documentation, including national and international digitization standards documentation resides on the CSUL staff wiki where it can be accessed by all employees. The wiki includes a wide range of information related to creating CSUL digital collections, including how to operate the digital scanners by format and instructions for creating project-tracking Excel spreadsheets that record the work of each staff member. The information gathered on these spreadsheets enables the supervisor to monitor and evaluate the work of the scanning staff, identify inefficiencies, and keep the project on schedule. Workflow analysis helped support our proposals to hire additional student scanning staff, purchase additional scanning equipment, and identify changes in workflow that will improve future digitization projects.

Project Planning

UHPC digitization project planning began in early 2007, with discussions and project meetings between the project archivist, the digitization librarian, and the metadata librarian. The project's participants knew what would be digitized, what metadata was needed, and where the collection would reside, but we had to develop a road map to help us achieve these goals.

That road map began to take shape with the UHPC finding aid, created by the UHPC project archivist. The digital projects librarian created the UHPC digitization project-tracking documentation and identified staff for scanning, created staff scanning schedules, and arranged for staff access to the Archives Annex where the materials were housed. The metadata librarian, working with the project archivist, developed a plan to use the information in the finding aid for the metadata. Then the digital services librarian developed the procedures for loading them into our content management system.

In September 2007, the UHPC digitization project scanning started with a small group of test scans to determine the best procedures for creating the digital images. Using CSUL's standards-based digitization guidelines, staff created approximately one dozen images. These scans were reviewed for accuracy and quality by both the project archivist and the scanning supervisor; when the pilot images met the requirements for the project, scanning began.

Utilizing Untrained Staff

Initially the number of trained digital scanning staff at CSUL was relatively small, with a Library Technician I and a Library Technician II, who worked on earlier digitization projects and had experience with scanning photographs and text documents, and a Library Technician II, with limited scanning experience. A Library Technician III supervised the work. These four staff also had other job assignments: the Library Technician I assisted in preparing materials for the bindery and assisted with a large inventory project; and the Library Technician IIs performed database maintenance tasks and also assisted with the inventory project. The Library Technician III, who reports directly to the digital projects librarian, supervises CSUL's in-house digital scanning, the database maintenance unit and the inventory project. She is responsible for creating and adjusting scanning staff schedules, monitoring scanning progress, contacting Library Technology Services (LTS) staff to maintain and repair scanning equipment, and performing quality control reviews of the scanned images.

The project began with 56 hours of scanning per week. Unable to hire additional staff, we examined staff duties to identify tasks that could be streamlined or eliminated altogether. A decrease in the number of print journal subscriptions and a reduction in the number of titles sent to a commercial bindery meant those saved hours could be applied to digitization. The same was true with tasks associated with database maintenance. For example, when approached by the CSUL Government Documents Unit to transfer the government documents database maintenance tasks to the Government Documents unit, we agreed and made the change. There were also some basic database maintenance tasks that could be performed by students, saving more time for digital activities.

We identified one of our Library Technician IIs whose knowledge of and experience with scanning, combined with her skills as an instructor, made her an excellent teacher. With these skills she trained our staff to create the high quality digital images we needed and now trains all our scanning staff and students.

Experience has shown us that the level of training needed for creating digital images varies by individual and must be tailored to the individual. Each person brings various levels of experience and understanding to digital scanning. Aside from the level of experience, the unique nature of the materials, coupled with unfamiliar models of equipment, requires individualized training. Training begins with scanner instruction and viewing Cornell University Library's *Moving Theory Into Practice Digital Imaging Tutorial* (Cornell University

Library, 2003.) Our digital imaging trainer spends 2-3 weeks teaching the trainee the local, national, and international standards and best practices, how to operate all of the digital scanning equipment, how to handle the materials being digitized, and any necessary project-specific scanning requirements. It usually takes staff, with multiple job responsibilities, one year to acquire the skills to create high quality archival digital images.

In December 2007, a couple of months into the project, the scanning was not progressing as quickly as expected. We hesitated to consider using student employees due to the fragile condition of the glass plate negatives and magic lantern slides, but there was no other option; the project needed to keep on schedule. We trained our most experienced and mature student employee first and eventually hired more students to assist with scanning. The first three hourly student scanners spent a combined average of 36 hours per week scanning. As summer approached we asked and received permission to offer summer employment to two of the students. The ability to keep them working during the summer, at a total of approximately 60 hours per week, helped us keep the project on schedule.

Midway through the project, in the spring of 2008, four members of the copy cataloging staff joined the UHPC digitization project. They were trained to assist the metadata librarian with metadata creation, a natural progression of their duties. The copy catalogers spent approximately 20 hours per week throughout the project assisting with metadata.

The UHPC project archivist, our authoritative resource for the project, was also our daily contact for the project. Creating images at the Annex proved to be a benefit for the scanning team because the project archivist's office is located at the Annex. She was available to answer questions about the extremely fragile materials and instruct staff on how they should be handled. At the start of digitization, the project archivist was responsible for performing quality control reviews of the images, but we soon discovered this arrangement was not feasible. The project archivist was still in the midst of processing the collection's 500,000 images, and the logical solution was to have the scanning supervisor review the scans. To reduce the number of possible errors, scanning staff perform a review of their own scans prior to the end of their work day. Staff are expected to correct any errors found before a review by the supervisor. If the supervisor discovers images that need to be rescanned those are given back to the person who created the image. Correcting scanning errors became a learning opportunity and the person responsible for the scanning error was responsible for rescanning the image. If the problems were a result of malfunctioning scanning equipment, quality control reviews were performed on 100% of the images until the problems were corrected.

Additional changes in job responsibilities occurred in the spring of 2008 when we replaced most staff working on the large inventory project with student employees. The change gave us approximately 32 additional hours per week to devote to the UHPC digitization project. To accommodate the increase in hours we met with the archivists and the Archives and Special Collections Coordinator to request an extension of the hours at the Annex. The Archives staff was understandably reluctant to have others in the Annex when an archivist is not present, but they agreed to adjust the schedules of staff in the Annex and to extend the hours. The increase in the rate of production made meeting the project deadline a more realistic goal.

By July 2008 all of the glass plate negatives and magic lantern slides had been scanned and once the quality control reviews and all rescans were complete we notified the metadata librarian. She began the process of preparing the metadata for the copy catalogers. Upon completion, the metadata librarian reviewed their work and requested corrections where needed. The metadata librarian then notified the digital services librarian, who began the process of ingesting the images and metadata into the digital repository.

During the life of the UHPC digitization project we lost and gained staff and student employees. The impact on the project was challenging at times. In the late spring and again in the fall of 2008, two Library Technician I staff undertook several weeks of intensive training to acquire the skills to fill void of created by the loss of two employees. The new staff were unfamiliar with digital scanners, they had little or no experience handling fragile photographic materials. Fortunately they quickly became proficient and by the end of 2008 we added 24 hours a week back to our scanning schedule.

The final format to be digitized was the gelatin nitrate prints. Work on digitizing this format began in August 2008 when we hired eight work study students to perform the gelatin nitrate print scanning. We began the fall semester with 132 hours per week: 80 hours of student scanning time, 32 hours of staff scanning, training, and quality control review, and 20 hours of staff metadata creation. We hoped the students would be able to work largely on their own after training. The scanning supervisor worked closely with them for the first couple of weeks; she then let them work on their own. A short while later, while performing quality control reviews of their work she noticed the students were making a large number of errors, many of them basic scanning errors. Our experiment to reduce the close supervision of the students was not a success. Distractions, or perhaps the lure of the holidays, resulted in a lack of concentration.

Scanning the UHPC collection took place at a site across campus. Saving the images to the Libraries' server from this remote site, and searching the web at the same time, caused the computers and scanners to slow and occasionally created serious technical problems. We now block internet access at all our scanning stations and more closely supervise the students' work.

There are advantages and disadvantages with using students to work on digitization projects. The advantages include lower labor costs, a more flexible workforce, and the opportunity to give students valuable skills and good work habits. One disadvantage is the substantial investment in teaching students the skills and knowledge needed to create high-quality digital images only to have them graduate after a year or two of employment. Due to the repetitive nature of the work, it is difficult for some students to concentrate on scanning images. Many times students are not able or willing to work during school breaks. In spite of the disadvantages, we found that the positives of employing students outweigh the negatives.

It is difficult to firmly estimate the number of hours of scanning time you will need when planning a digitization project. To compensate for staff leave and the uncertainty of student employment during breaks in the academic year or during final examinations, it is a good idea to budget extra time for digitization. Project downtime may occur because of equipment problems. In our case, while the scanners were being repaired we had to bring the scanning to a halt and reassign staff and students to other projects at CSU's Morgan Library. In addition to the scheduling problems on the UHPC digitization project, staff scanning schedules had to include 15 minutes to walk across campus to the Archives Annex, where the scanning was done. By using our project-tracking documentation we were able to assess the progress of the project at various points and make any adjustments needed to keep us on schedule. The willingness of everyone involved to adapt and remain flexible was a major factor in the success of the project.

Overcoming Equipment Problems

The project began with just two Microtek Artixscan 1800f flatbed scanners. The Microtek scanners were purchased prior to the project startup and were chosen for their design, which includes a drawer where the glass plate rests emulsion-side up without touching glass or the light source. This separation is desirable when scanning fragile glass plate negatives. The scanners were installed and calibrated by the LTS staff, the equipment experts. During the first four months of scanning we encountered numerous equipment problems, including having to recalibrate the scanners every day, sometimes several times a day to eliminate colored lines on the digitized images.

Equipment problems plagued us through much of this project and adding staff to scanning team did not help the situation. With more people scanning the scanners were in operation for 50 or more hours per week. This high rate of production took a toll on all the scanning equipment and the scanners were showing the stress of overuse. We needed more scanning equipment for both technical reasons and to increase production. The digital projects librarian recommended staff operate two scanners at a time, as one way to increase production. With 20 minutes to scan one glass plate, staff had time to prepare one image for scanning while the other was being scanned. We decided to follow this recommendation and requested that CSUL purchase two Epson Expression 10000 XL scanners, a model that best suits our needs. The scanners arrived in January 2008 but then we had to wait. It took LTS a couple of weeks to install the scanners. At the same time one of our Microtek scanners malfunctioned. Attempts to repair the scanner were unsuccessful and the only option was to return it to the manufacturer for refurbishment. The equipment installation delays and failures caused us to suspend the UHPC scanning for two weeks. We had to reassign staff and students to other projects in the interim.

By February 2008 the four scanners were in place and working, but then we were experiencing other problems. Our new Epson scanners were producing Newton's Rings, a series of concentric, alternating light and dark rings centered at the point of contact between the glass surface of the scanner and the glass plate negative, on the scanned images (Illueca, Vazquez, Hernández, & Viqueira, 2002). The older scanners were beginning to produce banding artifacts (straight lines) on the images. As this only happened with the glass plate negatives, we switched from scanning glass plate negatives to scanning the magic lantern slides until we could determine a solution to the problems. A resolution to the Newton's rings problem came from the digital projects librarian, who thought an acid-free paperboard (barrier board) frame, similar to mat boards used in picture framing, might resolve the problem. The frame raises the glass plate from the scanner glass just enough to allow air to circulate between the plates of glass and eliminates the Newton's rings. During the digitization of the University of North Carolina at Chapel Hill's William Blake Archive, scanners encountered Newton's Rings when creating images from transparencies. Their solution was to scan the images directly and not through glass (Viscomi, 2002). This solution was not practical for us. Using a frame to separate the glass plate negatives, which are extremely fragile, from the scanner glass provided a safe method to protect the emulsion side of the plates. The banding artifacts problem was resolved when we began a daily cleaning and re-calibrating of the scanners.

There was also the challenge of creating quality images from over-exposed and under-exposed glass plate negatives. We adjusted the scanner to capture either a darker or lighter image to correct the poor exposure. One point of pride for us was that we did not break or damage any of the fragile glass plate negatives in the collection.

Improving Interdepartmental Communication

Prior to the UHPC digitization project most digitization work was small ad hoc projects that did not require planning meetings, project-tracking documentation, detailed condition assessment guidelines, or extensive quality control reviews. As a result, not everyone participating in creating digital projects was aware of a project's status. Our digitization procedures changed with digitizing the UHPC collection. During the digitization project not all of us worked in the same location. The project archivist worked in one building, the metadata librarian, the digital projects librarian, and the digital services librarian worked in another. We needed to develop a project management structure that could foster communication and promote collaboration. Project communication, which was taking place via email, often resulted in further 'follow-up' emails. We realized that everyone involved in the project needed to know what was happening and why.

In early 2008 the Repositories Matrix Team, CSUL's administrative and policy-making team for digital activities, created the Digital Projects Management Plan Working Group (Working Group). The Working Group's charge is to monitor the progress of all digitization projects. It includes representatives from Archives and Special Collections, Metadata and Preservation Services, and Digital Repositories Services; every department participating directly in digitization. The Working Group began meeting weekly in February 2008. The initial focus was on the issues and problems surrounding the UHPC project. Now members report on digitization project news, digital equipment problems and equipment purchases, staffing issues, and conclude with a 'round robin' of project status reports. All policy questions are forwarded to the CSUL Repository Matrix Team. Building on the Working Group model, we now schedule pre-project planning meetings for all new digitization projects. These meetings focus on the scope of the project, staffing needs, equipment needs, and the creation of a digitization timeline. Attendees include faculty and staff who will be involved in the creation of the digital collection.

The collaboration that formed during the UHPC project contributed much toward improving interdepartmental communication. The project required a close working relationship along with frequent meetings and emails between the project archivist, the digital projects librarian, the metadata librarian, and the digital imaging staff. Group members were willing to share their knowledge and skill with others and remain flexible while workflows shifted and changed course during the life of the project. Those involved with building digital collections at CSUL have learned that building quality digital collections requires planning, good communication, and a commitment to a collaborative endeavor.

Summary/Lessons Learned

Digitization of the UHPC collection provided several lessons. Within months of commencing the project, with enough data to create an accurate picture of our progress, we realized that we needed more staff, more equipment, and more time to complete the project. While hiring additional digitization staff was not possible, our option was to train staff in other units to assist with portions of the work. As mentioned above, the willingness of everyone involved to remain flexible was a major factor in the success of the project.

When budgeting time for a digitization project, experience taught us that 20% more time should be added to the timeline, to allow for problems of all types to be resolved. Developing a realistic project budget and project timeframe will also help administrators and others understand the true costs of building a valuable digital collection. A short pilot project, conducted prior to the start of the project, can reveal quite a lot. It will show you how much time it really takes to scan the materials; which scanner settings should be used for a particular format; and whether it is possible to make textual documents searchable. Although we did conduct a short pilot, it was designed to learn how to operate the scanning equipment. We should have gathered other information, such as how long it takes to scan a glass plate negative, because soon after the scanning began we realized that we had wildly underestimated the time we thought was needed to scan these negatives. The 5 minutes scheduled per scan in fact turned into 20 minutes. A more comprehensive pilot would have revealed, among other things, what was technically feasible.

The UHPC digitization project underscored for us the importance of regularly sharing information with the project's participants. Good communication, as mentioned above, was vital to understanding the UHPC project's goals and unique digitization requirements. With more than 40 people involved in its creation, sharing information helped us understand how to handle the fragile archival materials, avoid many image rescans, understand the reasons for many of our equipment problems, create solutions, and keep on track to meet the project's deadlines.

Conclusion

By June 2009 the photographs in the first phase of the project were digitized, and the images and metadata began to be loaded into the digital repository. Each digitization project is unique, and each has the potential to present new challenges. Though it might not be possible to anticipate every outcome, there are some things that can be done to prepare the project for success. Obtain the support of your administration or funding agency for the project; develop good project planning skills and implement them; create tools for communicating with all project participants and document all the processes and workflows of the project. Subsequent digitization projects from this vast collection will benefit from what we learned during the first phase of the UHPC digitization.

References

Boock, M. (2008). Organizing for digitization at Oregon State University: A case study and comparison with ARL libraries. *Journal of Academic Librarianship, 34,* 445-451.

Boock, M., & Vondracek, R. (2006). Organizing for digitization: A survey. *Libraries and the Academy, 6,* 197-217.

Cornell University Library. (2003) *Moving theory into practice digital imaging tutorial.* Retrieved on March 31, 2010 from http://www.library.cornell.edu/preservation/tutorial

D'Andrea, P. & Martin, K. (2001). Careful considerations: Planning and managing digitization projects. *Collection Management, 26*(3), 15-28.

Digitization of Local Collections Task Force. (2005). *Digitization of local collections.* Retrieved on March 31, 2010 from http://digitool.library.colostate.edu/

Illueca, C., Vasquez, C., Hernández, C., & Viqueira, V. (2002). The use of Newton's rings for characterizing ophthalmic lenses. *Ophthalmic and Physiological Optics, 18,* 361-362.

Sutton, S. (2004). Navigating the point of no return: Organizational implications of digitization in special collections. *Libraries and the Academy, 4,* 233-243.

Viscomi. J. (2002). Digital facsimile: Reading the William Blake Archive. *Computers and the Humanities, 36,* 27-48.

Western States Digital Standards Group. (2003). *Western States digital imaging best practices. Version 1.0.* Retrieved on March 31, 2010 from http://www.bcr.org/dps/cdp/best/wsdibp_v1.pdf

Entering the Digitization Universe: One Catalog Librarian's Experience at an Academic Library

Mary Rose (Southern Illinois University Edwardsville)

Abstract

This chapter describes a catalog librarian's experience with an academic library's digital collection initiative. The author discusses how the library handled technical challenges and established policies and procedures during the process of creating its first digital collection. The effects of external pressures from consortial requirements and organizational change are also discussed. The author describes technical decisions specific to the first project and more general technical issues like customization decisions and decisions about filenaming convention. The processes involved in establishing selection criteria and rights and permissions policies are described. The author also provides a brief overview of three subsequent digital projects. The author concludes by speculating on how the library's digital presence will grow in the future.

Keywords: Academic libraries, Catalog librarians, CONTENTdm, Digitization, Digital collections.

Lovejoy Library at Southern Illinois University Edwardsville (SIUE) entered the universe of searchable digitized collections in 2008. We encountered several issues along the way to completing our seminal project. There were technical challenges to be met, and we had to establish procedures and policies. We also encountered external pressures due to our reliance upon consortial services and as a result of organizational changes at the University. This chapter is a narrative of this experience and a speculation about the future.

Background: the preliminary steps toward establishing a digital initiative and vision

In 2006-2007, Lovejoy Library administration took the first steps toward establishing a digital projects initiative by forming a CONTENTdm committee and acquiring access to CONTENTdm software as a member of the Consortium of Academic and Research Libraries in Illinois (CARLI). The software is installed and maintained on CARLI's server. Two Lovejoy staff members received training in the use of CONTENTdm; however, neither staff member was empowered with a mandate to create a digital collection. The initiative essentially stalled. When I joined the University as the Library's first catalog and metadata librarian in May of 2007, I recognized that getting Lovejoy fully engaged in the creation of digital collections was a main priority of the position. The aforementioned staff members immediately and gratefully handed their CONTENTdm workbooks over to me and notified the consortium that I was now the primary contact for coordinating the Library's use of this software. I had never previously used CONTENTdm but became intimately familiar with it over the course of the next several months. Lacking training or experience, I relied heavily on support services at CARLI to effectively leverage the software. I also took a generic metadata creation workshop and studied Dublin Core.

I quickly became aware that two digitization projects were being spearheaded by two tenured faculty librarians as candidates for our initial digital collection: one somewhat aggressively as a grant project and the other more casually without the impetus of a grant. Being naïve with regard to the politics of the organization, I deferred to others who decided to give precedence to the grant-funded project. The CONTENTdm committee subsequently decided that the Library needed a process for evaluating and prioritizing potential digital collections. Perhaps this was a response to the way in which resources had been committed to the first project because of a schedule driven by external funding. Or perhaps it was the usual librarian caution that any new undertaking will grow to unmanageable proportions if fed too liberally. Perhaps the desire for oversight was motivated by recognition that the shape of our accumulated digital collections over time would define the character of the Library to a significant degree, and whether this was ad hoc or directed was not a matter of chance but of choice. Whatever the reason, a digitization selection subcommittee to the collection management committee was proposed by a tenured library faculty member at the first CONTENTdm committee meeting I attended.

The digitization selection subcommittee became entwined with the Library's vision regarding digital initiatives. The subcommittee's charge was officially established as being the body responsible for receiving and evaluating digitization project proposals and making recommendations to the parent collection management committee regarding acceptance and prioritization of said proposals. The advisory group comprising the subcommittee included all of the library faculty administrators plus the Director of Development (essentially the marketing administrator) and the Director of Academic Computing. The subcommittee was rounded out by the Catalog and Metadata Librarian (me), the Electronic Resources Librarian, the Archivist and Special Collections Librarian (serving as chair), and whichever subject librarian was participating in a specific digitization proposal. The group resolved to create a proposal form to guide proponents in describing the subject, extent, rationale, funding, etc. of their project ideas. Selection would be accomplished by carefully evaluating the relevance of a project to the Library's mission and the advantages a digital platform was expected to provide for the particular included items, such as wider accessibility for heavily used resources, easier use of delicate or cumbersome materials, and improved access to text-rich content through electronic searchability. Selection criteria suggested by the Northeast Document Conservation Center were incorporated into the subcommittee's official position. The Center frames selection around three basic questions (Gertz, 2007):

- *Should* [the materials] be digitized? Is the collection important enough, is there enough audience demand, and can sufficient value be added through digitization to make it worth the cost and effort?
- *May* they be digitized? Does the institution have the intellectual property rights to permit legal creation and dissemination of a digital version?
- *Can* they be digitized? Will digitization achieve the goals of the project, given the physical nature of the materials and their organization, arrangement, and description? Does the institution have the technical infrastructure and expertise to create digital files and make them available to users now and in the future?

Challenges encountered during the first digital project

Our pilot digital collection was the KMOX sheet music digitization project. Lovejoy Library's Music Special Collections includes a gift from KMOX of over 48,000 music titles compiled by the St. Louis-area radio station: the live studio orchestra's complete performing music library. The titles date from the early 1900s. A subset of this collection, identified as being published prior to 1923 and hence in the public domain, became the target digital collection. Academic Computing, an entity under the administration of the Library's dean, scanned the sheet music in color at 600dpi, enlarged 400% during scanning and saved as uncompressed tif files. I began working on the project in earnest in January of 2008, with my first real technical task being to understand CONTENTdm enough to design a structure to showcase the collection effectively. Eventually I settled on a strategy: Each piece of sheet music would be what is known in CONTENTdm terminology as a *compound object*. Metadata would be supplied at the object level, meaning each piece of sheet music would have its own metadata but the individual pages comprising a given title would not be described separately.

The Fine Arts Librarian had obtained grant monies to hire graduate student assistants to help with the project. I trained the graduate assistants how to provide what catalogers consider *descriptive* metadata. This is the metadata that is transcribed from the piece being described. In this case, descriptive metadata included the song title, first line of the refrain, and publication information. I also showed the students how to search the Library of Congress's free online authority file (*Library of Congress*, 2009) for authorized forms of names for the lyricists, composers, arrangers, performers, and/or illustrators credited on the pieces. Finally, I created standard notes for the student assistants to apply, such as "piano, vocal" for an instrumentation note, "One color (purple)" describing the cover art, and "Includes advertisements" as a miscellaneous note. I reviewed their work and completed the metadata with subject analysis, detailed cover art description, and additional notes.

Learning how to use CONTENTdm required a tremendous amount of time and energy during this first project. The effort was amply rewarded, however, since the functionality provided by the software suited our application perfectly. The software supports batch population of a collection via tab-delimited files. This facilitated collaborative metadata creation, since the graduate student workers could create Excel spreadsheets with preliminary metadata for groups of titles and then pass them on to me to complete. I subsequently converted the spreadsheets into tab-delimited files and uploaded the metadata into CONTENTdm along with the corresponding images. The compound object structure, in which several images comprise one digital entity, elegantly matches the character of multi-page sheet music. The software also provides the means for creating index boxes, which enhance access to the content beyond full text searches of the metadata. We decided to use this functionality to create index boxes for composers, lyricists, and subjects for this project.

As stated previously, Lovejoy Library's digital collections are created under the consortial umbrella, using CARLI's CONTENTdm server. CARLI's collection of member libraries' digital collections is OAI-harvestable, and CARLI provides a means for member libraries to obtain usage statistics. But with these advantages come some constraints. CARLI requires all of their hosted collections to contain certain metadata fields, including (among others) *Rights* and *Language* fields mapped to the corresponding Dublin Core elements and a *Collection* field mapped to *Relation*. The *Rights* field requirement motivated our CONTENTdm committee to address the thorny issues of intellectual property more promptly than we might perhaps have otherwise; as it was we needed to formulate a policy before publishing the KMOX collection. This proved to be the committee's most important task. The consortium specified that the *Rights* field should identify the intellectual property rights status of the digital resources in the collection and provide direction for users to contact the owner. This field could also be used to inform users of fair use laws. The committee consulted with the University's legal counsel to develop a rights and permissions policy in conformance with these guidelines. The digital rights and permissions statement that eventually evolved through the committee's deliberations authorizes "fair use" of the digital resources, provides references describing the legal limits of fair use, specifies the form of attribution, and provides the means for applying for additional permissions (Lovejoy Library, 2009).

SIUE is responsible for the resources comprising our digital collections. Before we begin a digital collection project, we need to establish our right to create these component digital resources. This can be accomplished by using source materials in the public domain, securing permission for digitization and publication from the owner of the source materials, or actually purchasing the right to digitize and publish source materials. However, the rights status of the source materials is not always unambiguous. For the KMOX sheet music project, items within the public domain were identified as such by having a copyright or publication date prior to 1923 printed on the item. However, as I completed the metadata I noticed that some of the covers exhibited images clearly indicating that they were created after that date. For instance, the cover of "Come to the Fair" featured a photograph of the Trylon, Perisphere, and Helicline at the 1939 New York World's Fair, despite the fact that the music bore a copyright date of 1917. The cover for "The World Is Waiting for the Sunrise" depicted singer Mary Ford, who was born in 1924. Other pieces of music included advertisements for songs displaying later copyright dates. The Fine Arts Librarian consulted with legal counsel about the status of these items. It was decided that we could include these pieces of sheet music in the collection if we didn't provide access to the individual pages that were not in the public domain, an approach that wouldn't affect the usability of the music itself.

Another consequence of using CARLI's server is that our digital collections are subject to CARLI's "look and feel" requirements for uniformity. The consortium allows very little flexibility, as it wants to maintain a consistent look between the collections of member organizations. For our first project, this was actually a blessing. Designing a branded image is a lengthy process requiring resources (graphic design talent and technological tools and adroitness) and research (complying with the look and feel requirements of the SIUE website as a whole). As it was, the decisions I presented before the CONTENTdm committee were straightforward and simple. I made some mockups featuring the school colors in various combinations in the permitted areas; the voting process was fairly painless. I worked with Academic Computing personnel to get an official logo that conformed to CARLI's size constraints with the exact color specified by SIUE marketing guidelines.

Challenges encountered during subsequent digital projects

My second digital collection experience, the digitized presentation of a Civil War diary, was achieved in collaboration with the Social Sciences Librarian and a temporary staff worker under her supervision who had transcribed the entire diary. I learned how to use the transcription function in CONTENTdm and worked with the staff worker to render the transcription she had created into files that CONTENTdm could manipulate, i.e. individual text files with file names matching the corresponding image files.

In the spring 2009 semester, I was the instructor of record for a student's Senior Project course. The student, who had worked in a library for several years and was considering going to library school after completing his bachelor's degree, wanted to learn about Dublin Core metadata and digital collections. Together we designed a project for him to create a Civil War collection under my supervision using digitized letters and ephemera loaned to the Library by an emeritus professor of history. After completing background readings and papers, the student spent about five hours a week at the Library. He collaborated with me to make metadata decisions and learned how to use the CONTENTdm software, successfully completing the project in a semester's time. Working on this collection revealed a shortcoming of CONTENTdm in the way it supports managing metadata for disparate types of materials within a single collection. This project, which my student ultimately named the American Civil War Collection, is comprised of three different types of digital entities: letters, military orders, and songsheets. Adequately describing all three required a total of 27 different metadata fields. CONTENTdm does not have the functionality to organize metadata separately into subsets determined by their relevancy to particular included objects. Metadata manipulation (mapping, editing, etc.) after uploading is performed in a single interface in which all the metadata fields are displayed together. Fortunately in our case the small overall size of the collection meant coping with this limitation wasn't prohibitively awkward.

The same spring the library administration hired a second catalog and metadata librarian, and together we began work on a fourth digital collection. This project featured digital photographs of architectural artifacts designed by architect Louis H. Sullivan and owned by SIUE, accompanied by digitized historic photos of the buildings on which the ornaments originally appeared. We worked with the Fine Arts Librarian and her graduate assistant to plan the organization and presentation of the images and identify the metadata we wanted to include. The graduate assistant gathered the raw metadata which my colleague and I translated into controlled vocabularies. We used the Getty Art and Architectural Thesaurus (AAT) (Getty, n.d.) for terminology for the ornaments themselves, materials of construction, and types of buildings of origin, supplementing the latter with Library of Congress Subject Headings when we felt it would be helpful. We began populating the digital collection in April, a process that took four months due primarily to delays in obtaining some of the images and associated descriptions. Leveraging CONTENTdm to create a meaningful structure for objects in this collection proved challenging. We ultimately decided upon what CONTENTdm calls a *monograph* structure. A CONTENTdm monograph is a compound object with hierarchical levels, analogous to chapters in a book. We organized each of our digital entities to have two subsets (chapters) of images: artifact images and building images. Users click on one of these headings to reveal the images in the next hierarchical level. Although this structure isn't inherently intuitive, we felt it was the best fit from among the options available in the CONTENTdm software. The structure works well when browsing the collection as a whole or via the index boxes we supplied for artifact type and building of origin, but we are less enthusiastic with how it translates into retrieval from keyword searches. CONTENTdm has options for customizing the retrieval display that address some of our concerns, but the fact that the software isolates document- and page-level metadata in the search and display customization functionalities prohibits us from achieving our ideal result.

In summary, the four digital collections that Lovejoy has created to date using CONTENTdm are:

1. KMOX Popular Sheet Music , comprised of 118 objects and 558 jpg files.
2. William R. Townsend Civil War Diary, comprised of 14 objects and 356 jpg files.
3. American Civil War Collection, comprised of 9 objects and 40 jpg files.
4. Louis H. Sullivan Ornaments, comprised of 64 objects and 191 jpg files.

The completion of each project was marked by announcing its availability to the University community and adding a link to the library website. I also created a catalog record in OCLC for each collection, and added all four collections to the CONTENTdm Collection of Collections database (*CONTENTdm*, n.d.).

Issues to be addressed in future projects

Organizational change has provided a source of external pressure concurrent with and affecting the progress of our digital initiatives and priorities. Lovejoy Library's dean left near the end of 2007 after a long tenure as both Dean of Library and Information Services and Associate Vice Chancellor for Information Technology. Academic Computing had reported to the Dean in his latter capacity. Upon the Dean's retirement, the Provost decided to change the organizational structure so that the new library Dean would not have this dual responsibility. Academic Computing merged with the Office of Information Technology Services and now shares with it a new reporting structure separate from library administration. The new system began in July 2008. The interim Director of Technical Services began exploring a team approach to digitization. His plan centered around two major initiatives: purchasing a large format scanner for the library and hiring a digital imaging specialist, which were accomplished in 2008-2009. Library digitization projects could consequently be created without relying on Academic Computing personnel to scan materials. However, all of the aforementioned projects were digitized by various people before the purchase of the library's large format scanner and subsequent hiring of the Digital Imaging Specialist. The team approach has not yet been developed for producing CONTENTdm digital collections.

In fact, creation of the image files began prior to my involvement with each of the projects except the first. As a result, a filenaming convention was never established. We discussed filenaming for the first project, the KMOX sheet music collection. We decided to use a transparent method: The images were named using a combination of the song title, composer name, date, and page number. An example is ByTheLight_Edwards, Gus_1909_001.jpg. This approach doesn't support generalization to future projects. As I researched the issue further, I grew to prefer a more systematic approach to filenaming. This idea inspired me to create an *Image ID* field in the metadata for each sheet music title in the collection, which I populated with an alphanumeric collection-specific accession number. But the actual file names corresponding to the jpg files weren't included in the final metadata: an inadvertent oversight resulting from my inexperience with how CONTENTdm handles tab-delimited files. The problems with file names persisted for all four of the projects described previously in this chapter. The Digital Imaging Specialist is working with me and the other catalog and metadata librarian to establish a convention that works with our scanning equipment defaults. We have decided to adopt a cross-collection systemized convention similar to that described in the *Wisconsin Heritage Online Digital Imaging Guidelines*:

> File names for digital masters and derivatives need to be established before the scanning process. Systematic file naming helps not only to manage the project, but also ensures system compatibility and interoperability. It is generally recommended to assign an eight-character file name and a three-character extension, e.g. aa000001.xxx. This is sometimes called 8.3. File names should adhere to some general requirements. They should be:
>
> - Unique and consistent
> - Alphanumeric (consist of only letters and numbers)
> - Lowercase
> - Free of spaces and tabs
> - Numbered sequentially using leading zeroes (i.e. 001, 002, 003, not 1, 2, 3)
>
> The files can be named after an original source collection or per project, depending on the needs of the local institution. Up to four letters can represent the project abbreviation or original collection name, e.g. hf for Harrison Forman Collection or sccl for Shawano City-County Library. The remaining digits indicate a unique file number. This is often simply sequential numbers prefaced with leading zeros. For example, digital images from the Harrison Forman collection project are named hf000001, hf000002, etc. (p. 5-6)

I reached the end of my digital collection backlog with the completion of Lovejoy's fourth CONTENTdm-based collection in September 2009. I subsequently met with some of my colleagues to brainstorm ideas for additional digital collections. The result was a fantastic array of proposals employing audio and video files, featuring collaboration with other local institutions, and creating scholarly research products on a digital platform. The proposals were presented to the selection subcommittee. The constituency of the subcommittee had been modified to reflect the organizational changes described previously in this chapter. The Director of Academic Computing was no longer a part of the subcommittee and the new Digital Imaging Specialist had been added. Although the majority of the subcommittee greeted the new project proposals with enthusiasm, the role of the selection subcommittee is currently being reconsidered and thus the project approval process is on hold.

We are planning to purchase a server in cooperation with our IT department. Not only will this relieve severe storage problems during digitization workflow, it will also give us the option to explore creating portal pages to our CARLI digital collections or to host some collections locally. The Digital Imaging Specialist has a graphic design background and is highly interested in exploring creative ways to showcase our collections.

Sorting out the process of green-lighting digital projects and the graphic and technological design of locally-hosted portals and collections will doubtless incur long and passionate discussion. The committee-driven process that is the default for all decisions at Lovejoy is not a painless one. Consensus-seeking, while attractive in theory, is impractical in many ways. But it is the culture of this institution and I suspect the culture of many similar institutions as well. Some issues along the way to realizing our digital initiatives thus far have been thoroughly discussed and resolved with thoughtful regard for the future, and some were hastily addressed with the main goal of overcoming a stalling impediment. Some of the best ideas proved insufficiently nimble to adjust to unforeseen developments. Some of the bad seed sown in the interests of forward motion has yet to bear the anticipated troublesome crop. Regardless, we are moving forward into new kinds of projects with a sharper focus on who we are and how we want to present ourselves.

References

CONTENTdm Collection of Collections. (n.d.). Retrieved December 1, 2009, from http://collections.contentdmdemo.com/

Gertz, Janet. (2007). *Preservation and selection for digitization.* Retrieved December 10, 2009, from http://www.nedcc.org/resources/leaflets/6Reformatting/06PreservationAndSelection.php

The J. Paul Getty Trust. (n.d.). *Art & Architectural Thesaurus Online.* Retrieved December 8, 2009, from http://www.getty.edu/research/conducting_research/vocabularies/aat/

Library of Congress Authorities. (2009). Retrieved December 1, 2009, from http://authorities.loc.gov/

Lovejoy Library. (2009). *Digital rights and permissions.* Retrieved December 1, 2009, from http://www.siue.edu/lovejoylibrary/about/digital_rights_and_permission.shtml

Wisconsin Heritage Online Digital Imaging Guidelines (Version 2) (2009, September). Received December 2, 2009, from Wisconsin Heritage Online Wisconsin Library Services.

From Argentina to Zambia: Capturing the Digital A to Z's of a Child Art Collection

Kathleen C. Lonbom, Milner Library (Illinois State University)

Abstract

The International Collection of Child Art, residing at Illinois State University's Milner Library, is a collection of artworks produced by children and adolescents across a range of cultures and time periods, primarily mid to late 20th century. This chapter discusses the collection's background and its role as a culturally expansive primary source. Information is provided about the Library Services and Technology Act grant funding awarded through the Illinois State Library to support the digitization project, *Imagine Illinois and Beyond: Celebrating Creativity Through the Eyes of Our Children!* The benefits and challenges of the digital conversion are discussed. Finally the chapter will look at alternate methods of image access, specifically audio description, to facilitate information discovery for viewers with a print disability such as vision impairment.

Keywords: Academic libraries, Art, Audio description, Children's art, Cultural heritage materials-digitization, Descriptive metadata, Grant funded projects, Illinois State Library, Institute of Museum and Library Services, Library materials-digitization, Metadata, Special collections, Visual resources.

Collection Background

The International Collection of Child Art (ICCA) is a resource comprised of artworks created by children and adolescents from around the world. This cultural heritage collection reflects the visual expressions of young artists who capture themes from the fantastical to the familial and a myriad of themes that fall between. The collection was initiated more than forty years ago at Illinois State University (ISU), Normal, Illinois, and is now curated and administered by the University's library. This primary source includes over 8,600 accessioned children's artworks, from approximately 58 countries and cultures. The collection celebrates the creativity and innovative work produced by children with a multicultural perspective. The resource serves multiple audiences including students, academic scholars from across disciplines, and a wider public interested in viewing, learning about, and appreciating the imaginative vision that shapes a child's creative pursuits.

ISU's Milner Library acquired the ICCA in 2000 from the ISU School of Art, which inherited the resource following the closing of the University Museum in 1991. The collection had been stored in a classroom until the college could no longer accommodate it due to space constraints, lack of support staff, and less than optimal conditions for storing and maintaining this resource.

Virtual Shift: The Digital Project's Genesis

University libraries holding collections with parallel cultural and historical value have grappled with similar challenges and opportunities presented by the digital conversion of a unique resource. Questions, both philosophical and practical, invite those embarking on a digital project to entertain a range of considerations perhaps not previously attached to the physical collection. Digitization of the Eastern North Carolina Postcard Collection project members recognized the ambiguous nature of assigning subject headings to a stand-alone image, relatively free of contextual information. The postcards in this collection usually were accompanied by text caption, but did not always have context provided by a monograph (Dragon,

2009). Colorado State University's project to digitize the University Historic Photographic Collection emphasized the collaborative process of converting a historic resource under a controlled timeline. The conversion involved a variety of project partners learning to speak each other's professional language including archivists, metadata librarians, and digital project managers (Hunter, Legg & Oehlerts, 2010).). A Latin American political poster collection, part of the University of New Mexico Libraries Center for Southwest Research and Special Collections, speaks to digitally documenting the transient nature of a resource by preserving ephemera such as posters. Similar to children's art, posters are not typically created to last through time, but document a specific and often meaningful moment in time situated at the edge of societal mainstream perspective (Stephenson, 2006). Clifford Lynch's discussion of digitizing cultural heritage materials comments broadly on the discovery aspect of placing resources in an open electronic environment where unexpected and at times serendipitous communities form around such a collection. Lynch posits it is the objective of a digital library, expansive in its capacity to "enable and facilitate implicit communication" to provide a construct for the community building that develops around a collection (Lynch, 2007).

The move to consider digitization of the ICCA was rooted in curricular needs to accommodate a generation of users already vested in electronic access. By virtue of the resource's sheer size, aging condition, and location, physical access is limited. The collection of two dimensional artworks is stored in a multi-use university warehouse that also serves as the library's storage site for a collection of less frequently used volumes and is the home of University Archives. The warehouse is off campus and largely off limits to the public. Although slides of the artworks were created in the 1970s to support teaching and study of the collection, the analog format was no longer a viable option to support use of the collection in the 21st century academic environment. Included in the collection are sixteen thematic traveling exhibits that have been displayed widely and have garnered attention for the resource. Several hundred of the slides, selected from the collection's traveling exhibits, were converted to digital format in 2003, but overall the condition and quality of the slides was questionable and each image required color correction. The conversion of this small sample to a digital format brought attention to the collection when the images were mounted on the ICCA website and provided the spark that ignited the pursuit of funding to digitize the collection. Art, art education, English, and children's literature faculty actively using the collection in classes were supportive advocates for moving the resource into a fully accessible digital format.

Setting the stage for digital conversion in the fiscally constrained environment of a public university requires strategic use of limited funding for library resources and creative thinking to move forward with a digitization project. Milner Library began researching grant options to move forward with the digital conversion of the ICCA in response to faculty feedback.

The value of a grant award is not limited to the funding awarded to support a project. Significant gains are gleaned from a successful external grant award including the opportunity to work outside your own institution with the awarding agency, related publicity, promotion, and recognition of a collection. The external recognition has the potential to bring additional funding as a project's status is heightened, providing a scaffolding effect on which to build and enhance the project and its outcomes. Additionally, faculty librarians working towards tenure and promotion are keenly aware of the professional distinction associated with the potential of a funded competitive external grant and the implications for building a record of scholarly and creative activity.

Grant awards also provide resources to fund hiring student assistants who collaborate and contribute to a project's success. In an academic environment a grant funded library digitization project can advance a student's academic career by affording opportunities to work on the multiple facets afforded by such a project. Grant funded projects, such as the proposed digitization of the ICCA, offer a wide range of opportunities for students from a variety of academic disciplines, testing and developing students' strength as a researcher in art, art history, history, foreign language and culture. Students who have worked with the ICCA come from a variety of majors: art, art history, arts technology, English, and language. A student can also learn about time and project management skills and supporting the goals and objectives of a project through their own contributions.

Writing a successful grant proposal reflects a commitment of time, thought, and energy while providing an opportunity to compete and be recognized through the external agency awarding the grants. The Illinois State Library's (ISL) Library Services and Technology Act (LSTA) grant program, using funding made possible by a grant from the Institute of Museum and Library Services (IMLS), appeared to be a fitting choice for a proposal submission. The IMLS is the main provider of federal support for museums and libraries in the United States working with state and local organizations, its primary mission to strengthen the capacity for these institutions to link people, information, and ideas in a meaningful way. The fiscal year 2009 LSTA grant offerings by the ISL were available in three categories: technology programs and services, resource sharing, and digital imaging projects. The digital imaging category suited the needs for the potential ICCA digitization project.

The ISL's LSTA grant application and review process is competitive and requires the principal investigator to make the case for the value of the collection being considered for funding. Grant reviewers—experienced with digitization projects, past principal investigators, or project directors—evaluate proposals using a review rubric. The rubric is made available to grant writers and offers clear language about components of the grant application: project description, action plan, target audience, outcomes, timetable, personnel, and project sustainability (LSTA Grant Review Criteria, 2010). The ISL provides further support to grant writers by hosting workshops designed specifically for digital imaging projects prior to the grant proposal deadline. The workshops cover planning the grant project, elements of the proposal, and the evaluation rubric.

Developing the grant proposal afforded an opportunity to closely examine the ICCA's forty year history at ISU and to justify the significance of the collection in terms of how it related to historical and cultural trends on a state, national and international level. The resource, initiated by ISU's former University Museum Director, Dr. F. Louis Hoover, began with a collection of over 300 artworks gathered from the children of Illinois. Artworks from North American countries represent 55% of the current collection. Although ultimately international in scope, the seeds for the collection were sewn with creative works by the children of Illinois. With support from the University, the collection's scope grew under ISU art education professor Dr. Barry Moore (now emeritus), including artworks from children and adolescents of six continents, Antarctica being the only continent not represented. Relationship building and networking with international organizations such as the Christian Children's Fund reflected the University's longstanding record of supporting global engagement through activities including study abroad programs for students and welcoming international students to the ISU community.

The LSTA grant application required detailed attention to planning the ICCA digital conversion including proposed timelines, personnel, and supporting resources. The project planning guidelines suggested through the proposal process largely reflect the detailed information for the digitization of cultural heritage materials thoroughly outlined in the Digitization Activities Project Planning and Management Outline document disseminated by the U.S. National Archives and Records Administration (Still Image Working Group, 2009).

Milner Library's Digitization Center, established in 2005 to primarily provide for the digitization needs of the University community, proved the logical choice for the digitization of the ICCA. The Center, equipped to digitize a variety of analog formats, provided contractual services for successful projects funded by LSTA grants awarded through the ISL: the *Towanda History Project*, a partnership between the Towanda District Library and Historical Society, and the *Native American Collection*, held at the McLean County Museum of History. These projects established the Center's reputation for partnering on LSTA grant funded digitization projects. Additionally, Milner Library and ISU's School of Art work collaboratively with the

Center to produce an image database, ILSTUDIA, providing images for art, art history, design, and visual culture hosted on the library's CONTENTdm server. Further experience was gained with the digitization of two dimensional artworks when the Center digitized more than 250 prints from the New Editions Workshop project funded by the School of Art.

The grant proposal emphasized the collection's value to provide primary source materials across disciplines including art, history, social sciences, education, English and psychology. The educational value of the collection was already established by the documented study and use of the resource by researchers (ICCA: Research, 2008). The digitized collection was not meant to replace the original artworks, but to facilitate access to a larger audience. Titled *Imagine Illinois and Beyond: Celebrating Creativity Through the Eyes of Our Children!* the grant proposal was submitted in May 2008 to the ISL's LSTA digital imaging grant program. In August the total amount requested, $85,934.00 was awarded for the project to digitize 8,600 accessioned pieces in the ICCA. The grant cycle began October 1, 2008 with all funds to be expended by June 30th 2009.

Constructing the Project

The original grant proposal was submitted, approved, and awarded, allotting the majority of the funding for contractual services from the Digitization Center at Milner Library. Although the grant proposal was reviewed and approved at all required levels at ISU, the University's Grants Accounting and Comptroller's Office requested a budget amendment be filed after the grant was awarded, belatedly noting the Digitization Center named for contractual services could not be designated as a separate agency. An amendment to the grant budget needed to be filed to reflect expenditures to support the project. The budget amendment was submitted and approved by the University and the State Library. It was an unexpected hurdle to cross and created delays hiring grant funded personnel and ordering equipment. Additional complications were created by the reorganization of the of the Digitization Center, just weeks prior to the grant awards being announced. The director of the Digitization Center was reassigned to work full time on a separate external grant funded project, essentially leaving the ICCA project without a project director and the Center without a director. Without prior notice or planned options for time release from academic workload, the principal investigator took on the additional responsibility of project director for the digitization project. As author of the grant, the principal investigator had drafted the project planning that was already in place and the funded grant moved forward.

Developing the Data

When Milner Library began administering the ICCA, the resource came with a textual database holding museum generated information, as available, about the artworks including object identifiers, titles of the pieces, date created, artist gender, artist age, artist location, provenance, materials, dimensions and subject headings. The textual database laid the groundwork for collaboratively developing metadata schema, mapping, and standards used in the digital image database. Due to personnel turnover and position reassignments three different metadata librarians worked on the project during the planning phase of the grant, through the grant cycle, and after the grant cycle came to an end. The library supported filling the vacated positions so that metadata development continued to progress.

Initially, guidelines for the LSTA grant required funded projects to upload their digital files and related metadata into the Illinois Digital Archives for dissemination. Milner Library was already using CONTENTdm to manage several other digital collections, and it is the choice of the Consortium of Academic and Research Libraries in Illinois. CONTENTdm has proven to be a reliable data storage solution for a variety of formats including images, documents, and audio. This is not a small consideration for an institution, not only due to cost, but also to preserving cultural heritage collections with concerns for moving the digital data attached to these resources reliably and robustly into the future (Van Den Bosch, Van Den Herik, & Doorenbosch, 2009).

Vocabulary for the subject headings was most closely aligned with the Getty Art and Architecture Thesaurus (AAT). The project team continues to add and adjust subject headings as needed using the ATT as a guide, although not all terms are included in the thesaurus. For example, the terms "angels" and "ghosts" are excluded in AAT but are useful terms to apply in a children's art collection. Metadata for the collection was scrutinized closely after the images and information were matched and viewable simultaneously. Gaps in information were revealed. Descriptive metadata, such as titles for the artworks, were occasionally truncated due to the migration of data from one database format to another. This was an irregular occurrence which was remedied by consulting the original records or the artwork to complete the information.

A related grant was written concurrently with the LSTA proposal requesting funding from the University's Research Grant program to support additional enhancement and development of descriptive metadata fields for the collection. For example, as the collection grew, accompanying artists' comments were documented on old key punch cards, sometimes typed, sometimes handwritten, in the 1970s and 1980s by staff from the University Museum. The paper records, stored with the collection in the offsite library storage facility, provided no viable method of access for researchers. The awarded grant provided funds to hire a student who reviewed all paper records and transcribed more than 600 comments into a spreadsheet. Providing access to accompanying artists' commentary in addition to the images themselves provides researchers enhanced primary source material.

When paired with the image of the artwork, the accompanying artist commentary enriches the descriptive metadata available to users and also potentially provides illuminating context for the image (Figure CHILD-1). The commentary from the young artists had not been made fully available in an accessible format to users in the past. This same grant also partially funded student assistants to transcribe and translate a collection of post World War II Germany artworks donated to the ICCA in the 1970s.

Figure CHILD-1. *To Live Under the Sea*, boy, 11 years old, Philippines, 1976. © International Collection of Child Art, Milner Library, Illinois State University, Normal, Illinois. Used with permission. Artist comments: "I wish to be friendly to all fishes under the sea so I could see the beauty and surroundings under the sea. I wish to stay forever under the sea. I will ride on the back of the shark. I will help the poor people and I will give them pearls."

After the LSTA grant was fulfilled, a University Research Grant was awarded to support an ongoing project to write concise—one to two sentence— descriptions for the digital images from the ICCA. Descriptions were a missing piece in the information provided by the textual database. The accompanying descriptions will serve as an additional path to the end user, enhancing access and discovery. By Dublin Core definition, the *description* field provides a textual description for an image, such as a piece of children's artwork in this collection (Dublin Core, 2009). End-users, including students, educators, and researchers, will benefit from having additional access points available as supporting and valuable descriptive metadata for the digital collection of multicultural children's artworks. Although the majority of the 8,600 artworks converted under the LSTA digitization project have at least one term in the *subject* field for descriptive metadata, no information is available in the *description* field. The lack of information in this field limits the end-user's capacity to fully explore the resource for the purposes of teaching, learning, and research.

The library's digital imaging specialists captured images of the artworks with the center's Betterlight Super 8K-HS camera working on a Tarsia 40 x 60 inch vacuum table which accommodated most of the pieces. Required specifications for scanning the artwork were provided by the State Library and were compatible with other digital projects the library had developed. The image files have an uncompressed TIFF master file (300 PPI), compressed JPEG image files (300 PPI), and a thumbnail GIF image (72 PPI). The digital imaging specialists and project student assistants resized and edited image files using Adobe Photoshop CS2.

The Road More and Less Traveled

The Digitization Center's location required the children's artwork to be transported from the university warehouse approximately three miles off campus to the library. Over the course of the grant cycle, approximately forty weeks, weekly trips were made to move artwork to the library and then return the artwork to the warehouse.

Despite being located in the Midwest, climate never played a significant role in transporting the artwork, not a small consideration. A vehicle was able to drive into the warehouse for pickups and deposits to the library were delivered at a service door with a large overhang. The two dimensional works were transported in portfolios designed and crafted by the library's preservation staff. Each portfolio held 25-50 pieces depending on the size and material from which the artworks were made.

In the last months of the grant cycle the project team began processing the traveling exhibits, about 500 artworks, framed and stored in shipping crates. These pieces required extra time and attention because many of the pieces had to be unframed, digitized, and then reframed. The exhibits posed more of a challenge for transporting back and forth because transportation had to be arranged in advance for University facilities staff to deliver the crates to the library and then return them to the warehouse. The process of transporting, uncrating, digitizing, reframing, general handling, and re-crating the artworks was more time consuming than anticipated.

Library preservation staff worked with the project team from the planning phase and throughout the project cycle helping to identify workable solutions to related preservation and conservation issues. The overall condition of the artwork in the collection is fair, considering the age of the collection, some artworks more than fifty years old, and the materials used for children's artwork, typically not archival quality paper for example. A potential problem considered, during the planning phase, was the possibility that some of the artwork might have preservation or conservation concerns that would need attention. Working collaboratively with the library's preservation staff, the digitization staff handling the artwork created a rubric of potential preservation concerns and documented observations made about the condition of the artworks as each piece was handled that was unusual or in need of attention. As a result, the collection now has a record describing the condition of each piece that was marked for conservation attention. For example, several hundred of the artworks were in acidic mat board frames that necessitated removal as the pieces were handled. Excessive amounts of tape made this a more tedious, and time consuming, process than anticipated. Typical notes documented included: some water damage, tacky oil paint, fragile materials, acidic paper, tears, glue, tape etc. The digitization staff documented the preservation concerns throughout the process and consulted closely with preservation staff to make bridge fixes as needed. This documentation will be used to pursue grant funding for conservation and preservation of the artworks sometime in the future.

Miscellaneous Malfunctions and Positive Project Outcomes

Unanticipated technical problems can and will happen throughout a project period. Alternatively the positive outcomes provide an overpowering counterbalance.

Scanning came to a halt for several days just one month into the LSTA project, when the Betterlight Super 8K-HS camera used to capture the artwork malfunctioned and had to be shipped to California for repair. The library's main server containing all of the project image files went completely down toward the end of the grant cycle resulting in six work days that proved difficult for processing, digitizing, and scanning the artwork. The project team adapted, saving files to the work station hard drives for temporary storage, until the servers were restored. After a change in library network configuration, the digitization center staff encountered an unexpected increase in the amount of time it was taking to open a TIFF file from the server. Moving image files between servers or from the server to a local hard drive was slowed significantly.

Positive outcomes of the ICCA grant project and the increased level of digitization activity directly and indirectly influenced and contributed to changes in the Digitization Center. Repeated bending and lifting at the low level of the pre-fabricated scanning bed created ergonomic concerns. A frame to raise the scanner bed was designed and fabricated, raising the scanning bed to 30 inches thus improving the ergonomics of the setup and creating a more comfortable workflow. The library committed to supporting additional space by moving equipment and personnel from a cramped, shared area (which staff had uncomplainingly made functional) to a larger work space dedicated solely to the needs of the Digitization Center. The move also solved the slowed time to manipulate image files as the network ports and servers were upgraded from one hundred megabyte Ethernet to one gigabyte Ethernet in the renovated space. Staff increased as a second digital imaging specialist hired under the LSTA grant continued employment full time after the grant cycle ended. Two ISU students from the arts technology program were hired to work part time on the LSTA project. They assisted with scanning artwork, resizing images, and helped transport the artwork from the warehouse to the digitization center.

Areas of Growth

In 2007 Illinois Public Act 095-0307 altered the fabric of State awarded digitization grants. The newly enacted Illinois Information Technology Accessibility Act (IITAA) requires the preparation of audio descriptions to accompany digital images to enhance access for individuals with a print disability such as vision impairment. Due to the incongruous timeline of the fiscal year 2009 grant awards and the enactment of the IITAA, FY09 grant recipients, Milner Library included, were only asked to submit audio files to accompany twelve digital images. Funded applications henceforth are required to prepare audio descriptions for 100% of digital images. After attending an audio description (AD) workshop hosted by the Alliance Library System, the project director became intrigued by the concept of providing an alternate source of access to a visual resource. A small grant from the University was secured and provided seed money to hire a student assistant and begin researching the implications and mechanics of audio describing a digital image collection. Using the ICCA digital collection as a beta model, a pilot project has been initiated by the project director with the primary objective to investigate the challenging aspects of developing audio descriptions for an image collection.

Audio description is defined as a "narrative technique that makes visual images more accessible to blind and low-vision people by producing audible written descriptions of non-verbal visual information" such as the digital images in the ICCA. The history of AD is rooted in the performing arts and dates back to the 1960s when a vision impaired employee from the United States Department of Education suggested preparing audio descriptions for films as well as the captioning already being provided for hearing impaired individuals. The idea was not supported however until the 1980s when advocates gathered and initiated an ongoing program sponsored by the Washington Ear, a group recording newspaper and magazine articles for the vision impaired and continued by providing descriptions for performing arts venues (Snyder, 2008).

Employing basic principles for preparing AD suggested by the workshop, work began on writing transcripts for a selected number of images from the ICCA. The transcripts are brief, providing up to a one to two minute description averaging 200 words. Descriptive language, not analysis, attempts to provide a listener with a concise understanding of the image. The basic elements for the description use an introduction to the image, identify the primary theme or elements, and then describe in detail what is featured in the image (Figure CHILD-2).

Figure CHILD-2. *A Beautiful Afternoon with Birds. boy, 12 years old, Vietnam, 1972.* © International Collection of Child Art, Milner Library, Illinois State University, Normal, Illinois. Used with permission.

Audio Transcript: This artwork, a painting titled *A Beautiful Afternoon with Birds Returning to Nests* was created by a 12-year-old boy from Vietnam in 1972. The centerpiece of this painting—composed primarily with blue hues—

is two birds flying across a lightly speckled sapphire blue sky. A larger bird is painted in the upper left side of the artwork closely followed by a smaller and similarly painted bird. The beaks have only been suggested by a jagged line and the visible eye of each bird is a simple white dot. The avian bodies are sleek and graceful with plumage that subtly moves from light to deep turquoise. The birds blend closely with their inky blue-black shadows emphasizing their forked tail feathers, reminiscent of long fluttering coat-tails. This image is published by Milner Library at Illinois State University as part of the International Collection of Child Art Digital Collection.

Approaches to uncovering resources and options for developing, writing, and recording narratives for images, grant funding, and working with units across the university are being explored. An option being initiated is building collaborative partnerships with teaching faculty to integrate the creation of audio description for digital images in the child art collection, into course curricula in related disciplines. The outcome of the pilot project research, still in the beginning stages, will inform future digital imaging initiatives integrating audio descriptions with digital images. The children's artwork presents a captivating invitation to construct an accessible and meaningful representation of an image with language.

Conclusion

When discussion about digitizing the ICCA began the motivating drive behind the idea was to provide improved access to support teaching, learning, and research. With approximately 97% of the collection digitized at the time of this writing, the ultimate objective of the project has been fulfilled, although outcomes have expanded and were influenced by a fluctuating climate of change that involved personnel, equipment, and content (ICCA Digital Collection, 2009). Because change is a constant in this environment a key component of a digitization project is a creative, cohesive, and flexible project team invested in the project. It is impossible to deny the overarching appeal this collection of children's art extends to all, including the staff and faculty across multiple library units who contributed to and supported the project. From a pedagogical perspective, the project provided an opportunity to engage numerous ISU students who contributed their time and talents to multiple aspects of the process including collection maintenance, digitization skills, translation of artworks, conservation work, and transcription of metadata. The students who worked with the collection were thrilled to have the experience of working with primary source materials and were quite excited to be a part of the process that brought the collection to digital life. In the academic environment, and especially at ISU, which prides itself at placing the learner at the heart of teaching and scholarship, the level of student engagement was an unanticipated and truly positive outcome.

The project will continue with the ongoing refinement and enhancement of descriptive metadata, including expanded subject headings and description development. As the collection's identity shifts to the virtual, the responsibility to assure optimum access and searchability for continued use and research of this resource will remain at the forefront of its mission. Broadening the scope of access for a range of users by providing audio access will continue to be explored as the project moves into classrooms and provides collaborative opportunities for students to continue to contribute in meaningful ways to the project. The library will consider the forward direction other cultural heritage collections are moving in the virtual world (Ronchi, 2009). Embracing hypermedia to push the boundaries of the collection through virtual storytelling, gallery exhibits, and reconstructing the creative, historic, and cultural environment of a child artist are all possibilities. Ultimately this will serve the goal of remaining a meaningful and vibrant teaching and learning collection that will continue to inspire users researching the visual expressions of children.

References

Audio description Illinois. (2009). Retrieved March 13, 2010 from http://www.alsaudioillinois.net/

Best practices for creating digital files. (2010). Retrieved March 9, 2010 from http://www.cyberdriveillinois.com/departments/ library/ what_we_do/servicestechnologygrant.html

Dragon, P. M. (2009). Name authority control in local digitization projects and the Eastern North Carolina postcard collection. *Library Resources and Technical Services. 53* (3), 185-196.

Dublin core metadata initiatives; Dublin Core metadata element set, version 1.0: Reference Description. (2009). Retrieved March 15, 2010 from http://dublincore.org/documents/1998/09/dces/ *Educating Illinois 2008-2014: core values.* (2008) Retrieved March 22, 2010 from http://www.educatingillinois.ilstu.edu/ plan_sections/core_values.shtml

Hunter, N.C., Legg, K, & Oehlerts, B. (2010). Two librarians, an archivist, and 13, 000 images: Collaborating to build a digital collection. *Library Quarterly, 8* (1), 81-103.

Illinois digital archives guidelines for images. (2010) Retrieved March 14, 2010 from http://www.idaillinois.org/cdm4/guidelines/

Illinois general assembly. (2007). *Illinois information technology accessibility act.* Retrieved on March 14, 2010 from http://ilga.gov/legislation/publicacts/95/PDF/095-0307.pdf

Illinois state library: Library services technology act review criteria and rubric. (n.d.). Retrieved on March 22, 2010, from http://www.cyberdriveillinois.com/departments/library/what_we _do/pdfs/lsta10_rubric.pdf

Institute of museum and library services: our mission. (n.d.). Retrieved on March 22, 2010, from http://www.imls.gov/about/about.shtm

International collection of child art digital collection. (2009). Retrieved on March 21, 2010, from http://tempest.lib.ilstu.edu/index_icca.php

International collection of child art: research. (2008). Retrieved on March 20, 2010 from http://www.library.ilstu.edu/icca/research/

Lynch, C. (2007). Digital collections, digital libraries, and the digitization of cultural heritage information. In D.Kresh, (Ed.) *The Whole Digital Library Handbook.* Chicago: American Library Association.

Stephenson, N. K. (2006). Preserving dissent: The Sam L. Slick collection of Latin American and Iberian posters. *Art Documentation. 2* (1), 20-24.

Van Den Bosch, A., Van Den Herik, J., & Doorenbosch, P. (2009) Digital Discoveries in Museums, Libraries, and Archives: Computer Science Meets Cultural Heritage. *Interdisciplinary Science Reviews,* 34, (2/3) 129-138. doi 10.1179/174327909X441063

Ronchi, A.M. (2009). *eCulture: Cultural content in the digital age.* New York: Springer.

Snyder, J. (2008). Audio description, the visual made verbal. In J. Cintas (Ed.), *The didactics of audiovisual translation* (192-197). Philadelphia, PA: John Benjamins Publishing Company.

Still Image Working Group. (2009). *Digitization activities project planning and management outline. U.S. National Archives and Records Administration.* Retrieved March 12, 2010, from http://www.digitizationguidelines.gov/stillimages/documents/Planning.html

Acknowledgments

Milner Library ICCA Digitization Project Team: Sara Caldwell, Digitization Center; Jim Caselton, Facilities; Anita Foster, Bibliographic Services; Ross Griffiths, Preservation; Erica Holden, Digitization Center; Christina Horna, Systems; Krena Hoyt, Systems; Leta Janssen, Administration; Heather Kosur, Preservation; Jason Paul, Systems; Patrice Andre Prud'homme, Bibliographic Services; Toni Tucker, Administration; Sharon Wetzel, Administration

Milner Library student research and digitization project assistants: Daniel Abdalla, Stephanie Finch, Sheila Majumdar, Peter Nelson, Gina Pantone, R.J. Tortoriello

Additional appreciations to Cheryl Asper Elzy, former Dean of University Libraries, Dr. Richard Satchwell, former Director, Digitization Center, and Alyce Scott, Digital Imaging Program Manager, Illinois State Library.

Special Collections, Digitization, and the Classroom: A New Model

Mark Phillipson (Columbia Center for New
Media Teaching and Learning)

Michael Ryan (Columbia University Rare
Books and Manuscripts Library)

Abstract

The Black Radical Archive is a small pilot project at Columbia University that leveraged digitization to involve students in the discovery and description of heretofore hidden collections (http://blackradicalarchive.ccnmtl.columbia.edu/). This project is the result of innovative collaboration between archivists, educational technologists, a faculty member deeply engaged with archival collections, and his students—who made selections of their own and added to the digital archive. In this chapter we describe cross-divisional support for the project, its implementation in a Spring 2009 seminar entitled "Black Radicalism and the Archive," and lessons learned from the informal, just-in-time digitization intrinsic to course-driven repository building.

Keywords: Activism, Activists, Archives, Customization, Digital repository, Teaching, Drupal, Hidden collections, Informal digitization, Learning, Multimedia, Pedagogy, Processing, Repository, Special collections, Support, User-contributed.

Introduction

Special collections in many ways define the character of an academic library. They are rich and sometimes undiscovered islands of unique materials amid an ocean of more generally available information resources.

Locally held archival materials help define the identity and character of their parent institutions, attracting and nurturing research affiliations and communities. Faculty members who have actively benefited from direct access to such materials in their own research are looking for practical ways to involve their students in the experience and excitement of working directly with primary source materials.

In this chapter, we discuss a pilot project at Columbia University, the Black Radical Archive (2009), that sought to integrate special collections into the classroom — redefining some traditional notions of the academic archive and its use. This project supported a Spring 2009 graduate seminar's focus on three special collections held by the Columbia University's Rare Books and Manuscript Library (RBML).[1] It facilitated a deeper level of materials-based discovery and research, providing students the means to discover, categorize, annotate, digitize, and share important holdings in the collections. In the process, the visibility of the holdings and archival practice was raised, along with further prospects for drawing on archives to support teaching and learning.

Though digital surrogates are sometimes faulted as a replacement for tactile contact with original material, the Black Radical Archive in fact leveraged digitization to encourage hands-on engagement. At the height of the project's implementation, the Black Radical Archive shifted in function from a repository of digitized items to a hub for uploads of additional items discovered and digitized by students. The project, then, emphasized the importance of physically inspecting unique materials, even as it cultivated the advantages that digital surrogates offer for convenient and repeated inspection, communal access, and non-invasive annotation.

---

[1] RBML's holdings and activities may be seen online at http://www.columbia.edu/cu/lweb/indiv/rbml/.

Exposing the Collections

When he conceived of a graduate-level seminar exploring the intersections of activism and archive called "Black Radicalism and the Archive," Brent Edwards, Professor of English and Comparative Literature at Columbia, tailored it to three collections held by RBML: the Hubert H. Harrison Papers, a fully cataloged collection with a published finding aid; the C.L.R. James Papers, a collection of heretofore disparate collections that was in the process of being assembled as the seminar met; and the Amiri Baraka Papers, a large unprocessed collection with only a preliminary carton survey. Despite these different levels of cataloging and indexing, Edwards wanted his students to discover, categorize, annotate, and compare material from all three collections—developing primary materials-based research skills in the process.

Edwards's course occurred at an opportune time for both RBML and the students in the seminar. Special collections librarianship has changed markedly in its emphases during the past decade or more. Without losing its curatorial, collections-based focus, the field has invested heavily in promoting outreach and in directly supporting the work of teaching and learning on campuses.[2] Special collections units are now more open to a diverse constituency than they used to be, more concerned with creating a broad base of users. Outreach librarians are now common in special collections units, as are class and seminar rooms. As library staff collaborate more with faculty on course design, primary source materials are increasingly integrated into undergraduate and graduate courses. At Columbia and many other institutions, curators actively reach out to faculty for the purposes of better integrating source materials into curricula; RBML hosts two or three classes per day during the academic term, each of which use rare books, manuscripts, documents, and other materials from the collections.

---

[2] For background on these efforts, see Traister, D. (2003), Smith, S. (2006), and Association of Research Libraries (2008).

As a result of such outreach efforts, archival materials are better integrated into courses as enrichment (library staff presentations of source materials being studied in a course in later editions and formats), research consultation (in connection with assignments requiring students to consult books or manuscript materials in special collections), or surrogate access (digital facsimiles of selected special collections material made available to students through course management systems, or CMSs). When Professor Edwards approached RBML about his Black Radicalism seminar, we assumed that he would be interested in the classroom support that RBML is now accustomed to providing: that is, a review of sources pertinent to the course, a display of some of them, and some arrangement for ongoing access to select materials in the RBML reading room or the course CMS. We were wrong.

Professor Edwards was thinking outside the box — or, more accurately, he was thinking deep inside *the box*, the archival storage unit. Edwards was interested in providing students with access to primary source materials before they were organized for use. He wanted his students to confront and try to make sense of historical objects that had not been rearranged by archivists. Of course it is common practice in research libraries not to open collections for use until they have been fully processed. But again, Professor Edwards approached RBML at an opportune time. Like other large research libraries, Columbia has its own formidable backlog of unprocessed and underprocessed archival and manuscript collections. Addressing these arrearages became an ARL priority in the late 1990s, and the subsequent momentum to provide new energy and funding streams resulted in the "Hidden Collections" initiative that continues to play a vital role in our research libraries.[3] Echoing ARL recommendations to "connect the exposure of hidden collections to ARL's strategic priority for Research, Teaching, and Learning," (Special Collections Task Force

---

[3] See, for example, Greene and Meissner (2005), and Association of Research Libraries: Exposing Hidden Collections (2009).

Final Report, 2006), Professor Edwards asked us to challenge a long-standing policy of processing a collection before opening it up for use.

Edwards, of course, was less interested in library policy than in pedagogical opportunity. His syllabus framed variously (un)processed materials as a chance for students in the seminar to make original discoveries and contribute to a scholarly effort to describe the collections: "Part of the unique challenge − and, hopefully, the excitement − of this seminar is that the three collections we will be working with are in different states of organization. At times, especially with the Baraka Papers, we will be investigating boxes with little or no information about what we might find in them. On the one hand, this means that to a certain extent we will have the opportunity to discuss the collecting practices (inchoate as they might sometimes be) of these intellectuals themselves, as they gathered and stored a range of materials over many years. On the other hand, this means that, by noting the layers of material in a given box, by tracking sources, by deciphering handwriting, by dating an artifact or manuscript, by annotating and explicating, in the long run we will be helping RBML in the effort to catalog and make available to future researchers these enormous and currently unwieldy collections. "

For Edwards's purposes, each collection was ideal for the sort of practical engagement and various theoretical issues attending the formation of archives that he had in mind. The C. L. R. James Papers were really an artificially constructed assemblage of materials by and relating to James that had been harvested from a variety of sources in North America and the UK. One of the most important social and political philosophers and activists in the 20th century, James led a peripatetic life. He was careless about his personal effects, choosing instead to put his energies into philosophy, literature, and global politics. Friends and acolytes salvaged what they could along the way, shaping his legacy in this way, and those efforts resulted in what forms the core of the James Papers at Columbia. At the other extreme, Amiri Baraka has lived in the same house in Newark NJ for more than fifty years. He is also an inveterate collector, harvester, and saver. But he is not a disciplined or organized one, and so his papers, while voluminous, reflect an idiosyncratic self-archiving that could be called comprehensive, organic, or simply disorganized.

Black Radicalism and the Archive, then, would be an ambitious and wide-ranging course. It would focus students on the material aspects of archives that document activist movements, as well as on a larger set of theoretical concerns entailing the formation of political and cultural identities. Working with the class on this level was a new and exhilarating task; the challenge was to derive from material archives the making of a broader movement. As Edwards planned his course and conceived of readings and assignments trained on these materials, it became clear that the collective research he had in mind would require its own unique and equally ambitious support. At the center of that support would be a digital workspace, allowing him and his students to select, organize, share, and appraise each other's findings from three very different collections.

A New Model of Support

Once Professor Edwards conceived of a virtual space in which to coordinate and analyze the range of materials that students in his seminar would be considering, he turned to another division of Columbia University Libraries' Information Services: the Columbia Center for New Media Teaching and Learning (CCNMTL). CCNMTL's mandate is to facilitate and advance teaching at Columbia through the purposeful use of new media. Over its ten years of operation, CCNMTL has grown into a service enterprise that supports over 4,000 instructors at Columbia University. [4] It was the natural group to help design and implement what would become termed the Black Radical Archive, a digital workspace for Edwards's seminar.

Serendipitously, CCNMTL's priorities had been evolving congruently to RBML's; each group was exploring new ways to incorporate collections into teaching and learning. In 2007 CCNMTL

---

[4] More information about CCNMTL's services and projects is online at http://ccnmtl.columbia.edu.

had launched a strategic initiative called Digital Bridges[5] specifically devoted to the development of innovative connections between curated collections and classroom-based study. Digital Bridges projects have resulted in a variety of educational environments and tools that draw on collections held by museums, public media producers, documentary filmmakers, scientific laboratories, and academic libraries. As it cultivates new ways to incorporate collections into teaching and learning, CCNMTL is increasingly reliant on collaborative relationships formed with Columbia University Libraries units such as RBML.

Supporting Edwards's course, in fact, drove new levels of coordination between RBML and CCNMTL. Though each division digitizes materials as part of its service mandate, the purposes, time-frames, and quality levels of such digitization vary to a great extent. Digitization of source materials is, of course, intrinsic to CCNMTL's work supporting multimedia instruction at Columbia, and yet much of this digitization is conducted 'just in time' within the context of an individual semester or project; it does not conform to archival and preservation standards. At the same time, RBML conducts a robust digital program of its own. Partnering with Columbia's Libraries Digital Program Department (LDPD) and the Preservation and Reformatting Department (PRD), RBML's digitization is performed to high quality standards and often tied to extracurricular exhibitions and events. Setting up and stocking the Black Radical Archive, then, entailed coordinating these various digitization practices across CCNMTL, RBML, and units in the library supporting preservation-level digitization.

Shortly before the semester met, Edwards worked with RBML staff to identify items that he wanted to make available by dates pegged to his syllabus. The standard workflow for digital exhibition of RBML materials involves selection by curators, digitization to

---

[5] Background on Digital Bridges and description of various projects developed by this initiative is available at http://ccnmtl.columbia.edu/digitalbridges.

preservation standards by PRD, and design and presentation of derivative versions of the content by LDPD. But in this case, the tighter deadline was more typical of CCNMTL's course-specific digitization or an e-reserves process than a standard high-quality digitization workflow; Edwards needed a turnaround of materials scanned and posted to the digital archive in as soon as one week, in some instances. This compressed timetable was partly due to the unprocessed condition of some of the items: it took Edwards and RMBL staff some time to conduct an informal survey of uncataloged materials that would be pertinent to the course.

When there was enough lead time, Edwards's initial selections from the collections were processed in the traditional way: digitized in the libraries' preservation lab to archival standards, with a derivative version passed on to CCNMTL to post to the Black Radical Archive. In many cases, though, the pressing deadlines of Edwards's syllabus meant that shortcuts and workarounds were necessary. Edwards's engagement was crucial here: whenever necessary, he was ready to spend time in the collections himself, taking digital pictures for the Black Radical Archive. He was thus able to give his class online access to items from collections whose traditional digitization would have taken a long time – if it were even attempted. For example, Edwards was interested in a series of scrapbooks assembled by Hubert Harrison; these scrapbooks helped underline the course's emphasis on this activist's quirky and suggestive arrangement of materials. However well-suited such scrapbooks were for the course, archival-level digitization of such complex objects is a daunting, labor-intensive prospect, necessitating correlation of page components and layers. Assisted by RBML curators, Edwards conducted his own, decidedly non-archival imaging of these scrapbooks.

While this survey was taking place, CCNMTL was also consulting with Edwards to set up the Black Radical Archive, the website in which digital surrogates generated for– and eventually by– the class would collect. As a digital hub supporting student investigation of these collections, the Black Radical Archive was structured to help students quickly find as well as contribute items. Selecting an easily modifiable platform, CCNMTL built the archive using a lightly skinned instance of the open source Drupal content management system. Drupal allowed for quick set-up and modification of content types, as well as suitable administrative access for the fifteen or so students enrolled in the course, some of whom were visiting from other institutions.

The website was set up and integrated with Columbia University's authentication system shortly before the semester began. An alternate form of registering was also appended to the site in order to accommodate the visiting students. Authenticated students were allowed to search and access all content posted in the archive, post comments, browse and edit metadata, and upload files. A higher level of administration was reserved for CCNMTL so that the archive could be further designed, modules updated, and user roles managed. The interface was set up so that students could filter records by collection, scan all collection locations, and quickly browse assets by column sorting of titles and media types.

To support locating and indexing items from the collections, and the box descriptions that would be the seminar's capstone assignment, CCNMTL agreed to structure the repository with a simple and customized data model. In this model, every asset uploaded into the archive had to be connected to a *location*. Usually these locations were boxes (with a numbering convention defined for the class). Because assets from outside the three collections might also be uploaded to the digital archive, a generic "Outside" location category was also created. Metadata for the assets was kept as simple as possible — far simpler than typical library description — to help make the eventual student input of new assets into the archives as frictionless as possible.

Shortly before the class met, CCNMTL worked closely with Edwards to stock the archive with the many pictures he had shot of scrapbooks and other material he had photographed in the Hubert Harrison collection. Since some of these files were too large to be directly uploaded into the Drupal, CCNMTL arranged supplementary server space through the Libraries Digital Program (LDP) at Columbia. This too was a first: LDP had never before stored files that were not generated by professional staff at preservation-level standards.[6] Since Edward's selections for the digital archive included aging audio and video tapes of various formats, several other variations on traditional digitization processes occurred during the semester as RBML and CCNMTL staff continued to add assets to the digital archive, using Edwards's syllabus as a roadmap. RBML sent old audio tapes out to a third-party vendor; CCNMTL, more experienced with video processing, digitized some VHS tapes and, in the instance of some badly damaged tapes, also commissioned an outside vendor. All of these assets, generated through various means, were uploaded into the Black Radical Archive in time for students to access for specific class sessions. The Black Radical Archive, then, grew as a result of diverse support interactions and inputs, ranging from archivists to the instructor to various preservation specialists to educational technologists and, finally, the students in this unique course.

Classroom Support and Implementation

Class sessions were all held in a conference room in RBML, and supporting these sessions was a logistical challenge in its own right — involving coordination of cartons of material, presentations by students of their discoveries, and collective access to the Archive during class discussions. Participation of RBML staff in the class was critical. Since almost none of the students in the course had any significant experience with or exposure to primary source materials prior to the course, an RBML archivist who was assigned to supporting the course gave the group as a whole a short primer in archives and archival management, reviewing with them the fundamentals of acquiring, surveying, processing, and providing access to archival collections. In addition, she met with students individually throughout the course to answer their questions and help

---

[6] In moving in-house library digitization support towards more informal ground, this project resonated with calls from Davidson (2009), Dooley (2009), and many others to prioritize services for an expanding user base for special collections; Dooley urges us to "digitize with abandon."

them with their assignments. In effect, she served as a TA without portfolio. This as-needed support was provided in lieu of more formal training of Edwards's students in archiving practice, which would have overloaded a syllabus already rich with cultural theory and historical background about the seminal activists being studied. The goal of the course, after all, was to get students engaged with archival practice as a point of entry into more theoretical study of the practices and influences of Harrison, James, and Baraka.

Another component of class support was the accommodation of important guest speakers. In addition to noted scholars and experts, Baraka himself visited one session and explained his own "archival techniques," thus providing a further layer of documentation and information to add to the Black Radical Archive. Each of the guest sessions was taped, and the tapes became part of the evolving narrative of activism and archiving constructed on the foundations of the actual primary source materials, affording further material for the growing digital archive accompanying Edwards's course.

In the second half of the semester, Professor Edwards gave the class instruction on uploading items into Black Radical Archive. Students were then ready to undertake the culminating assignment: each one was assigned a box in the unprocessed Amiri Baraka collection and then asked to inventory the contents of their box. To do so, they would consult with RBML archivists, take digital pictures of particularly interesting items they discovered in their box, and upload box inventories and item photographs into the digital repository. Though Edwards felt that this assignment could yield some interesting information for RBML, in the form of preliminary inventories of uncatalogued boxes that were modeled on inventories of processed collections, the goal was not to produce authoritative documentation. Instead, students were asked to produce lists of contents, with as much contextual information (such as the date of an event, or the identity of a figure in a photograph) as they could ascertain. These unofficial selections and annotations by students joined the more professionally catalogued and digitized material already uploaded into the Black Radical Archive.

Even though Edwards's seminar met regularly in a conference room in RBML and could retrieve and display physical collections, digital surrogates from the archive were often displayed instead of actual objects during class. This was a matter of convenience and efficiency; discussion could engage details from many objects and could proceed in spontaneous directions without being bogged down by physical retrieval and replacement of items. Some items were simply too fragile and cumbersome for the students to pass around; the digital archive facilitated quick pinpointing of specific parts of these objects during discussion, without loss of the visual complexity that would have been hard to perceive in, say, photocopies. Digitization of a variety of old audio and video formats meant that the class could collectively consider such multimedia items without having at hand various playback instruments. The digital archive also facilitated convenient distribution of long manuscripts in the collections, which were typically printed out by individual students for reference before class and brought in for group perusal.

Students later described the "contagious" energy of their own uploading to the Black Radical Archive of discovered items from the Baraka boxes: their digital staging of material that would then be contextualized by findings in other boxes. This staging spurred discussions about theoretical and practical considerations of archiving. Items with particularly complex provenance gave rise to particularly lively conversation during the seminar. For example, the Baraka boxes included audio tapes with liner notes scrawled on them by the likes of Nina Simone and Allen Ginsburg—tapes that may very well have been owned by these other luminaries at some point.

Collective appraisal of such objects, facilitated by the Black Radical Archive, helped students think about the complexities of provenance, the layers of interventions in any archive by original collectors and subsequent organizers of material, and the artificiality of any one preserved state of a collection. One student ambitiously documented each "layer" that he uncovered in his box as he dug through it rather like an archaeologist, and shared these layers with the rest of the class to spur discussion of patterns of proximity across the Baraka collection—patterns that a classmate went so far as to term the "poetics of the archive." More simply, in-class consideration of items uploaded by students helped them compare contents of their assigned box to those in other boxes, and therefore gain various chronological, thematic, and material views of the unprocessed collection.

Participation in the course not only immersed Edwards's graduate students in the practice of archival research, it also suggested to them the usefulness of digital surrogates as a component of such scholarly practice. One student discussed the way that a preliminary inventory of items scanned by the instructor and classmates helped him to identify patterns and target investigation of specific objects in the archive — in short, to make more efficient use of his time with the physical collections. Another student was prompted to think about the benefits of informal, collaborative digitization for research in a subject area she is researching, modern Egypt; items of interest for this topic are as likely to be discovered on the likes of eBay as in a formal archival collection, and a digital hub, this student speculated after working with the Black Radical Archive, could help scholars distributed around the world coordinate findings.

Though in-class use of the Black Radical Archive was heavy, very few annotations of individual objects were posted on the site, despite the site's capacity to connect annotations to uploaded items. This was partly due to the structure of assignments in the class; by the time students were engaged in digitizing items from the unprocessed Baraka collection and comparing the contents of their assigned boxes, the semester was drawing to a close; annotation of various objects happened verbally as a matter of class discussion. In addition to a main projector and screen, several individual laptops anchored discussion with reference to various items in the digital archive. Class discussion anchored theoretical readings to the items stocked by Edwards in the Black Radical Archive and, as the semester proceeded, it was increasingly concerned with targeted identification of similarities and patterns across the collections. Student annotations that were uploaded into the archive, then, tended to be appraisals of groups of objects rather than of individual objects themselves.

As one of the few student who came into the course with previous experience with archives stated, the digital archive served as a "collective interpretive project," not a "collective digitization project." Had the class's emphasis been on building an online library, rather than on sharing an arena of interpretation, students would have concentrated on assembling and posting deeper metadata. Certainly the metadata in the Black Radical Archive is at present too sparse to serve researchers outside the course; it is limited to item titles, collection and box locations, and supplementary notes. Asking students in a future class to enrich the digital archive with more rigorous and informative descriptive metadata could be an interesting further educational use of the archive, should Edwards wish to further develop it as a resource for other researchers, or it could be a task assigned to a graduate student working with RBML archivists. Edwards's students were intrigued by the idea that their selections could help inform subsequent work with the three Columbia collections, though they agreed that subsequent cataloging would be necessary to make the digital archive useful to researchers beyond their class. Their most substantial legacy posted to the Black Radical Archive was, in fact, item-level description of unprocessed boxes, descriptions that ran to notable length in some cases and proved detailed enough to assist RBML in its eventual processing of the Baraka Papers.

The Archive beyond the Class

The Black Radical Archive survives the course it was built for, not as a comprehensive representation of the collections it draws on, but, rather, as an expanding documentation of engagements with these archives. It will thus raise awareness and interest in these rich collections, and, we hope, entice more teachers, students, and researchers into direct contact with archival holdings.

From the perspective of a special collections unit nested within a research institution, the lessons learned were several and significant. First, it challenged two major sets of operating policies and practices: to wit, that unprocessed collections should not be made available prior to processing, and that digitization projects should only by designed and undertaken for fully processed materials with stable metadata. Opening up unprocessed collections to students proved to be pedagogically and archivally important. In giving students access to primary sources prior to library mediation, the class allowed students to participate in the literal making of the historical record. At the same time, it generated descriptive information at a highly granular level that will eventually be of great use to processing archivists. The detailed box content lists provided by the students proved to be of a high quality; given the fact that the students brought to their tasks a depth of subject knowledge not typically available to a processing archivist, their contributions to the future organization of these collections will be important. Although it will not be possible to do this across the board in the future, involving students and scholars in the description of collections prior to their processing is an option we should try to exploit on a more regular basis — whether or not it is tied to an actual course.

Digitization projects in the Columbia Libraries are complex, formal, and labor-intensive. Standardization across the system is rigorous and necessary if the products are to be integrated into a larger common pool of digital assets. "Scan once not twice" is dogma. Such projects are thus developed in a team environment, subjected to a demanding vetting process, and implemented in a highly controlled fashion. These projects typically reflect some consensus within the Libraries as to which materials would be of most use to researchers when presented on the web. The assumption is that if we build it, the research community will find it and use it.

The lesson we learned from the collaboration is that we need to accommodate a more diverse set of needs for the generation of and access to digitized material. Aside from the benefit of surfacing previously hidden holdings, there may be good pedagogical reasons for doing so. Digitizing for the Black Radical Archive was entirely user-defined; RBML staff had no role in the selection process other than facilitating access and offering advise in response to the course instructor and students. The scans that resulted were of considerable value to the course, and they will always be available in the future should they need to be repurposed in some way. RBML has worked with CCNMTL on many occasions in the past in contributing to web-based course support. What was new here was that the content of that support was driven by users, not librarians. This project was bottom-up, and its success encourages us to look for future opportunities to re-engineer RBML's workflow to dovetail with CCNMTL's digital facilitation of learning activities.

This type of project is especially staff-intensive and time-consuming. Archivists assigned to the course had to invest considerable time working with Edwards on selecting materials, with other staff helping to process digitization, and with students in Edwards's course using these collections on a weekly bases. Moreover, they needed to attend every session of the course. CCNMTL staff had to be in constant communication with Edwards, RBML, other library units, and outside vendors to keep the digital archive coordinated to an unfolding syllabus. In the age of "sustainability" and "less process, more product," this customized support sins in many ways. But while it is not a working model for day-in, day-out course support, it does provide interesting options for boutique projects, and it serves to remind us how badly we need the boutique along with the mainstream and the generic. Research institutions are congeries of expertise, and special collections units need actively engage with complementary types of expertise —such as that cultivated by instructional technology groups, as well as the faculty and students we all serve—as part of their routine work.

Developing any course *ab ovo* is arduous and challenging; as anyone who has ever taught knows. But now that it has been developed and a model of it remains via the Black Radical Archive, the course — and intradivisional relationships formed in support of it — can be reused in various ways and for various purposes. We look forward to trying similar approaches with other faculty using a different menu of materials for different purposes. In the meantime, informal digitization and annotation of unprocessed material contributed to the forming of a unique engagement with our collections, and our task going forward is to preserve and make accessible this effort of interpretation as part of the Harrison, James, and Baraka papers.

Special collections and educational technology units considering these types of partnerships should be prepared to devote significant staff resources to them. In our view, the effort is well worth it, since it directly integrates unique holdings, faculty and students, and the diverse capacities of support units into the heart of our institution's academic mission. And that, after all, is why we are here.

The authors would like to thank Brent Edwards, Susan Hamson, Laura Helton, Lea Osborne, Patricia Renfro, and Lytton Smith for their assistance with this article.

References

Association of Research Libraries. (2006). *Special collections task force final status report, 2006.* Retrieved March 29 from http://www.arl.org/rtl/speccoll/spcolltf/status0706.shtml

Association of Research Libraries. (2006). *SP296 Public services in special collections,* November 2006. Retrieved March 29 from http://www.arl.org/bm-doc/spec296web.pdf

Davision, S. (2009). If we build it, will they come? Strategies for teaching and research with digital special collections. *RBM, 10*(1), 37-49.

Dooley, J. (2009). Ten Commandments for special collections librarians in the digital age. *RBM, 10* (1), 51-9.

Greene, M. And Messner, D. (2005). More product, less process: Revamping traditional archival processing. *American Archivist, 68*(2), 208-263.

Prochaska, A. (2009). Digital special collections: The big picture. *RBM, 10*(1), 13-24.

Smith, S. (2006). From "treasure room" to "school room": Special collections and education. *RBM, 7*(1), 31-9.

Traister, D. (2003). Public services and outreach in rare book, manuscript, and special collections libraries. *Library Trends*, *52*(1), 87-108.

Part IV – One Plus One is Greater Than Two:

Collaborative Projects

Digital Treasures: The Evolution of a Digital Repository in Massachusetts

Dodie Gaudet (Central MA Regional Library System)
Kristi Chadwick (Central/Western MA Automated
Resource Sharing System)
Jan Resnick (Western MA Regional Library System)

Abstract

Digital Treasures is a digital library collection of the history of central and western Massachusetts. It is a collaborative project among Central/Western MA Automated Resource Sharing System (C/W MARS), Central MA Regional Library System (CMRLS) and Western MA Regional Library System (WMRLS). Initiated by C/W MARS in 2006, Digital Treasures began as a pilot program when C/W MARS purchased equipment and software and set up a scanning lab at its headquarters in Worcester. Currently Digital Treasures has 36 collections from libraries, with over 1,300 accessible images. C/W MARS, CMRLS and WMRLS continue to collaborate on ways to bring funding, selection guidance and metadata expertise to their member libraries and bring access to the wealth of cultural history of the Commonwealth.

Keywords: Central Massachusetts Regional Library System (CMRLS), Central/Western Massachusetts Automated Resource Sharing (C/W MARS), Digital Barn Raising, Digital Treasures, Digital Commonwealth, Western Massachusetts Regional Library System (WMRLS)

History & Background

In the early 1960s, three Regional Library Systems were formed in Massachusetts to provide a variety of services directly to the public libraries in the western, central, and eastern parts of the state. The services were (and still are) provided at no cost since the Regions are funded by the state. When automation began entering libraries some 20 years later, the WMRLS (Western Massachusetts Regional Library System, 2010) and CMRLS (Central Massachusetts Regional Library System, n.d.) were instrumental in helping to establish a fee-for-service automated network available to all types of libraries named Central/Western Massachusetts Automated Resource Sharing or C/W MARS (C/W MARS Inc, 2009).

In 1998, the Regional Library Systems became multi-type. All public libraries are automatically members of a Massachusetts Regional Library System (MRLS). All academic, school, and special libraries are eligible for membership if they meet basic qualifications. Any WMRLS or CMRLS member can join C/W MARS by paying the membership fees. Not all libraries choose to join C/W MARS: some are small and cannot afford the fees; others are larger, have their own network staff and prefer a stand-alone Integrated Library System. The number of libraries in WMRLS and CMRLS is larger than the number in C/W MARS. As of March 1, 2010 membership in the three organizations broke down as follows

	CMRLS	WMRLS	C/W MARS
Academics	17	19	11
Publics	72	103	130
Schools	120	164	2
Specials	26	25	4
Total	235	311	147

With the imminent development of Digital Commonwealth, a state-wide portal and digital repository, CMRLS and C/W MARS were both interested in setting up a small lab so that libraries could begin scanning photos, documents and other items which could also be discovered via the state-wide portal. A Regional Library System and an automated network in the eastern part of the state had each purchased a scanner and offered instruction on its use, but few libraries took advantage of the opportunity. Considering this, C/W MARS proposed that one of its tech-savvy staff members who had an interest in digital photography be in charge of the lab and do the actual scanning if local library staff supplied the metadata. CMRLS had a cataloger on staff who could conduct workshops on Dublin Core and be available for metadata consultation. Since the offices of the two organizations are a mere seven miles apart, joining forces to support a single repository made the most sense and Digital Treasures (see *Digital Treasure*, 2009) was born.

The Scanning Lab

Due to some new memberships and some existing members upgrading, C/W MARS had enough discretionary funds to purchase hardware and software and create a new part-time position. The Executive Hardware for the new lab consisted of an Epson Expression 10000XL flatbed scanner with an 11" x 17" bed. A new server had recently been purchased for the network's regular activity and the old server was used for Digital Treasures. After much research, OCLC's CONTENTdm was chosen for the creation, storage and access to digital materials. Anticipating the future growth of Digital Treasures and the inclusion of text, OCR extensions were purchased at that time. Other programs loaded to the digital lab workstation included Adobe Photoshop CS2 for creation of derivative files, Adobe Acrobat for PDF conversion, and Datacolor Spyder 3 for display color calibration.

The Pilot Project

The principals involved in the Pilot Project were Michael Bennett, the new part-time Digital Initiatives Librarian at C/W MARS; Dodie Gaudet, Consultant for Bibliographic and Technical Services at CMRLS; and Jan Resnick, Assistant Regional Administrator for WMRLS. Dodie and Jan worked directly with the libraries in their respective Regions; Michael, who had previously attended the

Northeast Document Conservation Center's (NEDCC) School for Scanning, did all of the scanning and was available to answer the technical questions.

First some ground rules were established for the project. It was decided that the subjects of Industry and Agriculture would allow for maximum participation yet give the repository a focus. Concentrating on pre-1923 objects would avoid copyright issues. Each library would be limited to 20 scans. Materials were to be two-dimensional, no larger than 11" x 17", and in good enough condition to be handled without falling apart. Once library staff had created the metadata, they would be responsible for transporting their items to and from the C/W MARS headquarters in Worcester.

Information sessions were held in each Region to promote Digital Treasures and explain the Pilot Project. Next, Michael, Dodie and Jan developed an online questionnaire which was sent to the directors of all Regional member libraries. Directors were asked if they were interested in participating in Digital Treasures, how much material they owned, what kinds of materials they owned, how much they ultimately planned to contribute to Digital Treasures and related questions.

As the cataloger, it was Dodie's responsibility to learn Dublin Core and develop a two-hour workshop. In preparation for the project, she attended Introduction to Digitization offered by NEDCC in October of 2005 and their Persistence of Memory Conference in November of the same year. Using the Dublin Core Metadata Initiative (DCMI) site (Dublin Core Metadata Initiative, 2008) and the Bibliographic Center for Research (then Collaborative Digitization Program) Best Practices Document (CDP Metadata Working Group, 2006) she synthesized material on Dublin Core for Digital Treasures participants.

Simple Dublin Core was used so as not to overwhelm the staff creating the metadata since most of them were not catalogers. The handouts are available on the Digital Treasures site. Workshops were scheduled in both the Western and Central Regions. Participants brought examples of the objects they planned to have scanned and practiced their Dublin Core descriptions on paper forms.

The first library to complete the metadata for 20 images was the Jacob Edwards Library in Southbridge. The descriptions were keyed into an online form and e-mailed to Michael at C/W MARS. The photographs were delivered to C/W MARS for scanning and matched to the metadata. By the end of the Pilot Project in August 2006, 24 libraries, twelve from each Region, each had a digital collection of 20 images on Digital Treasures. Libraries also received a CD of their images to use for publicity or any other purpose they chose.

To allow the repository reach beyond the Commonwealth's borders, Digital Treasures metadata have always been compatible with the OAI standard (Open Archives Initiative, n.d.). The metadata are harvested both by the Digital Commonwealth and OCLC's OAIster project.

When specifications were being developed for Dublin Core records, the principals decided to use Library of Congress Subject Headings so that the records would integrate well with the MARC records in the online catalog. After the Pilot Project launched, Michael began working with staff at OCLC, C/W MARS and member libraries to crosswalk the Digital Treasures Dublin Core metadata into MARC format that could be loaded into OCLC Worldcat. As a subscriber to OCLC, C/W MARS would not only have their digital records available online, but would be able to export the records into their own public catalog with referring links back to the collections. Collections available in October 2007 were harvested and their MARC records are now available through WorldCat and the C/W MARS online public catalog as well as Digital Treasures.

After the Pilot Project

Up to this point, all costs for Digital Treasures had been assumed by C/W MARS, but the organization could not justify supporting this service exclusively with membership fees. The decision was made for C/W MARS to subsidize Digital Treasures, and charge participants a portion of the costs involved in scanning and maintaining the digital repository. With a vote of the membership, the following fee schedule was instituted and is still in effect:

All C/W MARS members are allowed 20 free scans. Each scan beyond the first 20 is $8.50 (50% of the actual cost to digitize an object). After scanning, the library pays $1.00/image annual maintenance fee. Libraries who are not C/W MARS members receive no free scans, pay $12.75/scan (or 75% of the actual cost) and $1.50/image annual maintenance fee.

The annual fee is assessed for the maintenance of each digital image's permanence over time through future platform migrations and regularly scheduled data refreshment cycles. It also covers maintenance of online delivery through CONTENTdm and the allowance of OAI metadata harvesting.

Once the Pilot Project ended, activity in Digital Treasures slowed down drastically. A couple of additional information sessions were held along with another Dublin Core workshop. Everyone liked the idea of having photographs and documents from their local history collections digitized, but had difficulty finding the time to select objects and describe them in a useful way. Even though the financial situation was relatively healthy at the time, some libraries found they could not justify the scanning fees. In the fall of 2007, Dodie applied for and received a grant from the Greater Worcester Community Foundation (GWCF) to cover scanning fees for libraries. The grant was called the Central Mass. Memory Project.

More importantly, the grant from GWCF funded a metadata specialist to work with the libraries selecting and describing their objects for digitization. Jeff Monseau, a Library and Information Science student at Simmons College who also worked part-time with the Archives of Mount Holyoke College, was hired as a "circuit rider." Because of the mission of GWCF, funds could only be used to help libraries within the Central Region. For those libraries, Jeff's experience, even the mere fact that he was available to help, was a tremendous boon and several new libraries added 20 images while other libraries increased the size of their digital collections. The grant funds enticed some non-C/W MARS members to participate in Digital Treasures which broadened the collection.

In early 2008, Michael moved on to the University of Connecticut and Kristi Chadwick became the administrator of Digital Treasures.

Digital Treasures on the Road

Digital Treasures had been up and running successfully for over two years. Digital Commonwealth had developed a repository as well as a portal and was publicizing its services, stimulating more interest in digitization. For libraries that had not yet taken the step, the Technical Services Section of the Massachusetts Library Association (MLA/TSS) organized a one-day conference in the fall of 2008. The committee chose the topic *Introduction to Library Digitization* and invited several people from throughout New England to talk about their projects, how the projects were started and to describe the practical, day-to-day aspects. Kristi, Dodie and Jeff were asked to talk about Digital Treasures, its technical details, and the Central Mass. Memory Project.

A Digital Barn Raising

As one travels westward through the Commonwealth, the area becomes more sparsely populated. Most towns have libraries, but the libraries are often small and some are staffed by a single person. The median population in western Massachusetts is 1900. Springfield, the largest community, has over 150,000 residents, meaning some of the other communities are significantly below the median. The towns are also rather dispersed by New England standards, and there is little or no public transportation. The western Massachusetts approach to Digital Treasures – as with many projects - relies on team work.

In May 2008, Digital Commonwealth received a grant from the H. W. Wilson Foundation for conversion efforts. The timing was fortuitous as WMRLS was in the process of organizing a "digital barn raising", a cooperative effort to get libraries started. To follow the theme, everyone contributed. Kristi Chadwick brought an introduction to Digital Treasures. A member of the Digital

Commonwealth Board, contributed information about the Digital Commonwealth and described the grants available from the Wilson Foundation. A librarian from the Berkshire Athenaeum in Pittsfield reviewed the major copyright issues involved in digital projects. Dodie Gaudet presented the basics of Dublin Core and how libraries would use it. Member libraries brought a few of their local documents. Jan Resnick coordinated the program and arranged a few extra catalogers to assist in the process.

The program consisted of presentations, questions and discussion, and concluded with a work session in which participants from member libraries began to develop Dublin Core metadata. This structure worked well for the group. They had the opportunity to ask questions (there were lots about copyright issues) and then had the chance to develop initial Dublin Core records for their documents in a supportive environment. WMRLS hopes to offer additional "barn raisings" expanding the skill base to a wider group of small libraries. Their collections contain a broad variety of treasures to be digitized. Buckland Historical Society, which participated in the barn raising session, went on to apply for and receive one of the Digital Commonwealth's Wilson Grants. Collaborating with the Buckland Public Library, they submitted over 50 objects to Digital Treasures. The Erving Public Library also received a Wilson grant and contributed 20 objects to the repository. The idea of the barn raising generated so much interest that participants were asked to contribute to a panel discussion at the day-long Digital Commonwealth conference held in the spring of 2009.

Workflow

Libraries with an interest in having objects digitized contact Dodie, Jan or Kristi. Items are limited to two-dimensional, 11" x 17" maximum size for scanning, or audio files in MP3 format. The original scope of agriculture or industry was lifted, so the theme of the collection is up to the library. For libraries that are not familiar with Dublin Core, Dodie assists with training, if based in the Central

Region. Jan and Kristi assist libraries in the Western Region. This can be done by e-mail, phone, or in-person consultation.

When the library has selected the objects they wish to add, Kristi gives them access to the password-protected online form. This form can be printed as a worksheet for initial descriptions, then entered online and submitted to Kristi by e-mail. The library also receives a copy for its own records. Once the library submits the first record for review, then all metadata can be sent.

Once the metadata are received, an appointment is made to go to the C/W MARS headquarters in Worcester, where the scanning lab is located. Depending on the number of objects to be scanned, a two-hour or more block of time is reserved for the library. If the collection is new, preparation for the library's appointment will include setting up folders on the CONTENTdm server and workstation and verifying the administrative metadata, which are kept in a Microsoft Access database.

When the library representative arrives with the images and/or documents, all items are matched by the identifier assigned by the library to the one listed in the metadata. Scanning on the Epson printer is done with its native program. All images are scanned in TIFF format for the "master" files, with a long side of 3000 pixels. Resolution of TIFF files range between 300 to 600 dpi, to achieve desired pixel dimensions. During the scanning, information from the metadata workform is copied into the MS Access Administrative Metadata database, including the title given to the object and the identifier assigned by the library.

After initial scanning is complete, the TIFF files are manipulated in Photoshop and converted into the derivatives. This includes autoleveling and creation of JPEG files. Two separate JPEGs are created, a full-size image and one at access size for CONTENTdm with a long side of 600 pixels and 72 dpi. The full size JPEG is loaded to the CONTENTdm server directly, and the access images are loaded through the CONTENTdm workstation, where the rest of the metadata are loaded in from the workforms then uploaded to the server for web presentation.

Stumbling Blocks

From the beginning, there has been some resistance from a few libraries to the digitization of their collections. The reasons vary widely. Some staff and trustees are concerned that by making documents available digitally, people will no longer feel the need to visit their libraries. Only experience will breach this barrier.

There is fear among a few people that digitizing library holdings and making them available on the World Wide Web exposes a library's materials to being used fraudulently. There is no evidence of this happening, but those who feel this way are not easily convinced otherwise.

The copyright issue of post-1923 material is one that concerns library staff. Many photographs have been donated to libraries, and their origins are unknown. As Digital Treasures expands and libraries have more of their hidden collections scanned, this is an area that needs more research, more specific direction on what can and cannot be digitized and how to proceed if there is a complaint. In the meantime, concern over possibly breaking the law limits what objects libraries are willing to contribute to Digital Treasures.

The digitization process has developed into a "three-legged" stool, comprised of Selection of Materials, Descriptive Cataloging/Development of Metadata, and Financial Resources. Without support for all three, digitization does not happen. Carving out time for staff to select objects for scanning has become more difficult since Digital Treasures started. The world-wide financial crisis quickly trickled down to libraries and many libraries have had to lay off staff and reduce the working hours of others. Selecting materials for inclusion in Digital Treasures is time-consuming even when the local history collection is well organized and many are not.

There are fewer people who feel comfortable with original cataloging. Even after objects have been chosen, it is easy to get bogged down in the process of descriptive cataloging. Digital Treasures participants have always been encouraged to create thorough metadata so that their images are more easily found via keyword searches. Unfortunately, the process is overwhelming to many, especially those who already feel time pressures.

No one thinks that the scanning fees, which are subsidized by C/W MARS, are unreasonable. However, with tight budgets, every penny is scrutinized. For a C/W MARS member library, adding 20 more images to its collection not only costs $170, but the annual maintenance fee is increased by $20 - a commitment that some libraries are unwilling to make. Financial incentives in the form of grants can help, especially when the grants include an experienced person to help with selection and metadata.

The Future of Digital Treasures

Currently the repository stands at 36 collections, with over 1300 items. The digital repository's contents are searchable through the native Digital Treasures front end, the Digital Commonwealth portal, OAIster, major Internet search engines such as Google and Bing, WorldCat and the local C/W MARS online public catalogs. New digital file formats, such as audio recordings, have been included in the repository. The Digital Commonwealth presented a grant round in 2009 to small institutions in Massachusetts, allowing some libraries to match funds to create new collections for the coming year. Another grant round is in the works for 2010.

Knowing how much personal assistance with the selection and metadata process can benefit libraries, C/W MARS has added the Digital Treasures project to the University of Rhode Island (URI) Graduate School of Library and Information Studies (GSLIS) Site Experience database for a possible internship. While statistics show that Digital Treasures is accessed, with nearly five million hits and over 550,000 unique visitors in 2009, the success for the future lies in continuing contributions and promotion of the repository.

References

C/W MARS Inc. (2009). *Connecting libraries in Central and Western Massachusetts*. Retrieved on May 2, 2010 from
http://public.cwmars.org/

CDP Metadata Working Group. (2006). *Dublin Core metadata best practices*, version 2.2.1. Retrieved on March 31, 2010 from http://www.bcr.org/dps/cdp/best/dublin-core-bp.pdf

Central Massachusetts Regional Library System. (n.d.). *Homepage.* Retrieved on May 2, 2010 from http://www.cmrls.org/.

Digital treasures: A Central & Western Massachusetts digital library project. (2009). Retrieved on May 2, 2010 from http://dlib.cwmars.org/.

Dublin Core Metadata Initiative. (2008). *DCMI metadata terms.* Retrieved on March 31, 2010 from http://dublincore.org/documents/dcmi-terms/

Open Archives Initiative (n.d.). *Standards for web content interoperability.* Retrieved on March 31, 2010 from http://www.openarchives.org/.

Western Massachusetts Regional Library System. (2010). *Western Massachusetts Regional Library System - Libraries Cooperating Communicating Sharing.* Retrieved on May 10, 2010 from http://www.wmrls.org/

Collaborative Digitization Goes Local

Ken Middleton, Mayo Taylor
(Middle Tennessee State University)

Abstract

This chapter describes our efforts to build a digitization program in spite of limited funding. By obtaining small grants and forming partnerships with other campus units and institutions in the Middle Tennessee region, we have developed modest yet engaging collections and planted the seeds for additional partnerships. The article will also highlight the use of graduate students, efforts to streamline the digitization process, and lessons learned.

Keywords: Collaboration, CONTENTdm, Collaborative digitization; Oral histories; Work flow, Community projects.

Introduction

In an era when many libraries are struggling to stay relevant to today's Facebook generation, digital projects have injected new purpose into Middle Tennessee State University's Walker Library. Staff members are excited about digitizing oral histories of pioneering women on campus, documenting the agricultural history of a neighboring county, or preserving seminal research on local rare plants. The digital collections under development by the Library have required collaboration with other campus entities and external institutions. Few of the digitized objects have come from the Library's own collections. In this chapter, we will describe the benefits of these partnerships and how they can be nurtured. We will also explore many of the practical issues that new digitization programs face, such as securing staff, streamlining the digitization process, handling diverse file formats, and customizing collections.

Efforts to collaborate with area institutions began as a natural extension of Walker Library's involvement in Volunteer Voices (http://volunteervoices.org), Tennessee's statewide collaborative digital project. MTSU librarian Ken Middleton served as the co-principal investigator of a three-year "Building Digital Resources" grant from the Institute of Museum and Library Services (IMLS) that coordinated the gathering of historical materials from organizations and institutions statewide. That project, based at University of Tennessee-Knoxville, focused on Tennessee history. Staffs were placed in each area of the state (west, middle and east) with a charge to collect unique photos, documents and other materials from cultural institutions. Selected items featured both major trends and figures in Tennessee history (e.g. early settlement, Ida B. Wells), and significant local items (e.g. Bradley County Courthouse). An important component of the project was to relate the digitized objects to the curriculum followed by schools in Tennessee. Walker Library was a satellite digitization center for the middle Tennessee region (Conner, Middleton, Carter, & Feltner-Reichert, 2009), with several librarians and staff participating.

As the IMLS grant project ended, Walker Library began exploring ways that it could build its own digital skills while continuing to assist area archives, libraries, and museums to digitize unique collections. We would quickly lose skills and momentum if we did not build on our Volunteer Voices experience by securing the institutional support to initiate our own projects. Noting that a key mission of the University is to develop "mutually beneficial partnerships" (Middle Tennessee State University, 2002) we examined appropriate models among more experienced institutions.

In 2002, The University of Pittsburgh's Digital Research Library began a two-year project to digitize a collection of 7,000 historic Pittsburgh images in partnership with the Historical Society of Western Pennsylvania, the Carnegie Museum of Art, and the

University's Archives Service Center (Galloway, 2005). As evidence of the continued success of this approach, they have added three more partner institutions over the last five years and now have more than 14,000 images in the collection (University of Pittsburgh Digital Research Library, 2010). The Digital Research Library has also collaborated with University of Pittsburgh faculty to create such projects as *American Left Ephemera and Visuals for Foreign Language Instruction* (Galloway, 2009). This program offers home pages for each of its 70 digital collections; each collection home page offers search and browse options, and a link to the partner institution's home page.

IUPUI Library's Program of Digital Scholarship has collaborated with an impressive array of campus and local institutions. The collection websites and promotional material give every indication that the Program of Digital Scholarship treats these institutions as equal partners: the "Partners" page provides background information about each institution; logos of relevant partners appear on each collection home page; and a link for contact information appears in each record. Its list of partners continues to grow. Building on its initial collaboration with Conner Prairie Museum that features textiles from the museum's collection, the Library recently announced two Conner Prairie collections based on 3-D imaging technology.

After touting the benefits of such collaboration (e.g., cost-effectiveness), Bishoff (2004) offers further guidance for librarians who want to forge lasting partnerships with other cultural heritage institutions: involve all partners from the start; respect each institution's mission and culture; and ensure that each partner benefits from the end product.

Building on these models we outlined a vision for our own digital project design and received the support of our Dean to purchase a server, large flatbed scanner and a license to CONTENTdm software. We then leveraged that support to secure a $5000 grant from the University Special Projects Committee to fund graduate students for our first project, MTSU Memory. More on that collection will follow.

Institutional Context

Walker Library serves 25,000 students on a rapidly-growing campus. Its funding and staff levels are significantly lower than most comparable institutions within Tennessee and nationally – approximately 60% of the average of our designated peer institutions on a per-student basis in 2005-2006 (W. Black, unpublished data). Digital work has been accomplished by reassigning small portions of time for several librarians and one staff member, making extensive use of graduate students and purchasing equipment and software on an as-needed basis, usually at the end of the fiscal year when other needs have been satisfied. Digital projects management has been added to the load of our small staff. We have no programming support for customizing CONTENTdm or working with open source programs. This has hindered our ability to implement advanced features such as embedded audio and video players.

Staffing

The situation for digital projects did improve recently when the Library administration designated our working group as "the Digital Initiatives Team," thus formalizing our role in the Library, and clearly recognizing the roles of the team members: Ken Middleton, Reference/Microtext Librarian (Team leader); Mayo Taylor, Reference/Access Services Librarian; Fagdeba Bakoyema, Reference/Web Librarian; Lynda Duke, Microtext manager; and Jo Williams, Cataloging Librarian.

Because these team members can only devote limited, irregular chunks of time to digital work and because they are drawn from different departments of the library, communication is the key to moving forward. We work hard to avoid problems by holding weekly meetings that also include our student workers, maintaining a wiki for the management of meeting minutes and other information, and by sending monthly reports of major activities to the Library Dean and Coordinators of both Library departments.

We are able to balance the restrictions on our professional staff time by liberal use of graduate students from the Public History program on campus. They bring to the work an awareness of the historical and cultural significance of the collections, a desire to gain skills that are highly relevant to their discipline and a facility with the technology involved. Because many of these students will enter careers in history museums or archives they also make ideal liaisons to local historical agencies. Our graduate students have been supported primarily by small grants received in support of specific collections, as discussed below. We have supplemented this labor force with an undergraduate scholarship student from the Electronic Media Department, at no cost to the Library, and by utilizing students employed at the Microtext service desk for projects that can be done when they are not busy with patrons.

Software /Hardware

Staffing issues also heavily influenced our decision to purchase the CONTENTdm digital content management software. Although its shortcomings will be duly noted, CONTENTdm offers institutions the ability to quickly create digital collections with minimal systems support. In addition at least six institutions in Tennessee are using the system, creating opportunities for collaboration.

The Library has purchased a good mix of digitization equipment. An Epson Expression 10000 flatbed scanner is large enough to handle most photographs and documents that we have selected for scanning. The Library recently purchased a Bookeye 3 planetary scanner with OPUS software. Intended primarily for the Interlibrary Loan department, it is available for digital projects outside standard business hours for fragile books and large format materials. We also have two portable scanners and a laptop computer to assist area institutions in digitizing their materials.

Collections

Campus Partnership: MTSU Memory

In anticipation of MTSU's centennial year in 2011, MTSU Memory (http://library.mtsu.edu/digitalprojects/mtsumemory.php)

will include photographs, documents, books, and oral histories that document our institution's growth from a small Normal School to a doctoral university with Tennessee's largest undergraduate enrollment. The Library's Special Collections hold many items of interest, including the institutional copies of yearbooks, faculty directories and the student newspaper. However, a larger repository of essential items is at the Albert Gore Research Center, which serves as a de facto campus archive. An early emphasis was to consult with the Director of the Gore Center to establish a working relationship and procedures for pulling and scanning materials.

Collection Focus

The digital projects team wanted to maximize usage of the collection by focusing on topical areas: the Great Depression, World War II and aftermath (e.g., GI Bill), the Vietnam War and student activism, and African Americans and women on campus. We expected the majority of items in the collection to be photographs, but wanted to include other types of primary sources (artifacts, newspaper articles, and oral histories) to present a multifaceted portrait of the University's history. The selection process for this collection has in fact been rather unusual because we initiated it without knowing what we would find, adjusting our expectations as new materials have been revealed.

Early Implementation

Walker Library launched its installation of CONTENTdm in late summer of 2007. Installation of the dedicated server and implementation of the software was handled by our Systems Librarian. Initial configuration of the CONTENTdm software was done by Ken Middleton when our first collection, MTSU Memory, was established. The remainder of the Digital Initiatives team members had been recruited and we had received guidance from our Dean on the direction that he would like us to take. Everyone on the team had some experience with digitization projects but none had worked with CONTENTdm. In an ideal world we would have enjoyed a beta period of testing the system and training the graduate students. In the real world, the clock was already ticking on a grant project and the graduate students needed work to do. They worked on the project more hours in most weeks than did their supervisors, leaving the professional team members hard pressed to hone their own skills to keep up with the graduate students. The students began selecting materials and scanning materials before any of us were proficient in using CONTENTdm and before we completed the configuration of the MTSU Memory field structure. One example of the consequences: as each record is created it is put in an approval queue to be reviewed and approved by one of the librarians. If the librarian isn't able to keep pace with the student, simple errors are repeated many times before they are corrected, which exacts a toll in terms of time wasted on corrections.

To slow down the rate at which items were loaded into CONTENTdm we gave the students guidance on the types of items we were looking for and sent them over to the Albert Gore Research Center. They concentrated on selecting items, but without the benefit of prior experience in completing metatadata they didn't know exactly what information they needed to capture to assure complete documentation of the items. The result was that many objects were loaded with incomplete data and improper form. Predictably, we are still returning to some of the earlier records to fill gaps and fix inconsistencies.

By summer of 2009 we again posted a job notice with several graduate programs on campus and again selected two Masters candidates from the Public History program. This time we started each of them with an introduction to the collections they would work with and the metadata guidelines available on our wiki followed by CONTENTDM tutorials and documentation. Finally, they began by importing and creating metadata for objects selected by our previous workers. Only after these initial projects were complete were the students free to find new materials for the collections.

Expanding Opportunities

Our original vision for MTSU Memory was a collection composed primarily of photographs and documents. However, we adjusted that concept when given the opportunity to include excerpts of audio and video interviews and oral histories.

Audio materials: As our graduate students investigated materials at the Gore Research Center they discovered an excellent set of oral histories that had been conducted with alumni from past decades. From that extensive collection, twenty-five were selected because of their relationship to the lead themes of our collection, such as World War II, Civil Rights, etc. Our initial plan was to digitize and display the typed transcript of each interview and then offer selected audio excerpts as a supplement. When a new Director joined the Gore Center he decided that the transcripts needed additional work to be ready for online publication. We adapted by finding a work around to offer only the selected audio excerpts. It consisted of loading MP3 files to our server, but not within CONTENTdm, importing a photo of the subject as the digital object for the CONTENTdm record, and then creating a metadata field to include links to the MP3 files. The work of selecting, reviewing and excerpting the oral histories was done by one of our graduate student workers as an internship for course credit. She selected and downloaded the freeware program, Audacity, to manage the sound files and participated in designing the customized process for creating the records. We hope to include the entire transcript of each record at some point. At present our CONTENTdm records direct users to the items available at our partner across campus.

Video materials: Another treasure trove at the Gore Center was a collection of interviews that were broadcast on the campus television station in the 1980s and 1990s. Of particular interest was a series of four lengthy interviews with Miss Mary Hall, an Education professor important to MTSU and the related University demonstration school from 1929 to 1963. We again turned to one of our graduate students who had recently completed a course in documentary filmmaking. She was able to use her personal computer (a MacBook) and software (iMovie) to create a series of video excerpts that encapsulate important phases of Miss Hall's life.

Book-length publications: As we researched our own campus for the MTSU Memory project, we frequently consulted The First Fifty

Years, a campus history written by alumnus Homer Pittard, that covered the period 1911-1961. Because MTSU held the copyright for the book we decided to digitize the entire volume. This initiated an intensive learning experience about the pros and cons of compound objects and ultimately the process of creating complex PDF files. The process of scanning the pages and doing OCR through the Abbyy Fine software was quite straightforward. A definite learning curve was encountered in figuring out how to structure a compound object from the hundreds of page images. However, once the book was loaded into the MTSU Memory collection, we were dissatisfied with the results, largely because queries could return dozens of individual pages intermingled with other materials. In addition, when we figured out the compound object expense in terms of licensed objects used, we rethought our original approach. In brief, a 200 page book exacts a cost of 201 objects utilized, 200 for the images and one for the combined record. By comparison, a book imported as a PDF made from the same original image files costs only one licensed object. While this may seem an arcane concern, with a licensing level of only 10,000 items we could envision our capacity diminishing quickly if we continued to do book-length items. So, The First Fifty Years was reloaded as a PDF as was our second book, The Raider Forties, and a thesis. Smaller multi-page items continue to be treated as compound objects.

It is worth mentioning that the experience of the user is quite different for audio, video and large PDF text files in our collections when compared with objects loaded as single JPEG files, compound objects or small PDFs. Whereas those files provide a display image immediately upon opening the record, the other file formats all depend upon software programs external to CONTENTdm (e.g. Adobe Acrobat or Quicktime) to open the file. In the case of large media files or PDFs the process can be relatively slow. The record display is also marked by the rather unimaginative default message of "Access this Item," which is not far removed from the archaic "click here" message of early web pages. We hope to find a partial solution to this problem through embedded media players.

Customizing Our Flagship Collection in CONTENTdm

Although CONTENTdm is an excellent tool for creating digital collections quickly, it does not provide a particularly user-friendly public interface. All searches retrieve results from all collections, which can be problematic when you have collections as varied as university history and ecology. We have created a separate entry page for each collection with a brief description of the collection, a search box, a link to an advanced search, and browsing options.

The lack of default browse options for subjects, time periods and formats has been particularly frustrating. CONTENTdm requires us to create the browse lists manually by running "custom queries" for every subject, for instance, that appears in a list. This process requires a significant amount of time. We have recently discovered Elias Tzoc's web-based tools for creating CONTENTdm browse lists (Tzoc, n.d.). Creating the list of 200 subject headings in MTSU Memory would have taken approximately 10 hours if we had used custom queries. After learning a few fairly simple steps, we created the list in just a few minutes using Tzoc's tool.

One extremely useful feature of a recent CONTENTdm upgrade is that search results now include facets that help users narrow their searches. For example, a simple search retrieves a list of records that can be narrowed by time period, subject, and genre. However, making changes to the default facets required too much time. Rather than simply check the desired facets in an administrative module, one has to find the relevant line of code in a PHP file, use correct PHP syntax, and determine the correct code for each facet. Many libraries may lack the technical staff to make such changes.

We are making efforts to attract users through additional access methods. Our metadata librarian has set up a profile in OCLC's digital collection gateway to streamline the creation of WorldCat records for our digital items. We are working at the state level to use the CONTENTdm Multi-site Server, which would create a central site for searching across CONTENTdm collections in the state.

Community Partnership

During 2009 the Digital Initiatives team received a $1000 grant from the MTSU Public Service Committee to assist several community associations with digital projects. Selected organizations were invited to propose projects; the first application received was from the Arts Center of Cannon County (ACCC). They had been given a collection of nearly 1000 photographs that were taken between 1944 and 1977 by William L. Clements, District Conservationist for the Soil Conservation Service (SCS). He served Cannon County, a small agricultural community just east of Murfreesboro and MTSU. The photos documented the farming methods that were disseminated by the SCS in that period. Significantly, each photo had descriptive information typed onto the image back, which made the task of describing each image quite easy.

The Clement Collection was much larger than our initial idea of what would be handled for each project with our small grant, with nearly 1000 photos available, but it was so compelling that we worked to find a way to accept it. The answer came through a supplemental $300 grant from our local Gannett newspaper and through use of a student worker who needed to fulfill work hours for his scholarship. The Cannon County, Tennessee Collection (http://library. mtsu.edu/digitalprojects/cannon.php) includes approximately 400 photographs selected from the total available.

We accepted the Clement photos because they beautifully illustrate and describe the details of the County's predominant occupation, farming, over a period of three decades. In addition, the collection was an ideal test case for working with area institutions to create digital collections:

- The Arts Center is an essential institution in a community where farming is still economically and culturally significant.. Many of the families pictured are still on their farms today.

- The Arts Center staff had already worked on a promotional plan for the collection and have developed plans for creating an exhibit based on the photos.

- Additional rich contextual material is available. Three hours of recent oral history interviews with the photographer will be included along with an interpretive essay from Evan Hatch, folklorist with the Arts Center.

- There were no copyright issues because the photos are the product of a federal employee.

- The photos have been relatively easy to scan and process because the photographs are all the same size. Moreover, detailed metadata is already recorded on the back of each photograph.

The homogeneity of the collection also provided an opportunity to develop streamlined processes, for example by loading nine images at a time onto the large format scanner, then utilizing Photoshop tools to deskew and adjust each image before saving it individually. We also were able to make optimum use of the template option within the CONTENTdm Project Client to automate the entry of identical information into selected metadata fields as each object is imported. In this manner large groups of records could be created in the Project Client and then uploaded in a batch operation for approval. The approval process itself was efficient because only the relatively few unique fields in each record (e.g. title, LC subject heading) needed to be carefully checked by the approver.

We have also used Elias Tzoc's web-based tool to create a tag cloud based on subject headings in the collection. Tag clouds offer a useful alternative to traditional subject heading lists because they provide users with a quick sense of the major subjects in a collection.

The Digital Initiatives team has made every effort to involve the Arts Center of Cannon County in developing the collection. Initial meetings with Evan Hatch, the Center's folklorist, covered everything from selection issues to scanning standards. The Center's logo appears on the collection web site, and links to the Center's web site. Treating the Center as an equal partner improved the quality of this initial digital collection, and it has also increased the likelihood of future partnerships. Early success of the project has encouraged discussions of additional materials that may be forthcoming to document the history and deep crafts tradition of Cannon County.

New and Forthcoming Projects

Buchanan Collection - will document the history of a local family that has included a Nobel Laureate MTSU alumnus, a governor, and an early settler of Nashville. The collection is being compiled in cooperation with family members.

Cedar Glades Studies Collection - a partnership with the MTSU Center for Cedar Glade Studies will digitize research on the rare cedar glade ecosystems of Middle Tennessee. Most notably the 1948 doctoral thesis of Dr. Elsie Quarterman was digitized with support from a small grant passed through the Biology Department. Her thesis was handled by two practicum students from the UT-Knoxville School of Information Science.

Shades of Blue and Gray: Reflections of Life in Civil War Tennessee - will include digital images of 250 artifacts from small archives, libraries, and museums across the state. In partnership with Celia Walker, director of Vanderbilt University's Peabody Library, we will create a metadata template in CONTENTdm, enter metadata, and customize the CONTENTdm database for items collected by other entities.

Stones River Battlefield Historic Landscapes - is digitizing deeds and other materials to document the largely forgotten African American community of Cemetery, which developed after the Civil War on land that would become the Stones River National Battlefield. Created by MTSU history professor Rebecca Conard and her graduate students, it is hosted by the Library and Digital Initiatives staff have played an advisory role.

Lessons Learned

The Digital Initiatives team's collaborative approach has made it possible to take on more projects. In turn, our list of lessons learned is comparatively long and keeps growing as we face challenges specific to new projects. However, as the list below illustrates, many of the lessons apply either to every digital project.

- Libraries that lack a digital projects department (and the corresponding budget line) should consider applying for small grants. In our case, the three grants have been enough to fund students doing the scanning and metadata entry.

- Recruit student workers / interns with relevant skills, and offer them a rewarding work experience. Recognizing that our public history interns are indispensable to the success of our digital projects, we have treated them as equal partners on the Digital Initiatives team. We have encouraged them to attend our weekly meetings, welcomed their suggestions for the improvement of digital projects, and tailored their internships to their interests and skills as much as possible.

- Be flexible. One of our best decisions has been to include interviews in audio and video formats in MTSU Memory, in spite of production delays. In addition, we adjusted our very modest approach to working with area institutions when we saw the potential of working with the Arts Center of Cannon County.

- An effective communication structure is essential, particularly for new digitization programs. By having weekly meetings, we have addressed metadata and technical problems before they become so large that they are difficult to correct.

- Communication is important when working with collaborative partners; tact, patience, and ability to explain both the process and benefits of digitization can not only help put partners at ease, but also pave the way for additional joint projects.

- Invest time in strategic planning. By focusing so much on the details of specific projects, we have not devoted sufficient time to plan for a robust approach for digital preservation.

Conclusion

Perhaps the most important lesson learned mirrors our experience with the statewide Volunteer Voices project. Small libraries, archives and museums have valuable collections, and often want assistance in digitizing these collections. By sharing our successes and growth pains in working with an academic archive, a small arts center/museum, and a growing list of other partners, we hope to encourage other institutions to proactively seek out collaborative digitization partnerships at the local level.

References

Bishoff. L. (2004). The collaboration imperative. *Library Journal 129* (1), 34-35.

Conner, T.R., Middleton, K., Feltner-Reichert, M., and Carter, A. (2009). *Volunteer voices: Tennessee's collaborative digitization program. Collaborative Librarianship, 1* (4), 122-132. Retrieved from http://collaborativelibrarianship.org/index.php/jocl/article/view/38/26

Galloway, E. (2005). *Historic Pittsburgh image collections. D-Lib Magazine, 11* (11). Retrieved from: http://www.dlib.org/dlib/november05/11featured-collection.html

Galloway, E. (2009). *Challenges of creating digital libraries: Digitizing, organizing, storing, accessing content.* 2009 CSE Annual Meeting, May 5, 2009. Retrieved from: http://www.councilscienceeditors.org/events/annualmeeting09/presentations/galloway.pdf

IUPUI University Library. (2009). *Library grant makes more Indiana history accessible to all.* Retrieved from http://www-lib.iupui.edu/node/1306

Middle Tennessee State University. (2002). *Academic master plan: Middle Tennessee State University 2001-2012.* Murfreesboro, TN: Author.

Tzoc, E. (n.d.). *Re-Indexing CONTENTdm metadata.* Retrieved from http://staff.lib.muohio.edu/~tzocea/files/CONTENTdm/re-indexing/

University of Pittsburgh Digital Research Library. (2010). *Historic Pittsburgh image collections.* Retrieved from: http://images.library.pitt.edu/pghphotos

Picturing the Past and Planning for the Future: Central Florida Memory

Lee Dotson, Selma Jaskowski
(University of Central Florida Libraries)

Abstract

Central Florida Memory is a collaborative digitization project to create a collection of primary sources related to Central Florida's history that provides a compelling look at Central Florida before the area became a tourist destination. Through cycles ranging from limited resources to ample grant funding, the collaboration has grown from a small pilot project with three partners to over 80,000 images contributed by seven partners. Organized for the user, the website has been enhanced to create more user friendly methods of access and includes storylines, lesson plans, and links to other sites of interest. This paper provides lessons learned about how to incorporate a variety of materials from diverse institutions into a single digital collection.

Keywords: Academic library, Bethune-Cookman University, Central Florida Memory, Collaboration, CONTENTdm, Digitization, Historical Society, IMLS, LSTA, Museum, Museum of Seminole County History, Olin Library of Rollins College, Orange County Library System, Orange County Regional History Center Public library, Stetson University, University of Central Florida Libraries.

The Beginning – 2002

When the directors of the University of Central Florida Libraries and the Orange County Library System came up with the idea for Central

Florida Memory (CFM) over drinks in 2001, it seemed like a friendly way for the two institutions to collaborate on a project that would serve both academic and public library patrons and foster inter-institutional understanding.

With the addition of the Orange County Regional History Center, the three institutions had the necessary resources to begin building an exciting digital collection. In 2002, the group began meeting to evaluate the collections of the three partners and determine what materials in each collection would provide the most compelling and engaging look at Central Florida's history.

Coming from very different missions and working environments, the partners recognized early on that this collaboration would take some work. Staffing, funding, and the capacity for participation needed to be discussed and an understanding of each institution's identity and purpose gained. Through quarterly meetings where brainstorming was center stage, the group identified the strengths each partner could bring to the project. Committees were formed and populated with members from each institution to foster communication among participants as well as organize functional responsibilities. While the full group discussed and agreed on overall structure and support, the committees focused on operational tasks such as selection, metadata and cataloging, storyline, marketing, and evaluation and assessment. The scope of the project was defined, collections examined and material chosen for inclusion in what was hoped would become the definitive site on the history of Central Florida.

Pilot Project – 2002

With the goal of applying for grant funding, the partners conducted a pilot project to prove the viability of such a collection. It would also serve to lay the foundation for scanning materials at a centralized location and create a website dedicated to Central Florida's history. Since their vision included building a digital collection with contributions not just from the original three partners but from libraries, historical societies, and museums throughout Central

Florida, the pilot project would be the beginning of a regional effort to expose hidden collections in small institutions. By digitizing materials from organizations with wonderful collections but no digitization resources, Central Florida Memory would be the vehicle to make these rich resources available electronically.

To begin, materials created from 1880 to 1930 were selected from the collections of all three institutions. The UCF Libraries offered their digital imaging facilities and servers, Orange County Library System lent the services of their graphic designer, and the Orange County Regional History Center contributed an abundance of material to the collection. The partners agreed to deliver materials for scanning to the Digital Services unit at the University of Central Florida Libraries. With one part-time scanning assistant, a flatbed scanner, and a digital camera, work began on digitizing thirty-five items totaling approximately 2,000 images from materials such as maps, letters, city directories, monographs, and ephemera. Overall, Central Florida Memory adhered to the recommendations set forth by the Publication of Archival, Library, Museum Materials (PALMM) and Cornell University. PALMM guidelines were routinely referred to for copyright concerns and digitization standards (PALMM Documentation, 2010). In addition, Cornell's *Moving Theory into Practice Digital Imaging Tutorial* provided a strong foundation for making decisions regarding image creation, file management, quality control, and digital preservation (Moving Theory, 2010). Size, condition, content, and intended end use of the item to be digitized were several of the factors taken into consideration when determining the most appropriate method and equipment.

Since the materials provided by the Orange County Regional History Center and the Orange County Library System were often fragile or rare materials, an environment of trust was essential to the success of the project. This was especially important for the History Center as it was not ordinarily their practice to allow materials to leave their reading rooms much less travel across the city. Representatives from the partner institutions were invited to spend a day with the scanning assistant to alleviate any concerns about the care and handling of materials as well as have a front row seat to the scanning process. With the small number of items involved in the pilot, tracking materials was easily performed using spreadsheets and email, and delivery and return of items was handled in person.

The next step was to choose a content management system for storing, searching, and retrieving the digital images. CONTENTdm was chosen because it could either be set up rather quickly and used easily by all levels of staff as an out-of-the-box installation or customized to create a unique look and feel for the collection (Lavoie, 2005). During the pilot, the installation was customized and objects were loaded into three distinct institutional collections. When contributing materials, partners were asked to fill out forms describing their materials. This information was used to create the metadata when the images were added to the collection. With a CONTENTdm collection of close to 2,000 images and a website in production, Central Florida Memory was born.

In order to present the collection in a way that was most appealing to a wide audience, "stories" were included to provide background for the images found there (Success story, 2009). The storylines were divided into sections – Dreams and Schemes; Roads, Rivers and Rails; and Critters, Crackers and Cottages. Each of these sections was divided into subsections and included topics like tourism, health, hotels, railroad, water, roads, nature, social life, people, and place. In these subsections users would learn why people moved to Central Florida, how they traveled, and what they experienced in this new, harsh climate (Gronlund, 2005). Users could search and browse the collection itself or get to images of interest through the stories.

The logo for the project and original website design were contributed by the Orange County Library System. The pages existed separately from CONTENTdm itself and supported the Florida Stories, Teachers, Site Map, Contact Us, and Links parts of the site. The link to Collection and any links in the other sections to images in the collection took the user from the website to CONTENTdm.

Figure CFM-1. Central Florida Memory Website, 2003 (Central Florida Memory, 2003)

On 21 May 2003, the Central Florida Memory website and collection were unveiled at a reception at the Orlando Public Library. After presentations describing the Central Florida Memory concept, how it was created, and plans for its future, refreshments were served and attendees were shown how to navigate the collection on multiple workstations set up in the meeting area. Included in the audience were representatives from area libraries and historical societies, as well as members of local government. Response to the new digital collection was very favorable. Contact information for potential future contributions was offered by several attendees.

Upon completion of the pilot project, the group applied for a Library Services and Technology Act (LSTA) grant but was unsuccessful. A year later, the group applied for and received a National Leadership Grant from the Institute for Museum and Library Services (IMLS) to expand the collection. The National Leadership

Grant was a perfect fit for Central Florida Memory given that the grant's goals included supporting "projects that have the potential to elevate museum and library practice" while advancing "the ability of museums and libraries to preserve culture, heritage and knowledge while enhancing learning" (IMLS National Leadership, 2010). As part of that grant project, additional partners were invited to join. The Olin Library at Rollins College in Winter Park, Florida and the Museum of Seminole County History in Sanford, Florida were welcomed to Central Florida Memory.

As part of the IMLS grant proposal, a formal mission statement was developed to illustrate the partners' ongoing commitment to building Central Florida Memory.

The mission of Central Florida Memory is to create, through collaboration among museums, libraries, historical societies, and archives in Central Florida, a comprehensive digital collection, serving the needs of scholars, students, teachers, and residents. Here they will access textual and graphical images and objects that document the region's historical and cultural heritage.

In order to fulfill its mission, CFM established the following goals:

- Provide access to the rich and varied content of libraries, museums, historical societies, and archives throughout Central Florida.

- Create an extensive digital resource for scholars, students, teachers, genealogists, Central Florida residents, visitors, and the general public, promoting lifelong learning.

- Assist museums, historical societies, and libraries in digitizing their collections and become a forum for sharing expertise and technical knowledge.

- Offer a digital archive to those museums, historical societies, and archives unable to establish their own digital infrastructure.

- Provide an innovative digital resource for K-12 teachers and parents to bring alive the region's history into existing and new lesson plans.

- Expand, enhance, and disseminate the collaborative structure model developed during the CFM pilot phase.

- Contribute to the larger body of knowledge of Florida history via access to the CFM website through other statewide project sites.

From the narrative of the IMLS grant submitted 3/31/2004 (Central Florida Memory Grant Writing Committee, 2004).

IMLS Grant – 2004

The IMLS grant phase provided a tremendous boost for Central Florida Memory. The funds received from IMLS made possible a commitment to increase the collection by up to 50,000 images. Additional activities included creating lesson plans to support K-12 education, expanding and enhancing the storylines and website, marketing the collection through promotional materials and a video, and presentations and poster sessions at conferences. At this juncture, deciding how to organize the collection was critical in affecting how the end user would search and retrieve items. Should we continue to divide the materials based on the contributing institution, by some other criteria, or not at all?

CONTENTdm allows creating multiple collections based on locally-determined parameters, or the ability to have one large collection and allow metadata to create subsets of materials for users as they browsed or searched. Having created three distinct collections as part of the pilot project, we knew that there could easily be confusion in searching and difficulties in upgrading. In the pilot model, each time we upgraded CONTENTdm, it had to be performed 3 times, once for each collection. With the addition of 2 new partners, it would be 5 times. Given those issues and understanding that the original intention of Central Florida Memory was to be a collection of a variety of materials representing all institutions, we combined the institution-specific collections into one single collection. This would make searching across all formats and all collections simpler and applying upgrades less complicated. However, we soon found out that combining collections had its own challenges. Working with a wide variety of materials in a single combined collection would impact production processes and necessitate new approaches.

With these changes and an ambitious workload ahead, some adjustments to the committee structure and work processes were needed. A Steering Committee was formed of the directors of the partner institutions for administrative purposes. An Operations committee was composed of institutional representatives who then served on one or more of the seven working groups.

The Curators Working Group was responsible for selecting materials for digitization. Taking our initial cues from the pilot project, materials were tracked on a shared spreadsheet and itemized lists accompanied delivered materials. It was soon discovered that one of the differences between scanning 2,000 images and 50,000 images was how quickly Digital Services became inundated with materials lacking descriptions or a process for tracking their progress (Dotson, 2005). Boxes of loose photographs seemed to appear from out of nowhere and books with similar titles were easily confused. A Digitization Request Form was created and partners were responsible for submitting a form for each item and arranging for delivery of the materials to the University of Central Florida Libraries Digital Services unit (Digitization spec kit, 2005). The form helped to consistently track materials through the use of uniform bibliographic information and a computer generated unique identification number. It allowed for entry of information pertaining to the lending institution's contact information; physical item information such as title, author, subject, description/notes, date original, publisher, number of pages, format, call number/identification number, and storyline; and digitization information including number of images to digitize and notes regarding special handling or other circumstances. The lending institution received a confirmation page upon submission of the request form to be printed and delivered along with the appropriate item. The confirmation page and unique identifier accompanied the item throughout the process from material inventory check in to scanning to metadata. In addition to providing a well organized tracking system, these measures resulted in a meaningful transition from a physical item to a digital image.

It was soon discovered that the scanning, metadata, and upload processes for some of the materials varied from the normal production processes. As general practice, when materials were received they were reviewed to determine the appropriate equipment to be used for digitization. The item was scanned, metadata created, and the images and accompanying metadata uploaded to CONTENTdm. However, special requirements for some materials necessitated a "projects within a project" approach to be developed. In all, five different "projects" (as discussed below) with unique characteristics were completed and added to the collection.

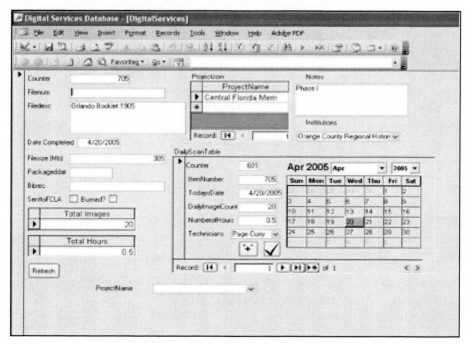

Figure CFM-2. Screenshot of the Digital Services Tracking Database (Digital Services, 2005)

Newspapers

The challenges presented by including the newspapers in a collection of mixed materials included inconsistency in the physical size, large format scanning, and optical character recognition for full text search capabilities. While several newspapers were digitized during this time, the most extensive experience was with the *Sandspur*, the student newspaper of Rollins College. The *Sandspur* began as a literary journal in 1894. Digitization of the first seventeen volumes proceeded normally as each issue ran 20 to 40 pages and measured in size from 27x20 cm to 23x15 cm. With volume 18, the format changed to that of a more typical newspaper length and size. These fragile bound newspapers measured anywhere from 38x27 cm to 41x28 cm and required scanning on a Kaiser rePro graphic stand with Karden-Linhof camera. Additional time and attention to detail were required to complete the digitization of the newspapers. Once scanned, the images were loaded into CONTENTdm as jpegs. Lacking OCR capabilities at the time, the metadata cataloger painstakingly created page level metadata to describe the contents for each image (Dunlop, 2005).

Funeral home records

The Undertaker's Memoranda from the Carey Hand Funeral Home records was an important collection used extensively for genealogical and historical research on Central Florida's people and places. The collection contained records and ledgers on services provided at the Carey Hand Funeral Home from 1891-1955. Forty-four books of the Undertaker's Memoranda covering the time period from June 15, 1891 through November 10, 1927 were made available on Central Florida Memory. In order to make the records searchable online, the handwritten fields had to be transcribed and linked with the appropriate image. A set was created for page level, field-by-field metadata, to represent information about the person, death, family, and burial. Efforts were coordinated between Digital Services and Special Collections so that as the books were being scanned, information from the handwritten fields was entered into a spreadsheet. Prior to uploading the materials, the appropriate rows on the spreadsheet were turned into text files that contained the associated metadata for each page. The end result was a collection of records searchable by name, date of death, cause of death, age when deceased, place of residence, gender, race, parents' names, and burial place.

Voter's registration records

The Orange County voter's registration records collection was also of great interest to genealogists. It contained the voting records of registered voters in Orange County cities from 1912-1934. All ledgers were numbered as volumes. Each volume contained the voter's name, age, race, occupation, local residence, party affiliation, whether a poll tax had been paid, and nativity or place of birth. Other information may have included the voter's declaration of naturalization, date of voter's registration with a political party, and remarks concerning disabled veteran voters, registration changes and deceased voters.

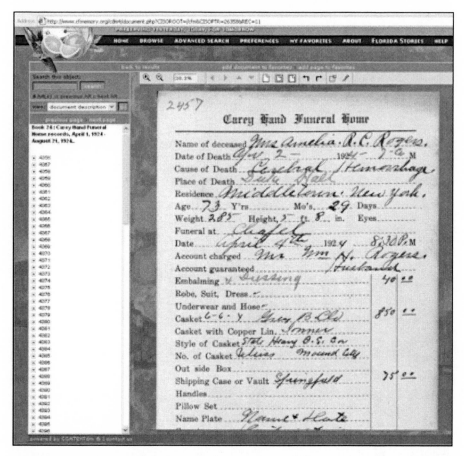

Figure CFM-3. Carey Hand Funeral Home Undertaker's Memorandum ("Book 24: Carey Hand," 2005).

The voter's registration records were slated to be digitized from microfilm to reduce the scanning workload. Unfortunately, the only microfilm copy available had received a great deal of use in a public library resulting in unreadable poor quality images. The original records had been in storage for many years and they had been randomly stored in boxes. It took several days to sort and organize the books by voting precinct before scanning or metadata creation could begin. A graduate student was hired to assist with metadata for the 257 books that contained over 8,000 records. Since the records were in an oversized ledger book format that read left to right across both pages, it was quickly realized that scanning procedures would need to be adjusted. Using the overhead scanner proved to be too time consuming for the 8,000 plus images.

Figure CFM-4: Magnified image of Orange County Voter's Registration Record ("Orange County Voter Registration," 2005).

The most efficient method of scanning these images was determined to be scanning the left and right pages individually and manually merging the two into one cohesive image. For each of the voter's registration images available, 3 images were created. The end result of zoomable jpeg2000s allowed the user to see an overall view of the page and zoom in to read the information line by line.

Handwritten letters

Two sets of handwritten letters, providing great insight into the lives of settlers in early Central Florida, became the fourth "project." The first set was penned by Arthur William Catesby Smyth. Smyth wrote letters to his fiancé and first cousin, Beatrice Alice Smyth, while she was living in England and he was living in Orlando. Smyth was a partner in Smyth and Co. Orange Packers and Shippers. The letters focus on the developing relationship of Arthur and Beatrice, but also include some general information on the citrus industry, property prices and social events. The other set of letters was written by a newlywed transplant to Florida, Helen Warner, who regularly wrote home to her mother, Mrs. Haig, who lived in Buckinghamshire, England. The letters describe both personal matters, and those of larger interest, including the establishment of an orange grove and the development of the city of Narcoossee. Helen and Bill Warner moved to Florida around 1885 and stayed in Winter Park while waiting for their house to be built in Narcoossee. Once settled, they planted an orange grove. The letters trace their life through the birth of their daughter and Bill's job as a steamer captain. Employment troubles dogged the family and he attempted to sell the orange grove in June 1887. When the letters come to an end, the family had not yet made any plans on what to do next.

Many of the letters suffered from poor paper quality and bleed through from both sides of the pages causing the scanned cursive text to be hard to read. Time consuming and painstaking detailed image editing was conducted to enhance the natural lines of the text while omitting letters fading through from the opposite side. Once acceptable image quality had been achieved, the next step was to make the content of the letters accessible by a full text search. Since the letters were handwritten, no OCR software was available and limited full text options to uploading text transcripts to a large free text searchable field. Luckily, CONTENTdm provided such a field and the History Center had hard copy typed transcripts available with the letters. Lacking an electronic version of the transcripts, the transcripts were rekeyed and saved as individual text files appropriate for uploading with the images.

Outsourcing

The digitization of certain newspapers and college catalogs necessitated the outsourcing of certain functions such as microfilm scanning and optical character recognition. Lacking the original hard copies normally preferred for scanning, the microfilm versions of the Rollins College catalogs, St Cloud Tribune, and Lochmede newspaper were deemed to be of good enough quality for digitization. In addition to microfilm scanning, optical word recognition for some previously scanned newspapers and monographs, such as city and telephone directories, was outsourced as well. Several vendors were contacted and iArchives was selected to perform the services. With a proven history of creating high quality images and "highly accurate and patented OCR software which consistently produces higher accuracy results when compared to the 'off the shelf' OCR engines," iArchives stood out from the rest (iArchives, 2010). During early discussions about metadata and file naming conventions, it was quickly realized that normal outputs differed slightly from the outsourced deliverables. Several test batches of materials were processed to give a better understanding of what could be expected. While some accommodations could be made, other aspects were fixed components of the iArchives system. Additional processing was necessary to bridge the gap between what the vendor could provide and what the expectations were for adding material to Central Florida Memory. However, one of the most basic differences was one that was not anticipated. The vendor's final images were delivered in a compressed format. While it did not affect the quality of the images, software had to be acquired and extra time was required to extract the individual files.

During the IMLS grant phase, over 50,000 images were added to the collection and the website was redesigned. Focusing on creating a single collection rather than multiple collections defined by institution, the site itself began to rely more heavily on the contents of the collection. The first web design for CFM featured pages that were essentially a series of linked pictures that gave access to CONTENTdm and could not be easily updated. That design was improved upon in 2004 when the pages were integrated with CONTENTdm. This gave the website a more cohesive look and made changes to its content easier. Unfortunately, it was found that upgrading CONTENTdm usually "broke" the design and adjustments and testing needed to be done each time.

To cap off the grant year, a workshop was held for partners, potential partners, and others working in the digital collection field. Presentations focused on what had been and could be accomplished in building digital collections. The mission and goals of CFM were outlined and attention paid to how the project activities were organized and carried out. By providing examples of materials added, equipment and software acquired, and lesson plans created, institutions were shown how they could start their own projects.

Work continued on the project after grant funding ended. Orange County Library System designed and implemented a CFM presence in Second Life while the UCF Libraries maintained and upgraded CONTENTdm and continued scanning activities.

LSTA Grant – 2008

In 2008, we applied for, and received, an LSTA grant to expand the collection by 30,000 images and our geographical coverage to include Volusia County. Similar to the previously funded IMLS grant, the LSTA grant was a good match for CFM as it was "a state-based program with a broad mandate to use technology to bring information to people in innovative and effective ways" (Library services, 2008). Bethune-Cookman University in Daytona Beach, Florida and Stetson University in DeLand, Florida were invited to become partners and to contribute material. Bethune-Cookman's contribution of historically significant images to CFM would increase the representation of early Central Florida's African-American community. Stetson's contribution of images and materials expanded CFM's geographic coverage beyond Orange and Seminole counties. To manage new contributions and an increased variety of materials, the Digital Projects Management

System was updated. As before, the new system tracked materials through the use of uniform bibliographic information and a computer-generated unique identification number. Once an item was received, the new Digital Projects Management System then provided the means to monitor the item's progress by tracking staff input in the form of checklists and text entries at various stages of the production process. From monitoring data and statistics to exporting metadata, the system enabled skillful handling of a large number of unique requests.

During the LSTA grant, the UCF Libraries' Digital Services unit was responsible for scanning and processing over 28,000 images. Previous experiences taught flexibility regarding production procedures and to prepare for the unexpected. Images were routinely reviewed for quality control and adjustments made to equipment and lighting. Due to the complex nature of scanning photographic and visual materials, it was decided that multiple equipment options would be employed to guarantee the highest quality images while protecting the original materials. By the end of the grant, four different types of scanning equipment had been necessary to carefully and accurately capture each image. Kodak i200 flatbed scanners were used to scan photographs in good condition and loosely bound materials. A newly purchased CopiBook overhead scanner proved effective for dealing with large photographs, yearbooks, catalogs, and unbound newsprint. Oversized and highly reflective materials were scanned on the Kaiser rePro graphic stand with Karden-Linhof camera. Tightly bound and moderately reflective items, such as bound glossy newspapers, were scanned on the Avision FB6080E A3 Bookedge flatbed scanner.

Once materials were scanned and images corrected, metadata was created by reviewing both the physical item and the scanned images. Since efficiencies in uploading small compound objects (one or two images) were achieved early on by using tab-delimited text files to upload preliminary metadata, this method was applied to larger compound objects as well. Controlled vocabulary fields were applied to 18 fields including author, photographer, subject, subject-personal names, publisher, studio, format, format-medium, subject-topic, repository, repository collection, type, language, coverage-spatial, coverage-temporal, funding source, date contributed, and CFM storyline. An important benefit of using controlled vocabulary fields is that they allowed the end user to perform a new search by linking metadata as phrases rather than individual words. In addition to making the images available to the public, master images were submitted to the Florida Digital Archive, "a cost-effective, long-term preservation repository for digital materials in support of teaching and learning, scholarship, and research in the state of Florida" (Florida Digital Archive, 2010). Once images were uploaded to Central Florida Memory, metadata records were exported and coupled with the respective images to create packages to be sent to the Florida Digital Archive for long term digital preservation.

Figure CFM-5: Central Florida Memory Website, 2009 (Central Florida Memory, 2009)

The website was completely redesigned using a different color palette and employing a cleaner look. CONTENTdm displays were pulled into the web pages but kept separate from them. The site could be updated and content changed easily and not be affected by any upgrades to the CONTENTdm software.

The Future

If the partners of Central Florida Memory have learned anything over the last seven years it is that whether or not funding is awarded, the project goes on. In funding years an extraordinary amount of work has been accomplished, and equipment and resources acquired. During the lean years when there is no funding, the work continues on a much smaller scale, but it goes on. The partners of CFM continue to meet quarterly, formulate new ideas on how to build the collection, improve access to the collection, and spread the message that this resource exists. New funding sources are being identified, new grants will be written, and new ideas will be implemented. The partners of CFM continue to believe in their commitment to the project and to each other.

References

Book 24: Carey Hand Funeral Home records, April 1, 1924 - August 21, 1924. (n.d.). Central Florida Memory. Retrieved August 14, 2005, from http://www.cfmemory.org

Central Florida Memory grant writing committee. (2004). *Central Florida Memory*. [Institute of Museum and Library Services grant proposal]. Orlando, FL. Retrieved December 1, 2009, from http://www.cfmemory.org/Share/About/Narrative.pdf

Central Florida Memory website. (2003). Retrieved May 11, 2003, from http://centralfloridamemory.lib.ucf.edu.

Central Florida Memory website. (2005). Retrieved September 20, 2005, from http://www.cfmemory.org

Central Florida Memory website. (2009). Retrieved March 13, 2010, from http://www.cfmemory.org

Digitization Spec Kit. (2005). Retrieved March 20, 2010, from http://www.cfmemory.org/Share/Workshop/DigitizationSpecKit.pdf

Digital Services Tracking Database. (2005). *Internal tracking database used at University of Central Florida Libraries.* Orlando, Florida.

Dotson, L. (2005). *See how it's done. Central Florida Workshop for Museum & Library Personnel.* Retrieved March 5, 2010, from http://www.cfmemory.org/Share/Workshop/Behind%20the%20Scenes%20I.ppt

Dunlop, D. (2005). *How it all connects II. Central Florida Workshop for Museum & Library Personnel.* Retrieved March 19, 2010, from http://www.cfmemory.org/Share/Workshop/ Metadata%20Part%202.ppt

Florida digital archive. (2010). Retrieved March 8, 2010, from http://www.fcla.edu/digitalArchive/.

Gronlund, G. (2005). *Weaving the story. Central Florida Workshop for Museum & Library Personnel.* Retrieved March 27, 2010, from http://www.cfmemory.org/Share/Workshop/CENTRAL%20 FLORIDA%20MEMORY%20WEAVING%20THE%20STORY%209 %2030%202005%202.ppt

iArchives process. (2010). Retrieved February 20, 2010, from http://www.iarchives.com/process.shtml

IMLS National Leadership grants. (2010). Retrieved February 17, 2010, from http://www.imls.gov/applicants/grants/ NationalLeadership.shtm.

Lavoie, J. (2005). *Showing it to the world. Central Florida workshop for museum & library personnel.* Retrieved February 23, 2010, from http://www.cfmemory.org/Share/Workshop/ Showing%20it%20to%20the%20World.ppt

Library services and technology act grants. (2008). Retrieved January 14, 2010, from http://dlis.dos.state.fl.us/bld/grants/LSTA/ LSTAinfo.pdf

Moving theory into practice digital imaging tutorial. (2010). Retrieved March 15, 2010, from http://www.library.cornell.edu/preservation/tutorial

Orange County voter registration. (n.d.). *Central Florida Memory*. Retrieved August 15, 2005, from http://www.cfmemory.org

PALMM documentation. (2010). Retrieved March 11, 2010, from http://fclaweb.fcla.edu/node/572/

Success story: Central Florida Memory. (2009). In *A new story based approach to digital collection* [OCLC CONTENTdm brochure]. Retrieved March 5, 2010, from http://www.oclc.org/us/en/services/brochures/211595usc_F_CentralFloridaMemory.pdf

Apollo 13.0: Digitizing Astronaut Jack Swigert's Apollo Documents

Andrew Weiss (Fort Hays State University, Forsyth Library)

Abstract:

The Kansas Cosmosphere and Space Center and Fort Hays State University Forsyth Library joined together in 2008 to digitize the personal archive of Apollo 13 astronaut John L. (Jack) Swigert. The documents (1966-1970) include blueprints and proofs of the Apollo Operations handbook Malfunction Procedures, which Swigert was called upon to revise in the aftermath of the Apollo 1 disaster in early 1967. The partnership between the KCSC and Forsyth Library has been fruitful in the area of public relations and dissemination of digital collections online. Some of the obstacles related to the partnership have yielded positive results. As a result of the partnership we created a standard for uniform file names for Forsyth's Digital Collections, in adopting and customizing Goddard Core, a variation of Dublin Core, and in developing an External Partnership Protocol to improve future collaborative projects.

Keywords: Apollo Operations, Best practices, Collaboration, CONTENTdm, Digitization, Dublin Core, Goddard Core, Handbook, Malfunction procedures, Museum-library partnership, Space exploration.

Introduction

We shall not cease from exploration
And the end of all our exploring
Will be to arrive where we started
And know the place for the first time.

--T.S. Eliot, Four Quartets

While orbiting the moon in 1968, Apollo 8 astronaut Bill Anders photographed Earthrise, one of the iconic images of the Apollo missions. Fragile and tiny, the earth appears "almost as a disk" in a dark void and concretely shows that humans are more miniscule than imagined (Brooks, Grimwood & Swenson, 1979, p. 277). Although later missions would overshadow Apollo 8, including the successful moon-landing of Apollo 11 and the successful failure of Apollo 13, the lasting legacy of this mission was a sudden appreciation for the Earth itself (Brooks et al., 1979, p. 366). The irony that a photograph of the Earth would become one of the most lasting images of the Apollo Program was not lost on the astronauts. Anders later remarked, "We came all this way to explore the moon, and the most important thing is that we discovered the earth" (Dordain, 2009, para. 6).

This image, later adopted by environmentalists, eventually contributed to the general zeitgeist that the mundane should take precedence over impractical dreams. Indeed, once an American had walked on the moon—as much a display of American real-politik might as a display of American ingenuity—public and political interest in the Apollo Program waned. By 1973 its funding was on its last legs and never again would the Apollo Program send an astronaut to the moon (McKie, 2008) (Brooks et al., 1979, p. 366). Yet if media coverage is any indication of an issue's timeliness, the 40th anniversary of the successful moon landing in 2009 proves that the spirit of the time remains vital. General interest in space exploration remains high among specialists and the general public alike. Furthermore, the improvement of digital technology is allowing us unprecedented access to the primary materials of important historical events, making the discoveries of the time even more immediate as they appear online. In essence, this is an exciting time to revisit the solid-state era of the Space Race of the 1950s, '60s and '70s through the power of digital technology.

In its partnership with the Kansas Cosmosphere and Space Center (KCSC) to digitize the papers of John L. (Jack) Swigert, Fort Hays State University's Forsyth Library has had the privilege to work with documents of great importance to American and world history. At the same time we find ourselves looking inward and realize that an emphasis on the "mundane" still proves to be important. As a result of our work, we realize the need for a strong foundation in the development of sound policies and best practices that can work in reality. As the Apollo astronauts discovered, the point of a journey is not always to arrive; it's to find out where you've been.

Background

The Kansas Cosmosphere & Space Center (KCSC):

Second only to the Smithsonian's Air and Space Museum in terms of collection size, the Kansas Cosmosphere and Space Center (KCSC), located in Hutchinson, Kansas, is one of the leading collectors of space artifacts in the United States; the items collected, many of which have flown in space, provide a complete overview of rocketry and space history from its origins in Nazi-era Germany, to the Space Race of the 1950s and 1960s, and to the era of détente between Russia and America in the 1970s. Items housed include complete German V-1 and V-2 rockets, a Redstone Nuclear Warhead, a Titan rocket, a Russian Vostok Spacecraft, The Mercury 7 Liberty Bell spacecraft, and the Apollo 13 Command Module. Their holdings also include the largest collection of Russian Space Program artifacts outside of the former Soviet Union (Kansas Cosmosphere, 2009).

FHSU, Forsyth Library & FLDCI

Forsyth Library is a small academic library serving the needs of Fort Hays State University's 11,000 full- and part-time students and

275 faculty & staff members. Roughly 4,000 of those students are traditional on-campus undergraduate and graduate students. The other 7,000 students study through FHSU's Virtual College, an online degree program. The library is central to the Virtual College and provides assistance to those students in the form of a dynamic web presence that facilitates off-campus access to our OPAC, databases, and digital collections. This digital content includes the digitized Swigert documents, our Master's Thesis Collection, letters from Benjamin Franklin and historic glass-plate negatives collections. Our first collection of materials was digitized in 2004. The Forsyth Library Digital Collections Initiative (FLDCI) was established in 2008 in order to facilitate the development and preservation of digital content. Under the development of this framework of guidelines, we have been able to create full-fledged digitization partnerships both within our university, including the Sternberg Museum, and Graduate School, and externally with institutions in Kansas. Our modest digital collections are positioned to grow exponentially in the next few years, and the establishment of the FLDCI promises to simplify the growth process.

Partnership Details

The partnership between the Kansas Cosmosphere and Space Center and Forsyth Library began tentatively in 2003 with the proposal made by library director John Ross to digitize materials held by the KCSC. The primary goal for this first joint partnership was to scan, catalog and upload images from the Mercury Project Missions into an online content management system. The digitization team included the KCSC archivist, Kiersten Latham, Forsyth Library cataloger, Jerry Wilson, and Forsyth Library Archivist, Patty Nicholas. By the end of November 2004 the majority of images, which included photographs of the Mercury spacecraft, astronauts, and engineers, had been scanned.

Early enhancements to the project began with the use of Dublin Core, which would later influence the presently used scheme. The second development was the decision to purchase CONTENTdm as the vehicle for the online dissemination of digital content.

CONTENTdm was eventually purchased and installed for use in May 2005. However, personnel changes at the KCSC and time limitations for Forsyth Library staff impacted both the development of image metadata and digitization. Consequently, no digital images from the Mercury Project were placed online until the project was revisited in March, 2010.

In early 2008, in consultation with the new president and CEO of the KCSC, Chris Orwoll, and the new Collections Manager, Meredith Miller, another partnership was proposed by Forsyth Library director, John Ross, with the aim to digitize the archive of Apollo 13 astronaut John L. (Jack) Swigert. It was Swigert who had helped to revise the Apollo Operations Handbook Malfunction Procedures after the Apollo 1 disaster of January 27, 1967. This collection of 10 archival boxes, each dedicated to a single spacecraft system, included unique unpublished materials, and represented an opportunity to refuel our partnership. As soon as copyright clearance was secured, we were given the green light to proceed.

During the three years that elapsed between the two projects, CONTENTdm had been successfully implemented by Forsyth Library Systems Technician, Heath Bogart, and was being used for Forsyth Library Archives collections. Two digitization team members had been added to improve the organization and workflows of the suddenly burgeoning digitization projects, including new Cataloger and Digital Content Specialist, Sherry Severson, and new Digital Collections Librarian, Andrew Weiss. From August 2008 through May 2010, the entire collection of materials in Swigert's archive was digitized, and 95% of these items were fully cataloged using Goddard Core, an elaboration of the Dublin Core metadata scheme developed by NASA's Goddard Museum.

Digitization Goals

This collection will help researchers and lay-people alike to see the program as a work-in-progress, something which can get lost as the Apollo mission becomes cemented in history. Our wider goal is to develop a collaboration model that will establish a set of procedures to use between a small academic library and a major museum.   We believe this will eventually contribute to the foundation of a larger digitization project involving all phases of national and international space exploration extending from World War II to the mid-1970s.

Apollo Mission Background:

If we die, we want people to accept it. We're in a risky business, and we hope that if anything happens to us it will not delay the program. The conquest of space is worth the risk of life.

- Gus Grissom (Barbour, 1969, p. 125)

Along with John F. Kennedy's May 25, 1961 speech committing the United States to the "Space Race," arguably the most important date in the Apollo Program occurred on January 27th, 1967. On that tragic day, Virgil "Gus" Grissom, Ed White, and Roger Chaffee, became the first astronauts to die in the American Space Program. Their Command Module suddenly caught fire while the three were inside conducting a "Plugs Out" launch pad test one month before their scheduled mission (Bilstein, 1996, p. 340). Because of design flaws, the hatch could not be opened by the astronauts or blown open externally. The shocking part of the accident was that it occurred where none was expected: on Earth. Though a terrible disaster, the Apollo 1 accident fundamentally changed the Apollo Program and, in essence, prevented further accidents from happening while in space (Brooks et al., 1979, p. 214-225).

After the accident of January 27th, a full investigation was conducted in order to arrive at the cause of the accident. During the investigation each piece of the Command Module was removed, using an identical copy of the Command Service Module (#014) as a guide, the engineers at NASA and contractor North American Aviation, Inc. (NAA) narrowed the cause down to two main factors. The first factor: the tests were being done in excessively high oxygen pressure, increasing the potential for fire. The second factor: too much Velcro was being used to tie wiring together. The combination of these two factors along with the spark from a faulty wire and the flaw in the hatch design, ironically implemented as a safety precaution, was ascertained as the cause of the accident (Orloff, 2004, para. 61) (Brooks et al., 1979, p. 214-225).

The investigation marked a turning point in the development of the Apollo Program. In the early 1960s, when the mission to the moon became a national priority, NAA and NASA had agreed to a two-tiered project. Tier one would develop a Block I spacecraft (1962—1968), which was to be used for unmanned boilerplate missions and sub-orbital rocket testing, and tier 2 would develop a Block II spacecraft (1964—1973), which was to be used for manned earth- and lunar-orbital flights and the moon-landing missions (Brooks et al., 1979, p. 229). The two phases overlapped between the years 1964 through 1968, but once the Apollo 1 accident occurred, Block I was phased out, being used only for unmanned Apollo 4, 5 and 6 missions until early 1968 (Brooks et al., 1979, p. 232). In order to redesign Block II, both engineers and astronauts were called upon to completely review the blueprints, diagrams and procedures for every aspect of the Apollo spacecraft. Included among these specialists was Astronaut John L. (Jack) Swigert, who reviewed the Apollo Spacecraft Malfunction Procedures for the Command Module (CM), the Lunar Module (LM) and the Service Module (SM).

Jack Swigert joined NASA in 1966 after a long career as an engineering test pilot in the 1950s and 1960s for North American Aviation (NAA). He served with NASA until 1977, and was most famous for his participation in the April 11-17, 1970 Apollo 13 mission, which was famously dubbed a "successful failure," after the crew were able to return safely to Earth despite multiple malfunctions within their spacecraft (Brooks et al., 1979, p. 378). In the aftermath of the Apollo 1 disaster, Swigert worked to redesign the Apollo Block II Spacecraft's Malfunction Procedures.

Swigert's role in the process of redesigning the Apollo spacecraft is reflected in the documents that he saved. The collection of documents starts with the 1966 Block I Apollo Operations Handbook, which contains his own corrections and notes, and ends with diagrams and unpublished blueprints of the Block II spacecraft through July and August 1969. However, the bulk of the documents deal with the Malfunction Procedures for the Block II spacecraft.

Digitization & Partnerships

Despite the ultimate goal of creating a larger "Digital Repository of Space Exploration" with the KCSC, Forsyth Library has had to deal with the less glamorous internal issue of "keeping house." Dealing with the reality of a digital project required that we put aside our ambitious dreams and put in place the tools needed to complete the project. This necessitated an honest look at our shortcomings and a fresh look at what we had to change or, in some cases, completely reinvent. In this section, we will examine the real-world applications and adaptations we had to consider, and the innovations we had to develop, in order to complete our project.

Partnership Practicalities

As mentioned, the wider goal for the partnership between Forsyth Library and the KCSC is to develop a "Digital Repository of Space Exploration," which would house and preserve the digital versions and corresponding metadata of the archival collections held by the KCSC. Collections initially involved would include the Jack Swigert Archive and the Mercury Project Collection. Further expansion of the repository would include the KCSC's collection of Soviet Soyuz-era documents, their compilation of the history of rocket development from WWII, and the museum's new digital photographs of artifacts and objects such as space suits, equipment, and other paraphernalia.

The first attempt at collaboration, the partnership to digitize Mercury Project documents and materials, was discontinued due to internal issues between 2004 and 2005. However, a few basic tenets of the partnership carried over to the second collaboration, including the decision to use Dublin Core, the basic division of labor, and the assumption that digitization costs such as labor, equipment and supplies would be covered by Forsyth Library.

For the 2008 partnership, it was determined that Forsyth library would be responsible for the creation of digital images; a basic lending contract agreement would be drawn up for each time materials were transferred to Forsyth Library; and the data generated by the digitization would be temporarily housed at Forsyth Library on its local PCs and backed up on its section of the university's server. The digitized images would then be uploaded into CONTENTdm, a proprietary content management system designed for libraries and other cultural institutions. During the image uploading phase, the project staff at Forsyth would input the necessary Dublin Core metadata. On the administrative side, the KCSC would be responsible for creating a "splash page" for the new digital collection as well as handling general Public Relations for the project. During the course of digitization, the two institutions would meet and discuss the progress of digitization.

Partnership Benefits

Both of our institutions have extensive public-relations networks that allow us to effectively disseminate the message about our joint project. For example, the KCSC has been able to link our CONTENTdm site to its home page, which sees considerable traffic from specialist historians, hobbyists, and primary and elementary schools. The KCSC also played a central role the 40th anniversary commemorations of the Apollo 11 moon landing in the summer of 2009. The project's profile is enhanced by the close relationship between former NASA astronauts such as Neil Armstrong and Charlie Duke, who donated Swigert's materials. Being aligned as a "sister" site to the Smithsonian's Air and Space Museum as well as NASA's Goddard Museum further increases the PR potential.

On the FHSU side, the university has an extensive and powerful public relations department as well as dedicated faculty members who speak at conferences, grant interviews to news outlets, and publish materials related to the Swigert collection project or similar space-exploration topics. Through the FHSU website, we are able to attract college students, differing from the patrons the KCSC usually attracts. Our central role as information hub at the university allows us to create intimate relationships with professors on campus and to embed the library and the KCSC further within the curriculum.

Partnership Obstacles

During the early development of our collaboration, it had not been disclosed to us that the Swigert Collection was not fully archived. An archivist at the KCSC had begun working on the Swigert Collection but had left in 2005 without being replaced. As a result, we needed to make some executive decisions about the materials; one major question was how to develop a file naming scheme for both physical and digital collections using documents not fully-archived. Related to this, the contents of the collection were not entirely known until we received the boxes at the library. This required us to spend time developing a naming scheme to keep track of the documents we were handling. In the absence of an archivist on staff at the KCSC and a subject specialist at Forsyth, we have had to become versed in the structure of the Apollo Operations Handbook's Malfunction Procedures and the electrical and power systems diagrams it references. These difficulties impelled us to create stop-gap solutions that ultimately led to some of our permanent policies. These policies allow us to navigate between the ideals of established best practices and the hard realities of internal and external staff limitations, limited funding, and minimal access to necessary technological expertise and/or equipment.

Developing Uniform File-Names

Since the collection had not been properly archived prior to receiving the documents, we had to develop a way to link each physical document to its digital counterpart. Documents had been partially assessed in 2000 by a private appraisal company. During that time, they assigned documents to general archival boxes based on the spacecraft system with which they were aligned. Since there were nine spacecraft systems, there were nine boxes devoted to individual systems and one box for the original Apollo Operations Handbook and other miscellaneous documents that defined the nomenclature of the system blueprints and diagrams; also included was the appraiser's finding aid. The documents were crammed into the boxes without much thought for organization, our first step in archiving was to place documents in folders, respecting the physical context by keeping the original order in which they appear, as well as the intellectual context by keeping groups of bound documents together. We then assigned numbers to each folder, designated as f(x), and numbers to each document, designated as d(x). For example, the very first document in the Electrical Power Subsystem box would have the title assigned f1d1, referring to its position in the group. The next challenge was to use these document titles to create a conceptual bridge between the real document and its digital counterpart while following the best practices of digital file naming.

In order to keep file names from exceeding the recommended number of 31 characters, we had to develop a system of abbreviations that would locate the file names within the context of our collections and would be used as a referential name rather than as a descriptive name. Our rationale for this emphasis on the referential aspect was that metadata would provide the description of the digital file. File names would follow the pattern as shown in Figure APOL-1. Rather than describing a document's intellectual content, we focused on the document's physical context. For example, the Master TIFF version of the very first document found in the EPS box, named f1d1, would have the digital file name of: kcas204_eps_f1d1.tif; its compressed-for-web-jpeg counterpart would be: kcas204_eps_f1d1ow.jpg. Occasionally, a document would need to be scanned or photograph in parts, which would require the use of a part designator; in the example above, the optimized TIFF version of the same document would have <p2o.tiff> added at the end of the file name.

The overall effect of this new naming protocol has streamlined our ability to track digital data. Its success has compelled us to change all of our previously digitized materials' filenames, and develop patterns for naming all future digitization projects. With a few alterations we are able to use this file-naming tree for any internal or external digital collection we develop at FHSU.

Uniform File-Naming Convention for Swigert Collection

Naming Tree Part	Part Definition	Applied to Swigert Collection	Abbreviation
Institutional Name	[Parent organization]	[Kansas Cosmosphere]	kc
Part of Object ID	[Collection]	[Apollo 1 Investigation]	as204_
Part of Object ID	[Box within Collection]	[Electrical Power Subsystem]	eps_
Part of Object ID	[Folder within Box]	[Folder number x]	f[x]
Part of Object ID	[Document within Folder]	[Document number x]	d[x]
Part Designator	[Part within Document]	[Part number x]	p[x]
Part Designator	[Reverse of document]	[Reverse Side]	r
Version of Object	[File Optimized for Use}	[Optimized File]	o
Version of Object	[File altered for web use]	[Web-ready]	w
File Extension Name	[File Format]	[File Extension: i.e. .jpg / .tif etc.]	.[xxx]

EXAMPLES

kcas204_eps_f1d1ow.jpg   22 characters
kcas204_eps_f1d1p2o.tif   23 characters

A few rules of thumb:

Use lower case letters of the Latin alphabet; numerals 0 thru 9

Avoid punctuation marks; except underscores / hyphens

Include part designator after object ID

Keep File names less than **31** characters (including file extensions)

Be as referential as possible--not descriptive; let metadata describe the item

Figure APOL-1: Table showing uniform file-naming conventions for Swigert Collection; ©2009, Andrew Weiss.

Adopting Goddard Core

During the first partnership from 2003-2004, the primary members of the Mercury Project digitization effort decided upon using

Dublin Core as the main metadata scheme. Dublin Core was chosen because of its use by multiple institutions in both museum and library circles. Research further revealed that Dublin Core was being heralded as part of the discipline's best practices. Dublin Core was subsequently agreed upon as the basis for the Swigert documents as it "represents the lowest common denominator for creating metadata to facilitate maximum accessibility across a broad spectrum of institution types" (North Carolina ECHO, 2009).

During the course of the digitization process and the initial testing of the images put into CONTENTdm, it was discovered that simple, unqualified Dublin Core would be insufficient for our needs. A thorough cataloging of each document was considered ideal; unfortunately, many of the documents proved to be extremely complex in terms of both intellectual content and physical context.

The interplay of content and context also added to the meaning of each document. For example, many of the documents were bound together in sets arranged in numerical order that refer to specific symptoms of the spacecraft's malfunction procedures. The Electrical Power Subsystem (EPS) malfunction procedures show what should appear in the gauges on the Apollo Spacecraft's control panel indicating to an astronaut whether the power systems are normal or abnormal.

Adding to the complexity of these documents are notes, drawings, and comments written on the blueprints and proofs; there are also papers and redrawn diagrams attached to them that cover over the original base. Furthermore, the documents are often signed and dated by various people, including Swigert and other engineers involved with reviewing the Malfunction Procedures. The circumstances in which the documents were drafted or marked also add to the complexity of their meaning. These were some of the documents used in the AS-204 (Apollo 1) investigation held between January 27th and March 21st, 1967, revealing the review process for the Block I and Block II spacecraft.

Given complexities such as multiple dates, authors and uses, it was deemed that a basic Dublin Core scheme would not be sufficient.

The next step was to consider alternatives to the Dublin Core scheme that would not stray far from best practices, and that could be used by both institutions, and yet would explain the significance of these documents with the required level of granularity.

Our final choice was Goddard Core, which was developed by NASA's Goddard Museum; it is an extension of Dublin Core and an ideal bridge between the library world and the space museum community (Goddard Library, 2005).

Goddard Core differs from unqualified Dublin Core by featuring a little more granularity. For example, Goddard Core allows one to utilize the following subdivisions for Dublin Core Element Subject :

Subject.employee
    .organization
    .missionsProjects
    .disciplines
    .instrument
    .functions
    .industries
    .uncontrolled

The problem with multiple dates has been anticipated by the development of these subdivisions:

Date.created
    .available
    .modified

Using the more granular modifications of the Date field allow us to handle the more complex documents in the collection that went through various phases of modification during the AS204 investigation and subsequent creation of the new Block II versions of the space craft Malfunction Procedures.

One of our intentions with this project has been to use CONTENTdm as the nexus to our cataloging process; we see this as a chance to open up the cataloging process to multiple participants both within Forsyth Library and externally at the KCSC. We are not "rocket scientists," but we have access to those who are specialists in this field. The KCSC has access to the Smithsonian as well as former NASA astronauts and employees who are familiar with these types of documents. We envision a multi-faceted, multi-participant cataloging process with CONTENTdm at the center of this activity.

In order to help us reach our goal of a more cooperative cataloging process, we added a few customizations to Goddard Core to tailor the scheme to meet the unique needs of the Swigert Collection.

Our customizations dealt primarily with improving the granularity of the DC Element <Description>. We felt that since the <Description> field was too broad, we would need to add subdivisions that would convey not only a general explanation of the document, but would also provide the transcription of the handwritten notes on each document, as well as explain the significance of the document with respect to its placement within NASA and the Apollo Space program. In order to accomplish this task we have added to the granularity of DC <Description> thus:

> Description.abstract
> .freetext
> .analysis

<.abstract> gives a brief summary of the content of the document, explaining the meaning of EPS or certain other important terms found in the document; <.freetext> presents the transcriptions of the handwritten notes, dates & signatures, allowing them to be searchable in a database; finally, <.analysis> allows the expert or outside consultant to remark upon the historical context or significance of the document. Interoperability will be slightly compromised should all three subdivisions become conflated into a singular <Description> element in unqualified Dublin Core. However, for the purposes of our own project, we feel the possible loss of interoperability is outweighed by the collaborative potential of the customization.

Dublin Core - Goddard Core / FLDCI Customization Mapping		
Dublin Core	**Goddard Core Customization**	**FLDCI Customization**
TITLE	.alternate	
SUBJECT	.employee	
	.organization	
	.missionsProjects	
	.disciplines	
	.instrument	
	.functions	
	.industries	
DESCRIPTION		.abstract
		.freetext
		.analysis
CREATOR & CONTRIBUTOR	.employee	
	.code	
	.contract	
	.missionsProjects	
	.organization	
	.instrument	
DATE	.created	
	.available	
	.modified	
TYPE	.information	
IDENTIFIER	.persistent	
	.url	
COVERAGE	.projectPhase	
	.chronology	
	.spatial	
RELATION	.hasVersion	
PUBLISHER	.organization	

NOTE: DC Elements FORMAT / RIGHTS / LANGUAGE / SOURCE not changed

Figure APOL-2: Goddard Core. © 2009, Andrew Weiss.

Creating an External Partnerships Protocol

Along with the two innovations mentioned above, the most important development of our partnership with the Kansas Cosmosphere has been the creation of our External Partnerships

Protocol, which is intended to better anticipate the needs of Forsyth Library's digitization projects with regard to outside institutions. Entering into our partnership with the KCSC, a number of grey areas existed that we did not quite anticipate or iron out completely until after the project had begun. For the sake of future projects, we decided to codify our procedures in order to facilitate future partnerships.

The protocol is based partly on our experiences with another digitization partner, the Stafford County Historical Society Museum, for whom we are digitizing an extensive collection of glass-plate negatives. The protocol is made up of two separate missives. One is a series of steps outlining the full life-cycle of a partnership; the other is a series of guidelines and policies that clearly define terminology, policies and partner roles.

For the step-by-step procedures, we have outlined the following steps:

2) Meet Potential Partners; these meetings are meant to establish a willingness to participate and to negotiate framework agreements and partner obligations.

3) Determine Project Viability; both partners evaluate their collections using the Digital Collections Project Planner devised by us for objectively evaluating a target collection. Having both sides evaluate the project helps us to see any similarities as well as any differences in what is valued in a collection.

4) Determine the project's priority and place it within the Project Pipeline.

5) Pilot Testing; using a representative sample of materials we determine if any special needs, such as scanning or handling oversize documents, might arise during digitization or online dissemination;

6) Project Oversight: once digitization begins, we establish schedules for regular meetings to update partners. We also work on tweaking workflows, assessing digitization benchmarks and quotas, and perform quality control of images.

7) Post-project Wrap-Up, which involves checking that materials have been digitized; we also create a project summary to explain the results of the project and to enumerate any problems that occurred during the project. We finally seek avenues for PR.

A series of guidelines and policies, which exists to inform the step-by-step procedures, is the second part of the protocol. In it we define minimum standards for our partners and what roles and actions are assigned to them. The guidelines include:

1) Preparation Work, which outlines our requirements for cleaning and general handling of materials, requirements for safe storage and transport, requirements for metadata, and our recommendations for creating unique file names;

2) Digital Preservation, which outlines our methods of digital storage, and our policy for "weeding" the data once the project has been completed and files transferred;

3) Assumption of Responsibility for Damaged Materials, which outlines the liability for any materials damaged or mishandled during the project;

4) Assumption of Costs, which outlines our standard cost per image fees, the costs assumed by us and the costs assumed by our partners, and the services costs will provide;

5) Copyright, which outlines our policy of using only materials that have complete copyright clearance, and also explains our position that the onus of copyright clearance falls entirely on the partner supplying the source materials.

Both parts of the External Partnerships Protocol fit within our overall digitization initiative, the Forsyth Library Digital Collections Initiative (FLDCI), and provide us with a valuable aspect to our burgeoning digital framework. The External Partnerships Protocol functions in counterpoint to our Internal Collections and Intra-departmental Protocols, which outline our procedures and policies for digitizing collections from the library's Archives and Special

Collections and establishing partnerships to digitize materials from various departments at the university.

Conclusion:

We have been fortunate to work in close contact with the Kansas Cosmosphere and Space Center. Our experience in developing the Swigert Collection for a digital audience has taught us the value of communication between partners. We have also met the challenges of the project by creating solutions that have a positive effect on both our KCSC partnership and our overall Forsyth Library Digital Collections Initiative (FLDCI). The development of a uniform file-naming convention for the Swigert Collection had a direct impact on our other digital collections, helping to rein in haphazard naming by staff members in multiple departments. Adopting and customizing Goddard Core helped us to move a step closer to collaborative cataloging, a major goal for this under-staffed institution. Finally, Forsyth Library was able to develop a clear External Partnership Protocol to help us anticipate issues with future partnerships. We now view the obstacles in the KCSC-Forsyth Library partnership as nothing less than opportunities to create a solid and lasting digital collections framework.

References

Barbour, J. (1969). *Footprints on the moon*. New York: American Book-Stratford Press.

Bilstein, R. (1996). *Stages to Saturn*. Washington D.C.: NASA.

Brooks, C., Grimwood, J., & Swenson, L. (1979). *Chariots for Apollo: A history of manned lunar spacecraft*. Washington D.C.: NASA.

Dordain, J. (2009*). International cooperation in space. Universities Space-Research Association*. Retrieved November 1, 2009, from http://www.usra.edu/galleries/default-file/09Symp_Dordain.pdf

Goddard Library (2005, September 15). *Goddard core. The Goddard Library*. Retrieved November 10, 2009, from http://library.gsfc.nasa.gov/mrg/Goddard_Core.htm

Kansas Cosmosphere and Space Center. (2009). *History. Kansas Cosmosphere and space center.* Retrieved November 10, 2009, from http://www.cosmo.org/mu_history.htm

McKie, R. (2008, November 30). *The mission that changed everything. The Observer.* Retrieved November 2, 2009, from http://www.guardian.co.uk/science/2008/nov/30/apollo-8-mission

North Carolina ECHO (2009). *Digitization guidelines chapter 5: metadata. North Carolina ECHO, Exploring Cultural Heritage Online.* Retrieved November 1, 2009, from http://www.ncecho.org/dig/guide_5metadata.shtml

Orloff, R. (2004). *Apollo by the numbers: a statistical reference.* Retrieved November 14, 2009, from http://history.nasa.gov/SP-4029/Apollo_01a_Summary.htm

Collaborative-Centered Digital Curation: A Case Study at Clemson University Libraries

Emily Gore and Mandy Mastrovita (Clemson University)

Abstract

This article will discuss the authors' experience in building and outfitting a regional scan center to serve Clemson University and the South Carolina Digital Library (SCDL), the state's digital library initiative. The authors describe their experiences regarding the establishment of a new unit armed with the task of providing digital curation, imaging, and technological services within an academic library that previously had very few. A subset of their discussion regarding the overarching observations and challenges will also include issues that have arisen within their multiple imaging production workflows, content management, shared metadata, and preservation responsibilities. Throughout the article, the authors address the pervasive and complex relationships between collaboration, sustainability, storage, preservation and access that they have greeted on a daily basis.

Keywords: Archival materials, Collaboration, Cooperation, Digital images, Digital libraries, Digital preservation, Digitization, Distributed preservation, LOCKSS, MetaArchive, Metadata.

Introduction

Clemson University officially established its digitization initiative in the fall of 2007 by establishing a library unit for Digital Initiatives and hiring a unit head. Most large academic libraries like Clemson established digitization initiatives in the 1990s or early 2000s, but there are distinct advantages to beginning an initiative later. One distinct advantage was that we could learn from others and from the best practices and standards in an already established field. Another advantage is that we could begin to think about the blending of digitization initiatives, institutional repository development, data curation and the preservation of digital assets -- in other words, we began thinking in terms of data curation instead of simply digitization. A third, and possibly the greatest advantage, was that we could join existing collaboratives and be instrumental in starting others. In our opinion, collaboration is the key to building sustainable digital initiatives, so we wanted to make sure we took advantage of collaborative opportunities from the start.

Establishing the initiative

Learning from established best practices, prior experiences and contacts with vendors, Clemson University Libraries decided to equip a scan center and object photography studio as the production center for its new digital initiative. The concept behind the development of this scan center is that it would be used not only for projects centered at Clemson, but also for collaborative projects as part of our statewide digital library effort, the South Carolina Digital Library (http://www.scmemory.org). As one of the 3 core partners for the South Carolina Digital Library (with the University of South Carolina and the College of Charleston), Clemson's goal was to establish a scan center to meet the needs of cultural heritage institutions in the Upstate region of South Carolina. Staffing for these collaborative projects has been covered in part by funding provided by the State Library of South Carolina through Library Services and Technology Act (LSTA) funding. LSTA funding is awarded to states on a formulaic basis by the Institute of Museum and Library Services (IMLS). In addition to part-time staffing, LSTA funds have supported the purchase of one scanning station (Dell computer and Epson 10000XL scanner).

Hiring of Key Positions and Restructuring of Extant Positions

The Digital Initiatives unit began with only a unit head. The unit head identified the need to hire someone to be in charge of digital production as well as a programmer. In addition, one position already existing in the Systems department would become the CONTENTdm specialist since the need for desktop support in the library is decreasing. It was also decided that the Systems unit and the newly formed Digital Initiatives unit would merge under the direction of the Digital Initiatives unit head.

After examining positions in many other digital initiative units throughout the country, it was decided that the digital production position would be filled as a librarian faculty position and that the programmer would be hired as a staff member. The librarian would be sought first and the programmer would follow after equipment and processes were in place. Within several months of advertising the position, the Digital Production Librarian position was filled by Mandy Mastrovita. After Mandy's arrival, students were hired to support the production cycle. Currently, there are six student positions in the unit, with students working up to twenty hours per week. Our grant-funded student works additional hours when his schedule allows. Students come from a variety of backgrounds and majors, but all have in common attention to detail, technological aptitude and a willingness to learn. The programmer position has been more difficult to fill and is currently being re-advertised.

Purchase of Equipment, Installation, and Training

After having reviewed the holdings of Clemson University Libraries, we expected to have to digitize a good deal of maps, manuscript material, photographs, and negative film. Therefore, equipment was selected for purchase based on anticipated scanning needs and the incorporation of digitization best practice guidelines as established by leading institutions such as U.S. National Archives and Records Administration's *Technical Guidelines for Digitizing Archival Materials for Electronic Access: Creation of Production Master Files – Raster Images* (U.S. National Archives and Records Administration, 2004), *JISC Digital Media - Still images, moving images and sound advice* (2010) and IMLS Digital Library Forum's *A Framework of Guidance for Building Good Digital Collections* (IMLS Digital Library Forum, 2008) This included flatbed and large format scanning equipment to be purchased with a budget of $100 thousand dollars. While we anticipated some variation in the kinds of materials that we would receive as a regional scanning center, we did not expect our partner institutions and donors to have as much bound material as they have in their holdings, particularly oversized ledgers, scrapbooks, and yearbooks. Because of this, we may need to purchase a dedicated book scanner in the future or look to work with outsourcing vendors to digitize this material.

Small and Medium Format Imaging: Flatbed scanners

We have two flatbed scanners that can handle both transparencies and reflective media: a Kodak iQsmart3 scanner, and an Epson Expression 10000 XL, fitted with a transparency unit. The Kodak scanner is a higher-grade professional scanner that captures images at a much higher resolution, 5500 dpi. We chose the iQsmart3 nearly two years ago because of its reputation as a professional image scanner; it is one of the few scanners that was designed to accommodate the scanning of glass plates in addition to standard transparency and reflective media sizes. The iQsmart3 was well-represented in prominent libraries and projects at the National Library of Australia, the Wellcome Library, Iowa State University, Yale University, and Brigham Young University. Kodak software, support documentation and service, however, have fallen short. We have found that communication with professional listservs (such as the IMAGELIB-L listserv) has helped bring us in contact with other professional users who have helped resolve some of those issues.

The iQsmart3 was designed as a professional printer's scanner. Sometimes, professional print scanning solutions do not apply to the archival environment. In a photolithographic printing environment (the primary market for the iQ3), the film would be held down on the scanner bed with photographic oil. This optimizes contact with the plate glass and minimizes film flaws such as scratches, which disappear when oiled. Another option would be to tape the film down to the glass. Oil and adhesives are not acceptable when working within archival best practices. We have compromised by laying down residue-free gaffer's tape (adhesive side facing the glass, NOT the film), lining the film up with the mask windows, laying the negatives on the glass without adhesives, then laying the masks on top of the film. Other iQsmart3 practitioners have developed physical (temporary) modifications for project-specific demands.

Our second flatbed scanner is an Epson Expression 10000XL. Although the Epson does not yield such a high dpi count (scanning at 2400 dpi), its interface is simple to understand, and we find that because it looks and acts more like a consumer-level scanner that it is the simplest to learn how to operate. We start our newest trainees on this piece of equipment. Relative to our other scanners, the Epson comes in at a very reasonable price of around $3,000 dollars, for the Photo Edition, which includes a transparency hood unit. The Photo Edition comes with its share of cartridges, cut for 35mm negatives, 35mm mounted slides, medium format film, and large format film. The Expression will scan up to tabloid-size transparent or reflective media (27.94 cm x 43.18 cm), and is a real workhorse.

Large Format Imaging: Digital Scanback

After having established our equipment for small and medium format digitization, we determined our budget (approximately $100 thousand dollars) and room dimensions (6.096 m long x 4.88 m wide x 2.37 m high). Our low ceilings limited us to shooting material from our walls. We decided to work with Academic Imaging Associates (AIA), a value-added reseller (VAR) to help select a scanning unit that would be the best physical fit for our work environment. Working with AIA, we ultimately decided to go with a Better Light Super 8K-HS scan back and a TTI vacuum easel. The Super 8K-HS scan back unit is a capture device shaped like a large format film cartridge. It slips into the bottom of our large format camera (a TTI Digiflex 45ei), where it is tethered by a cable to a Mac Pro workstation. The scan back has a sensor that reads red, green and blue pixels, and is controlled by a motor that glides the sensor across the back of the camera to capture the image. The Mac workstation runs Better Light's ViewFinder software for focus, tone and exposure control and Adobe Photoshop CS4 for any further image review and optimization. (Collette, n.d.)

Our Better Light scan back system selection also necessitated the purchase of appropriate components and equipment from many smaller sub-vendors. The role of the VAR in articulating specifications and orchestrating the shipment of so much expensive and complex equipment was very important. It required trained professionals who have worked closely with these sub-vendors and built out the equipment themselves. The VAR staff's understanding of where traditional analog and digital photography are distinct and where the lines cross was also important, particularly with scanback units such as ours which are built to fit inside of large format analog cameras. They also supplied us with a trainer who was not only a professional commercial photographer, but had also built out many scanback units like ours. He was able to make adjustments, order additional pieces, and train our staff to work with the camera.

Although we had to arrange the installation of the vacuum unit, the remainder of the building and training was handled by the VAR. The Digital Production Librarian had received previous training and worked with a Better Light scan back system, but there were substantial variations in these two customized Better Light configurations. There were no identical pieces of equipment in the new setup, (new lights, tripods, vacuum easels, light tents, etc.) which made training an essential requirement, as she would be responsible for training staff and students. Training, retraining and refreshment of basic large format techniques were a huge help, and fostered confidence in our unit's staff and students who would be responsible for operating the Better Light scan back equipment.

Digital Imaging and Analog Tools

We were sure to reserve enough in our budget for this important part of our workflow. Although the use of analog cameras is on the wane, in digitization work, there are many digital-analog hybrids, such as our Better Light scanback, as well as analog tools that are still required for handling photographic materials. There is also the matter of handling of analog film-based media throughout the process of digitization. The extent to which materials that are to be digitized are handled or curated is determined locally.

The generation gap is widening with our students who were born in the late 1980s-early 1990s; they may be familiar with photographic prints, but require an introduction to analog film, negatives, and wet film processes. After we instruct our students to keep abreast of best practices by taking the Cornell University Library's *Moving Theory Into Practice Digital Imaging Tutorial* (Cornell University Library, 2003), we have to spend a good amount of time training our students about halftones, how film grain still needs to be checked with a loupe, that transparencies need to be placed on daylight-balanced light tables, and so on, so that they understand that image quality is not always determined by digital equipment or software settings. Teaching them to check analog film for irregularities throughout the process of digitization is an important part of our ongoing training processes.

Building and implementing workflows

We are thankful to have partnerships with cultural heritage institutions that have yielded a substantial amount of original material for us to work with; these relationships have been cultivated as an earlier part of the digitization process. Our newest challenges lie in building workflows that leverage the skills of faculty, staff and students in an effective way, especially in times when resources are tight. A need for more staff is perhaps the most common complaint of digitization practitioners, and has recently been recorded in the results from UNLV's library digitization survey report as the greatest challenge of its survey participants (Lampert & Vaughan, 2009).

Students and Staff

We have addressed staffing challenges in a way that is similar to digitization programs at peer institutions: we have combined resources and balanced the distribution of work between new and existing staff and units in the library. Digital imaging and metadata creation has been distributed amongst repurposed staff, faculty and students in Special Collections, IT, and Cataloging (Boock, 2008). The staff and faculty dedicate a portion of their time to work on our projects, so, as we begin, we really are only working with a fraction of time spent on our digitization projects. We have depended heavily upon student labor, and have structured many production tasks and responsibilities so that they can be fulfilled and monitored by students. Our senior students, for example, assist by performing quality control on the work created by junior students, followed up with further quality control work by staff and faculty. Some of our Upstate project partners in the South Carolina Digital Library have worked collaboratively with us in metadata creation, but they are often content experts, not metadata experts. Our operations and projects are still new, and these relationships will be negotiated continually over time; we hope we can dedicate more staff to the process of entering metadata, performing quality control, preparing content for upload into CONTENTdm and preserving our images and data.

New Materials and New Workflow Plans

In working with multiple collections, we have learned how to pace ourselves when assimilating new materials in new formats and developing new workflow plans. Thus far, our collections have been relatively small. While starting off with smaller projects is recommended for determining equipment and training benchmarks, it still takes time to develop plans for small collections that vary in dimension and format. Each collection requires the design of different sets of instructions based upon equipment specifications, and the research and analysis of best practices for different media formats (e.g. scanning images from an oversized bound ledger requires different handling and equipment than scanning an envelope full of negative transparencies). The preservation of a consistent workflow is balanced alongside the need to pay extra attention to establishing effective communication of detailed plans and best practices to all students, staff and librarians. Consistency in communication is challenged by having to negotiate the different hills and valleys in everyones' levels of technical training and best practice comprehension, a common problem when working with a diverse group of students, staff and faculty in different areas of specialization (Gueguen & Hanlon, 2009).

File Access and Preservation

Access and preservation are considered throughout the process of digitization. We have trained our students to capture and store master TIFF files locally on our production computers, each is backed up with a RAIDed data storage unit that protects all short-term work. Master images are then cropped and de-skewed, and color profiles are assigned. Students embed pertinent collection and keyword information to master TIFFs using Adobe PhotoXMP. When this is done, NISO Z39.87 technical metadata is extracted using the JHOVE API (*JHOVE - JSTOR/Harvard Object Validation Environment,* 2009). JPG derivatives are generated and moved to the CONTENTdm production server; master TIFF images are copied to our SAN (Storage Area Network) for long-term storage. If working collaboratively with partners at a geographic distance, JPGs are often stored where the partners can access them via the Web for metadata generation and quality control.

Descriptive Metadata

A descriptive metadata worksheet, designed on basic Dublin Core (Dublin Core Metadata Initiative, 2008) and South Carolina Digital

Library elements, is sent as an Excel worksheet to our project partners, or uploaded to GoogleDocs and shared with our student workers and catalogers. The students enter descriptive information about the original items and identify any South Carolina county/region information; this is entered in an unqualified Dublin Core spreadsheet. If the original collection belongs to Clemson, we work with staff in the Special Collections and Cataloging departments to complete the more complex Dublin Core fields (DC.Title, DC.Subject, DC.Description) that require subject and collection analysis to complete the fields appropriately. If the collection belongs to a project partner, we determine which aspects of metadata creation they are capable of handling on their end, and adjust accordingly. All involved work is performed in accordance with best practice guidelines as established in North Carolina Dublin Core guidelines (see North Carolina ECHO, Exploring Cultural Heritage Online, n.d.) and county and region information in accordance with South Carolina Digital Library data fields. When the Dublin Core-based spreadsheet is completed, it is later converted to a tab-delimited text file, uploaded to the CONTENTdm production server for display, and saved on the SAN for ongoing storage.

Web-Based Tools

In the past year, we have developed our production workflow by articulating necessary tasks and procedures, preparing training materials, and identifying bottlenecks. With our staff, students and partners working in different physical areas and requiring ongoing training and access to production data and instructional materials, we have turned to a departmental wiki and Google Docs in our work environment. Using these Web-based tools has alleviated IT networking burdens, facilitated group collaboration, and minimized workstation bottlenecks, especially with spreadsheet data entry. Both tools feature extensive history versioning, which adds an extra layer of security when working with groups; if any mistakes have been made, an earlier iteration of a document can be retrieved with ease.

Our departmental Wiki pages have been easy to update, and have simplified training by minimizing the need to re-explain complex instructions. Thus far, we have placed approximately 100 instructional documents in our wiki, covering topics that include: unit tasks, student scheduling, best practices guidelines, workflow models, training instructions for image capture, metadata entry, and uploading collections into CONTENTdm. We have shared our Web-based documents (training materials, equipment specifications, metadata guidelines, etc.) with our immediate colleagues, and portions of this content with wider networks of digital library professionals at conferences. As of yet, the low cost and accessibility of these tools has outweighed other options. However, we have begun to outgrow this arrangement, and are currently in the process of evaluating more comprehensive project management systems that will help facilitate more sophisticated workflow planning.

Content Management

We have not included a great deal about our CONTENTdm workflow. Our preliminary workflow procedures are more useful to the general reader because they thoroughly address the nature of a collaborative production environment that embodies elements of digital imaging and metadata input with forethought towards preservation. While CONTENTdm functions as a presentation management system, we have determined that over time we will need to manage more complex digital objects and associated metadata than a system such as CONTENTdm can handle. Because of this, we will be moving to an open source system, e.g. Fedora, that supports more robust digital object management and preservation.

Distributed Digital Preservation

By establishing a digital initiatives unit in 2007, Clemson was able to learn from field best practices that establishing a digital preservation plan is part of establishing an initiative. Not only was the establishment of a plan essential but so was the establishment of an infrastructure for preservation. After working with campus IT to secure storage on the SAN for our preservation master files, we investigated digital preservation systems. After identifying existing preservation systems, including OCLC's Digital Archive, SRB/iRODS networks, and LOCKSS-based networks (*HOME-LOCKSS*, 2008), Clemson joined the MetaArchive, a private LOCKSS-based network.

The MetaArchive, a National Digital Information Infrastructure and Preservation Program (NDIIPP) funded project centered at Emory University, utilizes private LOCKSS networks that dynamically replicate and distribute digitized items to multiple file servers in multiple locations (see MetaArchive Cooperative, 2010). Before Clemson joined the network in 2008, the network was established and tested for several years by its original member universities, Emory, Georgia Tech, Florida State, Virginia Tech, Louisville and Auburn. In addition, the network's original partners focused on the preservation of Southern digital culture, and Clemson's material certainly falls into that category. At present, Clemson is working to setup our LOCKSS node in order to place our digitized and born-digital content in the network. Soon the collections we curated over the past year will be replicated and distributed on the MetaArchive network to insure continual access.

References

Boock, M. (2008). Organizing for digitization at Oregon State University: a case study and comparison with ARL libraries. *The Journal of Academic Librarianship 34* (5), 446.

Collette, M. (n.d.). *Scanning backs. How they work.* Retrieved March 10, 2010, from http://www.betterlight.com/how_they_work.html.

Cornell University Library. (2003) *Moving theory into practice digital imaging tutorial.* Retrieved March 31, 2010 from http://www.library.cornell.edu/preservation/tutorial

Dublin Core Metadata Initiative (2008) *DCMI metadata terms.* Retrieved March 31, 2010 from http://dublincore.org/documents/dcmi-terms/

Gueguen, G. , & Hanlon, A. (2009). A collaborative workflow for the digitization of unique materials. *The Journal of Academic Librarianship 35* (5), 470.

HOME-LOCKSS (2008) Retrieved March 31, 2010 from http://lockss.stanford.edu/lockss/Home

IMLS Digital Library Forum (2008) *A framework of guidance for building good digital collections.* Retrieved March 31, 2010 from http://www.niso.org/framework/Framework2.html.

JHOVE - JSTOR/Harvard object validation environment. (2009). Retrieved on March 31, 2010 from http://hul.harvard.edu/jhove/

JISC Digital Media - Still images, moving images and sound advice (2010). Retrieved from http://www.jiscdigitalmedia.ac.uk/

Lampert, C., & Vaughan, J. (2009). Success factors and strategic planning: Rebuilding an academic library digitization program. *Information Technology and Libraries, 28*, 123.

MetaArchive Cooperative (2010). *About MetaArchive: collaboratively preserving our digital heritage.* Retrieved March 31, 2010 from http://www.metaarchive.org/about

North Carolina ECHO, Exploring Cultural Heritage Online (n.d.) *North Carolina Dublin Core guidelines.* Retrieved March 31, 2010 from http://www.ncecho.org/dig/ncdc.shtml.

U.S. National Archives and Records Administration. (2004). *Technical guidelines for digitizing archival materials for electronic access: creation of production master files – raster images.* Retrieved March 31, 2010 from http://www.archives.gov/preservation/technical/guidelines.html

The Craft Revival Project: Library Leadership in Creating Connections between Small Cultural Institutions

Anna R. Craft, Tim Carstens, Jason Woolf
(Western Carolina University's Hunter Library)

Abstract

The Craft Revival Project is a collaborative digital project partnering a mid-sized academic library with six small cultural heritage institutions in order to document the historic effort to revive handmade crafts in the western part of North Carolina during the late 19th century and the early 20th century. The partnership among these diverse institutions has allowed for the creation of a product that no one of the individual institutions could have created on its own. This article describes the benefits of the project to the partners in this collaboration including those of increased technological capacity, raised collection care standards, and increased publicity for and visibility of the institutions. It also describes lessons learned from the project including those regarding the workflow and staffing levels that are most appropriate for a collaborative project of this kind.

Keywords: Appalachia, Craft Revival, Digital project management, Digital projects, Digitization, Handicraft, Library-museum collaboration.

Introduction

The Craft Revival Project (http://craftrevival.wcu.edu) is a collaborative digital endeavor led by Hunter Library of Western Carolina University (WCU), partnered with six small cultural heritage organizations, all located in the mountains of western North Carolina. The project sprang from a successful 2004 North Carolina Exploring Cultural Heritage Online (NC ECHO) planning grant that led to four years of funding, beginning in 2005. Hunter Library's Special Collections, Penland School of Crafts, John C. Campbell Folk School, and WCU's Mountain Heritage Center formed the initial partnership, with the Southern Highland Craft Guild joining in 2006. Two Cherokee organizations, the Museum of the Cherokee Indian and Qualla Arts and Crafts Mutual, joined the project in 2008, bringing the total number of project partners to seven. The project documents the historic effort to revive handmade crafts in the western part of North Carolina during the late 19th century and the early 20th century; this effort helped to revive mountain traditions, create networks of artisans, and boost the economy of the area. The website and associated database tell the story of this movement and the people involved in it through images, texts, and other digitized documents from the collections of the partner institutions.

The partner organizations all have holdings documenting Craft Revival history and all provide the public with access to their collections. A team based at Hunter Library oversaw the project and worked with staff coordinators at each of the associated partner organizations. Hunter Library employs approximately 45 full-time staff. Western Carolina University, part of the University of North Carolina system, is a regional comprehensive university of approximately 9,000 students.

Most of the partner organizations are quite small, some with only a single staff member to manage their archival collections. The Mountain Heritage Center (MHC), part of Western Carolina University, is a regional museum. Established in 1975, the MHC works through its collections, programs, and publications to interpret current studies of Appalachia. The other project partners are separate from WCU. The John C. Campbell Folk School was founded in 1925 in Brasstown, North Carolina, and was modeled after traditional Danish folk schools, or folkehojskoler. In its early years, the Folk School offered instruction in traditional handiwork skills such as woodcarving, weaving, dyeing, and farmwork. These traditions continue at the Folk School today, along with new and more modern courses on topics including photography, storytelling, and cooking. The Museum of the Cherokee Indian is located on the lands of the Eastern Band of Cherokee Indians, in Cherokee, North Carolina. The Museum and its collections tell the story of the 11,000-year documented history of the Cherokees; the archives include photographs, books, and other materials associated with Cherokee history. Penland School of Crafts was originally founded as a community craft organization in 1923 in Penland, North Carolina, under the name Penland Weavers and Potters. Today Penland offers workshops in crafts including glass, metals, photography, textiles, and wood. Qualla Arts and Crafts Mutual (QACM) is also located on Eastern Band lands in Cherokee, North Carolina. This cooperative craft organization was founded in 1946 to preserve and advance Cherokee arts and crafts, and this mission continues today. QACM showcases historical and contemporary examples of Cherokee crafts and provides an outlet for members to sell their craft items. The Southern Highland Craft Guild was chartered in 1930 as the Southern Mountain Handicraft Guild, with a mission to educate people about traditional handicrafts and to market the crafts of its members. Today the Guild is located in Asheville, North Carolina and provides juried membership to over 900 artists and craftspeople in the southern Appalachian mountains.

A planning committee comprised of members from the partner institutions, Hunter Library staff, and outside advisors made technical choices early in the project's planning. This group based many decisions on the NC ECHO Guidelines for Digitization, which recommend Dublin Core as the basic metadata standard for digital projects in North Carolina (2007). The committee chose an OCLC-hosted instance of CONTENTdm for the digital collection management system, and for controlled fields adopted several standard thesauri, including Library of Congress Subject Headings, Library of Congress Name Authority Files, and the Getty Art & Architecture Thesaurus.

Numerous collaborative digital projects are documented in the library literature, including many that focus on regional or statewide engagement. The Colorado Digitization Program, now the Collaborative Digitization Program, is one such program that has created digital projects through relationships with museums (Bailey-Hainer & Urban, 2004). Digital Past, from the North Suburban Library System in Illinois, is another example of a project that has brought together libraries and museums of various sizes (Schlumpf & Zschernitz, 2007). The Southern Oregon Digital Archives has also pursued collaborative relationships for some of their collections, including the First Nations Collection, which brings together materials documenting the indigenous peoples of southwestern Oregon and northern California (2004). The Craft Revival Project is on a smaller scale than many of these projects and as such can provide some lessons learned about the challenges and rewards associated with small-scale digitization projects.

Learning from Project Challenges

The Craft Revival Project ultimately met its goals, but that success did not come easily. Along the way, the project encountered and addressed challenges related to limited resources, understaffing, technical problems, and geographic distance between the partner institutions.

When the project was first envisioned, one of the major intended outcomes was technological capacity-building at each partner institution. The original project workflow relied heavily on the partner institutions, involving them in nearly all steps of the process, including item selection, scanning, metadata creation, and upload into CONTENTdm. The role of Hunter Library was to coordinate and support the work of the partners, administer the database, ensure that metadata met project standards, and provide the contextual story and interpretation of the movement through the website. The intention was that the hands-on experience would position the partners to undertake digital projects of their own in the future. This workflow did produce some of the expected benefits for the partners, but it also created a number of difficulties for the project.

Heavy reliance on time commitments from staff at the smaller partner institutions presented the most significant problem with this workflow. Each original project partner had at most two individuals contributing to the project work of selecting and scanning items, creating metadata, and loading items into the CONTENTdm Acquisition Station. Additionally, several individuals worked in their institutions on a part-time basis, further placing constraints on their time. Project partner Michelle Francis, the archivist for Penland School of Crafts, was one such participant who worked on a part-time basis. Francis described the need for realistic staffing as a primary lesson learned. Describing any steps that she would take in undertaking a similar project in the future, Francis stated, "I think I would have a more realistic expectation if I did this again on what... the demands on my time [would be]" (personal communication, November 2, 2009). She noted that the project required "a lot of hours for a part-time person to work into a part-time schedule." Peter Koch, Education Coordinator at WCU's Mountain Heritage Center, also identified the longer-than-expected time commitments as an issue, noting that "it takes a fair bit of effort to put an individual item up [onto the database]" (personal communication, October 20, 2009).

This original vision of a project that would rely on partner institutions for much of the production was also directly tied to the level of staff resources that Hunter Library initially devoted to the project. Since the role of Hunter Library was initially to provide training, coordination, and review of the partners' work, rather than production of the work itself, a large in-house staff devoted to the project was not part of the original plan. The library director at the time planned to lead the project himself, a Craft Revival subject specialist was hired to provide interpretive content, a technical staff member was to work on the website and provide technical support, and part-time student assistants were hired as needed. These staff structure choices meant that no members of the permanent library faculty, except the director, were involved in either the initial planning of the project or as part of the original project team, and this was an oversight. Most notably, the failure to involve the library's Cataloging Unit deprived the project of a source of expertise and labor that might otherwise have been available. Even after a metadata librarian position was created to help with the project, the Cataloging Unit's contributions were limited during the early years of the project by difficulties with recruitment for the new position and by turnover within the position.

The project's staffing situation was further compromised when, shortly after the project began, the library director was assigned significant additional responsibilities within the university and consequently had little time to devote to the project. This reduction in the director's involvement meant that the project did not receive the high-level support and direction, additional resources, and institutional legitimacy that would have encouraged library staff to fully support the project. At this point, the subject specialist took on the leadership role in the project. For some time after this, the project continued to be understaffed, with as few as two Hunter Library-based staff members working on the project at any time. This staffing level was inadequate to fully support a project of this scope.

The project also faced differences in technological capabilities among the partner institutions and challenges in providing support to these geographically separate organizations. In contrast to prior assumptions, not all partners had reliable high-speed Internet connections at the time the project started, and connectivity was required for uploading data into the CONTENTdm system. Connectivity proved a concern for much of the first two years of the project. Additionally, the small partner institutions, many without IT departments, relied on training and support from Hunter Library when they needed assistance with project work. Because most of the partner institutions are in rural settings, some as far as 100 miles away from the coordinating library, any technical problems that could not be solved by phone or email contact could not always be addressed immediately by the Hunter Library Project Team. This underlined the importance of communication between the Project Team and the staff at each partner organization, and the importance of not making assumptions about existing technical capacity.

The partners' limited experience with digital projects and the previously mentioned restrictions on their time had implications for the quality of the work produced. Early in the project some partners struggled with metadata consistency, use of CONTENTdm, and scanning issues resulting in image crookedness, blurriness, lack of contrast, or incorrect resolution. Staff at Hunter Library had to correct these problems in a process that proved both time consuming and frustrating.

Hunter Library took a number of steps to deal with these difficulties. The library held training sessions for all partner staff and provided partners with individual training and technical support as needed. The project director developed two intensive training sessions supported by a 100-page workbook distributed to project partners. These step-by-step manuals guided partners as they worked through the steps of scanning, modifying images, creating metadata, and uploading digital files into the system.

Over time, a reworked, larger project team was put into place at Hunter Library. The Craft Revival subject specialist continued to serve as project director. Three members from the Cataloguing Unit—the head of cataloguing, the metadata librarian, and the metadata assistant—were also part of the team. Two technical staffers from the Systems Unit— a technical support specialist and a web specialist—participated as well. Three project assistants—a research assistant, an image specialist, and a project archivist—replaced undergraduate and graduate student workers. This larger team proved better able to handle the workload of the project.

Finally, with all partner institutions struggling with limited time and staff resources, the Project Team redeveloped its workflow to complete work without overburdening any of the partners in the collaboration. Hunter Library's Project Team recognized that each partner had different strengths and different needs for support. The library Project Team eventually assumed responsibility for more of the project work while tailoring tasks at the partner institutions to best reflect each partner's abilities. Partners continued to digitize their items and create metadata descriptions for them, but Hunter Library brought all of the CONTENTdm work in-house and had librarians in the Cataloging Unit check the metadata and assign Library of Congress Subject Headings to the records. This new workflow, implemented just before the Cherokee partners joined the collaboration, immediately brought more consistency to the project.

The Cherokee institutions, while interested in becoming part of the project, made it clear that they had little time or staff available to contribute to item selection, scanning, and metadata creation. To accommodate these needs, the Hunter Library Project Team made further modifications to the workflow at these institutions. The project director handled item selection and project assistants completed scanning and basic metadata creation tasks on location at the two Cherokee sites. Once items were scanned and basic metadata created, the project director wrote interpretive descriptions for the items. Finally, this information was passed on to the Cataloging Unit where staff entered the information into CONTENTdm and added subject headings.

While personnel from the two Cherokee institutions were not involved in the day-to-day production, they assisted in the item selection process when possible and were available to answer questions about their collections. Staff at these institutions, primarily liaisons Vicki Cruz at QACM and James "Bo" Taylor at the Museum of the Cherokee Indian, provided access to the Cherokee community that might not otherwise have been available to non-Cherokee project staff. These staff members at the Cherokee institutions spoke to the importance of the project in their community and made connections with relatives of craftspeople featured in the project and to others with knowledge of the Craft Revival era. These connections enabled fact checking and the gathering of additional information.

The Craft Revival Project experimented with different workflows evolving from one dependent upon partner staff to accomplish work into one relying more heavily on staff hired and supervised by Hunter Library. The fourth year of the project, using the lead-library-centered model, saw improvement in the number of items added over those in previous years. Project assistants, working closely with the project's director, received in-house training and day-to-day supervision in photography, scanning, image manipulation, and metadata creation. Since the project assistants were not juggling their duties with other work responsibilities, they could concentrate their full attention on the project. Image quality improved dramatically; images were scanned and cropped correctly, manipulated to the appropriate resolution, and saved in proper formats. Descriptive metadata provided to the metadata librarian was more complete and better organized. The metadata librarian ensured this metadata and the subject headings within the metadata were consistently applied, regardless of origin. In short, processes ran more smoothly and fewer things had to be redone using the workflow where Hunter Library took on more of the production tasks.

Project Successes

The Craft Revival Project's collaborative effort strives to tell the story of the movement and make it accessible to a wider audience through the World Wide Web. This mission has been successful and there were other unexpected, positive outcomes that came from the project. These successes varied by institution and included improved collection care and organization standards, increased knowledge of digital project practices, collection development opportunities, networking opportunities, publicity for the involved organizations, and the creation of a digital product that no one of these institutions could have made on its own.

One beneficial effect of the project was improvements in the way that some partner institutions manage their collections. Perhaps the greatest growth in collection management and development occurred at the John C. Campbell Folk School. When the project began, the school's folklorist, David Brose, handled project contributions. Realizing the scope of the project and the time commitment involved, Brose brought on Anna Shearouse as a scanning assistant and, in recognition of her skills and passion for the subject matter, Shearouse was promoted to the position of archivist at the Folk School. According to Shearouse, her work on the project as an archivist has had a tangible and lasting impact on the Folk School. Shearouse, in collaboration with Craft Revival Project director and a consulting archivist, developed the first collection policies and finding aids in the Folk School's history. Shearouse has since cataloged and created finding aids for collections not related in scope to the Craft Revival Project, stating, "I'm not sure that would have happened without the project's structure" (personal communication, October 30, 2009).

Similarly, Qualla Arts and Crafts Mutual had their collection cataloged for the first time through their participation in the project. The project director worked with the QACM director and a project assistant to photograph the collection, provide accurate documentation, and create and implement a numerical inventory system. To ensure the sustainability of this system, they developed a workflow to register new objects as they are added to the collection.

Even partners who entered the project with fully cataloged collections were able to improve their collection management. Deb Schillo, librarian for the Southern Highland Craft Guild, believes that her knowledge and management of the Guild's collection has also improved. According to Schillo, the Guild's archives had previously "been managed by volunteers in a hit or miss way and the project has given a real framework [to the collection]" (personal communication, November 2, 2009). Staff at the Mountain Heritage Center and Hunter Library's Special Collections also credited their project work with helping them to make new connections within their collections and update their records (P. Koch, personal communication, October 20, 2009; G. Frizzell, personal communication, October 29, 2009).

The partners also gained valuable technical skills and materials that benefited their institutions and collections. Each partner received a desktop computer, scanner, and external hard drive as part of the project. Several partners pointed to their experience with Adobe Photoshop, provided with each computer, as one very useful skill that they developed. George Frizzell, Head of Special Collections at Hunter Library, stated that his experience with Photoshop enabled him to better manipulate scanned material to increase readability (personal communication, October 29, 2009). Peter Koch and the staff at the Mountain Heritage Center honed their technical skills to the point that they provided training sessions to other partners.

Michelle Francis of Penland School of Crafts stated that an unforeseen benefit of her scanning and Photoshop skills has been her ability to fulfill requests for digital reproductions of material held in the archives at Penland. Francis also described the progress made in another important area:

I think it is important to mention that I'm one of the partners that is from a very small institution. Our archives are not located in a fireproof building with a sprinkler system and probably won't be any time soon, though [an archive] is in the master plan of the school. So, while having some of our oldest and most irreplaceable documents on a website, while not the ideal form of preservation, is far better than nothing and is a very welcome byproduct of this project. (M. Francis, personal communication, November 2, 2009)

In addition to technological steps forward, an increased awareness and visibility of the partners' collections has been another positive consequence. Schillo described the history of the Southern Highland Craft Guild's archives as "being shuttled from back room to back room for decades, but now it is seen as a real investment that has brought in scholars and has really added a lot to our place in the community" (personal communication, November 2, 2009). Penland's Francis also highlighted increased awareness in the local community as well as with researchers. The overall web presence and specifically the "Craft Today" and "History" pages located on the main Craft Revival website have given Francis the web presence she has desired throughout her eight years as Penland's archivist (personal communication, November 2, 2009).

The increased visibility of the collections involved also led to unexpected collection development opportunities. As the primary contact person listed on the website, project director Anna Fariello received several communications of interest from people who held private collections that related to the Craft Revival. The project's policy is that only items held in public collections can be digitized and made part of the project; so in these instances Fariello encouraged owners to consider donating these collections to one of the partner institutions. This encouragement yielded the donation of the Scroggs Collection to the John C. Campbell Folk School, a collection that fit in well with the scope of the existing Folk School holdings. This connection might not have been made without the visibility of the project.

Many partners established or strengthened relationships with the other partner institutions and discovered meaningful connections between holdings in their collections. Peter Koch of the Mountain Heritage Center provided the following anecdote:

One area in particular that it has worked is with the [subject] of corn shuck crafts. We have been able to connect that material together to tell a much more complete story of those crafters and their work because of the connections that we have made to the material that the Southern Highland Craft Guild has. The connection between our material and theirs has allowed the telling of a much fuller story. (P. Koch, personal communication, October 20, 2009)

Deb Schillo of the Southern Highland Craft Guild echoed this experience and said she especially values the personal connections that she has developed during the project. "I knew that Penland and John C. Campbell were members of the Guild and had some history with us but we never interacted very much," stated Schillo, who credited the project with allowing her to meet the other partners and, in her words, "see where things overlap and to fill in some of our holes [in our collection]" (personal communication, November 2, 2009).

In some cases, one institution holds objects made by a certain craftsperson, while other institutions might hold photographs, biographical information, or other documents or objects related to or created by that person. For example, Goingback Chiltoskey was one of the most celebrated Cherokee woodcarvers of the Craft Revival era. He taught wood crafts at the Cherokee high school and participated in regional events such as the Craftsman's Fair of the Southern Highlands. The collection of the Museum of the Cherokee Indian includes historical and contemporary photographs of Chiltoskey, as well as photographs of some of his family members, and items carved by Chiltoskey. The collection of the Southern Highland Craft Guild includes photographs of Chiltoskey participating in Craftsman's Fairs between 1948 and 1953, biographical information about Chiltoskey in the member files, and items carved by Chiltoskey. Additionally, the collection of the Mountain Heritage Center includes carved items attributed to Chiltoskey. Users of the Craft Revival website have the opportunity to learn about Chiltoskey's background, see examples of his work, and view both historical and contemporary photographs of him, including some showing him at work. Though physically held in different institutions, the digital collection brings these items together and lets users discover them in one place. Numerous similar examples exist throughout the Craft Revival collection. Through these combined collections, users gain a richer picture of the people, the crafts, and the movement as a whole.

Conclusion

The Craft Revival Project has successfully met its challenges and is now supported by a smoothly running organization equipped to create and lead digital endeavors. At the time of this writing, the project has completed its goals and wrapped up most production activities, as most of the partner institutions have exhausted the relevant items held in their collections. Hunter Library has a staff structure in place to continue accepting and uploading items on an as-needed basis so that the collection may continue to grow on a smaller scale.

The project also achieved many of the goals for capacity-building and improvements within the partner institutions hoped for when the project was first envisioned. Partner collections are better managed and staff members within the partner institutions have learned new skills. The project has also served as a means of preserving vulnerable partner collections. By making images of materials from partner collections available on the web, the project not only made these materials accessible to a wider audience, but also provided the institutions with valuable publicity. Partners have benefitted from connections they made with other institutions working on the project.

These successes only came about after some hard lessons. Partner institutions and Hunter Library learned that digital projects are labor-intensive and that adequate staff should be in place before such projects are undertaken. Project experience also taught that a workflow depending on the lead-library for the production of images and metadata runs more smoothly than a model dependent on partner contributions. While some small cultural institutions may have the ability to consistently deliver large numbers of high quality images and metadata, the limited resources typically available to small cultural institutions make it unlikely that all such institutions will be able to do so. A lead-library centered model is more likely to produce consistently positive results.

This experience also provided lessons about the lead-library model. Success of this model requires a strong institutional commitment. Library administration must make it clear that they are behind the project and expect all appropriate library staff to contribute to its success. Key individuals who will work on the project should be involved in the planning of the project, both to ensure their support for the project and to ensure that they understand their role within it. If the library is new to digital projects, top administration must expect to be called on to clarify roles, expectations, and lines of authority as the library develops its digital infrastructure. Whenever possible, more than one individual within the library organization should be capable of performing key functions, including leadership functions, to ensure continuity in case of turnover.

Any library seeking to start a major digital project must realize that digital projects are resource intensive and the library must be prepared to devote significant resources to ensure success. While many large research libraries can easily support a specialized digital project team, small-to-medium-sized libraries will likely have to work harder to put the pieces in place as they build their digital infrastructure. The medium-sized library should probably not consider taking on a major project without having already completed a number of small-to-medium-sized projects. Digital infrastructure needs to be in place at the beginning of the project.

The Craft Revival Project Team intends to apply the lessons learned to future digital endeavors. It is hoped that these lessons may also be useful to other libraries and small institutions seeking to collaborate in the future.

References

Bailey-Hainer, B., & Urban, R. (2004). The Colorado digitization program: a collaboration success story. *Library Hi Tech, 22*(3), 254-262. doi:10.1108/07378830410560044

Cedar Face, M. J., & Hollens, D. (2004). A digital library to serve a region. *Reference and User Services Quarterly (44)*2. 116-121.

NC ECHO. (2007). *Guidelines for digitization [Rev. ed.].* Retrieved from http://www.ncecho.org/dig/digguidelines.shtml

Schlumpf, K, & Zschernitz, R. (2007). Weaving the past into the present by digitizing local history. *Computers in Libraries, 27*(3), 10-15.

Hudson River Valley Heritage: A Journey in Collaborative Digitization

Jennifer Palmentiero
(Southeastern N.Y. Library Resources Council)

Abstract

This chapter presents a case study of Hudson River Valley Heritage, a decentralized collaborative digitization effort coordinated by the Southeastern New York Library Resources Council (SENYLRC). The case study documents the journey of a network of small organizations with limited resources and limited digitization experience in developing an online digital repository of historical materials housed in libraries and cultural heritage organizations in an eight country region in New York. The intent of the chapter is to describe the process-- from inception, through planning to full implementation-- and share what was learned for those who might be considering similar ventures.

Keywords: Collaborative digitization, CONTENTdm, Digitization, Digital libraries, Library materials – digitization, Museum and library collaboration.

Introduction

Libraries have always been about sharing--providing their user communities with access to information though a network of shared resources. The digital age has made sharing possible on a much wider scale than ever imagined. With these new opportunities comes the need for enhanced collaboration and an expanded notion of community. This chapter presents a case study of an effort to expand information sharing through a collaborative digitization project. The case study documents the journey of a network of small organizations with limited resources and limited digitization experience in developing an online digital repository. The intent of the chapter is to describe the process-- from inception, through planning to full implementation--and share what was learned for those who might be considering similar ventures.

Hudson River Valley Heritage (HRVH) is a collaborative digitization service coordinated by the Southeastern N.Y. Library Resources Council (SENYLRC). Several SENYLRC staff members were responsible for the conception, planning, and implementation of HRVH: John Shaloiko, Karen Starr, Patricia Carroll-Mathes, Christopher Hyzer, Tessa Killian, and Zack Spalding. I am also proud to be a member of this team as the Digital Services Librarian.

Our work would not be possible without the aid and support of a committee of regional professionals dedicated to helping move the service forward. The cultural heritage organizations that have risen to the challenge and enthusiastically learned to digitize their local history holdings make HRVH the valuable resource that it is today.

Background

SENYLRC is one of nine New York Reference and Research Library Resources Councils ("3Rs"). These multi-type library consortia, established and chartered by the NY State Board of Regents in the late 1960s, provide a variety of services to their members including continuing education, access to electronic resources, services to the health care community, consulting, information technologies, advocacy, and more recently digitization. Each New York 3Rs Council is "governed by a locally elected Board of Trustees and has substantial input from member libraries through a robust committee structure; and each receives operating and special program aid from the State of New York, along with locally generated funds." The overriding goal of these systems is to do "collectively what their constituent libraries and library systems cannot do individually or what can be done better together" (NY3Rs Association, Inc., n.d.). It was in this spirit that HRVH was born.

SENYLRC's mission is to support its members in the Mid-Hudson Valley in order to enrich their services and enhance access to information for their users. The council strives to achieve service excellence in libraries by:

- Thoughtfully applying emerging technologies to resource sharing, collection building, information access and communications;

- Providing imaginative, accessible and relevant development opportunities for staff at all levels;

- Becoming a focal point for the exchange of ideas, collaboration, the development of new tools and the promotion of the transforming power of libraries.

The Hudson River Valley of New York is one of America's most historic locales. HRVH provides free online access to historical materials from digital collections contributed by public, academic and special libraries, archives, museums, historical societies and other cultural heritage organizations in the Mid-Hudson Valley region of New York State. HRVH documents the history of this eight-county region from the early colonial period to recent decades and includes photographs, manuscripts, clippings, cookbooks, scrapbooks, 3-D objects, yearbooks, oral histories, maps and newspapers.

The success of HRVH results from the effort and enthusiasm of a network of people committed to its growth. The roles and responsibilities for the development of HRVH are shared among SENYLRC staff, the organizations that contribute their unique resources, and an advisory committee of dedicated professionals. Participating organizations are responsible for the entire digitization workflow with generous help and support from the HRVH team at SENYLRC. The Council provides the technical infrastructure, access to CONTENTdm® digital collection software, equipment, documentation, and training. It is this model of collaboration and shared responsibilities that make HRVH a successful digitization service for the region. There was very little digitization expertise in the region when this journey began a decade ago and everyone involved had a lot to learn. At times it seemed like a "two steps forward one step back" process. HRVH is now a thriving digital service as well as a community of trained professionals working towards a common goal of providing unparalleled access to our region's rich history.

Planning

Collaborative digitization became a program concept through SENYLRC's Regional Automation Committee in the year 2000. The following year SENYLRC embarked on a strategic planning process funded with a Library Services and Technology Act (LSTA) grant awarded by the NY State Library. Representatives from a variety of organizations in the region were invited to serve on a digitization task force to assist SENYLRC in developing a regional plan. Liz Bishoff, then Director of the Colorado Digitization Project, was hired as a consultant. She was instrumental in laying the groundwork for what would become HRVH.

The task force, under Bishoff's leadership, specified five objectives to be met during the planning process:

- Identification of regional collaborative partners building on current digitizing efforts.
- Identification of issues/challenges/roadblocks which will impact implementation of a regional digitization program.
- Identification of local collections which are candidates for digitization.
- Development of a coordinated funding strategy that addresses the need for support from both public and private sources.
- Coordination of a regional digital institute to train project participants in the areas of digitization.

Eric Roth, then Archivist at the Huguenot Historical Society, was contracted by SENYLRC to study the current digitization landscape in the region in an effort to address several of these objectives. He conducted interviews with staff members at organizations that were identified as possible partners in a regional collaborative effort including academic libraries, public libraries, and government agencies. He discovered that digitization efforts, future plans, and attitudes about digitization varied greatly among these different types of organizations. A few organizations had begun preliminary digitization projects. Others expressed interest in digitizing, but acknowledged many roadblocks including a lack of technical infrastructure and expertise, lack of staff, lack of funding, and a lack of intellectual control over their physical holdings. Intellectual property and copyright issues as well as selection were identified as challenges to overcome. Roth noted that smaller organizations--historical societies, schools, churches, and state historic sites--were understaffed and underfunded and would have difficulty digitizing given their limited resources. These smaller organizations could benefit greatly from partnerships with larger organizations (Roth, 2001).

The interview process revealed the roles that SENYLRC might play in a regional digitization effort. SENYLRC could develop and maintain expertise in digitization, foster communication, provide training and consultation, help select equipment, identify funding sources, and provide standards to organizations that wanted to digitize their own collections. The interviews also revealed that there was little interest in having a central organization, like SENYLRC, handing the digitization for other organizations (Roth, 2001). Eric Roth documented his findings in a report titled: *Opportunities, Challenges, and Priorities: Developing a Collaborative Digitization Plan for the Mid-Hudson Valley* (Roth, 2001).

SENYLRC developed and sponsored a Digital Information Institute funded with a LSTA grant. Experts from around the country presented workshops covering all of the steps involved in building digital collections. The first session provided an overview of the entire process. Subsequent full day sessions were devoted to scanning, metadata, project management, copyright, preservation, digital preservation, and storage and access of digital materials. The Institute was attended by 327 people from interested regional organizations between February and October of 2002.

SENYLRC released *The Digitization Program Plan for the Southeastern Region of New York* in April 2002 (Southeastern New York Library Resources Council, 2002). The Plan identified the following goals to be achieved:

- Organizational Infrastructure – Create a cross-organizational steering committee comprised of representatives from seven to nine key institutions in the region to guide the implementation initiatives for this regional digital effort.
- Collection Selection Criteria – Establish selection criteria and identify target collections to be digitized by cultural heritage institutions within the southeastern New York region.
- Standards – Agree upon and adopt standards for metadata and scanning that will facilitate collaborative digitization.
- Legal Issues – Identify the legal issues relating to digitizing collections and develop an awareness strategy to educate the staff of the regional cultural heritage institutions contemplating digitizing a collection.
- Accessible Collections – Create a regional collection of digital objects contributed by cultural heritage institutions within the southeastern New York region, which is open, distributed, and easily accessible by the public.
- Training – Provide training and consulting opportunities, focusing on the digitizing of materials and managing digital projects, for staff of the cultural heritage institutions (Southeastern N.Y. Library Resources Council, 2002, p.7).

Phase One: Implementing the Plan

A permanent Digital Advisory Committee (DAC) was established by SENYLRC's Board of Trustees at the end of 2002 to assist SENYLRC staff in implementing the goals of *The Digitization Program Plan.* Participants in the Digital Information Institute as well as staff from organizations that were already digitizing were invited to serve to ensure that there were members with some digitization expertise on the committee. With the assistance of the committee, SENYLRC was positioned to take on the roles of coordination, consultation, documentation, and communication.

Standards and Best Practice Development

The committee spent 2002-2003 developing documentation to address selection, digital imaging, and metadata drawing largely from standards and best practices already in use around the county. Documentation created by the Research Libraries Group was adapted and expanded upon to provide general selection criteria for potential partners. The *Western States Digital Imaging Best Practices* was adapted for the digital imaging guidelines (BCR's CDP Digital Imaging Best Practices Working Group, 2008). Dublin Core was selected as the metadata standard for the region. The committee determined that Dublin Core's simplicity would allow a diverse group of organizations with varying local practices to successfully contribute records to a shared repository. A brief metadata guide was developed drawing largely from the Dublin Core Metadata Initiative documentation (Dublin Core Metadata Initiative, 2003). SENYLRC's initial metadata documentation was purposely general and not too prescriptive.

A web site, Hudson Valley Heritage (HVH), was created to disseminate information about the project including background information, planning documents, and committee activities. An extensive digitization resource list was developed incorporating the documentation produced by the committee with links to online resources developed by and for projects around the country. Copyright resources, digital audio resources, general digital imaging and metadata resources, and a link to the Dublin Core web site were included as well as links to digital projects and collections that had already been created within the region.

Selecting the Platform

The Digital Advisory Committee explored a variety of software packages for digital collection building in 2003 including Greenstone, Luna Insight®, and CONTENTdm®. After evaluating these options, CONTENTdm®, a turn-key solution for developing, maintaining, and providing end-user access to digital collections, was selected. It was reasonably priced, came pre-packaged with the Dublin Core element set, and did not require a lot of technical expertise to implement. Additionally, server software, a user interface, client software for importing, describing, and uploading items, and a web-based administrative interface for managing and editing collections were all included with the license. The client software could be installed in different locations making it an appropriate choice for a decentralized regional project. SENYLRC would host the server and the web site, yet any interested organization could have access to the client software and web-based administrative site providing them with full control of the metadata creation and management process.

Getting Started

In the summer of 2004 SENYLRC and the Digital Advisory Committee were positioned to invite organizations to contribute digital collections to HVH. The Committee recommended that a "regional hand-holder" be available to support and assist organizations with their projects. SENYLRC staff had little experience or expertise in digitization. SENYLRC's Director, knowing my interest, allowed me to receive training and mentoring in order to take on this role. The early phase of the project provided an opportunity for me to gain hands-on experience building digital collections. I also received personal training from several staff members at the United States Military Academy Library at West Point who were already using CONTENTdm® to build digital collections. As the Director and Board of Trustees identified digital services as a valuable emerging program, I was encouraged to obtain an MLS degree. With the support of SENYLRC, I pursued an MLS at St. John's University and my degree was granted in 2007.

Three organizations were selected to be the pilot contributors: Vassar College Archives and Special Collections Library, Marlboro Free Library, and Wilderstein Preservation. The committee deliberately selected different types of organizations to explore various workflow options. Two laptops and a scanner were purchased to loan to early participants as needed. SENYLRC was not positioned to fund digitizing activities at these organizations, but helped to offset the costs of their projects with these purchases.

Vassar College Library already had a collection of digitized 19th century photographs available on its web site. Ron Patkus, Director of Archives and Special Collections, seeing the value of participating in a regional collaborative, suggested that SENYLRC staff migrate the collection to CONTENTdm®. The original metadata records were created in a MySQL database adhering to AACR2 cataloging rules and structured to appear as MARC records on the web. This project provided an opportunity for SENYLRC staff to determine the steps involved in moving a collection from one platform to CONTENTdm® as well as how to "map" or "crosswalk" AACR2/MARC metadata to Dublin Core metadata elements.

The Marlboro Free Library was selected to digitize and contribute a photograph collection documenting the history of this small Hudson River community. The Director, Jim Cosgrove, had already received digitization funding through a New York State Assembly member grant. He originally planned to host the collection on the library's website. When SENYLRC's Director heard about his plans, he approached Jim and encouraged him to load the collection onto HVH instead. The library used the $7,000 member grant to purchase a scanner and hire a professional cataloger to create the metadata. A local photographer volunteered to create the digital images.

Wilderstein Preservation, the third pilot contributor, is a historic house museum with an extensive collection documenting the history of the Suckley family who owned and lived in the house for over a century. Wilderstein digitized and contributed a theme based collection documenting the family's participation in World War I through the American Field Service. This collection includes a photo album, diaries, letters, postcards and 3-D objects. Duane Watson, archivist and curator at Wilderstein, provided leadership and support to a library school graduate student. With my assistance, and equipment from SENYLRC, the entire digitization process was done in-house.

It is difficult to determine in advance the amount of time digitization projects take, especially at the beginning when there is a steep learning curve. The Marlboro Free Library and Wilderstein Preservation projects took a full year to complete. Neither had digitized before and the project staff was only available part time. Vassar's collection was uploaded to HVH by August 2004, just as the other two organizations were getting started. The availability of Vassar's collection in HVH generated enthusiasm in the region. Several new organizations expressed interest in joining the project and began contributing material before the first three projects were fully evaluated. As a result, once an evaluation did occur and some necessary modifications were identified, these other organizations, in addition to the pilot organizations, were affected by the changes.

Lessons learned from Phase One

The first phase of the project revealed the need for two important changes: a web site redesign and an overhaul of the initial metadata guidelines. The initial project web site, which had been designed as an informational resource, became obsolete once CONTENTdm® was licensed. CONTENTdm® comes with a web-based user interface for searching and browsing the collections. A redesign, building on the CONTENTdm® foundation, would allow the collections to take primary importance and provide a consistency to the site while still including project documentation. The existing metadata documentation lacked input guidelines and examples as well as information about how and when to use specific fields. Early participants recommended that the metadata guidelines be more prescriptive, but the document also needed to meet the needs of a range of contributors: from the volunteer to the professional cataloger.

The web site redesign was completed in the fall of 2005. The second generation of the web site included a name change from Hudson Valley Heritage to Hudson River Valley Heritage to correspond with the designated Hudson River Valley National Heritage Area. SENYLRC hired a web development team to create a new logo for HRVH and to customize the CONTENTdm® interface.

Building the new site with CONTENTdm® as the foundation allowed the collaborative collections to be the focus of the site, but also would allow the designers and SENYLRC to add pages to the basic structure.

One of the issues that emerged during the pilot phase was the lack of individual organizational identity in CONTENTdm®. There was consensus that users should experience a consistent look and feel as they navigated through the site, but that individual organizational identity was also important. To address this issue we built "home" pages for each organization on top of the CONTENTdm® structure. These pages give each organization a place to describe their collection(s) and link back to their own web site. These pages also contain a search box that allows users to limit their search to the participant's collection.

The web design team suggested that a comments feature would add value to the site and wrote a program for that purpose. Allowing visitors to post comments to items in HRVH proved to be a complementary addition to the site by encouraging interaction with and among the user community. We intended this feature to be an avenue for users to provide additional descriptive information about resources. While this certainly does occur, we have found that it is used most often for sharing thoughts and memories about the people, places, and events documented by the collections.

The metadata revision, completed in February 2006, was accomplished through efforts of SENYLRC staff, the then chair of the Digital Advisory Committee, a contributor from one of the pilot organizations, and a consultant from OCLC. SENYLRC staff surveyed the metadata documentation created for many other collaborative projects in developing guidelines for HRVH.

We surveyed the metadata style guides, application profiles, data dictionaries, and online records of dozens of projects. Here are a two: Western States Dublin Core Metadata Best Practices was heavily consulted. The latest version, CDP Metadata Working Group Dublin Core Metadata Best Practices is available at: http://www.bcr.org/dps/cdp/best/dublin-core-bp.pdf (last accessed January 6, 2010). University of Washington Libraries Data Dictionaries is also a good source: http://www.lib.washington.edu/msd/mig/datadicts/default. html (last accessed January 6, 2010). Most CONTENTdm implementations can be accessed from this page on the OCLC web site and is a good place to start looking at how other organizations create Dublin Core records in CONTENTdm: http: //www.oclc.org/ contentdm/ (last accessed January 6, 2010).

The resulting *HRVH Metadata Style Guide* included expanded instructions for using fields, examples of field usage, and many additional fields that were not in the original document. For example, one added field, called Digital Collection, was needed to allow participants to group items from their main collection into sub-collections based on topics or themes.

By the time the new metadata style guide was complete, participating organizations were well into their projects. In fact, one organization had already contributed over 500 items. Fortunately these early participants understood that they were part of a new and emerging service and were willing to edit their records to reflect the changes in the metadata guidelines. Open communication between SENYLRC staff and the staff of these organizations was instrumental in identifying desired changes to both the web site and the metadata guidelines, allowing for necessary modifications.

Phase 2: From Project to Service

In the fall of 2005, SENYLRC and the Digital Advisory Committee began to discuss transitioning HRVH from an emerging project to an ongoing service. Among the issues that needed to be addressed were setting policies for the service, developing a sustainable funding model, and identifying strategies for recruiting and training new contributors to ensure the growth of collections.

Setting Policies

The early phase of the project reinforced the importance of individual support and consultation. SENYLRC established a policy to provide an organization up to 28 hours of on-site help by SENYLRC staff in the first year of contribution, and 10.5 hours in each

530   Hudson River Valley Heritage

subsequent year. As the availability of equipment was also identified as a need, a permanent scan center was established at the SENYLRC office and two additional scanners were purchased and made available to contributors on three-month rotations.

Funding the Service

Developing a funding model took some time. There was a strong desire in the beginning to encourage participation by not charging fees, however, SENYLRC's Executive Director and Board of Trustees realized that a free service with substantial personnel and technology costs would not be sustainable in the long term. They sought a solution that would achieve some cost recovery, while at the same time encourage participation. There were initial discussions about charging per digital object, but this model seemed complicated and difficult to manage. DAC recommended that membership in the council become a requirement for participation in the HRVH service. The Board established a new affiliate membership category with a lower annual fee than regular membership. This category would allow organizations that had minimal need for SENYLRC's other services to participate in HRVH. As a result, SENYLRC's membership grew beyond traditional libraries to include historical societies, museums and other cultural heritage organizations. The Board of Trustees decided that a minimal fee was appropriate when factoring in the associated benefits of training, consultation, support, software, equipment and hosting.

Recruitment and Training

Recruiting and training new contributors was achieved with another LSTA funded workshop series that ran from 2005-2007. The series was similar to the earlier Digital Information Institute except there was more focus on CONTENTdm® and HRVH as participants were required to upload 35 items to HRVH as part of the learning process. The series, *Training for Digital Asset Management through the Hudson River Valley Heritage Program*, was attended by 34 people representing 26 organizations in the region.

From October 2005 through early April 2006 participants attended workshops that provided them with the fundamentals of building digital collections: a session to introduce them to digitization and the HRVH service, project management, copyright, digital imaging, metadata, and CONTENTdm®. In April and May attendees created 5 digital objects (digital image and metadata) in HRVH with the assistance of SENYLRC staff. A mid-program review was held in June and participants presented their 5 items for review and discussion. Most participants achieved this mid-program goal, but a few did not and, in fact, were unable to attend the remainder of the series. Staff changes and insufficient time to devote to digitization were cited as the major reasons. In June of 2006 the Board of Trustees celebrated this successful new service by making HRVH the focus of SENYLRC's annual meeting. Representatives from two participating organizations spoke about their experiences and SENYLRC staff presented HRVH to a packed room of attendees, including members of the press.

From July 2006 through March 2007, the remaining participants attended workshops on digital preservation, sustainability, and promotion, as they worked to complete the required 35 items. The final session provided an opportunity for participants to share their experiences with each other and with SENYLRC staff. By this session, 18 organizations out of the initial 26 had uploaded items to HRVH and all 18 became members of SENYLRC. A few organizations, however, fell short of the required 35 items. The reasons for this vary, but the biggest obstacle was lack of time to devote to their projects.

Lessons Learned from Phase Two

Initially, individual organizational identity was important, so the user interface was customized to provide quick and easy access to resources by contributing organization. From the revised HRVH home page there were only three ways to access materials: searching by keyword, browsing by contributing organization or by broad resource type. Once there were more than twenty organizations represented, the need to be able to browse by broad topic became apparent. A small working group developed broad topic categories that could be assigned to each item. As with the creation of the *HRVH Metadata Style Guide*, we looked at other sites that had implemented broad topic categories for browsing to help us formulate our list of terms.

In developing our broad topic categories we consulted the following sites: Arizona Memory Project (http://azmemory.lib.az.us/cdm4/topicbrowse.php); North County Digital History (http://history.nnyln.net); and the Ohio Memory Project (http://www.ohiomemory.org/custom/ohiomemory/om/index.php?Guidelines.)

The initial list had twelve topics, but was soon expanded to seventeen after application and review. As a result of the metadata modification, all records needed to be edited. SENYLRC staff provided editing assistance for metadata records to reflect these new topic categories. The web site was enhanced to include a new "Explore" page to provide browsing by topic as well as browsing by personal names, corporate names, and locations indexed in the records. Users can now browse the collections in multiple ways by clicking on the "Explore HRVH" button from the home page. We also refreshed the look and feel of the home page to include a slide show with rotating images from each of the collections.

Group discussions at the 2005-2007 training workshops became increasingly lively as the series progressed. The participants enjoyed learning from each other through sharing their experiences, expertise, challenges, and successes. It became apparent that SENYLRC needed to foster this development by providing networking opportunities beyond the training series. A listserv had been established at the start of the series primarily as a way for SENYRLC staff to communicate efficiently with all HRVH participants. Participants were encouraged to use the listserv as a means of communicating with each other once the series had commenced. At the end of the training series a Users Group was established to encourage HRVH participants to gather periodically.

By the conclusion of the two year training series in 2007, the project had become more than just a service; HRVH was a community. SENYLRC staff had gained digitization, mentoring and teaching experience and had developed comfort in their roles as experts. The participants felt empowered and excited by their emerging skills and were eager to continue contributing to HRVH.

Current State of HRVH

The HRVH Community

Today, with comprehensive guidelines and documentation, an experienced and available staff, a funding model, and communication avenues in place, HRVH is a sustainable, thriving service. There is a wide range of digitization activity among the contributing organizations: some organizations upload items on a regular basis; others contribute sporadically as time allows, and a few projects have stalled because of staff changes.

The HRVH team at SENYLRC consists of four people who dedicate time and expertise to the service. The Executive Director is responsible for the overall direction of the service. The Manager of Technology and Administrative Services is responsible for management, training, grant writing, recruitment and publicity. As the Digital Services Librarian, I provide training and one-on-one consultation, support, and assistance to all participating organizations. The Systems Manager installs software, maintains the server and web site and provides technical assistance/trouble shooting to SENYLRC staff and all participating organizations.

The HRVH Users Group meets quarterly and provides an opportunity for participants to network with each other. These meetings allow SENYLRC staff to update participants on new directions, software upgrades, or to discuss the digitization of specific materials such as scrapbooks. The greatest benefit of these meetings is the opportunity to draw on the expertise and experience of all members of the group. For example one member led a discussion on developing fee and permission policies for reproductions because his organization handles many such requests. Another member led a discussion/demonstration on preservation of original materials drawing on his extensive expertise and experience. These meetings strengthen the sense of community in addition to providing

Responsibilities	HRVH Contributor	SENYLRC and DAC
Project Management	• Project Manager • Project planning • Determine workflow	• Guidance • Assistance • Training
Project Planning	• Project purpose • Audience/user needs • Mission/Goals/Objectives • Budgets: time and cost • Selection • Copyright	• HRVH Collection Selection Criteria • Identify organizational partners in the region • Identify and include unique collections that reflect the historical significance of the Hudson River Valley
Digital Conversion Process	• Digital conversion: in-house or outsource • Metadata creation • Quality control	• Digital Imaging Best Practices • HRVH Metadata Style Guide • Assist with digital conversion and metadata creation • Provide CONTENTdm® software • Digital lab at SENYLRC • Loan equipment • Quality control on first batch of items
Access to Digital Content	• Provide text for the organization's HRVH webpage • Create links from your homepage to HRVH • Online exhibits	• Host CONTENTdm® server and all of the digital objects • Provide a HRVH webpage for organizations • Provide high speed bandwidth • Host and provide links to online exhibits
Evaluation	• Evaluate collection use	• Usage statistics • Survey of users
Sustainability	• Funding • Update metadata • Storage/preservation of digital masters	• Committed to maintaining HRVH • CONTENTdm® upgrades • Server upgrades • Increase bandwidth as necessary
Marketing/ Promotions	• Promotions to organization's constituency and to local community	• HRVH Communications Plan • Press release templates • Bookmarks

Figure HRVH-1. Detailed breakdown of roles and responsibilities for HRVH. Table created by Tessa Killian, Manager of Technology and Administrative Services at SENYLRC.

educational opportunities. The division of the digitization responsibilities has been solidified (Figure HRVH-1 provides a detailed breakdown of roles and responsibilities.)

Recruitment

In order for HRVH to grow in scope, content and therefore, value, recruitment of new members is essential. To introduce HRVH and encourage participation, SENYLRC staff frequently attends meetings of library directors, historical society directors, and other regional meetings attended by cultural heritage professionals.

In 2008, SENYLRC was able to offer small grants, supported with state funds, to help organizations offset the costs of digitization. A sub-group of the Digital Advisory Committee worked with SENYLRC staff to develop a grant application and identify content areas that would be funded. These included the Colonial period, the American Revolution, and items related to the 1909 Hudson-Fulton Celebration in preparation for the 2009 celebration commemorating the 400th anniversary of Henry Hudson's voyage up the Hudson River. The grant application was purposely designed to be brief and simple because the amount of money being offered did not warrant a lengthy application. Four organizations--two current contributors and two new organizations--were awarded funds to digitize materials from those content areas. SENYLRC hopes to offer more grants in the future.

Training

In the fall of 2006 SENYLRC developed their own curriculum for training new contributors. *Training Basics for HRVH* is a four-day series that covers the fundamental skills needed to begin building digital collections in HRVH. The first day introduces the service as well as project management and copyright considerations. The remaining three days are devoted to scanning, metadata creation, and CONTENTdm®. This training series is offered twice a year over a several week period. The workshops are required for new contributors and are also open to current contributors who need a refresher or need to train new staff members.

Promoting HRVH

The importance of constant marketing and promotion cannot be understated. SENYLRC's marketing activities have included the creation of bookmarks and postcards, press releases, and promotional spots on public radio. HRVH collections have also been linked from appropriate Wikipedia articles bringing in users from the popular online encyclopedia. Additionally, SENYLRC's Systems Manager has optimized Google's ability to index HRVH content which has greatly improved access to the site through the search engine. It is not only important for us to promote the site as a whole, but it is equally important for HRVH contributors to market to their own target audience. The organizations that promote their collections have the most visitors and the most user comments posted to their items.

Recent Projects

In 2007 SENYLRC was awarded Library Service and Technology Act (LSTA) funds to digitize materials documenting African American history in the region from slavery to the early 20th century and to create associated lessons plans for educators. An online exhibit was created to complement the digital collection and provide context for the resources in the collection. *The Missing Chapter: Untold Stories of the African American Presence in the Mid-Hudson Valley* provides a visually appealing and informative journey through a collection of manuscripts and images that tell the stories of African Americans in the region going back to the colonial period. *The Missing Chapter* is very popular and widely used by teachers in the region (Hudson River Valley Heritage, 2010.)

A 2008-2010 LSTA funded initiative was a pilot project to digitize historic newspapers. The platform for HRVH Historical Newspapers is Greenstone, an open source software. SENYLRC staff had experimented with uploading newspapers to CONTENTdm® and discovered that newspapers overwhelmed the other content in HRVH and searching resulted in too many newspaper articles. The LSTA grant funded the customization of Greenstone and the digitization and creation of metadata for ten years of a daily paper. HRVH Historical

Newspapers is linked from the HRVH home page, but searching the newspapers occurs from a separate interface.

In 2008-2009 SENYLRC partnered with the Greater Hudson Heritage Network (formerly the Lower Hudson Conference of Historical Agencies and Museums) and the Sound and Story Project of the Hudson Valley on a collaborative project to plan for the identification, digital reformatting, and increased accessibility of oral histories housed in cultural heritage organizations in the region. This initiative was funded by the Institute of Museum and Library Services (IMLS). The major planning activity was a regional survey to determine what organizations held oral histories, what formats and condition they were in, and the topic areas covered by the interviews. Ten oral history interviews were digitized and included in HRVH as a pilot project to determine the steps involved.

Although SENYLRC was a pioneer among the New York 3R Councils in establishing a regional digital repository service, the other eight 3R Councils are in various stages of regional digital collaboration. CONTENTdm® is the platform for each of these services, thereby making it fairly simple to link them together using the CONTENTdm® multi-site server. New York Heritage (http://www.newyorkheritage.org), a web portal hosted by the Northern NY Library Network, provides one interface for searching the harvested metadata from all of the nine regional services. As a result, SENYLRC's HRVH contributors now benefit from the exposure of their digital content at the state level.

Digitization: Benefits and Challenges

Benefits and challenges of digitization have been revealed by SENYLRC and HRVH contributing organizations. One benefit for SENYLRC has been a new found role of the Council for historical societies and museums that previously would not have considered membership. Prior to HRVH, SENYLRC helped member libraries improve their services to patrons. Through HRVH, SENYLRC has created a service that directly benefits the public, thereby increasing visibility of the Council. Building digitization expertise in the region enhances the program tremendously as new contributors can learn from those organizations that have been involved in the service longer. It is a joy to watch people become empowered by their new skills and share their expertise with others.

One challenge from SENYLRC's perspective is achieving consistent quality in digital images and metadata across the collections. Even with the provision of documentation, the quality of digital images and the richness of metadata records vary from collection to collection. Another challenge is our desire that the collections grow at a steady pace. We do not require the adherence to timelines and we have noticed that collections grow with the availability of staff dedicated to the project. The biggest challenge faced by the Council is ensuring that we have the funds to keep the service moving forward. Funding consists of revenue from membership dues, a portion of New York State funding to SENYLRC, and federal grants when awarded.

An informal survey of HRVH participants was conducted to collect their thoughts on participating in HRVH. They were asked, in two open-ended questions, to reflect on their digitizing experiences and provide some insights that would benefit the readers of this chapter. They were asked to share the challenges and benefits of digitizing at their local institutions as well as the challenges and benefits of participating in a collaborative effort.

Challenges at the local level identified by the respondents include: the steep learning curve, copyright considerations, workflow and staffing issues, and the need for good planning and organization. Benefits of digitizing collections were identified as: learning new skills and feeling empowered by them and the rewarding feeling associated with knowing that once hidden collections are now available to a wide audience. For some, digitizing collections has provided opportunities to collaborate with local school districts on creating lesson plans; for others it's been identified as a source of community pride.

There were mixed reactions regarding the use of CONTENTdm® as the platform for HRVH. Some respondents indicated that it is cumbersome to use and therefore a challenge to participating in

HRVH, while others identified the software as a benefit of participation in the service. Respondents overwhelmingly shared benefits associated with HRVH participation including: group training, one-on-one assistance, the availability of equipment on loan, technical support, networking opportunities, world wide exposure of collections, and no requirement for a high level of in-house technical expertise. Another benefit is HRVH's ability to virtually unite disparate collections when several organizations hold complementary resources. In fact, several contributing organizations from the same locale collaborated on a physical exhibit, with an accompanying virtual HRVH exhibit, documenting the history of education in their town.

Conclusion

Ten years into our collaborative digitization journey, HRVH is an award winning service, having been formally recognized by two NY State organizations--the New York State Library awarded SENYLRC the 2006 Joseph Shubert Award and Nylink awarded SENYLRC with a 2007 Achievement Award. Also, in 2006, we received Greater Hudson Heritage Network's Award for Excellence recognizing HRVH as a valuable service to cultural heritage organizations. Participants continue to add items to HRVH, SENYLRC continues to recruit and train new members, and the Digital Advisory Committee is dedicated to supporting SENYLRC staff in identifying new directions for the service. Our collective efforts have created an active community of digitization experts in our region in addition to providing a wonderful resource where HRVH visitors can discover the rich history of the Hudson River Valley.

References

BCR's CDP Digital Imaging Best Practices Working Group (2008). *BCR's CDP digital imaging best practices. Version 2.0.* Retrieved January 6, 2010 from http://www.bcr.org/dps/cdp/best/digital-imaging-bp.pdf

Dublin Core Metadata Initiative (2003). *Dublin Core metadata element set, Version 1.1: Reference description.* Retrieved January 6, 2010 from http://dublincore.org/documents/dces/

Hudson River Valley Heritage (2010). *The missing chapter: Untold stories of the African American presence in the Mid-Hudson Valley.* Retrieved January 6, 2010 from http://www.hrvh.org/exhibit/aa07/

NY 3Rs Association, Inc. (n.d.). *What is NY 3Rs Association?* Retrieved January 6, 2010 from http://www.ny3rs.org/site/view/108

Roth, Eric (2001). *Opportunities, challenges, and priorities: Developing a collaborative digitization plan for the Mid-Hudson Valley.* Retrieved January 6, 2010 from http://www.hrvh.org/about/HRVHassessment.pdf

Southeastern New York Library Resources Council (2002). *Digitization program plan for the Southeastern Region of New York.* Retrieved January 6, 2010 from http://www.hrvh.org/about/HRVHplanfinal.pdf

Southeastern NY Library Resources Council. (2002). *Digitization Program Plan for the Southeastern Region of New York.* Unpublished manuscript.

Collaborating for Success: A Cross-Departmental Digitization Project

Sue Kunda (Oregon State University Libraries)

Abstract

In 2007 Oregon State University Libraries acquired the personal collection of Gerald "Jerry" Williams, a native Oregonian and former national historian for the U.S. Forest Service. The collection contains personal papers, historic images, serials, monographs, oral histories, maps, moving images, political posters, ephemera, and artifacts of the U.S. Forest Service and Civilian Conservation Corps. Four library units collaborated to catalog, digitize, and make available online more than 1700 (and counting) items from the collection. In this chapter are descriptions of the planning process, workflows, policies and procedures. The author documents technical and procedural obstacles, methods used to overcome these difficulties, and lessons learned in working through the barriers.

Keywords: Academic libraries, Collaboration, CONTENTdm, Copyright manifest, Data dictionary, Digitization projects, DSpace, Dublin Core, Gerald W. Williams, Institutional repositories, ScholarsArchive@OSU, Workflows.

Introduction

In 2007 the Oregon State University Libraries (OSUL) acquired the personal collection of Gerald "Jerry" Williams, a native Oregonian with a lifelong passion for Pacific Northwest history. Williams began his career with the U.S. Forest Service in 1979, working as a sociologist with the Umpqua National Forest located in southern Oregon. After stints with the Willamette National Forest and later the Pacific Northwest Regional Offices, Williams was appointed, in 1999, national historian for the U.S. Forest Service. Throughout his career Williams was a prolific author and avid collector of Pacific Northwest historical documents, images, and artifacts.

The Gerald W. Williams Collection includes 35 years of Williams' personal papers related to his more than 75 publications, 3100 monographs and serials, and over 6000 copies of documents from the papers of Gifford Pinchot, the first U.S. Forest Service chief. In addition, Williams collected more than 24,000 historic photographs, including photographic prints, postcards, sterographic images, and glass lantern slides. The voluminous collection also includes oral histories, maps, moving images, political posters, and ephemera from the U.S. Forest Service and the Civilian Conservation Corps. (2008). After inspecting the collection and consulting with on-campus stakeholders about its value to the OSU academic community, OSUL purchased everything but several works of art and a group of miscellaneous artifacts.

Once the collection was transported to OSU library administrators agreed digitization of the textual items and historic images would take precedence over the digitization of other components. Many of the monographs and serials had no copyright restrictions and the OSUL Digital Production Unit (DPU) already had a well-established digitization workflow for printed matter. The historical photographs were compelling and had considerable potential value for researchers. In addition, University Archives and DPU worked together on a daily basis to digitize and make available online photographs and other images.

Digitization Project

Project Pre-Planning

With the help of Digital Access Services staff and student workers, the subject librarian for Forestry went through Williams' shelf lists and notes for the library portion of the collection to ascertain which titles were currently owned by OSUL and/or which titles were possible candidates for digitization. The Forestry subject librarian created a detailed spreadsheet documenting this information and a more general digitization matrix indicating the number of holdings at OSUL and number of items eligible for digitization. These documents were shared with an administrative team (University Archivist, Digital Access Services Head, Cataloging Unit Head, DPU Head, Digital Production Librarian) in order to gauge library resources. The Cataloging Unit Head was assigned project manager while the University Archivist and Digital Production Librarian were given oversight of the digitization of the images and textual items, respectively.

The Cataloging Unit Head facilitated a meeting with Cataloging and DPU staff to hammer out workflows and responsibilities. Attendees brainstormed ideas, devised two separate cataloging workflows, and agreed to do a one-week pilot test of each set of procedures to determine which was more efficient. Workflow #1 required Cataloging staff to organize the library portion of the Gerald W. Collection into the four groups in the Digitization Matrix (Public Domain/Not Held at OSU, Public Domain/Held at OSU, Non-Public Domain/Not Held at OSU, Non-Public Domain/Held at OSU) before beginning the cataloging process. Workflow #2 allowed Cataloging staff to begin cataloging without organizing the collection according to the Digitization Matrix. DPU staff also developed digitization workflows that coordinated with cataloging workflows.

The University Archivist and Head of Special Collections perused the library portion of the collection and flagged items deemed rare and/or valuable. After processing, these items would reside in the OSUL Special Collections rather than the general circulating collection.

Digital Repository Platforms

OSUL currently supports two digital repository platforms: DSpace and CONTENTdm.

DSpace: an open-source institutional repository platform developed by MIT and Hewlett-Packard, was originally designed to manage, archive, and provide access to textual documents making it an obvious choice for the monographs and serials in the collection. DSpace provides full-text searching through the Lucene search engine, which is especially conducive for print materials, and its contents are routinely crawled by search engine spiders. DSpace also offers permanent URLs, licensing, flexible metadata, and multiple digital preservation features.

CONTENTdm: a proprietary-based digital content management system first developed at the University of Washington and later purchased by OCLC Online Computer Library Center, was originally conceived to store and provide access to digital images. The software automatically generates thumbnails, JPEG, and JPEG2000s from TIFF digital files. Users can perform basic editing functions (resize, rotate, sharpen, crop), pan and zoom JPEG 2000 files, bookmark favorites, and create personal slideshows. Because of these more image-based capabilities, OSUL chose to use CONTENTdm to store and display the historic photographs, slides, and artifacts from the Gerald W. Williams Collection.

Metadata

Textual Items

The Digital Production Librarian created a data dictionary for the Gerald W. Williams Collection's textual items, which was appropriate for both monographic and serial titles. The dictionary specifies the metadata elements, their definitions as well as their use policy (e.g., required or not, repeatable or not, etc.) Most of the metadata elements are derived from the qualified Dublin Core.

These approximately 900 titles would be housed in ScholarsArchive, OSUL's instance of DSpace. Dspace supports the Qualified Dublin Core Metadata Schema. Most descriptive metadata for the collection was fairly standard (creator, title, date, etc.) but several adaptations were made to align this collection with OSUL unique needs.

While the Gerald W. Williams Collection's titles were grouped under a collection by the same name in ScholarsArchive, OSUL also used the description field (dc.description) to add a note designating them as Gerald W. Williams Collection titles. By doing this, users finding an item through a search engine rather than entering directly through the ScholarsArchive user interface, would see the item came from the Gerald W. Williams Collection.

The Digital Production Librarian also added metadata elements specific to Oregon Explorer, OSUL's natural resources digital library and its associated portals. Oregon Explorer metadata generally consists of geographic and spatial information relevant to the state of Oregon, but a relation field (dc.relation) also allows items to be pulled into the appropriate Oregon Explorer portal. For example, "Bohemia Mining District: A Brief History" was assigned the relation field "Explorer Site::Land Use Explorer", allowing it to be included in search results in the Land Use Explorer.

Dspace automatically attaches administrative and structural metadata.

Images

The images from the Gerald W. Williams Collection are housed in CONTENTdm, which also supports the Dublin Core Metadata Schema; therefore, the metadata for this collection is similar to the textual metadata. Standard descriptive metadata (creator, title, and date) was used, but OSUL also added geographic metadata such as Rivers and Streams, Hydrologic Unit Codes (HUC's), and Longitude Latitude Identification (LLID).

Technical metadata describing the digitization process is found in the Transmission Data field and Administrative Metadata for this collection is found in the Restrictions and Contributing Institution fields.

Digitization Specifications

Textual Items

Textual items that could be debound were scanned in both tiff (600 dpi master files) and pdf (300 dpi access files) formats on a Canon DR-9080C. This production scanner has a feed capacity of 500 sheets and scans at rates of up to 90 pages-per-minute. Tiff files were scanned as individual files while pdf files were scanned as a single document. This allows future manipulations of single tiffs, if necessary, and provides a pdf file more appropriate for web viewing.

Textual items that could not be debound were scanned on a Bookeye 2 Planetary Book Scanner located in the Interlibrary Loan Department. Unlike the Canon DR-9080C, which can scan a document in either single-page or multi-page format, the Bookeye 2 can only scan documents as single images. In addition, this scanner does not have the capacity to scan at 600 dpi, the resolution OSUL normally requires for master (tiff) files. Because these files are used to recreate an access copy, if necessary, and not considered the preservation copy, a lower standard is acceptable. All textual pdf files were compressed and ocr'ed using cvision's pdfcompressor™ 4.0.

Images

A University Archives volunteer used an HP4370 ScanJet to scan all images (photos, postcards, etc.) currently included in the Gerald W. Williams Collection. Items equal to or smaller than 3 x 5 inches were scanned at 800 dpi while items larger than 3 x 5 inches were scanned at 600 dpi. The volunteer created both grayscale and color tiff files for each item and the University Archivist chose the image he felt was of the highest quality. The volunteer used Adobe Photoshop Elements 4.0 to make any necessary edits.

Workflows

Cataloging

Cataloging staff had devised two possible workflows for processing the collection and planned to spend one week following each set of procedures to determine the most efficient workflow. It quickly became apparent that the more expedient workflow was the second one, which did not require any further organizing of the collection before cataloging. The first workflow was dropped.

Library technicians responsible for adding monographs and serials to the library collection started by retrieving items, one book cart at a time, from University Archive compact shelving. Working from the book cart the cataloging technician checked the library OPAC to see whether or not the item was currently held at OSUL and, if not, cataloged the item. Additionally, the cataloging technicians used a variety of online sources (Google Books, Internet Archives, organizational websites) to ascertain whether or not the title had already been digitized elsewhere.

If a digital copy existed, and it met OSUL general quality standards, the cataloging technician inserted the appropriate information into the record and either sent the piece out to the circulating collection (items not held by OSUL) or the gift shelves (items already held by OSUL). The cataloging technician then placed items not found online or found online but of a very low quality, on a shelf marked "Gerald W. Williams Collection" outside the Digital Production Librarian's office.

Either the Digital Production Librarian or a trained library technician checked each item's copyright information to determine if it was eligible for digitization. Figure OREG-1 (next page) outlines the matrix used to determine each item's digitization eligibility.

The Digital Production Librarian created a copyright manifest to track copyright decisions and contact information. This Excel file was kept on a shared server so anyone involved with the project could access it at anytime.

Items not eligible for digitization were returned. Items eligible for digitization were placed on one of two shelving units. If the title was new to OSUL, and could not be debound because it was going to be added to the collection, it was placed on a shelf for scanning on the planetary book scanner in ILL. Items already in the OSUL collection, and could therefore be debound, were placed on a shelving unit reserved for sheetfed scanning.

Copyright Matrix: Gerald W. Williams Collection

Date of Publication	Conditions	Copyright Term/Digitization Eligibility
Before 1923	None	None. In the public domain due to copyright expiration. Digitize item.
1923 through 1977	Published without a copyright notice	None. In the public domain due to failure to comply with required formalities.[1] Digitize item.
1923 to Present	Prepared by an officer or employee of the U. S. government as part of that person's official duties[2]	None. In the public domain. Digitize item.
1923 to Present	Title is of Pacific Northwest or Oregon nature	Contact copyright holder for permission to digitize item. Document permissions in copyright manifest. Digitize items with permission.

Figure OREG-1. Digitization eligibility matrix

Textual Digitization

A DPU student scanner retrieved items that could be debound from the appropriate shelf. After debinding the item the student scanned the text block on the Canon sheetfed scanner and saved it as both individual tiff files and a multi-page pdf file. Hardback covers were also scanned and saved as individual tiff and pdf files. The student used Adobe Acrobat 9 Pro to combine the covers and text block to make one complete pdf file. The pdfs were then compressed and ocr'ed using cvision's pdfcompressor™ 4.0.

An ILL student scanner retrieved items that could not be debound and needed to be scanned on the ILL planetary scanner from the appropriate shelf. The student scanned each single page and double-page spread into one tiff file and used BScan ILL 2.0 software (packaged with the Bookeye scanner) to split double page spreads, deskew any crooked pages, crop the borders, and remove any thumb images captured during the scanning process. The student checked the quality of the resulting tiff file, made any necessary modifications, and used Adobe Acrobat Pro to convert it to pdf. Both files were saved and placed into a folder on a DPU server.

Textual items, both bound and debound, were added to ScholarsArchive using the customized DSpace metadata. Because each item had already been cataloged and added to the library's OPAC the student simply copied and pasted the information from the catalog into the metadata textboxes and attached the corresponding compressed and ocr'ed pdf file to the record.

After submitting the digital copy to ScholarsArchive the student returned the physical piece to the cataloger who had performed the initial work on the item. The cataloger checked the student submission, uploaded the item to the Internet, and added the ensuing URL to both the library's OPAC and WorldCat catalog. Debound items were recycled while bound items were added to the library's collection.

As of this writing all items destined for scanning on the sheetfed scanner have been digitized and added to the collection. Items that need to be scanned on the ILL planetary scanner continue to be added at a rate of approximately two per week.

Image Digitization

Each week the University Archivist pulled eight to fifteen images from the Gerald W. Williams Collection prior to the volunteer scanner's arrival on Wednesday. He completed a Word table for each weekly session, which included the image file number (written on the back), scanner settings, and descriptive metadata. The volunteer created two or three digital files of each image based on the provided specifications, saved all images to a jump drive, and placed it on the University Archivist's desk.

After the University Archivist reviewed the scans and chose the best images, a University Archives student worker gave the originals to a DPU staff member and copied the files to a shared drive located on a workstation in the DPU. This allowed the DPU staff member to pull a copy of the file off the server and into CONTENTdm's Acquisition Station. She used the original image when creating the necessary metadata, uploaded the item, returned the original to University Archives, and transferred the file to a permanent server.

Project Challenges, Successes and Lessons Learned

Challenges

It is impossible to take on a project of this magnitude and not encounter obstacles. Listed below are several challenges OSUL encountered during the process and the methods used to overcome those "bumps in the road".

Challenge #1: The DPU had limited experience scanning older monographs such as those found in the Williams Collection. Image printing processes used during the production of the books made it difficult to produce a high-quality copy of both images and text using standard DPU procedures. Trying to balance the desire for high-quality images with a fast-paced production environment – and without appropriate software – frustrated student workers and staff.

Solution #1: Unfortunately, this is still an obstacle when scanning older monographs. Moire patterns appear on some photographic images, making them less than ideal, but rarely does it affect whether or not an item can be viewed effectively. The Digital Production Librarian is now working to purchase scanning software that will lessen, or completely remove, these imperfections.

Challenge #2: Project organizers wanted all books eligible for digitization to be scanned, but the only DPU scanner that could be used for unbound books was a flatbed scanner. It would have been extremely inefficient if used for this purpose, especially with a number of books containing more than 300 pages.

Solution #2: DPU and ILL had a history of collaborating to solve digital access issues and of sharing student workers during calendar breaks. When approached by the Digital Production Librarian about the possibility of using the ILL planetary scanner for the Gerald W. Williams Collection, ILL staff agreed without hesitation. The two units worked out a schedule and workflow that allowed ILL students to digitize the books, edit the digital files, and save them to a DPU server.

Challenge #3: Student workers had limited access to the ILL planetary scanner due to its heavy usage during the workday and its continual malfunction.

Solution #3: Student workers were allowed to scan beyond the eight-to-five workday and on weekends. After repeated repairs the vendor eventually replaced the planetary scanner.

Challenge #4: Because of the complexity, detail, and number of people involved in the project, it was nearly impossible at times to remain consistent with workflow policies and procedures.

Solution #4: The project manager scheduled regular "check-in" meetings to review and, if necessary, update procedures. As the project progressed and staff became more familiar with practices and workflows, meetings were scheduled further and further apart until they were eventually discontinued altogether.

Challenge #5: Original workflow designs did not account for a copyright-checking step between catalogers and student workers nor identify a location for catalogers and students to place processed or digitized items.

Solution #5: Catalogers and DPU staff created additional workflow steps to include copyright checking and assigned shelves for items at various stages in the digitization process.

Successes

Digital Access Services, the department tasked with completing the vast majority of this project, is well known for managing and accomplishing large multi-step endeavors without much fanfare. The Gerald W. Williams Collection was no exception; the work was completed efficiently even as staff continued handling normal day-to-day responsibilities. Other measures of success include:

Success #1: Five library units (Cataloging, Digital Production, University Archives, Interlibrary Loan, and Special Collections), 17 staff members, and nine student workers collaborated to add more than 3,000 valuable, historic volumes to OSUL, 850 digitized monographs and serials to ScholarsArchive, and nearly 1000 images to the online Gerald W. Williams Collection. One would expect difficulties coordinating policies, procedures, and workflows with a collaboration of this size, but other than the complications surrounding the planetary scanner, few project disruptions occurred.

Success #2: Download statistics for the textual items in ScholarsArchive illustrate the amount of interest in this collection, both nationally and internationally. In 2009 the 686 items in the collection received nearly 40,000 downloads from more than 100 countries (Usage statistics retrieved December 10, 2009, from Gerald W. Williams Collection https://ir.library.oregonstate.edu/jspui/handle/1957/9112.)

Success #3: On February 14, 2009, timed to coincide with the 150th anniversary of Oregon's statehood, OSUL made its debut in

Flickr Commons with a launch of close to 125 images from the Gerald W. Williams Collection. The series, focusing on the Civilian Conservation Corps, was an instant hit with more than 8000 views within the first twenty-four hours. As of December 10, 2009, OSUL has added an additional 156 items and plans to continue increasing to the collection on a regular basis.

Success #4: Oregon Public Broadcasting twice visited to access historic pictures for two episodes of Oregon Experience. Civilian Conservation Corps chronicles the story of the New Deal program by the same name, and The Logger's Daughter explores the history of African American loggers in northeast Oregon.

Lessons Learned

Every large digitization project brings with it a unique set of challenges and obstacles. Adhering to a few basic principles can often mitigate the impact of these barriers:

Lesson #1: Pre-plan, pre-plan, pre-plan. While it may be tempting to skip the pre-planning phase, especially if an organization has previously undertaken numerous digitization projects, this step cannot be overemphasized (see Lesson #5). For most sizable digitization projects OSUL organizes and completes an inventory of the items in the collection, creates one or more data dictionaries, establishes workflows, and conducts meeting to discuss policies and procedures with appropriate personnel.

Lesson #2: Involve those people responsible for completing the work in the pre-planning phase. Students and staff on the front lines often have a better understanding of, and a more efficient method for, completing tasks. Their insights can be invaluable.

Lesson #3: To identify potential obstacles, process a few "test" items through the entire workflow prior to formally starting a project. It is much less disruptive to modify policies and procedures before the project gets fully underway.

Lesson #4: Do not start a project of this magnitude at a time when key decision-makers are unavailable. There are always questions and workflows modification early in the process, and not having the person(s) with the authority to make those decisions not only disrupts progress but can also frustrate workers.

Lesson# 5: Be (and stay) flexible. No two digitization projects are the same and each one has its own idiosyncrasies. Be prepared for policies and procedures from previous projects to fall short when applied to another. When obstacles do arise – and they will – encourage others' suggestions and keep an open mind when considering possible solutions.

Lesson# 6: Ask for help. Many cultural heritage organizations have considerable experience with digitization projects and most are willing to share their strategies and techniques with others.

Future Plans

As of this writing, OSUL has approximately 125 volumes to scan and add to the Gerald W. Williams Collection in ScholarsArchive, which will bring the total number of items in the institutional repository to just less than 1000. The image collection in CONTENTdm now houses 910 images. The digitization of textual items will most likely be finished in 2010. OSUL will continue digitizing the more than 24,000 historic photographs for many years to come. As time permits the University Archives staff will pull together groupings deemed of interest based on professional judgment and patron requests, and place them in the standard digitization queue.

Another possible future digitization project from the Gerald W. Williams Collection include Williams' own personal papers. His collected working papers, unpublished manuscripts, articles, and conference papers are valuable research documents in and of themselves. Finally, with Williams still collecting and now donating many of his acquisitions to OSUL, it appears the Gerald W. Williams Collection could be growing for a long, long time.

Supplementary materials can be found in ScholarsArchive@OSU at http://hdl.handle.net/1957/16758

References

Copyright Information Center. (2009). *Copyright term and the public domain in the United States, 1 January 2009.* Retrieved November 2, 2009, from: http://copyright.cornell.edu/resources/publicdomain.cfm

Oregon State University Libraries, University Archives (2008). Guide to the Gerald W. Williams Collection, 1855-2007. Retrieved November 27, 2009, from http://digitalcollections.library.oregonstate.edu/cdm4/ client/gwilliams/index.html

Peterson, K. (2009). *OSU enrollment jumps more than 8 percent to nearly 22,000. Retrieved November 28, 2009,* from http://oregonstate.edu/ua/ncs/archives/ 2009/nov/osu-enrollment-jumps-more-8-percent-nearly-22000

Simmons, T. (2006). *OSU recognized as Oregon's leading research university.* Retrieved November 28, 2009, from: http://oregonstate.edu/events/newsevents/carnegie.html

Springer, M., Dulabahn, B., Michel, P., Natanson, B., Reser, D., Woodward, D. et al. (2008). *For the common good: The Library of Congress Flickr pilot project.* Retrieved November 27, 2009, from http://www.loc.gov/rr/print/flickr_report_final.pdf

Stauth, D. (2006). *OSU College of Forestry viewed as number one in North America.* Retrieved November 28, 2009, from: http://oregonstate.edu/dept/nce/newsarch/2006/Oct06/forestryrank.html

The Commons. (2009). Retrieved November 27, 2009, from flickr Web site: http://www.flickr.com/Commons? GXHC_gx_session_id_=6afecb2055a3c52c

United States Copyright Office. (2009). *§101. Definitions, Copyright law of the United States of America and related laws contained in Title 17 of the United States Code.* Retrieved November 2, 2009, from http://www.copyright.gov/title17/92chap1.html#101

Using Omeka to Build Digital Collections: The METRO Case Study

Jason Kucsma (Metropolitan New York Library Council)

Kevin Reiss and Angela Sidman (City University of New York)

Abstract

In September 2008, the Metropolitan New York Library Council (METRO) began work building a directory of digital collections created and maintained by libraries in the metropolitan New York City area. METRO built the directory using Omeka, an open source collection management system, as a test to determine the viability of this platform for member libraries interested in using Omeka to build and deliver their own collections. This paper addresses Omeka's strengths and weaknesses as a software platform for creating and managing digital collections on the web. The analysis includes an examination of original record creation, and the extensibility of the system through the use of plug-ins.

Keywords: Content management system, ContentDM, Digital asset management system, Digital directory, New York City, Digital services, Digital workflow, Metadata management, Non-profit organization, Omeka, Open source software, Plug-in development, User experience, WordPress.

Project Background

The digitalMETRO project was born from the Metropolitan New York Library Council's (METRO) 2007-2010 Digital Library Services Plan. The plan serves as a guiding document for METRO's work in helping member libraries build and maintain unique digital collections and provide access to them online. Since 2005, METRO has provided over $300,000 in digitization grants to fund over 30 digitization projects. METRO also provides a diverse curriculum of workshops focusing on digital conversion, metadata for digital collections, digital collection management software, and related areas of emerging technologies for libraries. In addition to ensuring these programs continue to provide training and resources to member libraries, the Digital Library Services Plan also recommends the creation of a directory of digital collections in the METRO membership.

With the charge of creating a directory of digital collections, Jason Kucsma, METRO's Emerging Technologies Manager, served as Project Manager and assembled a small project team to begin working on the directory in October 2008. He recruited Angela Sidman, then a Metadata Librarian at the Mina Rees Library at City University of New York's Graduate Center, to serve as the Metadata Librarian for the project. Kevin Reiss, then the Systems Librarian at the Mina Rees Library, was recruited as the project's Web Developer.

Choosing Omeka

One of the first decisions we had to make was which collection management system we would use to build and deliver the directory on the web. We considered three different options. METRO licenses a hosted CONTENTdm (CDM) instance from OCLC, so that was first considered as an option. Sidman and Reiss had worked extensively with CDM to build the METRO-funded Digital Murray Hill Project. While CDM is a system that supports collections with robust metadata and that contain a wide array of digital formats it lacks some characteristics that are desirable in a modern web digital exhibition tool. The out-of-the-box CDM user interface makes it difficult to browse collections by subject and set, and CDM does not support any of the interactive features that many users expect in a web interface such as tagging, social networking, and a mechanism to accept end-user feedback on the web. Though CDM does provide a basic Application Programming Interface (API) that allows for some modification of default CDM behavior, we felt that this API was an inadequate tool for building the types of features we wanted to include in the digitalMETRO website.

Our interest in deploying a feature-rich digital exhibition tool next led us to consider Omeka, a relatively new open source collection management system that was created by the Center for History and New Media (CHNM) at George Mason University. The Omeka software was the closest option to another open-source web content management system, WordPress, that we considered using for our project. WordPress has well-documented theme mechanisms for customizing the display of WordPress content, and an expanding pool of plug-ins that be used to modify content behavior. Unfortunately, WordPress does not have a well-developed mechanism for supporting the types of collection-building workflows and metadata-creation common to archives and libraries, and creating a plug-in to support these activities was beyond the modest scope of this project. Our exploration of potential content management systems overlapped with the Fall 2008 release of the 0.10 beta version of Omeka, and the growing number of projects using the system in beta made it worth considering.

Additionally Omeka's developers appear to have taken design inspiration from the highly successful general purpose open-source content management system Wodpress. Wordpress is widely known for it's ease of install and high-level of functionality. In this vein, Omeka developers have touted the platform as a "next generation web publishing platform for museums, historical societies, scholars, enthusiasts, and educators." Our project team thought libraries might also fit into that family, particularly smaller libraries with limited technical staff or financial resources to build and deliver digital collections online. The simplicity of installing and configuring the Omeka system rivaled WordPress's ease-of-use, leading CHNM Director Dan Cohen to suggest Omeka is "Wordpress for your exhibitions and collections." Omeka also utilizes the same theme and plug-in mechanisms Wordpress utilizes to provide omeka users a means to customize and create new system behavior.

According to the CHNM website: "Omeka provides cultural institutions and individuals with easy-to-use software for publishing collections and creating attractive, standards-based, interoperable online exhibits. Free and open-source, Omeka is designed to satisfy the needs of institutions that lack technical staffs and large budgets."

Omeka was also an attractive choice because the strong and flexible approach to metadata representation built into the software. Additionally, Omeka Developer Dave Lester affirmed an advantage Omeka has for use in libraries and archives over a general-purpos CMS like WordPress on his blog, Finding America, "WordPress doesn't use structured metadata the way that scholars, libraries, and archives do. We have controlled vocabularies, 50 ways of classifying the same thing, and need a system that allows us to easily do that."

While Omeka does not currently support controlled vocabularies in the sense that catalogers use to maintain authority control for records, comments like this marked what we felt was a shift within the Omeka developer community from a focus on archives and museums to the digital collection building pursued by libraries. This, combined with the fact that Omeka appeared to be quickly developing a community of users and developers actively creating new features and posting improvements to the software, reinforced our decition to adopt Omeka for the digitalMETRO platform. Also, this relatively low-risk project would allow us to test the viability of Omeka as a collection building and exhibition platform that could be recommended to METRO members and othes small and medium libraries and archives.

The Omeka theme and user experience

Choosing Omeka as digitalMETRO's platform allowed us to present digital collections in an interface that provided the features which users expect from a modern, interactive website. Omeka users can easily customize the display and behavior of their websites using a number of pre-packaged Omeka themes or by manipulating the well-designed basic CSS that controls the basic look and feel of an Omeka theme. Looking at the existing digitalMETRO site (which utilizes the Omeka "Winter" theme) for illustrative purposes, we can explore some of the more useful standard Omeka features. The "Winter" theme is one of 11 out-of-the-box themes available, and the system affords a good deal of flexibility through CSS customization.

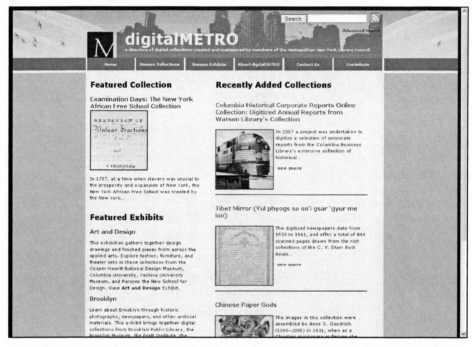

The screenshot above displays the main page of our Omeka instance. Visitors to the site are given a number of options which they can use to begin exploring the site. Casual browsers may be drawn to the "Featured Collection," which is randomly generated by Omeka each time the home page is refreshed. Site administrators can determine which items will be included in this rotating cast by simply checking a box in the item record. The site can also be set to feature "Recent Added" items to a collection, and the number of items can be set according to a specific collection's needs. Users may do a simple search using the "Search Box" in the top right corner of the page, or they can conduct an "Advanced Search" using the link just below the simple search box. While the current search tools offer expected, though limited access to the collection, Omeka 1.1 promises to feature a more robust search tool.

Omeka generates both RSS and Atom feeds to support syndication of item content. A series of tabs affords the user several additional options for navigating the site. In addition to expected administrative tabs that direct people back to the home page or to the about page to learn about the site, the Browse tab is perhaps the most useful. This directs users to a page where they can browse the directory via ordered lists of tags, collection creators, or dates that collections were added to the directory.

Sharing resources from an Omeka collection is easy as well. The clean and simple URLs generated for items in Omeka make it easy for users to share an item from the system via email or other social networking tools. This stands in direct contrast to most proprietary digital content management systems such as ContentDM or Ex Libris Digitool which typically generate obtuse lengthy URLs that are hard to share and parse with many email and social networking tools. Depending on the browser being used, additional sharing options will be featured in the URL window as well. Omeka has a COinS (ContextObject in Spans) plug-in that embeds bibliographic metadata in the HTML of the page, making the site compatible with bibliographic research tools like Zotero. Additionally, a Social Bookmarking plug-in allows users to share a given resource on any number of social bookmarking sites like Delicious, Facebook, Digg, Yahoo!, Technorati, and more. The Omeka theme mechanism makes it easy to deploy and customize these types of features to provide the type of experience most users expect on today's web.

digitalMETRO Scope and Specifications

The digital collections directory project (digitalMETRO) that we executed using Omeka began with a survey of digital collections in the METRO membership that continued as the project took shape.

Kucsma built an initial list of discrete digital collections created and maintained by METRO member libraries. We established a collection policy rooted in the desire to represent as many collections as possible given our limited personnel and time. A collection would be included in the digitalMETRO directory if:

- the creating institution is a member of the Metropolitan New York Library Council

- the institution owns these resources and has permission for them to be accessed freely online

- the collection includes at least 30 resources (images, audio files, finding aids, etc...)

The last criteria was established to exclude small exhibitions that featured only a handful of digitized resources. To facilitate user-submitted collections that could be added to the directory once the project was made available online we anticipated taking advantage of Omeka's "Contribute" plug-in to allow libraries to submit collections to the directory that might not have been included in the first phase of surveying. Additionally, we also created a simple spreadsheet template that libraries could be used in the future to submit multiple collections for inclusion in the directory using Omeka's CSV Import plug-in.

Metadata Management with Omeka

Throughout the project we made extensive use of one of the richest and most fully realized aspects of Omeka: its metadata support. Omeka supports the standard dublin core metadata set by default. Omeka also makes it easy to develop and implement project-specific metadata sets as-needed and have them easily feed into the Omeka display and editing infrastructure. There are two ways to do this:

- Through the creation of Custom Omeka Item Types (http://omeka.org/codex/Managing_Item_Types)

- Though the creation of new Element Sets (http://omeka.org/codex/Creating_an_Element_Set)

These two options mean Omeka can support the creation of a locally defined metadata set or easily add support for an existing metadata standard. An example of this is the inclusion in the Omeka 1.0 release of a plug-in that makes the Extended Dublin Core Metadata Set available as a metadata or element set choice for any Omeka project. A plug-in could be created for any metadata set desired by an Omeka user. This extensible metadata architecture ensures that Omeka will work well with future metadata initiatives since they can be easily supported using either one of these mechanisms, a key factor in deciding whether Omeka is right for an institution's collections. Both Custom Item Types and Element Sets are easily displayed and manipulated in both the Omeka public end-user display theme and from within the backend Omeka administrative environment.

We used this customizable infrastructure to build our own unique collection metadata schema using a Custom Omeka Item Type. Our item descriptions of collections in digitalMETRO are based on the Basic Dublin Core Element Metadata Set and the built-in Omeka Additional Metadata Set. Omeka provides for additional item-type metadata using pre-defined elements for a variety of digital formats including moving image, website, oral history, email, still image, lesson plan, and more. Because we were essentially creating a directory of digital collections, as opposed to creating records for individual items within a larger digital collection, we opted to create a custom "Collection" item type and add the the following project-specific elements to each record:

- Local Project URL
- Alternate URL
- METRO Funded Project (whether or not this project was funded by a METRO digitization grant)
- METRO Funding Year (if applicable)
- Institution Type (academic, public, or special library)
- Full Project Title
- Sample Item URL (for representative images from a given collection)

Building digitalMETRO with Omeka

The digitalMETRO Omeka instance is hosted commercially by Bluehost an Apache 2 Web Server running on Linux. The project runs in a PHP5/MySQL5 Environment. Omeka is built upon a robust, open-source PHP web application programming framework. It uses the Zend Framework, a Model View Controller (MVC) application which has enabled Omeka to be designed for extensibility out-of-the-box. Omeka has two means for extension: the theme and plug-in. If these sound familiar to many web developers, these are the same constructs used within WordPress.

We modified one of the existing available Omeka themes for the display (Winter), which can be easily downloaded from the themes section of the Omeka site. Our modifications included some minor changes to the text size and color scheme as well as adding a custom header created from royalty-free vector art licensed from iStockphoto. To add additional functionality to the site, we installed the following plug-ins http://omeka.org/add-ons/plug-ins/ within our Omeka instance:

Atom Output	Adds the Atom Syndication Format to the list of available output formats.
COinS	Adds COinS metadata to various item pages, making them Zotero readable.
Contribution	Allows collecting items from visitors
CSV Import	Imports items, tags, and files from CSV files.
Dropbox	Allows Omeka users to 'batch upload' a large quantity of files at one time, creating unique items in the archive for each file.
Exhibit Builder	Build rich exhibits using Omeka.
Google Analytics	Adds Google Analytics tracking code to the header of every page.

HTML Purifier	Protects Omeka from XSS by filtering HTML/XHTML using the HTML Purifier library.
Lightbox2	Adds functions for themes to add image overlay functionality to Omeka themes using Lokesh Dhakar's Lightbox2 Javascript library.
OAI-PMH Repository	Exposes Omeka items as an OAI-PMH repository.
Simple Contact Form	Adds a simple contact form for users to contact the administrator.
Simple Pages	Allows administrators to create simple web pages for their public site.
Social Bookmarking	Inserts a customizable list of social bookmarking sites below each item in your Omeka database
Sort Browse Results	Allows sorting of results on browse items page.

The growing community of Omeka developers is actively contributing to the functionality of the software through the development of new existing plug-ins and improvement of existing ones. Plug-in development is happening at a rapid rate. Plug-in deployment is also very simple since plug-ins are written as drag and drop extensions to the Omeka application. All that is required to deploy a plug-in is to load it to the "plug-ins" directory of any Omeka application and fill in any required local customization paramters for the plug-in within the Omeka administrative interface. In fact at the time we were compiling this report, a new Social Bookmarking plug-in was made available, and we were able to add it to digitalMETRO in less than five minutes. There are a number of additional Omeka plug-ins that will be of particular interest to libraries, archives, and museums including OAI-PMH Harvester (OAI Harvesting Support) and Geolocation (adds location information and maps to Omeka).

Given our assertion that Omeka's extensible design and the emerging and expanding set of plug-ins that enhance functionality make it an exciting and potentially empowering tool for cultural institutions who have web development skills on staff, the existing Omeka project developer documentation has the potential to be a major limitation to theme and plug-in development at the moment. The project documentation has lagged quite a bit behind actual development that has occurred in the nine months we have been working with the system. This will need to be improved upon if Omeka is going to serve the needs of the audiences drawn to its flexible infrastructure and low barriers to implementation. There is an active developers' list and help forums on the Omeka site, but the Omeka Codex http://omeka.org/codex/Documentation needs to improve to the level where a competent departmental Web Manager or Web Librarian can easily start hacking the code using clearly defined examples to get started. At the moment, much of the customization work requires combing through source code to find a suitable example or an explanation of a given function's parameters. This is a stark contrast to the much larger pool of documentation and examples available for systems like WordPress.

Plug-In Modification

Our plug-in work to-date with Omeka falls into three categories. First, we deployed a number of plug-ins that required no modification aside from basic configuration within the administrative interface. Second, we modified a few of the plug-ins. The Lightbox plug-in written for Omeka 10 required some slight modification to run on the Omeka 1.0. We also modified the Contribution plug-in so that libraries could recommend collections to be added to the directory. These modifications allow the plug-in to record basic metadata for the "collection" Omeka Item Type we defined for the digitalMETRO directory. Lastly, we are engaged in some new plug-in development that will attempt to increase the findabilty of digital objects within Omeka collections.

As written, the contribution plug-in was not particularly suited to our project design since it was built to facilitate self-archiving by object authors. For digitalMETRO, we configured the form to solicit some basic metadata about collections that visitors would like to see added to the directory. Once the form is submitted, a skeleton "non-public" omeka item record is created and queued for the Metadata Librarian to complete and make public on the site. It is easy to see how a feature like this can allow cultural heritage institutions to quickly and easily create sites to collect information and resources from individuals around a certain topic or event. For example, The April 16 Archive site,which is dedicated to collecting and preserving stories about the Virginia Tech tragedy, uses the contribute feature to solicit stories, pictures, and audio files related to the campus shooting.

This type of modification to an Omeka plug-in is relatively easily achieved, with a few caveats. Omeka has been implemented as an MVC application within the PHP Zend framework, so each plug-in conforms to the same framework familiar to today's web application developers. Plug-ins are composed of a directory structure that mirrors the MVC framework with a "view", "controller", and for more complicated plug-ins a "model" directory. The modification for the contribution plug-in mostly happened at the view level, though the internal data structure that stores information about contributions needed to be adjusted to be capture the data from submitters that we wanted. The "controller" file also needed to be modified in order to map contributions directly to the custom "Collection" Omeka item type we used to code each digital project description.

New Plug-in Development

In order to advance the project's goals of highlighting the collections within digitalMETRO we are developing two plug-ins, a Sitemap generator and an Category Browser that turns any Omeka metadata element into a browsable category. The first will enhance the site's discoverability by exposing Omeka content in a simple XML format defined by the sitemaps protocol http://www.sitemaps.org/. This file can then be submitted formally to search engines like Google or Yahoo!. The major challenge in building this plug-in was ensuring all Omeka content, exhibits, items, and static content were represented in the sitemap output. A plug-in hook was also added so that the creation of new content or updates to existing data was recorded in the sitemap.

Browse Collections (7 total) Sound recordings			
Browse by Title	**Browse by Tag**	**Browse by Creator**	**Most Recent**

Sample Image	Title	Creator(s)	Tags
	Academic Podcast Initiative	St. John's University (New York, N.Y.)	Queens, Colleges, Sound recordings, Education, Outreach, St. John's University, Podcasts
	Jewish People's University of the Air	Touro College	Judaism, Jewish life, Sound recordings, Education, Touro College, Jewish People's University of the Air, Radio programs, Outreach
	Childhood in the Bronx	Herbert H. Lehman College	Photographs, Bronx, Lehman College, Sound recordings, Social conditions, Childhood, Oral history

The second plug-in in development will enable Omeka to behave in a fashion similiar to the "category" mechanism. The plug-in will allows any Omeka element to become an active browsing option and ensure that the option is represented with a clean URL that can be used effectively by search engines and end-users alike. We took a first pass at this by manipulating the Omeka advanced search screen to enable the Creator, Format, Subject, and Type, elements to be browsable. This delivers cumbersome URLs that look like this:

```
http://nycdigital.org/dmetro/items/browse?search=&advanced[0][elemen
t_id]=51&advanced[0][type]=contains&advanced[0][terms]=Sound%20r
ecordings&range=&collection=&type=&tags=&submit_search=Search
```

The plug-in will instead produce URLs that will take the following form:

```
http://nycdigital.org/dmetro/items/browse/format/sound+recordings/
```

The plug-in will provide an adminstrative screen that will enable an Omeka administrator to select which specific elements will become part of the new browsing options made available through the plug-in. The long-term goal is to make functions available to theme authors so they may easily create tree-like navigation structures for desirable browsing elements. This will substantially increase the number of different access points users have to items in an Omeka collection. The resulting "categories" will also be printed out in the sitemap generated by the aforementioned sitemap plug-in.

digitalMETRO Workflow and Technical Issues

Creating and adding item content within Omeka occurs primarily in the web browser via the password-protected administrative interface. Like the public-facing side of the Omeka instance, the admin interface is implemented using a theme architecture that can be customized to meet the needs of a particular Omeka project. While we haven't explored this option it is certainly available and could be a means to address some of the adminstrative user interface issues we encountered during our collection building and metadata creation activities that will be discussed in the next section.

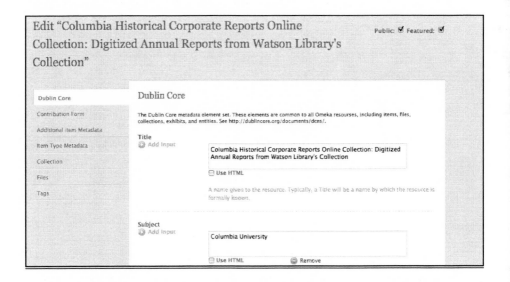

There are low barriers to getting started with record-creation in Omeka. Individual records may be authored in the administrative interface by filling out a tabbed customizable metadata template. There is a "files" tab where media associated with a given item can be uploaded using a web form with a file input form. Larger groups of records and media may be batch loaded from CSV files, which we discuss below. However, in the earliest stages of the METRO project, the Metadata Librarian entered individual records directly into the administrative interface using the web template. This template is divided into six sections which reflect the intellectual organization of the project's metadata:

1. Dublin Core: Basic Dublin Core Metadata Element Set common to all Omeka projects

2. Contribution Form: Contains data elements pulled from the Contribution plug-in used by member libraries

3. Additional Item Metadata: Custom metadata fields added by project staff to augment the standard DC data elements

4. Collection: Project-specific metadata associated with the custom item type "Collection"

5. File: Associates digital image files with metadata records for display purposes

6. Tags: Allows for the addition of uncontrolled or loosely controlled vocabulary to aid in subject analysis and collection description

The bulk of the Metadata Librarian's work occurred in the Dublin Core (DC) tab of the item creation form. It was here that project description (Title, Creator, Format, Description) and subject analysis (Subject) took place. For librarians with experience in creating records using DC the item creation template is familiar and intuitive. For librarians accustomed to creating records using the rigid structure and numeric field tags of MARC, the Omeka interface offers a soft entry into new types of metadata creation. The web form provides a blank field for each data element and users may build from there, adding fields through a simple click on a "plus" button labeled "Add input." Under each data element is a definition of the element's purpose and examples of proper usage. These data element definitions would be particularly useful for projects in which there are multiple record creators, including students or interns, and for librarians with limited experience in creating non-MARC metadata.

While it was easy to begin authoring records in the administrative interface, the limitations of the system became clear as we started working with a greater volume of records. For example, there is no mechanism for populating related records with common data within the administrative interface. To ensure consistency between records, the user must rely on time-consuming tactics such as copying and pasting from previously created records or from source sites like the Library of Congress authority files (LCSH for subject authorities and LCNAF for names) or the Art and Architecture Thesaurus (AAT). Additionally, navigating within a single record was time-consuming, as the template's layout required a burdensome amount of scrolling. This scrolling could not be avoided as the "Save Changes" button appeared only at the bottom of the screen and regular saving was key to successfully authoring records in Omeka. The item creation template was, of course, web based and if a user accidentally navigated away from the active record, either to another tab within Omeka or to one of the many sites from which data had to be copied and pasted into the form, then any unsaved content within the record disappeared. The system does not offer a preventative warning asking if the user would like to save any unsaved changes before closing the record. On several occasions we lost time and detailed intellectual work by accidentally navigating away from the item creation form.

These issues make Omeka problematic as a serious choice for a project that will involve large-scale and or detailed metadata creation, since using it in the fashion digitalMETRO attempted revealed serious data consistency issues. However, considering the strong, extensibile MVC architecture Omeka is built on top of, all of these issues seem to be within reach of being fixed if the development community would take notice. As better documentation of the Omeka adminstrative theme and Omeka plug-in develop, these issues could be addressed. For example, support for controlled vocabularies could come via a plug-in developed for a given vocabulary. A more streamlined editing interface that supports both record templates and data-typing of metadata fields could be accomplished through rewriting some of the

MVC code within the administrative theme. A more robust search and retrieval mechanism using the Lucene search engine available within the Zend framework is currently under development by the core Omeka development team.

Project staff quickly moved to batch loading records as a means of bypassing as many of the administrative interface's shortcomings as possible. The project manager created an Excel spreadsheet and populated it with key data elements which could be determined through a preliminary viewing of a potential site: Creator, Title, URL, METRO funding status, etc. The Metadata Librarian then reviewed the spreadsheet and ensured that the completed fields complied with LCNAF before the web developer loaded the file into Omeka. This process created a queue of skeleton records which the Metadata Librarian could then enhance through description of subjects, formats, additional authors, and other data before making the records viewable on the public side of the site. The benefits of moving to batch loaded CSV files were immediately clear. The use of spreadsheets allowed the Metadata Librarian to easily populate fields with shared data, which improved consistency within and between records and also decreased the time spent on cutting, pasting, and scrolling. This, in turn, led to a decrease in the number of records lost through browser navigation errors.

Intellectual Control and Tagging within Omeka

Even with batch loads, control over data within Omeka is loose. Catalogers more comfortable with the tight intellectual control offered by a traditional library information system or a digital content management system like CONTENTdm may be disappointed by the weak search and retrieval features and the inability to carry out basic find/replace tasks or other global changes within the record-creation module. The weakness of the intellectual control provided by Omeka means that for a project of any size or scope it is crucial for librarians to get their records right the first time around, when they author them. This is not necessarily easy, as Omeka does not support controlled vocabularies such as LCSH, AAT, or the Thesaurus of

Geographic Names. Metadata authors must work around the system to ensure that they enter correct, consistent, and authoritative data into their records. For this project multiple strategies were employed to control headings, including cutting and pasting directly from authority files, loading standardized data through batch loads, cross-checking through keyword searches on the public site, and exporting alphabetical lists of subject headings and tags into tab delimited files for review by hand. In addition to the difficulties faced in creating consistent data content, there was an additional hurdle in that Omeka does not include a record validation function to make sure that core fields are populated.

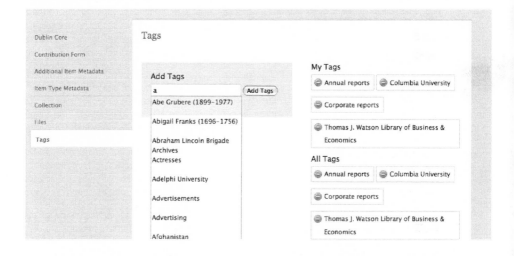

The tagging mechanism built into the item creation module offers a bright contrast to the difficulties of working with controlled data. With the move to Omeka 1.0 an unlimited number of tags can be added to each record. Our project staff opted to take full advantage of the tags, building them into a robust companion to the more structured DC data. The same core metadata fields found in the item records are repeated in the tagging, only this time instead of relying on controlled vocabularies, natural language terms are used. Compare, for example, the structured and unstructured terms used to describe John Jay College's collection "Crime in New York 1850-1950," http://nycdigital.org/dmetro/items/show/18.

	Controlled vocabularies	Tags
Creator	John Jay College of Criminal Justice	John Jay College
Additional creators	Turkus, Burton B.	Burton B. Turkus
	Lawes, Lewis Edward, 1883-1947	Lewis Edward Lawes (1883-1947)
Subjects	Homicide	Homicide
	Organized crime	Organized crime
	Criminal investigation	Criminals
	Sing Sing Prison	Sing Sing Prison
	Death row inmates	Inmates
Materials	Forensic photographs	Crime scene photographs
	Identification photographs	Mug shots
	Transcripts	Trial transcripts

A keyword search on the public site will pull up content added through controlled vocabularies as well as the tags. In the absence of traditional see/see also references, which are built into library catalogs and databases, the hope is that this combination of structured and unstructured data will help lead non-expert users to the information they seek. Even an experienced librarian might not immediately think to search for "Identification photographs" but the more commonly used "Mug shots" will guide users to the same authoritative data and with a deal less frustration or confusion.

Experiments in Exhibition Building

Omeka was developed with the express needs of museums, historians, and educators in mind. The software's origins in the arena of cultural institutions could account for what is, by library standards, weak intellectual control within the admin site. However, its development at George Mason's Center for Social History and New Media also directly led to one of Omeka's greatest strengths: exhibition building. Once users have created records within the system they can, with great ease, put together exhibits which shine a brighter light on related groups of material. A site editor fills out a web form to determine top level data such as Title, Slug, and Theme, then assigns section metadata, and finally adds individual records to the section. A given exhibition may have multiple sections, thus allowing for more complex relationships between digital objects. Templates make the layout of individual records semi-customizable within exhibits. Some templates give precedence to images while others allow for a greater expanse of exhibition-specific didactic text.

Exhibition-building fell on the margins of METRO's project goals and digitalMETRO does not fully exploit this feature's true potential. Nevertheless, project staff did create two exhibits which appear on the lower left side of the homepage as "Featured Exhibits." The "Art and Design" collection offers a good example of how the exhibition feature can be used for educational or curatorial purposes. This exhibit gathers together design drawings and finished pieces from across the applied arts. Site visitors may explore fashion, furniture, and theater sets through multiple librarys' collections, including the Cooper-Hewitt National Design Museum, Columbia University, Yeshiva University Museum, and Parsons the New School for Design. In this case, the exhibition was built around the unifying theme of design history and illustrated the range of materials owned by METRO's member libraries. The strength of the exhibition feature is in its ability to convey a curatorial perspective in a dynamic, interactive setting which guides users from object to object while providing expert contextual information alongside standardized metadata and social tagging.

Conclusions

Omeka has great potential to effectively and efficiently support small and medium-sized digital collection building and online exhibitions for libraries and archives. The software is well-suited to enable librarians, archivists, and curators to work effectively in the context of their disciplines. The core Omeka software architecture and design are well-suited to allow the software to expand and improve as the user community grows. It is also well-positioned to serve as a tool institutions can use to repackage existing digital collections in a new, modern web exhibition framework with the availability of a robust CSV import option that can bring both metadata and media into the system.

Continued improvement of the Omeka administrative interface within this architecture will help it become a more viable digital collection building solution for libraries and archives. We experienced a good deal of frustration navigating through the interface to create records. We also had serious concerns about the ability to create consistent and detailed metadata within the administrative interface. The ability to create and manipulate metadata in a spreadsheet and populate skeleton records in Omeka works around some of the administrative interface issues, but there is still room for improvement in how a user creates records online. Omeka's search and retrieval capabilities also need to improve for it to become a more fully realized digital collection management tool. At this writing the Omeka development is working to utilize the Apache Lucene support with the Zend framework to provide a more effective full-text search interface for Omeka. It is hoped this effort will result in a new "Lucene" plug-in for the Omeka 1.1 release.

Despite these limitations Omeka is certainly well-positioned within its target market of small to medium-sized institutions that need an easy-to-deploy, effective, professional tool to make digital library, archival, and museum content available on the web. It is important to measure Omeka's functionality, features, and limitations against some of the same functionality, features, and limitations of a proprietary system. We hope that our experience will help other institutions evaluate Omeka as a possible collection management system for their digitization projects and anticipate and overcome any of the obstacles we encountered.

References

2006_digsurveyreport.pdf. (n.d.). Retrieved September 22, 2009, from http://www.metro.org/images/stories/pdfs/ 2006_digsurveyreport.pdf

2007_digplan.pdf. (n.d.). Retrieved September 22, 2009, from http://www.metro.org/images/stories/pdfs/2007_digplan.pdf

Cohen, D. (2008, February 20). *Introducing Omeka.* Dan Cohen's Digital Humanities Blog. Retrieved September 22, 2009, from http://www.dancohen.org/2008/02/20/introducing-omeka/

Dave Lester's Finding America. New Omeka Release 0.10 Beta. (n.d.) Retrieved September 22, 2009, from http:// blog.davelester.org/ 2008/11/12/new-omeka-release-010-beta/

digitalMETRO. (n.d.). Retrieved September 22, 2009, from http://nycdigital.org/dmetro/

Explore Murray Hill through images and maps. Digital Murray Hill. (n.d.) Retrieved September 22, 2009, from http://murrayhill.gc.cuny.edu/

Model–view–controller - Wikipedia, the free encyclopedia. (n.d.). Retrieved September 22, 2009, from http://en.wikipedia.org/ wiki/Model%E2%80%93view%E2%80%93controller

Omeka | Documentation - Omeka How To. (n.d.) Retrieved September 22, 2009, from http://omeka.org/codex/Documentation

Omeka | Home. (n.d.). Retrieved September 22, 2009, from http://omeka.org/

OpenURL ContextObject in SPAN (COinS). (n.d.) Retrieved September 22, 2009, from http://ocoins.info/

The April 16 Archive. (n.d.) Retrieved September 23, 2009, from http://april16archive.org/

WordPress Blog Tool and Publishing Platform. (n.d.) Retrieved September 22, 2009, from http://wordpress.org/

Zend Framework. (n.d.) Retrieved September 22, 2009, from http://framework.zend.com/